French and Indian War Aftermath

Notices Abstracted from Colonial Newspapers

Volume 5
January 1, 1761-
January 17, 1763

Armand Francis Lucier

HERITAGE BOOKS
2007

HERITAGE BOOKS
AN IMPRINT OF HERITAGE BOOKS, INC.

Books, CDs, and more—Worldwide

For our listing of thousands of titles see our website
at
www.HeritageBooks.com

Published 2007 by
HERITAGE BOOKS, INC.
Publishing Division
65 East Main Street
Westminster, Maryland 21157-5026

Copyright © 2000 Armand Francis Lucier

"A sketch of the Cherokee Country" from George Bancroft's
History of the United States, 1874, Little, Brown.

All rights reserved. No part of this book may be reproduced or transmitted in any form or by any means, electronic or mechanical, including photocopying, recording or by any information storage and retrieval system without written permission from the author, except for the inclusion of brief quotations in a review.

International Standard Book Number: 978-0-7884-1535-2

CONTENTS

MAP iv
FOREWORD v
CONTRIBUTORS vi

JANUARY 1761 1
FEBRUARY 1761 11
MARCH 1761 33
APRIL 1761 43
MAY 1761 59
JUNE 1761 69
JULY 1761 77
AUGUST 1761 95
SEPTEMBER 1761 109
OCTOBER 1761 135
NOVEMBER 1761 145
DECEMBER 1761 153

JANUARY 1762 163
FEBRUARY 1762 173
MARCH 1762 185
APRIL 1762 195
MAY 1762 213
JUNE 1762 231
JULY 1762 243
AUGUST 1762 257
SEPTEMBER 1762 279
OCTOBER 1762 297
NOVEMBER 1762 317
DECEMBER 1762 327

JANUARY 1763 339

INDEX 345

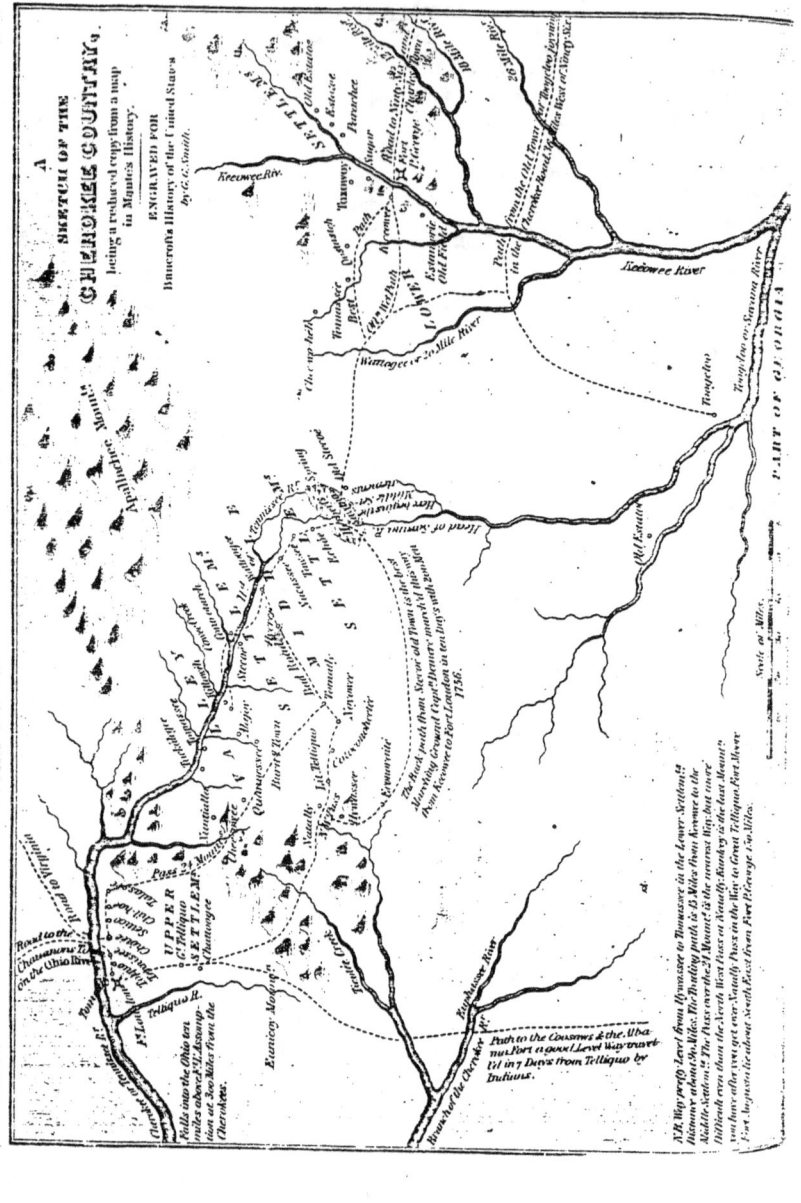

FOREWORD

The French and Indian War for all practical purposes ended with the capitulation of Canada by the French and Canadian troops to the British and American forces. Yet hostilities still continued, and the following is a chronicle of newspaper articles concerning the people of the American provinces, starting January 1, 1761 and concluding with a speech given at the Council Chamber at Boston on January 12, 1763 by Governor Francis Bernard. He declared that the preliminary articles of peace had been signed by the Ministers of England, France and Spain.

Much to the disappointment of the inhabitants in the American colonies the capitulation did not bring complete peace to the continent. The Cherokee and Creek Indians were still creating havoc on the southern frontiers. Along the east coast the French and Spanish privateers increased in their activities, in response the colonial port towns refitted some of their vessels into privateers.

The expeditions to French Martinico, Spanish Havannah and Newfoundland by British and some Provincial troops were of much concern. The publishing of dispatches, eyewitness accounts, private letters in the weekly newspapers being their main source of information.

Speeches, proclamations, commentaries, want-ads and trivial affairs are all inserted in order to understand life in the American provinces without mutations to composition and spelling, except where it was thought necessary for clarity and understanding.

Armand Francis Lucier.

CONTRIBUTORS

Boston Gazette. Boston Massachusetts.
The Boston Evening Post. Boston Massachusetts.
Connecticut Gazette. New-Haven Connecticut.
Gentlemen's Magazine. London England.
Halifax Gazette. Halifax Nova-Scotia.
New-Hampshire Gazette. Portsmount New-Hampshire.
New-London Summery. New-London Connecticut.
London Chronicle. London England.
London Gazette. London England.
Newport Mercury. Newport Rhode-Island.
Providence Gazette. Providence Rhode-Island.
Maryland Gazette. Annapolis Maryland.
New-York Gazette [Weyman's] New-York, New-York.
New-York Mercury. New-York, New-York.
North-Carolina Gazette, New Bern North Carolina.
Pennsylvania Gazette. Philadelphia Pennsylvania.
Pennsylvania Journal. Philadelphia Pennsylvania.
South Carolina Gazette. Charlestown So. Carolina.
Virginia Centinel. Williamsburg Virginia.
Virginia Gazette. Williamsburg Virginia.

JANUARY 1761

HALIFAX Jan. 1. By the honourable Jonathan Belcher, Esq; President of His Majesty's council and Commander in Chief of His Majesty's Province of Nova Scotia, Accadie, &c. &c.

A PROCLAMATION

Whereas the late Governor hath granted several Townships within this Province under certain conditions; and amongst the rest that within a certain limited Time such a Number of the Grantees should remove with their Families and Effects; And as several said Grants by the said conditions would be forfeited; particularly a Grant on the Townships of Cumberland, Amherst, Sackville, Onflow, Truro, and Yarmouth; and whereas many of the said Grantees were in his Majesty's Service, employed in the Reduction of Canada at the Time when the said Townships were to be settled; and others for other reasons signified to the late Governor, and approved of by him, have not complied therewith: ――― I have therefore thought fit, by and with the Advice and consent of His Majesty's Council, to issue this proclamation hereby declaring to all the said Grantees that no Advantage will be taken of any forfeiture hitherto accur'd but their respective Interest shall be secured to them either by Deeds separately upon their Removal into this Province or jointly to the Grantee as shall be agreed upon by them. And the Committees of several Townships are hereby ordered to call a Meeting of their respective Proprietors as soon as may be, to inform the several Grantees thereof and they are further desired to transmit to me, as soon as may be, the number of Families, and Persons in each Family and of their stock, for each Township respectively, and what number will be ready to embark in the ensuing

Spring and I shall be ready to give them all Assistance and Protection which is or may be at that Time be in my Power, Provided always, that the said Grantees do remain themselves and their Families, and their Effects into this Province, on or before the First Day of June next and in default thereof, it is hereby further declared, that they are to expect to benefit from this proclamation.

   Given by Order of the commander   J. Belcher. in Chief. R. Buckley, Secr'y.
         God save the King.

   BOSTON Jan. 5. Thursday Morning all the Bells in this Town began to toll on Account of the Death of His Majesty King George the Second, and, continued tolling most Part of the Day.
——— And at ten o'Clock Minute Guns, to the Number of 77, the Years of His said Majesty's Age, were discharges at Castle William.

   The same Day His Excellency the Governor, and the two Houses of Assembly, attended divine Services at the Old Brick Meeting House where a Sermon was preached by the Rev. Mr. Cooper upon the sorrowful Occasion of the Death of our late most Gracious Sovereign George the Second, and, in the Afternoon of the same Day a Sermon was preached by the Rev. Caner, at King's Chapel, where His Excellency and the Members of the Court Attended.

   Boston Jan. 5. We hear from Stonington in Connecticut that a transport Brig belonging to Rhode Island, lately arrived in that harbor from Albany, with a number of Soldiers on board, among which were 12 persons who had the Small Pox; that soon after their arrival the people on board who had the distemper left the vessel. (among whom were the Captain and Mate) soon after which the people on board cut the cable, when the vessel drove ashore and bilged: The sick people were taken out and put into a hospital, but not withstanding the care taken care of them, only two out of twelve servived the distemper.

   We hear from Wallingsford, that last Friday se'nnight, one Lieut. Culver, went to a retailer in that place for a gallon of molasses, but it being late at night, and the retailer in bed, he refused to let him have it till morning; but Culver insisted on having it then, and haul'd him out of bed, when the retailer called for help, upon which Doct. Hall of that Place, came to his assistance, but upon his entring the door, Culver struck him on the head with a stick which kill'd him on the spot. ——— Culver was soon after taken up and put under confinement.

NEW-York Jan. 5. The several Independent Companies of Soldiers lately arrived from England, and quartered in New-Jersey, embarked last week, at Port Amboy, in small Vessels and were carried on board Transports lying near Sandy Hook, 'tis said, in order to proceed to South Carolina.

Yesterday Capt. Groves arrived here in a Schooner in 14 days from South-Carolina: He says the Indians continue in their Old Ways: but that Major Thompson has again thrown into Fort Prince George, a large supply of provisions, and that there are near a thousand men in and about the fort.

On Saturday morning last sailed from the Hook, his Majesty's ship Dover, Capt. Pearsal, also several cartel ships for France with prisoners.

CHARLESTOWN S. Carolina Jan. 6. Some Mohawk Warriors are come in the transport that arrived this morning: a great many parties of those and other Indians are gone out against the Cherokees; some of them have carried both Cherokee scalps and prisoners to Pittsburg or Fort Pitt.

CHARLESTOWN S. Carolina Jan. 10. On Tuesday and Thursday arrived five large Transports from New-York (under convoy of his Majesty's Ship Nightingale, Campbel) having on board upwards of 1100 Rank and File of His Majesty's Troops under the Command of Lieut. Col. James Grant. These Troops are destined to act against the Cherokees, and will stay here no longer than absolutely necessary, Six Mohawks are also arrived with the Troops.

PHILADELPHIA Jan. 15. We hear that Major Rogers has taken possession of Fort Detroit, and that the garrison are now coming down to this city. The Major is gone to Lake Superior, a journey the French say, never undertaken at this season of the year.

We hear that the French Garrison of Detroit are at Lancaster, on their way down here; as are likewise a Number of people, that were prisoners there.

CHARLESTOWN S. Carolina Jan. 17. On the 25th ult. arrived here in town from Virginia, in good health (considering the great hardships he has undergone) Capt. John Stuart, the only officer of Fort Loudoun garrison that has had the good fortune to escape being massacred by the Cherokees.

On Thursday some unfavourable accounts were received from Augusta, dated the 5th instant. The Wolf has had been there 13 days, but seemed to decline the visit he intended to make to the Governor of Georgia and this Province. His Return to the Creek nation may be attended with very bad consequences.

The Sloop Sally, of and from Jamaica, Stephen Perkinson master for Cape Fear foundered at sea: The master and crew, with 11 negroes, and some valuable effects, were saved, and carried to Georgia by Capt. Howard, in a Schooner from Philadelphia.

It has been reported (but wants confirmation) that some Mohawks have taken several Cherokee scalps, and a prisoner, and carried them to Pittsburgh.

BOSTON Jan. 19. A letter from London dated Oct. 13 1760, with Part of a Letter by way of a Journal, from an Officer in Gen. Amherst's Army, Sept. 5, 1760.

Friday, ——— At eight I was presented at a sight which quite overcame me: the rangers bro't to the head quarters a number of families, consisting of old men, women and children, who had come in for fear of our Indians. As soon as they located the General, the women with prodigious number of children, some at their breast, got round him, crying out, Les Savage, &c. He said to them in French, they had nothing to fear, for he commanded an English Army; and his orders were so strong, and he was so fully convinced of Sir William Johnson's humanity, that none of them would be hurt by our Savages. The tender manner in which he spoke to them melted me before I was aware, but looking round, I found all the spectators in the same condition. —— Here was a Grandfather presenting his numerous offsprings to the General, a mother, with a child at her breast, and two or three at her knees, bawling and crying, the mother weeping, while the father was endeavouring to console them.

—— The General order'd victuals and drink for them; a large fire was made before his tent, and they set all around; the men began to light their pipes, and there appeared a satisfaction in the countenance of the whole: Many of these were sent into the deserted houses (for these families lived on the other side of the bay) but a great many of the women and children chose to stay at the fire before the General's tent, and indeed he had a numerous Family. —— The cruelty committed on our frontiers were at once forgot, every one was melted into compassion at the miserable sight; and even the very Rangers whose hearts are none of the softest, seemed glad when they were ordered back without their prisoners.

BOSTON Jan. 19. Extract of a Letter from Albany, January 10, 1761.

"A few Days since Mr. Morrison, Capt. Wait's Clerk, arrived here by Land from Major Roger's Party, whom he left well at Presque Isle the second Day of November last, after they had returned from Pittsburg. —— Capt. Jonathan Brewer with a Party was to drive 40 Bullocks by Land to Detroit, from Presque Isle. —— The Major expected to have been at Albany by the New Year's Day.

By a Letter from New-York it is said, that they have heard from Major Rogers, that he was well, and was expected —— but whether their News from him is of a later Dated the above. I am not able to determine.

P. S. There was a Vessel lost on Lake Erie in a Storm, with 100 Barrels of Provisions; the Crew and about 12 Barrels saved; which obliged Major Rogers to send Capt. Wait back to Niagara for 100 Barrels more; but the reason of Scarcity of Boats at Niagara, he did not take but 36."

BOSTON Jan. 19. Since our last we have had extreme cold weather, whereby, our harbour is almost fill'd with Ice: ———— We have within this time had several alarms by the cry of fire; which were soon extinguished, without any considerable damage occurring, and Tuesday evening last, when about half an hour after nine o'clock a violent fire broke out in one of the shops opposite the north side of Faneuil Hall Market, on Dock Square, which entirely consumed all the row of wooded buildings from the store occupied by the Hon. Thomas Hubbard, Esq; to the Swing Bridge: These buildings belonged to the Town and were leased to a number of Tradesmen, some of whom had their whole stock therein, most of which was either consumed or lost: There were several small schooners in the dock, but they received little damage; nor did the fire proceed to the north side of the dock, on the contrary it communicated itself to that stately edifice, Faneuil Hall Market, the whole of which was soon intirely consumed, excepting the brick walls, which are left standing; the fire then proceeded to a number of shops on the south side of the market, consumed them also; The wind rising about this time carried the flakes of the fire over the houses towards Kingstreet, and the warehouses and stores on the Town Dock, & Long Wharf, wherein were the greatest quantities of richest merchandize in the Town: The Inhabitants having devastations of the fire of last Spring recent in their minds, they were apprehensive of a further destruction especially as the Tide was down, the dock filled with Ice and some of the pumps in this neighbourhood failing: many people removed their goods, some of which received damage thereby; The severity of the weather was such that many persons could scarce stand it; and the water which issued from the Engines congealed into particles of Ice before it fell: Altho' the flames and flakes of fire fell on many houses and stores, yet no dwelling house was consumed; one or two near the market were considerably damaged ———— Never were slate on houses discovered to be of so much advantage as at that time; for when great flakes of fire fell thereon, they immediately run off without doing any mischief.

   The loss of Faneuil Hall Market must be great to this Town, as it was a noble building, esteemed one of the best pieces of workmanship here, and an ornament to this Town: It was built near 20 years ago the sole expence of the late generous Peter Faneuil, Esq; the capacious Hall which bore the Founder's name, would contain above 1000 of the inhabitants at a meeting: —— There were convenient apartments for the officers at the East end of the lower floor, one of which was improved as a Naval Office, and the other a Notary Publick's: The other part was very commodious for a Market. —— The records, papers, &c. with such other things as could be removed, were mostly saved.

   There are near 20 Tradesmen deprived of their shops by this fire, which must make it extremely difficult for them at this severa season; especially when it is considered that many of those who lost their shops in March last, are not yet supplied with proper places to carry on their respective business in.

   The frequent fires in this town in winter, are occasioned oftentimes by the great quantity of charcoal which are burnt in pots: wherefore people are reminded to see that their pots of fire are well extinguished before they leave them; and that they have their chimnies swept, and particularly to be careful of ashes which are generally carried into the cellar.

   BOSTON Jan. 19. Whereas great quantities of Goods and Merchandize were remov'd from several Warehouses and Stores on the Dock, when the fire broke out there on Tuesday Night last, to different Parts of the Town, a large Proportion whereof is not return'd to the Owners, nor can they tell who has 'em; and as many Persons may be possess'd of those Goods who would gladly return them, if they knew whose property they were; these are therefore to desire all Persons who have any such Goods & Merchandize in their keeping, to send 'em to the Warehouse of Mr. Thomas Bremfield, Merchant, on the South Side of the late Market, on the Dock, where proper

Persons will attend to receive and take care of 'em, for benefit of those to whom they belong.
—— And if any Persons willfully conceal said Goods and Merchandize, with an intent to defraud the Owners thereof, such may depend upon being prosecuted with the utmost severity of the Law.

At the Desire of the Merchants, and by Order of the Selectmen,

       Ezerkiel Goldthwait, Town Clerk.

CHARLESTOWN S. Carolina Jan. 21. The Cherokees and Creeks seem determined to kerp up the War, which will no doubt end in the destruction of both.

CHARLESTOWN S. Carolina Jan. 24. We hear that Capt. Quintyne Kennedy, of the 17th regiment, is to command the body of Mohawks that are to act against the Cherokees.

BOSTON Jan. 26. A Ship and Snow with about 250 of our Provincial Troops, who had been for near two Years past in his Majesty's Garrison at Louisbourg, and sailed from thence in November last, are not as yet arrived: It is probable, if they have not made a Harbour to the Southward, they were obliged to go off the Coast in the late severe Season; as also a Vessel from Glasgow, which was spoke with about a fortnight ago on the Coast.

Capt. Furlong late of the Schooner bound from Quebec to New-York, arrived here last Wednesday passenger in a Vessel from Halifax, and informs, Thar after he had left the River St, Lawrence he met with very bad Weather, which obliged him to lay to, whom on the 15th of November at ten o'Clock at night his Vessel drove on Isle Sable. He had on board Major Elliot with his Lady, and a Party of about 50 Regular Troops, who all got on Shore safe. excepting two of the Seamen that were drowned: When they landed, they found the Company of another Schooner which had been cast away a few Days before, one Porter Master, belonging to Ipswich and was bound from Louisbourg for Boston: There being no place for Habitation, or Wood for Fuel, on the Island, they took the Sails of the Vessels to make a covering, an pieces of the Wrecks, served for firing, it being exceeding cold Weather: There were a number of live Cattle on the Island; but, they save little or no Bread, nor indeed scarce any Thing that belonged to the Vessels. After being 7 Weeks in this deplorable Condition, they discovered a Marblehead Schooner making towards them; but the Sea running high and the weather very boisterous, only the above Capt. Furlong and some Seamen could get on board; they immediately sailed for Halifax leaving the Major with his Lady and about 50 others behind, who were in Health, except Capt. Porter.

The above Marblehead Schooner was fitted out by the People of that Place in quest of one of their Fishing Schooners, which had been missing from the Banks the last Fishing Season, and supposed to be on the above Island Sables; but tho' they had not the Pleasure of finding their Brethren there, yet they came very opportunely for the Relief of others in Distress. ——— Upon Arrival of the above at Halifax, Commodore Lord Colville ordered one of the Tenders to accompany the Marblehead Schooner, which was taken into Pay, to proceed immediately to Island Sables, to bring off those that were left behind.

BOSTON Jan. 26. The following Advice from St. Johns's (in Antigua) Dated Nov. 26. His Majesty's ship Stirling Castle, of 74 guns, Capt. Everit, arrived here last night, and Bro't in a Brig, laden with sugar and coffee from Hispanoola.

From Santa Croix, and the neighbouring islands, we hear, that the French privateers are very numerous thereabout; hardly a day passes without some of our Northwardmen being carried in there, and are generally sold the next day.

It is strongly reported and is generally believed, that the privateer Sloop Sanders, Capt. Stevenson from this place has been sunk by two armed vessels from Curracea, who willfully suffered all the crew to perish.

We are informed that upwards of 30 French privateers have lately sailed from Martinique chiefly in quest of Philadelphia vessels, of whom they have already taken several: And that they formed a chain quite from the Northward of Barbuda to the Virgins.

NEW-YORK Jan. 26. We hear there is several vessels ashore between the Capes of Delaware and Sandy-Hook, one was known to be a brig inward bound from the West-Indies, Brown Master, belonging to this port.

Capt. Corne, in a snow belonging to this port also, bound from Jamaica, is also ashore on the South Side of Long Island.

We are credibly Informed, That a privateer sloop, belonging to Jamaica, late the Fox, of this port, in an engagement with a French privateer of 6 guns, off Hispaniola, was blown up, and her whole crew, one man excepted, perished.

CHARLESTOWN S. Carolina Jan. 28. Saturday last the Governor was pleased to appoint Lauchlane Mackintosh, Esq; Captain-commandant of Fort Prince George Keowee.

We hear Capt. Mackintosh set out immediately for the camp at Congarees, and thence to Ninety-six and Keowee, where he will relieve Mr. Miln, who has been Commandant of Fort Prince George ever since the death of Mr. Coytmore.

On Friday last his honour the Governor sent an express to the Governor of North Carolina and Georgia, with dispatches said to be concerning the intended operations of the ensuing campaign to the westward, &c.

BOSTON Jan. 31. Whereas a Quantity of Tea, and other Goods by law prohibited to be imported, were landed in some Part of this town on Sunday the 11th Current: We the Subscribers, two of the principal Officers of his Majesty's Customs for the Port of Boston, so hereby promise to any Person who will inform be thereof, so that we may seize the said Goods, or any part thereof, and prosecute the same to Condemnation, that he shall receive from us, upon demand, after said Goods, or any part thereof, are condemned, one Third Part of the Appriz'd Value.

       Rob. Temple, Comptroller.
       Cha. Paxton Surveyer.

FEBRUARY 1761

BOSTON Feb. 2. By His Excellency Francis Bernard, Esq; Captain General and Governor in Chief in and over His Majesty's Province of the Massachusetts-Bay, in New-England, and vice Admiral of the same.

A PROCLAMATION

For the Encouragement of Piety and Virtue, and the Preventing of Vice, Prophaneness and Immorality.

His most gracious Majesty having an early attention to the Welfare of his People, and being sensible how much their religion and moral Duties, hath been pleased, among the first Acts of his Reign, to issue his royal Proclamation for Encouragement of Piety and Virtue, and for preventing of Vice, Prophaneness and Immorality in which He declares by Royal Purpose and Resolution to punish all Persons guilty thereof, of whatsoever Degree or Quality, especially such as are employed near his royal Person; and that, for the Encouragement of Religion and Morality. He will upon all Occasions, distinguish Persons of Piety & Virtue by Marks of his Royalty to our.

And He strictly enjoins all his Subjects, of what Degree and Quality soever, from playing on the Lord's Day at Dice, Cards, or any other Game, either in public or private Houses or other Places whatsoever: and require and commands them decently and reverently to attend the Worship of God on every Lord's Day, on Pain of his highest Displeasure, and of being prosecuted against with the utmost Rigour that may be by Law.

And, for the most effectual reforming all such Persons who, by reason of their dissolute Lives and Conversations, are a Scandal to his Kingdom,

His further Pleasure is, that all Judges, Mayors, Sheriffs, Justices of the Peace and all other Officers and Ministers by very vigilant and strict in the Discovery, and the effectual Prosecution, and Punishment of all Persons who shall be guilty of excessive Drinking, Blasphemy profane Swearing, Lewdness, Profanation of the Lord's Day, or other dissolute immoral and disorderly Practices; and that they take Care also to effectually suppress all publick gaming Houses, and other lewd and disorderly Houses.

And, to the end that all Vice and Debauchery may be prevented, and Religion and Virtue be practiced by all Officers, private Soldiers, Marines and others who are employed in the service by Sea and Land: all Officers and Commanders whatsoever are commanded to avoid all Profaneness, Debauchery and other Immoralities; and that by their own good and virtuous Lives and Conversations, they set good Example to all such as are under their Care and Authority; and likewise to Care and inspect the Behaviour of such as are under them, and punish all those who may be guilty of any of the Offences of their Neglect therein:

I should be greatly deficient in my Duty, If I was to neglect exerting the Power, with which I am vested to the good Purpose aforementioned: Wherefore I have thought fit, by and with the Advice of His Majesty's Council to publish and declare, That it is my firm Resolution to use my utmost Endeavours, that His Majesty's most gracious Proclamation be duely observed within this Province, as well according to the true Intent and purpose as to the strict Letter thereof.

I do therefore command and enjoin all Judges, Justices, Sheriffs, and all other Magistrates and Officers whatsoever, that they take dire Care that all the Laws for the promoting true Religion and Virtue, and for the restraining of Wickedness and Vice, be duely observed; and that all Offenders against the same, be brought to condign Punishment. And recommend to all Ministers of the Gospel, that they be assisting in this good Work, as well by their public Ministry as by their private Council and Advice. And I exhort all the good People of the Province, that they contribute what they can towards general Reformation of Manners by their Example, by their Influence, and by all Means in their Power; remembering what great Things God hath done for them, and how much they are indebted to Him, for the manifold Mercies upon them.

And I further declare, That in the Disposal of the Offices of Honour and Trust within this Government, it is my Intention, that an exemplary Life and a Religious Conversation ahall be considered as necessary Qualifications of the Persons to be appointed thereto, as be placed among the best Recommendations to the public Service.

And I do hereby require the Justices of Assize and Justices of the Peace in the Session, to give strict Charge for the Prosecution and Punishment of all Persons guilty of the aforesaid Offences; And that they do in their several Courts cause the Proclamation to be publickly and immediately before the Charge is given.

Given at the Council Chamber on Boston, the Twenty sixt Day of January 1761, in the First Year of the Reign of our Sovereign Lord George the Third, by the Grace of God, of Great Britain, France and Ireland, King defender of the Faith, &c.   Francis Bernard.
By His Excellency's Command,
    A. Oliver, Secr'y.
          God save the King.

BOSTON Feb. 2. All Persons that have had their Vessels taken up by Leonard Jarvis, Esq; by Order of His Excellency General Amherst, for the Year 1760 to transport Cattle to Quebec are desired immediately to come and settle their accounts with said Jarvis, that they may receive Certificates of their having complyed with there Charter-Parties. ——— And all Persons that have returned Certificates is Impress Bills are also desired to come and advise with him.

BOSTON Feb. 2. Notice is hereby given to all who have subscribed to settle upon Lands reserved for me in Nova-Scotia, that they send in a list of their Names to the following Persons, employed as Agents, viz. In the Province of Massachusetts-Bay, Mr. Andrew Gambell of Milton, at Lieut. Oliver Peibody of Andover. In the Province of New-Hampshire, to Matthew Parron, Esq; of Bedford, Mr. William Fisher, and Mr. David Archibald of Windham. ———

It will be likewise necessary, that they signify the Time they shall be ready to embark, and at what Ports, that Vessels may be provided accordingly.   Alexander McNutt.

Boston Feb. 2. Extract of a Letter from South Carolina, dated Decenber 24, 1760.

" We have received advice that his Excellency Gen. Amherst has destin'd 600 men to be taken from Gen. Whitmore's regiment, 200 from Gen. Mockton's, and 400 from other old regiments, all choice troops, season'd to America, to assist in chastising our perfidious Indian enemies besides four companies of Maj. Hamilton, who seem likely to remain, orders being received to discharge the transports that were left for them. Since the departure of Gov. Ellis, the Lieut. Gov. Wright, has had 25 headmen and 140 Creek Indians, who all made the strongest profession of Friendship, and went away in very good temper. The General Assembly of North Carolina are dissolved, and the troops disbanded. The Assembly had presented a bill for continuing their forces and augmenting them to 600, but had tack'd an Agent to it, which has obliged the Governor to refuse his assent, and occasion'd their dissolution. Letters from Georgia, says, they are in great expectation that Gov. Ellis will intercede with Gen. Amherst, that the troops which may be sent for their protection, may be provided with quarters, &c. at the expence of the Crown, the province being yet unable to support such a burden.

That Gov. Wright gives the greatest satisfaction imaginable; and that as the terror from the Creeks subside, the people begin again to look out sharp for vacant lands on the Frontiers."

NEWPORT Rhode Island Feb. 3. From Carolina we learn, That Major Thompson with 470 Rangers, arrived at Fort Prince George on the 3d of December, and had thrown in a Supply of Provisions, viz. 8000 Wt. of Flour, a Waggon Load of Salt, and 58 Head of Cattle; together with Cloathing, Firewood, and other Necessities. And further, that the Little Carpenter had delivered to Col. Byrd 10 Prisoners taken at Fort Loudoun, and reported that 40 more on the Way.

CHARLESTOWN S. Carolina Feb. 4. On Sunday last his Honour received dispatches from Mr. Miln, at Fort Prince George.

Fort Prince George, Jan. 22. "Nothing wort notice since my last of the 11th, only yesterday an officer and a party being out to cut wood, Hugh Jutt and William Townsend, two of the provincials, staid behind unknown to the party, and were shot and scalp'd within sight of the fort, by a party of Indians. I gave all the timely assistance possible, but on one approach the Indians made off, leaving behind them a Creek warrior. ─── The Indians have now abandoned those lower towns almost entirely. ─── Several white people (greater villains than the savages themselves) who remain among the Indians, persuade them not to deliver up their prisoners telling them we shall never carry on war against them while they keep them in confinement. ─── The Creeks continue to give them assurance of assistance. Since Oucannosstota returned from the French with the goods and ammunition, and had those assurances from the Creeks he says 'What nation or what people am I afraid of? I do not regard all the forces the great King George cans send against me among those mountains."

"The Mankiller of Newcasih, who went home on the 6th instant, promising to return in 8 nights, with at least 5 prisoners, which he said he had bought from his own towns and lodged in his house, has not appeared since. I have seen a great character given of this Indian in one of the gazettes, wherein it was said, that every one here looked upon him as a true friend Indian in the nation. This was certainly a mistake of writer or printer; for I never had (as you know) a good opinion of him, especially after the plot he laid with Serowih. I could give you many intances of his being a bad man; and am fully persuaded, that most of his late frequent visits here were made only in expectation of meeting with or hearing of, some of those people whom he had sent down to the settlements with leather, &c. to purchase goods for him: I doubt whether he will come any more; if he does, I Think it must be on some new-concerted scheme, and can be on no good design.

What will be the fate of out prisoners in the nation, God knows. I wish they were well out of it; They are mostly painted and dressed like the Indians. ——— I am glad to hear Mr. Mackintosh may be expected up here, for the Cherokees in general have truly the greatest regard for him, of any white man that ever was in their nation; in short, his conduct when here formerly, has made him a great favorite of theirs, and I believe they will put much confidence in what he tells them."

According to some late advices from the Northward, it is probable, that the army in this province may soon be augmented with more regular troops; and that the famous Major Rogers, with some other partizans of merit, and as many Indians as can be procured, will likewise be sent this way, to act wherever they can be of the most service. And there are some hints, that we may perhaps sooner see peace and security restored to these southern provinces than Expected.

Philadelphia Feb. 5. The sloop Sally and Polly, Capt. Dennis, of this Port was taken off Teneriffe by a French privateer; and the schooner Seaflower, Capt. Winter, was also taken off the same place, but returned to the Captain after 10 pipes of wine were taken out of her.

We have Advice from St. Christophers, That Capt. McPherson, of the Britannia privateer of this port, has retaken two snows, one from London to Antigua, with King's stores; the other from Marblehead for Guadeloupe with fish and lumber: That he has taken a large Dutch ship in her ballast, from Martinico: That he took a Dutch brig from a small privateer belonging to St. Christophers, suspecting some Collusion between the Captains: And that he had informed the Colloden man of war of a Dutch ship bro't into Sandy Point by the same privateer; which ship the Calloden cut out and carried to Basseterre.

PRINCE Town (New-Jersey) Feb. 5. Yesterday at about two o'clock in the afternoon died, at his house in this town, the Reverend Mr. Samuel Davies, President of the college of New-Jersey, in the thirty-eight year of his age. He was seized, last Monday se'nnight with a violent inflammatory fever, which greatly affected his brain, and continued so obstinate as not to be controul'd by power of medicine.

ANNAPOLIS (Maryland) Feb. 5. A few days ago, a Widow on Kent Island, having left two small children at home by themselves, while she went to a neighbour's, the eldest a little girl about 3 years old, being cloathed in callico, by some accident her cloaths took fire, and she run out of the house; the mother soon after returning home, and seeing a smoke in the snow, went to it, and to her great Astonishment, found it to be her little daughter burnt to death.

BOSTON Feb. 9. The Publick are hereby inform'd that the Lad who has lately had small-Pox in Middle-Street is recover'd, that the Negro woman at the Pest House is almost well, and there is no other Person in Town that has this distemper, and there is now the greatest Probability it will spread no further: And as the small-Pox has been and still is in several Towns in the Country and Nurses have gone from hence to attend the sick there, some of whom may be now returning. —— It's desir'd the Select Men of such Towns would give Directions that those Nurses take particular Care to leave all their Apparel in those Houses in the Country where they have been nursing; and that they do not attempt to come into Town but in such Apparel only, in is altogether free from Infection, and they may depend upon being confin'd if they do, the Select Men apprehending the greatest Danger at present is from the Nurses who are soon expected here.   By order of the Select Men,
          Ezekiel Goldthwaite Town Clerk.
Province of Massachusetts-Bay. Feb. 5, 1761.

BOSTON Feb. 9. This Day came to Town John Malcom, from Quebec in Canada, and desired one Thomas Power a Suttler at Halifax, Immediately to come to Boston and settle all Accounts with said Malcom without fail, as his Tarry at Boston cannot be long, his business immediately calling him back to Quebec before the Lakes break up.

By Capt. Whitty, who arrived here last wednesday in 8 days from Halifax, we learn, that Major Elliot, with a number of troops who had been cast ashore on the Isle of Sable, on their passage from Quebec to New-York had been taken off, and brought to that place.

BOSTON Feb. 9. I the subscriber one of the Agents for Capt. Alexander McNutt, for settling the Lands reserved for him in the Province of Nova-Scotia, desire the Subscribers for said Land to meet with me on Thursday the 26th of this Instant, at 2 o'Clock in the Afternoon, at the House of Mr. Joseph Morton Tavern-Keeper, at the Sign of the White Horse in Boston; so I may know when we shall be ready to embark, that the Vessels may be got ready.   Andrew Gemmel.

NEW-YORK Feb. 9. We hear from Colt's Neck in New-Jersey, that a few days ago, three or four men dug out on the side of a hill, from whence a fine spring issued, fifty-two large rattle snakes, and nineteen black snakes, all twisted together in one bunch or knot. The cold weather prevented there making any resistance tho' the rattle snakes were so lively as to be able to rattle pretty briskly: ——— They cut their heads off the rattle snakes and then skinn'd them. ——— The digging was purposely after them, and a great number had been seen near the spring the summer before.

Friday the garrison from Detroit arrived here from Philadelphia, about 40 in number, and were immediately sent to Long Island.

NEW-YORK Feb. 9. Capt. Marshal who arrived here from Bristol about 14 days ago, informs, that on the 23d of November last, he spoke with his Majesty's ship Loo, who after a few days before retook the brig Ruby, from Maryland to London, who was taken on her passage by a French privateer; on the same day also; Capt. Marshal fell in with his Majesty's ship the Hero, or 74 guns, The Captain whereof informed him, that he had taken, in a short space of time before, 7 privateers belonging to Bayonne.

By an exact list of the royal navy of Great Britain, just published, it appears, that 40 French ships were taken this war, and now added to it; and 60 more of theirs have been destroy'd, or casually lost, since 1756, so that their navy is lessened 100 sail since the beginning of the war.

BOSTON Feb. 10. Arrived at Albany, Captain Jonathan Brewer, Captain Wait. Lieut. Hazzen and one other Lieut. with some Rangers from Major Rogers: The two Captains were gone to New-York with an account of the Proceedings of that Party, to his Excellency General Amherst. ———— They were informed there, That the Major in his Way to Detroit met no Opposition from the Indians; on contrary, they laid down their Hatchets and willingly submitted themselves to the British Government: ———— That the Major having taken Possession of Detroit, he sent the French Garrison to Pennsylvania; and the above Officers with a detachment of 75 of his Party with advice to Albany; almost all the Men were considerably frost bitten: one was frozen to Death in the Woods: ———— The British Troops being in Possession of Detroit, Major Rogers set from thence with about 50 of his Rangers, and intended to proceed 400 Miles further, some say he intended to come out in the Province of South-Carolina.

CHARLESTOWN S. Carolina Feb. 11. By letters from Augusta, on the 5th inst. we learn, that the Choctaws have kill'd three Creeks and one Euchee whom they took for a Creek. The Creek Indians in general, are in great distress for provisions. One of the Creeks killed by the Chactaws, named Mistifico, was among those who paid a visit to his Honour the Governor. A party of Creeks were lying in wait for those Choctaws who were lately here. It is thought war between the Creeks and Choctaws will be consequence.

On Sunday last the Wolf-King, with some others of the Creek headmen, arrived here from Savannah, in the Charlestown scout-boat, and yesterday morning had a publick audience of the Governor and Council.

The general Assembly voted the thanks of the House, and the sum of 1500 pounds currency, to be presented to Capt. John Stuart, as a gratuity for the many important services rendered by him to this province in the Cherokees; and for his conduct and perseverance, in the defence of Fort Loudoun; and has also recommended him in the warmest manner to the Lieutenant Governor, as a person highly deserving the favour of his Honor, and promotion in the service of this Province.

PHILADELPHIA Feb. 12. On Monday last the brave Major Rogers, with Captain Breme, arrived here from his long and fatiguing March to Detroit, where he was sent by His Excellency General Amherst, in order to take Possession of the French Forts there; and from whence he was to have proceeded to Michillmachinac, 360 Miles beyond it, to bring off the French Soldiers that were in Posts at that Place (as mentioned in former Paper) But that he could not accomplish on account of the Ice, so was obliged to return after having got 200 Miles of it ——— The Major met with no Opposition, the People laying down their Arms, to the Capitulation of Canada, and seemed in general, well satisfied with being under an English Government. ——— At Detroit he found betwixt Four and Five Hundred Men Capable of bearing Arms; 'tis a fine level rich Country, where before the war, there was a great deal of Wheat raised, Plenty of Cattle and the Inhabitants lived very comfortable; tho' they have not done so of late, most of the Cattle being killed, and their fields not cultivated as usual ———
As soon as the Arrival of this Gentleman was known, the People here, to testify their Sense of his distinguish Merit, immediately ordered the Bell to be rung and shewed hi other Marks of Respect. ——— Yesterday he set off for New-York.

BOSTON Feb. 14. Province of Massachusetts-Bay,

Court of Admiralty, Boston, February 14th 1761.

To be sold by Decree of said Court, at publick Auction, to the highest Bidder on the 26th Instant, at Twelve o'Clock at Noon, at the Royal Exchange Tavern in Boston, the Ship Squirrel, burtherned about 260 Tons, whereof Lewis Turner was late Master, with all her Sails, Rigging, and Appurtenances, for the Payment of Mariners Wages.   per Curiam,   Wm. Story, D Regr.

CHARLESTOWN S. Carolina Feb. 14. King Hagler has been at the camp at Congarees, and given Lieut. Lawrens a good talk, containing nothing more than promises of firm attachment to the British interest, and that he and his warriors would be ready to join the army upon the first notice. The Lieut. Col. acquainted him in answer, with the present situation of affairs, and recommended several matters to him and the nation's observation.

Major Thompson, Capt. McDonald, of Colonel Middleton's regiment (who accompanied Captain M'Intosh to fort Prince George) set out from the Congerees Thursday last for Ninety-six 'twas thought they would arrive on Sunday; and as the Major expected to find all the companies of Rangers compleat there, and every thing ready to proceed to Keeohwee, It is probable he moved frome Ninety-six last Tuesday.

Last Sunday the Wolf King and 5 other Creeks Indians that accompanied him to Savannah, arrived here from thence in a scout-boat; and he has since had several conferences with his honor the lieut. governor, and one with the Mohawks that came from New-York with the King's troops.

The same Evening Col. Middleton arrived in town from the camp at Congarees; where Lieut. Laurens, Lieut. Savage, &c. were arrived with the recruits from North-Carolina before he came away.

Saturday last the Governor was pleased to appoint Launchlane Mackintosh, Esq; Captain commandant of Fort Prince George Keowee, where he will relieve Mr. Miflin, who has been Commandant of that Fort.

CHARLESTOWN S. Carolina Feb. 14. A Gentleman who is well acquainted with the disposition and affairs of Indians, write as follows;

"It is certain that the Creek nation, are much divided; that we have many friends among them, that the Mortar and some others are very strongly attached to the French and Cherokee interest; that many young people are thirsting after war names and would do any thing to obtain them; that many Creeks from Oakehoys and Oaksuskees in the upper country, and from the Cowetah's in the lower are generally and may be now, amongst the Cherokees, and some will probably join them; yet I am of opinion that the sober part of the nation have no scheme in view, at least not for some time, for they will wait to see how you act against the Cherokees first. Don't be under any apprehension of the lower Creeks supplying the Cherokees with corn, for what you said before on that subject is undoubtedly fact. ——— I hope to hear of the troops destined to humble the Cherokees, being in motion soon, for the Indians must know of their arrival, by this time, and having no notion of improper seasons, not of the provisions on that must be amassed for such a body of men, will think and say they are afraid to go against them, in which error I wish they may continue till Col. Grant can surprize 4 or 500 of them."

A great many traders from Augusta has gone to the Creek nation.

Charlestown S. Carolina Feb. 14. Last Tuesday an express that had been sent to Augusta returned from thence, by whom we have advice, that Fool-Harry, and Young-Twin and the Young Lieutenant of the Coweta's; three Creek Indians of note much attached to the French and Cherokees, were in the woods with the Cherokees, in a joint hunting-ground of both nations, not much beyond 40 miles from Augusta: That something of moment was supposed to be concerting at these interviews, which is suspected to be no less than an attack, the coming spring, on the forts at and about Augusta, too well known by the Creeks to be filled with goods, great quantities of provisions, and warlike stores, and almost destitute of men: That some of the Creeks had meditated such an attempt, and even had made some preparation for it, last spring; but by some means or other, were prevented carrying that scheme into execution then: And, that many Creeks are continually coming in from their hunts with leather to trade the stores about Augusta, which may be a very pernicious consequence, not only enabling those Creeks to dispose of the Cherokees leather, and procure for them supplies of whatever kind they want, and thus baffle our measured to distress, humble, and reduce that perfidious nation to reason.

Considerable magazines are forming, and every necessary measure is pursuing, for forwarding and facilitating the success, of the intended expedition against the Creeks; so that there is scarce a probability that it will be in the least delayed, or unsuccessful.

BOSTON Feb. 16. Since our last came to Town from Quebec & Montreal &c. Capt. John Malcom of the Sloop Wilmot, and Capt. John Holmes of the Sloop Sally.

The Advices from His Majesty's Dominion of Canada are such as with Pleasure we can give the public, viz. ——— That all British Troops stationed in the several Parts of that Country, together with the English and French Inhabitants, are well and in high Spirits, having Supplies of almost all sorts of Provisions: ——— That great Harmony subsist among the whole. Those Inhabitants who lately were under the Tyrannical Yoke of France, now exult in the Liberty they enjoy under the British Government: No greater Burden is laid upon them than they can bear: ——— The British Troops are quartered upon the Inhabitants in proportion to their Circumstances; and whatever they have to dispose of they are paid for with strictest Honor, which attaches them greatly to their new Masters, or rather Fathers: ——— Any who are in want are supplied with the necessaries suitable for them: ——— Particularly we hear, That of considering the Circumstances of many of the poor Peasants and others, who suffered the Loss of all their Effects, and being under Arms most of the Summer could not raise Grain necessary for their Families, a Contribution was sent on Foot at

Quebec and a large sum of Money contributed by the Officers of the Garrison, the English Merchants, &c. &c. to support those Poor during the Winter.

Provisions it is said bro't into Montreal and sold very cheap: Poultry being in great plenty, and sold at Quarter of a Dollar, For a Turkey and Dunghill Fowls 3 for a Pistereen: and Wheat at 3 Pistereens per Bushel.

BOSTON Feb. 16. The following is the rout taken By Capt. Malcom and Holmes, from Quebec to this Place. ——— on the 8th of January they left Quebec in a Sleigh, in company with 12 other Sleighs having Goods for Montreal and travell'd on a good Road to Trois Riviere. From thence they went up the River on the Ice, and passing over Sereil, arrived at Montreal in 2 Days: ——— After tarrying there 2 Days they proceeded in their Sleigh to Chamble, St. John's and Isle au Noix, which they reached in 3 Days more: During this Time the Season was moderate for Winter. ——— From Isle au Noix they travel'd 45 Miles on Lake Champlain in one Day, but next morning after going some Miles, finding the Ice grow weak, they left their Sleigh, and went ashore with their Horse and Baggage on the South-East Side of the Lake; it being bad Travelling in the Woods. It was 5 Days and as many Nights before they arrived at Crown-Point. ——— On their Way the met an Officer with Dispatches for the Governor of Montreal and Quebec; with Accounts of the Death of his late Majesty King George the Second, & Accession of the present Majesty King George the Third to the British Throne. At Crown-Point they tarried one day, and having procured another Sleigh they proceeded another to Ticonderoga, and over Lake George to Fort George: Thence proceeded to Fort Edward, but the road not being broke they travelled with only their Horse: ——— From Fort Edward they went in a Sleigh to Albany: From whence they came to Town by Land on Monday last the 9th of February.

BOSTON Feb. 16. Capt. Swabridge in a large Schooner, rich laden from this Place, was not arrived at Quebec: The Indians reported that a

Schooner was cast Ashore 12 Leagues below Isle Bec on the North side of the River; having no Persons on board it was tho't at Quebec, she might be above mentioned Schooner.

BOSTON Feb. 16. IX o'Clock A. M. These are to inform the Publick that on Thursday last a Child at the northerly part, and And Yesterday a Negro Woman at the North Part of Town broke out with Small-Pox, and both were remov'd to the Hospital; and no other Person in Town has the Distemper. And for further Satisfaction on Friday last general Visitation of the Inhabitants was made by His Majesty's Justices of the Peace the Selectmen and Overseers of the Poor, and by Report it appears that the Small-Pox is not in any other Place in Town but at the Hospital as above. By Order of the Select Men,
Ezekiel Coldthwait, Town-Clerk.

NEW-YORK Feb. 16. Friday last Major Rogers came to Town by Way of Philadelphia from Detroit situated between Lake Erie, and Lake Huron, where he had been to bring off the French Garrison.

Whereas, a surprizing Monster, was caught in the Woods of Canada, near the River St. Lawrence, and has with great difficulty been tamed, and brought to the House of James Elliot at Curler's Hook. This is to inform the Publick. That it will be exhibited at said House till the Curious are satisfied. This Monster is larger than an Elephant, of a very uncommon Shape, having three Heads, eight Legs, three Fundamentals, two Male Members, and one Female Pudendum on the Rump. It is of various Colours very Beautiful, and makes a Noise like the Conjucture of two or three Voices. It is held unlawful to kill it, and is said to live to a great Age. The Canadians could not give a name till a very old Indian Sachem said, He remember to have seen one when he was a Boy, and his Father called it a Gormagut.

HALIFAX Feb. 21. The 11th Inst. being the Proclamation of King George the Third, as the Fireworks were played off by the Artillery from the Governor's Battery. Edmond Smith Matross, belonging to said Corps as he was standing on the aforesaid Battery, had the Misfortune by accident to be shot in one of his Thighs, of which Wound he died a few Hours after.

BOSTON Feb. 23. IX o'Clock A. M. The Publick are hereby inform'd that on Saturday a Soldier lately come to Town from Crown-Point was taken with the Small-Pox, and remov'd to the Hospital, that Yesterday two others were taken with it, one was immediately remov'd to said Hospital, and the other is to be carri'd their this Morning. These are the only Persons in Town who have the Small-Pox, except three who have been at the Hospital some Time, and are all getting well.   By Order of the Select-Men.
Ezekiel Coldthwait, Town-Clerk.

We hear from Waterbury in Connecticut, that one Abygail How, aged about 8 years, (an adopted daughter to Mr. John Slaughter of that place) having some time had a hankering for rum; Mr. Slaughter inform'd the child's friend of it, who advised him, (the next time she ask'd for any) to give her as much as she would drink. Accordingly on the 3d instant, some of the family told the little girl she might dring as much as she would. she was well pleased with the offer, and readily accepted the Rum; which was given her in a pint cup: and having drank almost a pint, she declined drinking any more; and being ask'd if she had enough; she answered, she wanted more, but was afraid she should be drunk; they told her she might drink what was in the cup, (which compleated the pint) and they believed it would do her no harm, upon which she readily drank it: Soon after she fell into a sound sleep, from which she could not be waken, but expired the next day; tho' all possible means were used for her recovery.

BOSTON Feb. 23. Extract of a Letter from Monto Christo , January 13, 1761.

The following was an abstract from the Journal of an officer on board one of the transports from Louisbourg, blown off to the West Indies, Viz.

"Dec 4, 1760. Sailed from Louisbourg bound to Boston in the Snow Hibernia, John Troy, Master, having on board two companies of Col. Bagley's regiment, viz. Capt. Stephen Whipple's and

Capt. Peter Parker's, in all 72 men, in company with two other ships with troops; at three next morning, being off St. Esprit, the wind blowing a hurricane at N. W. which cast the three ships on their beam ends, where we lay for some tome before we could wear ship, after which we past the other vessels, and in a few moments left them on their beam ends, and have not heard from them since; we then scudded before the wind and had our maintopsail split to pieces, and it was with difficulty we saved any of them; the wind continued blowing hard for several days, which poop'd us three times, knock'd in our cabin windows, and floated every thing in it; ———— From the 18th to the 1st of Jan. beating on the coast of New England to no purpose, the troops growing sickly, by means of their being confined between decks for near 20 days, the cabouse being washed overboard the first night, provisions could not be dress'd nor any thing got warm for the sick, it was agreed to try for any part of the continent, but the wind continued to blow hard against us, were obliged to put away for the West Indies: ———— Jan. 7. In lat. 20. 31. at 8 at night, going the rate of $5\frac{1}{2}$ knots, the forepart of the ship struck upon a rock or wreck, where she remained for some time; but by the skillfulness of the Captain we got off without any damage. We buried 3 men of a nervous putrid fever, one of which was Captain Stephen Whippel of Ipswich, when it was agreed to go to Monto Christo. At 10 o'Clock the same morning espy'd a boat in shore making towards us sailing and rowing with 8 oars; we got all the men under arms, that were able to bear them, and prepared for an engagement: At 3 in the afternoon she came so near as to send several shot over us, but did nor come near enough for our small arms; she then put about and stood for Isabella Bay. On the 11th, arrived in the bay of Monto Christo, and applied to the Spanish Government, who freely promised to supply us with any thing that we wanted on the Government's credit; we are landing our troops on an Island, and as soon as the troops can be a little recovered and the ship refitted we shall proceed to Boston."

NEW-YORK Feb. 23. By a Gentleman Officer who came to Town on Thursday last from Montreal, and who has been from hence to Quebec and back again since we had the Account of the King's Death; we are told, —— That all the French in Canada; of any distinction, went into mourning for the late King; —— That they have had a very mild Winter in Canada, the Troops all very healthy, and have all the necessaries of Life in Plenty. —— And, that Governor Gage has been Addressed by the Officers of the Militia, and Merchants of Montreal, on the loss of our Sovereign, in the following Manner, viz.

To His Excellency General Gage, Commander of Montreal, and its Dependencies.

The Address of the Officers of the Militia and Merchant of the City of Montreal.

Cruel Destiny has then cut short, the glorious Days of so great and so magnanimous a Monarch. We are come to pour out our Grief into the paternal Bosom of your Excellency, the sole Tribute of Gratitude, of a People who will never cease to exalt the Mildness and Moderation of their new Masters. The General who conquered us, has rather treated us like a Father than like a Vanquisher, and has left us a precious* Pledge by Name and Deeds of his Goodness to us. What acknowledgements are we not beholden to make for so many Favours? Ha! They, shall be forever engraven in our Hearts, in indelible Characters.

We entreat Your Excellency to continue us the Honour of your Protection; We will endeavour to deserve it by our Zeal, and by earnest Prayers we shall ever offer up, to the immortal Being, for your Health and Preservation.

*Pledge, in French is Gage.

Charlestown S. Carolina Feb. 25. On Wednesday Wolf-King, with several other Headmen and Warriors, being come into the Council-Chamber his Honour the Governor addressed them in that manner so agreeable to Indians, setting before them the power riches, and the number of warriors in the British nation, the happy state of those Indians who enjoy favour and protection of the British, and the poor and miserable conditions of those who had forfeited that favour. His Honour then mentioned the Cherokees, and told the Wolf that Nottowegas, who had ever been our true friend after accompanying the warriors to the northward in all their battles, were now come hither, six of them being actually arrived.

The Wolf-King began his speech with saying, "I never entered this room with so much concern or so ingloriously as I now do, neither did I ever speak with so low and feeble a voice; my speech will be on disagreeable matters, but disagreeable as they are, I will speak from my heart the truth. ——— I never came into nor sat in this house with so bad a grace; when I came formerly it was to make treaties for securing a plentiful supply of goods ——— I need not repeat the old disagreeable subject of the murder of some of the traders; I can compare it to nothing but a little piece of wood taking fire, and setting a house in a flame; it was soon put out. ——— I do assure your Honour, that the murder of the traders by some of the mad young men, was without the knowledge, and contrary to the will of the wise men. ——— He denied in the strongest terms, that the Creeks had any hand in the present disturbances between us and the Cherokees, who he acknowledged had frequently applied to them for assistance." We are aware, says he, "that the French likewise, as well as the Cherokees, are great Liars; they speak with forked tongues; and that all of their promises of friendship, and taking care of us and our children are nothing, for we know they are not capable of doing it. We already begin to feel the loss of the trade; our own interest in this respect, will bind us to the English." He then solicited that a quantity of goods might be sent up, and concluded with telling his Honour that Duvull's Landlord was gone out against the Choctaws for their killing some Creeks, and that he was uncertain whether this might not occasion a war between the Choctaws and Creeks.

The same day the Governor, had the Wolf-King and his Warriors at his own house, together with Silverheels, and three other Mohawks, who arrived here with Col. Grant from New-York.

The ceremony of the pipe being over, his Honour opened the conference; and addressing himself to the Indians said, "That he was glad to see so many of his Brothers present at his house; that the one came a great way from the West, and the other a great way from the East, to see him; that the latter has a great deal to relate of his part of the country, and his brothers the Creeks, might have something to say of the occurrences to the Westward, &c."

Silverheels, [a Mohawk] "I am no Sachem and therefore do not pretend to say any thing on behalf of my nation in a publick capacity, for that belongs to the headmen; I am only a warrior. I and my countrymen have been at war, by helping our brothers the English, for seven years past, against the French and their Indians. That war is now at an end, their is nothing more to do there, every thing is peaceable and quiet, we therefore turn our eyes to the Southward. We have heard of some noise of war to the Southward, therefore come along with my brothers the English to see what it was; and thought they are but a few of us Mohawks now here, I expect a considerable number more very soon, besides those that have already gone, and daily go by land to war against the Cherokees. I remember that an old treaty subsist between our nation and our brothers the Cowetaws; we are both friends to the English, and I would be well pleased to go hand in hand with them to war against the Cherokees; I will likewise assure the Cowetaws, that all Indians of Canada, and beyond the lakes have lately sent ambassadors to our country, desiring us to open the path and make it clear, that they might also go to war against the Cherokees, and the Cowetaws will hear of what I now inform them, this ensuing summer. I myself have been present where many bloody battles have been fought, a great many warriors killed, white men and Indians. The French began the war, but now they see the event, for there is not a strong fort nor a great town, but what the English have taken or destroyed, and sent the Governor of Canada, with his Captains and beloved men, prisoners over the Great

Water. Now there is profound peace from this place (Charlestown) to the northmost part of Canada, and all this land, and all the Indians that were formerly under the influence of the French, offer their service to the English; and there is nothing left to the French but the Missisippi. This is all I have to say to my Brothers of the Cowetaws, which I insist upon to be truth, and as a token that what I say is true, I give this string of Wampum."

WOLF. "I believe what my brother the Mohawk has told me. We the Lower and Upper Creeks have been at Peace for a long time past with our brothers the Six Nations, and an ancient treaty still subsist between us made by the Cowetaw-town; we observe it, and hope our brothers of the Six Nations do the same. I am glad to see them so unexpectedly and shake hands with them; with respect to the Cherokees, they have brought this war on themselves, by killing the English; they are now in great distress for want of ammunition and necessaries: They get some from the French at Alabama, notwithstanding which they will be obliged to abandon their country. Some of their towns are moved already, and others no doubt will soon follow. I desire to assure our brothers the Mohawks the Six Nations, that we [the Creeks] neither encourage nor take part with the Cherokees, and have nothing to do with their quarrel. Though we have been at peace with all nations for a long time, I hear the Choctaw Indians have killed four of our people; this probably will bring off a war between us and them. I depend on our friends the English to support us with arms and ammunition to defend us against our enemies.

This mixed black and white string of wampum, with the red string, which I have received from my brother the Mohawk, I suppose relate to the Cherokees which I will present to the Cowetaws, and acquaint them with the intent of it, I in the Name of the Lower, and Upper Creeks, desire the peace between us and our brothers the Six Nations continue firm, and that they may confine their operations of war to the Cherokee towns only, and not proceed beyond them towards our nation, and that they would also be good friends with the Chickesaws, I also desire my brother the Governor now present, that he will write to the commander and chief of all the Governor's to the northward, That no misunderstanding happen by the Indians who came to war with the Cherokees, and that and all the Indians that are friend to the English may continue in peace together. If they should be a few starving and distressed Cherokees happen to stray into our nation, and take sanctuary among us, I hope that will not be looked upon as countenance shewed to the Cherokees in general.

I likewise desire my brother the Mohawk warrior to take care of and carry this string of white wampum to his country; and there present it to the Sachems or Kings of his nation, as a taken to all their warriors that we have not forgot the treaty that has so long subsisted between us and them; as also that we want to keep fast hold of that treaty, that there may be no difference arise between us."

The Governor told the Wolf that he had already written to acquaint the General and the Governors to the northward, that the Chickesaws, Catawbas and Creeks were friends at the present to the English, and that if any of the cherokees who had not been guilty of the murdering the English were to go there, as quitting their guilty countrymen, it would not offend us; but if such as had the hatchet in their hands should mix among the Creeks, it possibly would the Indians who came to join the English against the Cherokees to do some mischief there, and therefore the Creeks should be very cautious what they did on that account.

MARCH 1761

BOSTON March 2. Wednesday last came to Town Benjamin Ingolls Ensign of Captain Motte's Company, who was on board the Snow Hibernia, and informs us, That he left Monto Christo the 20th of January last, That our Provincial Troops were remaining on an Island in the Bay, and the Vessel refitting; which as soon as they had finished would proceed to this Place: They were handsomely treated by the Spanish Governor and Officers suppli'd with Money to purchase Necessaries for the Men. ——— Capt. Hasset was likewise on board the said Snow: The three Men who died on the Passage were ——— Wallis & Sampson of Capt. Whipple's Company: ——— Clemens of Capt. Parker's. ——— They had heard nothing of the two Transports viz. Capt. Stewart's Ship; on board her was Capt's Davis, Corce, Newhall and Companies: ——— Capt. Rutlige's Ship; on board of her were Captains Blake & Peabody, & Companies.

NEW-YORK March 2. Extract of a Letter from Captain Byvanek of the Letter of Marque Brig Polly, of this port of 10 guns, and 18 men, and dated Guadaloupe, Dec. 7, 1760.

"I arrived here after a tedious passage of 26 days, owing to some measure to my meeting with several French privateers. The first two I met with, was a Sloop of 8 guns, and a schooner of 6, which happened on the 26th of November, at night, when we engaged them both for 3 hours, and 'twas with difficulty we got clear of them: The 27th we were chased by 4 sail in the latitude of St. Martins, who fired many broadsides at us, which we return'd as well as we could, and did them so much damage that they did not think proper to board us, and we were only on the defensive, made the best of our way, having our gunner and another man badly wounded."

Friday last a schooner arrived here in 9 days from Hampton, in Virginia; in her came passengers some officers belonging to the Boston provincials, that sail'd from Louisbourg last fall in the ship Nancy, they with great difficulty, after many weeks at sea, happily got in there. Several of their companies are come by land.

BOSTON March 9. Saturday a Sloop came from Norfolk in Virginia, The Master of which informs, that a ship called the Carey, bound from London for Louisbourg, put in there in distress, having lost some of her Masts at Sea; and that in the Road of Hampton, in weighing their Anchor, the boat overset, by which accident the Mate and 7 Hands were drowned.

Boston March 9. One of the two Transports with some of the Provincial Troops on board from Louisbourg, mentioned in our last to be missing is arrived in one of the Rivers in the Colony of Virginia, viz. Capt. Rutilege's Ship, having on board Capt. Peabody, and Capt. Blake, with their Companies. ———— As soon as the Ship had repaired the Damages, which she had sustained on the Coast in the severe weather last january, she was to proceed to this Place with the Troops. This advice we have by a Vessel from Virginia, arrived here since our last, who has brought three of Capt. Peabody's Men, and landed them at Cap-Ann.

The other Transport from Louisbourg is still missing; as also a Vessel from Glasgow that was on the Coast at the same time.

We have also advice of one of the Transports which sailed from New-York, with Part of Colonel Montgomery's Troops on board, last November, for Halifax; in a letter from a Gentleman in New-Providence, dated January 19th, viz.

———— "Latter end of last Week I was agreeably surprized on the Appearance of a Transport with Troops in this Harbour. ————November 10th, the Eight Companies of Colonel Montgomery's Regiment that was in Canada and the remainder of the Royal Scots, embark'd at New York on board six Transports under the Command of Col. Foster, bound for Halifax; this Fleet suffered greatly at Sea.

'The Transport come here is called the Mercury, Capt. Claston, Master, from New-York: the whole are of Col. Montgomery's Highlanders, 156 in Number, commanded by Capt. Alexander Mackkenzie; the other Officers are, Lieut. Archibald Robertson, MacNab, John MacDonald, Ensign Alexander Grant, and Mr. Munro their Chaplain. ——— They were beat down as far as Newfoundland, and the last twenty Days the whole were on short allowance, which was almost out the Day they made this Port. ——— The People of Providence has provided the Men with Quarters; the Officers are pleased and so are the Inhabitants, General Shirley received the Officers very politely."

Upon having advise at Charlesrown, South Carolina of the above Transports happily arrived at New Providence, Capt. Stote in his Majesty's Ship Scarborough, proceeded thither with the Ship Brotherly Love (Transport) Wm. Armstrong Master, with Provisions for the Troops. The Transport was sent lest the Mercury should not be in a Condition to carry those Troops to Charlestown immediately, Provisions being very scarce at New-Providence.

NEW-YORK March 9. We learn from Albany, that near 200 Sleighs set out from thence for Montreal, about a Month ago, with all sorts of Liquor and other necessaries for the use of the Army and the French in that Province.

Last Monday Evening Capt. Collins, late of the Schooner Sally, of this Port, arrive here by Land from Quebec, which Place he left the 4th of February last: He informs us, That the River at Quebec had not been Shut up this Winter; but that in general it had been thought a pretty mild winter there: That Forces in the Garrison of Quebec and Montreal were in good Health and Provisions plenty: And that there was great friendship between the Indians and the English. Capt. Collins was bound to Quebec but was cast away the 9th of November last, in a violent snow Storm, on the North Shore, a few Leagues above the Isle of Bic, soon after entering the River: The Vessel was lost, but the Captain and Men saved: he says the Indians told him of a large

Schooner belonging to Boston being cast away the same time as he was, about 9 or 10 Leagues lower, but he could not learn the Name of either Vessel or Master.

NEW-LONDON March 13. Yesterday Morning about a Quarter of an Hour after 2 o'Clock, a considerable Shock of Earthquake was felt in this Town preceded by a rumbling Noise.

BOSTON March 16. Last Thursday Morning about Half an Hour after Two the People of this Town were awaken with an Earthquake, which lasted about twenty Seconds but without doing any damage to our Houses. ——— It was divided into two Shakes, with a short pause between; and the last was the greatest. ——— The Weather was moderate for the Season, like that of the preceding Day; and a perfect Calm rested upon both Land and Water. The Stars over-head shone clear; but the Horizon all around was covered with a whitish Fog which appeared as if there had a light behind it.

We also learn from Fishermen that were upon the Water coming in at that Time, that the course of this Earthquake was nearly from the S. W. to the N. E. and that they perceived the Noise, as a distant rising Wind, some considerable Time before the Shaking came on.

NEW-YORK March 16. We hear that the brave Major Rogers embarked this Week for South-Carolina in his Majesty's Ship the Greyhound.

BOSTON March 16. IX o'Clock A. M. The Public are hereby informed, That the Persons lately mentioned as having the Small-Pox, are now well; that another was taken with it at the corner of Vitner Street about a Week past, who was afterwards removed to a back Room, and has it favorably: And as this Person is the only one amongst us that has the Distemper, or the Symptoms of it, there is good Reason to hope that the Town will soon be free from this Infection.

By order of the Select-Men
William Cooper, Town-Clerk.

CHARLESTOWN S. Carolina March 21. On the 14th ult. Major Thompson set out with 550 rangers from fort Ninety Six with provisions, &c. for fort Prince George. The 20th they arrived at the fort, not having met with the least interruption, and delivered there 89 head of cattle, 95 hogs, 50 barrels of flour, and 4 waggon loads of goods to ransom the prisoners in the Cherokee nation. The 21st the rangers threw in a good supply of fire-wood, and the same evening encamped at Six mile creek, on their return. That night, as their horses strayed to some distance from their encampment, in quest for food 129 of them were carried off by the Indians; one was found killed, and 3 stabbed. And no noise was made by the Indians (who perhaps intended to have surprized the men instead of the horses, had they not found them on their guard, and too numerous) this loss was not discovered till the next morning when parties were sent out; but the enemy made off with such a precipitation, that they could not be overtaken. Mr. Miln, Mr. Wilkinson, and Mr. Bell, came away from fort Prince George with Maj. Thompson, having remained there a long time, but are now happily relieved by Lieut. McIntosh and Ensign McDonald. The men in garrison in that fort are not yet exchanged.

Last Sunday arrived in Town, Capt. James Colbert, with a Cherokee scalp and prisoner, which he, with a party of Chikesaws took near Prince George the 27th ult. The party he fell in with consisted of 5, 3 of whom, being on horseback, got off, but one of them, having a fall, lost his ammunition and blanket. The prisoner told Colbert, that he belonged to a gang of 30 with a white man, who had been down to Long Cane, and burnt all the houses and provisions they found there, but were otherwise unsuccessful; that on their return the divided into small parties; that the Little Carpenter still pressed the nation to accept or sue for peace, by which it is plain that he continued firm to his attachment to the English; and that the Cherokees rather incline to the peace than to continue the war, but were kept in action by repeated assurances from the Creeks that their nation would at last join them.

On wednesday last 4 transport ships having on board the heavy baggage of his Majesty's Troops to be employed in the approaching campaign against the Cherokees (in conjunction with forces of this province) under the command of Col. Grant, sailed up Cooper river, for Strawberry, where they are to land the same, in order to be immediately transported in waggons to Monck's Corner, And,

Yesterday morning early, the said troops set out on their march from hence, to begin the campaign: They consist of 4 companies of his Majesty's royal or 1st regiment, 2 companies of the XVIIth, 3 of the XXIII, and 8 of the new raised independents: To morrow evening they may reach Monck's Corner, where they will halt no longer than may be absolutely necessary.

The behaviour of the troops during their stay in Charlestown has given the greatest satisfaction to the inhabitants; who, on Friday and Sunday last week, were very politely complemented and agreeable entertained, by the officers of the army, with a comedy and a farce, in the Council Chamber.

The Hylanders, who arrived here from Providence, remain in town under Capt. Mackenzie.

BOSTON March 23. By a Letter from Guadaloupe we have an Account that 33 sail of Vessels from these Parts were taken and carried into Martineco from the 20th of January to the 15th of February; among whom was Capt. Ordiorny in a Ship from Pistataqua, who while the Frenchman and his People were ashore at Matineco, cut his Cable, and carried the Ship to St. Kitts, and call'd for assistance; but before they could bring the Ship at Anchor, she fell to the Leeward, and was obliged to put in Tortola.

BOSTON March 23. Ran-away on the 19th Day of February last from Captain Ezibilon Ross of Dover in Dutches County in New-York Government, two Negro Fellows, one of 27 Years old, 5 Feet 6 Inches high; had on an all Wool Coat, lined with Flannel, and a Red double Breasted Jacket, his left Leg is less than his right and his foot turned out: ——— The other about 17 Years old, and has lost one of his Fingers on his right Hand. Whoever shall take up said Fellows, and carry them to the Subscriber, in Dover aforesaid, or to Jaremiah Ross in Windham in the province of Connecticut, shall have Forty Shillings York-Money Reward, and all necessary Charges paid.   Ezibilon Ross.

NEW-YORK March 23. Extract of a Letter from Montreal. ——— "The Case of the poor Canadians is really deplorable, occasioned by the bankruptcy of the Crown of France, Many of them who had, with great-danger and labour, acquired estates worth 20,000 Pounds sterling by the Fur-trade, or otherwise, can now scarce procure a dinner. All their remittance from the mother country, consisted in bills on the French King, which are not now worth a farthing, as nobody whatever will accept of them in payment. It is computed there is above the value of 3,000,000 Pounds sterling of these useless paper scrips, circulated through the colony, which, as a reward to the wretched inhabitants for all their hardships and fatigues, most now supplied the place of affluence and Independence. Most, if not all of them, are perfectly reconciled to the British government, as they can now with security enjoy a little property they have; whereas formerly, Governor Vaudreuil made no ceremony of seizing the produce of the lands, their merchandize and manufactures of every kind, and after conveying them to the King's storehouses, paid to the proprietors any price he pleased, if the owner therefore had occasion for any of their commodities, they could not procure them under twenty times the price they had received.

"Montreal in general is a well built town, but incapable of any defence. The churches are elegant, and the houses of some of their principal men are really magnificent; though few in number. The Hotel Dieu is by far the finest hospital I ever saw, every thing in it extremely neat and convenient.

"The people here are extravagantly fond of dress; a stranger would think Montreal to be a city inhabited by none but the rich and idle: they are all finely powdered, walk with their hats under their arms, and wear long coats, adorned with tinsel lace and buttoned down to the extremity. Since I came here, I have not seen one man dressed like a tradesman. The ladies in general are handsome, extremely gay, and not well bred."

NEW-YORK March 23. Saturday Night last between Eleven and Twelve, the Town was alarmed greatly by the cry of Fire; It proved to be one of the Forts on the Common, known by the Name of Block House. As it was a Monument of Reproach, and an Asylum of Debauchery, the Inhabitants, so much noted for their Agility at Fires, remained tame Spectators till this Castle vanished in Fume to its native Air.

HALIFAX March 26. Sunday morning last his Majesty's Ship Powey, Capt. Tonya arrived here from Boston.

The same morning one Mary Bird, fell down dead in the street, 'tis said she was used very ill by some soldiers or sailors, at a house in this town.

BOSTON March 30. Friday last one Andrew Cayton received 49 Strips at the public Whipping Post in this Town for House robbing viz. 39 for robbing one House, and 10 for robbing another.

The Town of Boston at the late annual Meeting passed the following Vote, which is now published by order of the Select-Men, niz.

Whereas it would be for the better Security of the Town, if the several Fire Societies would provide three Ladders each, to be lodged in such Places as they shall judge most convenient: therefore Voted That this Provision be recommended by the Select-Men.

Att. William Cooper Town-Clerk.

BOSTON March 30. The Speech of his Excellency Francis Bernard, Esq; Captain-General and Governor in Chief, in and over His Majesty's Province of Massachusetts-Bay in New-England, and Vice-Admiral of the same.

To the Great and General Court of Assembly of said Province, met according to Prorogation at the Court-House in Boston, on Wednesday the 25th of March 1761, viz,

Gentlemen of the Council, and Gentlemen of the House of Representatives,

I have his Majesty's Commands, signified to me by the Right Honourable Mr. Secretary Pitt, That, His Majesty have nothing so much at Heart, as by the most vigorous Prosecution of to reduce the Enemy to the Necessity of accepting a Peace on Terms of Glory and Advantage to his Majesty's Crown, and beneficial in particular to his Subjects in America; and as nothing can so effectually contribute to the great and essential Object, in the King's being enable to employ as immediately as may be, such Part of the Regular Forces in North-America, as may be adequate to some great and important Enterprize against the Enemy, in order the better to provide for the full and entire Security of his Majesty's Dominion in North-America and particularly of the Possession of his Majesty's Conquests, during the Absence of such Part of the Regular Forces; It is his Majesty's Pleasure, that I should use my most Endeavours to induce you to enable me to raise with all possible Dispatch, within this Government, Two Thirds of the Number of men which were raised here for the last Campaign, and form them into Regiments, to be ready to march according to the Appointment of his Majesty's Commander in Chief.

The whole that his Majesty expects from you, is, the Levying, Cloathing and Pay of the Men; and on these Heads, that no Encouragement may be wanting in the great and salutary Service, The King is most graciously pleased to order me to acquaint you, that strong, Recommendations will be made to Parliament in their Session next Year, to grant a proper Compensation for such Expences as above, according as active Vigours and strenuous Efforts of the respective Provinces shall justly appear to merit.

The Orders I now lay before you differ from those, which have been before signified to you on the same Subject, only in this: ——— the former were to engage you to assist in the Conquest of Canada; the present are to require the like Assistance in preserving it. ——— It would be injurious to you, for me to use Arguments on this Occasion, that should express the least doubt, that the preserving that Country should be less the Object of your Concern than the Conquest of it has been.

You who have so chearfully born the Heat of

the Day, will not now decline serving in the Cool of the Evening; You who have so well expressed your Duty and Loyalty to the late King, who began, and so successfully carried on this necessary War, will not be deficient in the same Sentiments towards his Royal Successor, on whom is devolved the important Charge of putting a good End to it: especially when he expresses so earnest a Desire to establish Peace on Terms of Glory and Advantage to his Crown, and beneficial in particular to his Subjects in America.

This would be due to any Successor: but to the present, your best Services will fall short of your Obligations. Figure to yourself a Sovereign endowed with every Virtue, that can diffuse Blessings on human Happiness of his Life will ever consists in promoting the Welfare of his People; then say, who can set Bounds on their serving such a King, except what their own Ability must prescribe, or the Expediency of the Service required shall limit.

Gentlemen of the House of Representatives,

I shall lay before you all necessary information concerning the Service required; and as it is distinguishable from that which is gone before, I shall point out to you the Particulars in which the usual Provisions will want Alteration. I shall also order the Treasurer to lay before you the present state of the Treasury; and you will consider how far it will want a Supply.

Gentlemen,

There never was a Reign that opened so ouspiciously in the British Empire as the present; nor had ever America so large a Share in the public, Joy, or so great an Interest in the general, Expectation. Let us therefore be equally distinguished by our ready concurrence in, and vigorous Pursuit of every Measure, that is proposed for making the most of the Advantages, that have been gained by this successful War.

Council Chambers
25th March, 1761.   Fra. Bernard.

APRIL 1761

CHARLESTOWN S. Carolina April 1. This Day the Highlanders march from town for the Camp.

We hear from Virginia that several large parties of the Six Nations and other Indians have been seen going against the Cherokees; and that both Virginia and North-Carolina are raising men for the common cause. We hope soon to hear this confirmed.

BOSTON April 6. As every British Subject will undoubtedly be somewhat solicitous to become seasonably acquainted with the publick Administration and changes under our new King at Home, and with the influence of his Majesty's Government on the Province of Canada, and his other other Provinces and Colonies in America; as well as with the important Affairs of Peace and War in Europe; We would assure our readers that we shall endeavour faithfully to publish the most early Intelligence we shall receive from Time to Time on these Heads, by the several Ships Expected from Great-Britain and elsewhere. And likewise with due Fidelities shall communicate such important Advices as we shall receive from England and her Colonies respecting the further prosecution of the War in America. ——— The Operation thereof in Louisiania, Ect. and also against the several hostile Tribes of Indians yet remaining on the Continent; and shall be oblig'd to our Readers and others for what authentick Intelligence they can give us as to these Particulars.

BOSTON April 6. Whereas Phebe the Wife of me the Subscriber, has run me in Debt, and refuses to live with me as a dutiful Wife ought to be, and otherwise behaved herself in a very unbecoming Manner; This is therefore to forewarn, all Persons from trusting her on my Account, for that I will not pay any Debts she shall contract from date hereof, as Witness my Hand,

Bridgewater, April 1, 1761.   Abner Fobes.

NEW-YORK April 6. On Tuesday evening arrived here 9 French prisoners, being the remainder of the garrison of Fort Detroit, we hear they are to be sent to Long Island.

Monday last his Majesty's XXIId regiment of foot arrived here from Albany: The behaviour of this regiment, when here about 3 years ago, gave great satisfaction to the inhabitants: They are now commanded by Lord Rollo.

HALIFAX April 9. We hear that all Regiments that were formerly 1000 in Number are to be reduced to 700 each.

It is said on board his Majesty's Ships, that Commodore Swanton is on his Passage to relieve Lord Colvil, that the Destination of the Fleet will not be known until his Arrival here. ——— On Monday and Wednesday last embarked 700 of Col. Montgomery's Highlanders, some on board his Majesty's Ships, and some on board Transports; we hear they are to sail for New-York under the Convoy of his Majesty's Ships, the Sotherland, Falkland, Repulse and Lizard, their Destination from thence will not be known till they Arrive at the aforesaid Place.

PHILADELPHIA April 9. The houses of this City and Suburbs have been lately carefully counted, when the amounted to 2909. In the Year of 1753 they were only 2200; so that they have increased since that time 769.

CHARLESTOWN S. Carolina April 11. On last account frome Ninety-six are that 47 more prisoners have been purchased from and delivered up by the Cherokees, 36 of them soldiers. making in all 67 since Capt. M'Intosh had been there.

We hear for certain, that the brave Major Rogers is appointed to command the independent company in this province, lately Capt. Paul Demere's.

We hear the regular troops at Monck's Corner, were to march forward from thence this day.

The Highlanders with Col. Grant sent for from Providence are returned to town in order to embark for New-York, whither Gen. Amherst has ordered them.

Near 70 sick of the Independents came down at the same time.

BOSTON April 13. In the general letters and memoirs relating to the neutral, civil and commercial history of the island of Cape Breton, and St. John's (which will deserve the attention of the public) in the following remarkable paragraph. ——

We have six missionaries, whose continued employment is to spirit up the minds of people to fanaticism and revenge. I confess that these arms are turned against our natural enemy; but this enemy has not as yet violated the peace between the two nations; and I question whether the Christian religion admits of our raising, without a cause, such sentiments in the minds of the vulgar, as are conductive to envy and hatred, and destructive to our fellow creatures. I cannot bear these odious declarations, which our priest make every day to the poor Savages, 'The English are the enemies of God, and com-'panion of the Devil: Since they do not chuse 'to adopt the same way of thinking with us, you 'must do them as much mischief as you can. Our 'King could not avoid concluding a peace with 'them, which is not to be of long duration. But 'this peace does not relate to you at all. Go 'with your hostilities. 'till we think proper 'to assist you. To behave in this manner is your 'duty towards God, towards your neighbour, 'whose blood calls aloud for vengeance; and last-'ly towards yourselves, since they aim at nothing 'but your total destruction.'

BOSTON April 13. The Government of New-York hath made provisions for raising, paying, and cloathing One Thousand seven hundred and Eighty seven men, officers included, to be employed in securing his Majesty's Conquest in North America; the men are to receive Fifteen Pounds of bounty, besides a hat, coat, a pair of buckskin breeches, two shirts, two pair of stockings, two pair of shoes, and one blanket, and also furnished with tents and other necessaries for the service of which they shall be employed.

The assembly of the Colony of Connecticut, at

their session, on the 26th of March, made provisions for raising and equipping, for the ensuing campaign, twenty three hundred effective volunteers, including officers; to be formed into two regiments, and commanded by the Colonels Lyman and Whiting.

The General Assembly of Rhode Island, at their session at Providence, the 30th ult. (in obedience to his Majesty's command, signified to them by the Right Hon. Secretary Pitt) ordered a regiment to be immediately raised, to consist of six hundred and sixty five men, officers included, for the ensuing campaign; of which the following Gentlemen were appointed field officers, viz. John Whiting, Esq; Colonel: Samuel Rose, Esq; Lieutenant Colonel, and Christopher Hargill, Esq; Major.

Last Friday between one and two o'clock in the afternoon a canoe set off from the Castle for Dorchester Neck, with three men, and by a flaw of wind was overset and one of man, Jonathan Chandler, about 22 years of age, was drowned; the others were saved.

Yesterday arrived here Capt. Stuart from Antigua in 26 days; he was blown off this coast in the severe weather we had last winter, coming from Louisbourg, having on board the Captain Davis, George and Newhall, with about 80 provincials which had been doing duty there. Capt. Newhall died on the passage from Antigua, and have also buried 9 privates since the left Louisbourg: The above vessel in company with a Brig from Piscataqua, two Sloops for New-York, and a Brig from Cock, were convoyed 5 degrees to the Northward by the Levant man of war.

By Capt. Stuart we learn that the French privateers are still very thick in the West-Indies, and take vessels even at the mouth of our harbours there, notwithstanding the utmost care and diligence of Commodore Douglass's squadron to suppress them: That Capt. Frost in a Schooner from this place was lately taken by the enemy, but retaken by some of our cruizers and sent to Autigua, and that two or three French privateers were also sent into the same place a few days before Capt. Stuart sail'd, by some of his

Majesty's frigates on that station.

BOSTON April 13. Province of Massachusetts-Bay Court of Vice Admiralty,

Boston April 11, 1761.

All Persons claiming Property in the Snow called Anglesoy, her Boats, Tackle, Apparel, furniture, and Appurtenances, seized by Robert Temple, Esq; Comptroller, and Charles Paxton, Esq; Surveyer of his Majesty's Customs for the Port of Boston, for Breech of the Acts of Trade, are hereby notified to appear at a Court of Vice Admiralty to be holden in Boston, for said Province, on Thursday the Sixteenth Day of April Instant, at Nine o'Clock forenoon to shew Cause (if any they have) why the said Snow, Appurtenances &c. should not be adjudged to remain forfeit, pursuant to an information filed in said Court for that Purpose.

    per Curiam.   Wm. Story, D. Regr.

NEW-YORK April 13. Friday night some Villains entered a house of one Mr. Price, near the Whitehall, and carried off a chest, which they found in the entry, in which was 300 Pounds in cash, and divers other things; but the chest being soon miss'd a hue and cry was rais'd, and several went in quest of the rogues, when they found the chest unopen'd, in the water, by the battery, which they cast thro' one of the Embrazures.

ANNAPOLIS Maryland April 16. On the 7th inst. the following tragical scene was acted at Mr. Booth's plantation, viz. while he was gone from home, a negro man which he bought last summer attack'd a negro wench, and beat her head to pieces with a maul; and would have kill'd a negro boy, but he sav'd himself by running: He then went into the house and murdered his mistress, bating her head to pieces, and an axe split the head of a little boy, his master's son, as he lay in bed. He then went away, and is supposed to have put an end to his own life. Mrs. Booth, and the negro wench were both advanced in their pregnancy.

PORTSMOUTH New-Hampshire April 17. Last Tuesday came to town Mr. Randle, late Pilot of the Schooner Elizabeth (alias Old Monk) John Frost

late Master, who was suppos'd to be lost in the great Storm of October last, coming from Philadelphia to this Place: as we have not yet obtained the Particulars from Mr. Randle, we only can say from Report. That the said Schooner was wreck'd, and after being 13 Days on the Wreck, they were taken up by a French Privateer, which was afterwards cast away on the coast of Spain. Capt. Frost and his Son is daily expected home.
——— Mr. Randle came home via London. Thus thro' the Divine Favour, we have reason to hope that a useful Man, is still preserved in Mercy for the Support of a distressed Wife and a Number of small Children; and Benevolence on this Occasion can never be better placed than on such Objects, wherein both Honesty and Poverty centers.

BOSTON April 20. On Monday last arrived here Capt. Rutlidge in a transport ship from Louisbourgh with the remainder of the provincials who had been doing duty there: He sailed from Louisbourgh for this place the beginning of last winter, in company with two other transports, who were all blown off the coast in the severe weather we then had, but have since arrived here as has been mentioned. In the Ship came the Captains Blake and Peabody, with those of their companies that had not come away before, having lost but 4 men since they left Louisbourgh, notwithstanding the difficulties and hardships they underwent: They were 30 Days beating on this coast, and were several times within view of Casco Bay, but the seamen being much frozen, they were oblige to bear away, and get into Virginia, from whence they arrived in 23 days.

Capt. Stuart in a Sloop, belonging to this Place, bound for Maryland, was cast ashore on the back of Long Island; the Vessel we hear is entirely lost.

NEW-York April 20. The General Assembly of New-Jersey have voted the raising of six hundred effective men, officers included, to be employed in his Majesty's service the ensuing campaign.

HALIFAX April 23. On Sunday morning arrived here some of the Royal Americans from Pisquit, who had been on command at that place, and are now relieved by the grenadier company of the Royal Scots, we hear they are to join their respective regiment at Quebec.

BOSTON April 24. Province of Massachusetts-Bay Court of Vice-Admiralty to be sold pursuant to a Decree of said Court, by public Auction at Royal-Exchange Tavern in Boston, on the seventh of May next, at Twelve a Clock Noon, the Snow Anglesoy, her Boats, Tackle, Apparel, Furniture and Appurtenances, seized by Robert Temple Esq; Comptroller, & Charles Paxton, Esq; Surveyor, of His Majesty's Customs for the Port of Boston, for Breech of the Act of Trade and condemned (by said Court. Conditions to be seen at the Register's Office and Place of Sale.

Wm. Story, D. Reg'r.

BOSTON April 25. These are to give public Notice to all those who have engaged to settle at Truro and Orflow in Nova-Scotia. That the Honourable Mr. President Belcher, Commander in Chief of his Majesty's Province of Nova-Scotia, hath sent the Montague armed Vessel, Captain Sivanus Cobb, with other Transports sufficient to carry them and their Effects to said Places, that they will be allowed two tons to each Person, with their Stock: Said Cobb may be treated with on board his Vessel at Clark's Wharf; the Settlers are desired to be ready by the first of May to embark, or as soon after as possible, and forthwith to send in their Numbers with their Stock, and all necessary Preparations will be made to receive them,

Notice is also given that the People are to provide themselves with Provisions for their Passage, as well as for the Time to come, and that there will be troops ordered for their Assistance and Protection.

Letters and Lists may be left, and further Information had at Mr. Hancock's Store Boston.

Boston April 27. By His Excellency Francis Bernard Esq; Captain General and Governor in Chief in and over His Majesty's Province of the Massachusetts-Bay in New-England, and Vice-Admiral of the same.

A PROCLAMATION.

Whereas the General Court in Obedience to his

Majesty's Commands, signified by his Secretary of State, in order to provide for the Security of his Majesty's Dominions in North America, and particularly of the Possession of his Majesty's Conquest there, during the absence of such Part of the Regular Forces as shall be employed in an Enterprize against the Enemy, hath made Provisions for raising Three Thousand Men, to be formed into three Regiments, under the Command of Gentlemen of the Province to be commissioned for that purpose, and put under the supreme Command of General Amherst his Majesty's Commander in Chief in North America: I have thought fit to issue this Proclamation, as well to invite his Majesty's good Subjects to inlist in such Service, and to make Public the Terms of Enlistment.

The Men who are to be inlisted to serve till the first Day of July 1762, but will probably be dismissed much sooner, either upon return of regular Forces, or by the intervention of a Peace; in which last Case they will be discharged as soon after the Security of his Majesty's Dominions and Conquests in North America shall be effected: And they will not be employed or sent to the South-westward of the River Delaware.

They are to receive the Bounty of Nine Pounds each, Three Pounds fourteen Shillings and eight Pence of which will be paid in a handsome Suit of Cloaths, &c. the remaining, Five Pounds five Shillings and four Pence, in Money: And that they may be assured that the Suit of Cloaths is of full value of what is charged at, a Suit will be put in the Hands of every Captain to be viewed as a Pattern.

They will heve the same Pay, and be provided with Victuals, Tents, Camp Equipage and all other Accommodations in the same Manner as last Year: And all the Officers are appointed before they receive Beating Orders, they may in General depend upon serving under the Officers with whom the inlist.

Given under my Hand at Boston the Twenty first Day of April in the Year of our Lord 1761, and in the First Year of his Majesty's Reign.

                                        Fra. Bernard.

By his Excellency's Command
Tho. Goldthwait Secr'y of War.

BOSTON April 27. To the Publisher of the Boston Evening Post. Some remarks and observations relating to the Choice of Representatives, offered to the serious Considerations of the Freeholders and other Inhabitants of this Province, in the approaching Election in the several Towns.

Salem, in the County of Essex, April 20, 1761.

The English Constitution, or form of civil government, is so wisely contriv'd as to adjust and limit the prerogatives of the crown, and at the same time effectually secure the liberties of the people; and therefore has long been the admiration and envy of other nations. ——— The people of England have the same title to their rights and properties, and the same security for the enjoyment of them, that our kings have under their crowns, or for the defence of their regal dignity. For as they can plead nothing for what they enjoy, or claim, but fundamental and positive laws, so the subject's interest in liberty and prosperity, is conveyed to him by some terms and channels and senced about with the same hedges and pales, namely, the ancient and unalterable establishment of our laws. In England, the law is both measured and bond of every subject;s duty and allegiance; each man having a fixed fundamental right, born with him, as to freedom of his person, and property in his estate, which he cannot be deprived of, but either by his own consent, or some crime for which the law has impos'd such a penalty, or forfeiture. And such law every man consents to by his legal representatives.

This excellent constitution, and these happy privileges, are not confin'd to the British Isles, but are the birthright and inheritance of every British subject, in his Majesty's most remote plantations. And we, in this Province, besides our cannon share of these blessings, have many and great privileges convey'd to us by our excellent charter, perhaps more intrinsick value, than that which was formerly wrested from our fathers, in the reign of a tyrannical prince. ———— What remains now, but that we highly esteem, and wisely improve these valuable privileges, and endeavour by all proper means to transmit them as a sacred depositum to future generations.

And this I am brought insensibly to what I had principally in view, when I began this letter; to which I hope the foregoing observation will be thought a proper introduction.

As the time is drawing near, for the election of Representatives in our several towns; and as we are too apt to neglect our privileges, it is proper, at this season, to remind us of our true interests. And surly, it is great importance to ourselves, and the welfare of our posterity, what manner of choice we make. The House of Representatives, is our branch of the legislative power, so that the laws to secure our liberties, and by which we are to be governed, are of our making: Nor can any tax be impos'd, or monies drawn out of the treasury, but by the consent of our Representatives. And the election of his Majesty's Council by our Representatives is also a greater concernment to us than we are apt to imagine; which may be more particularly considered in the sequel of this letter.

It might reasonably be suppos'd, that from long observation, and experience, we had by this time a clear and full conviction, what sort of men we should, reject, as unfit, or, elect, as suitable persons to represent us in the General Court. But, I fear, our inattention to an affair of such great consequence has still left very much in the dark. In order therefore to point out those men who are most likely to serve our best interests, because I would not neglect the common rules of order and method, I shall first of all, say what persons are to be avoided in our choice, And certainly, men of prostituted consequences, of corrupt, morals, and prostigate lives, are to be rejected with disdain and horror. Such, surely, are unfit for civil society, and therefore not to be entrusted with our liberties and lives. Next to these, we must turn our eyes from all indigent and necessitous persons, and from all such candidates who offer to buy our votes, both promises of treats and entertainments, or, that they will serve their towns for nothing. Let us remember, that according to a vulgar proverb, Every man who puts water into the pump to fetch it, intends to pump it out with advantage. Such men are therefore to be shredly suspected, that they have some lucrative post in view; or, that they are concerned in jockeying our unimprov'd and unappropriated lands. Nor let us vote for men, who are like to prove pensioners, or in any shape receive salaries from secret services: For person of this character have always been penicious to a state, and consequently the object of popular resentment, as from the histories of our nation is abundantly evident.

Moreover, let us not choose men too young, who are raw and unexperienced in political affairs; men who have never learn'd the very first principal of civil government, and know little or nothing of our happy constitution. An ignorant politician is a contradiction in terms. So likewise in our choice, let us take care to shun persons of tyrannical cast of mind, who are for promoting arbitrary measures, and straining the prerogative beyong its due bounds; men, who would render to Ceasar the thing that are more of his, by any legal claim whatsoever. In a word, let us pass by, in our choice, those men who have served us the last, or many former years, if we have found them either ignorant or indolent with regard to out great concern: Or, while they have pretended to serve our best interests have really been driving bargains for themselves, and swapping away our invaluable privileges. Let us chuse no man merely because he is a justice of the peace, a colonel, a major, a captain, or any other officer, civil or military, if he be Destitute of grand essential qualifications of a good Representative.

I shall now pass from the negative part of this address, tho' much more might be added, for our advice and caution; and proceed to say, positively, what sort of persons are like to make the most useful Representatives. And in general let us look out for the best men we can

find. And such doubtless, are those gentlemen
in whom the statesman, the patriot and the
christian happily unite. The advice of the good
old proselyte, to the Hebrew lawgiver still remains in full weight and energy, and is therefore worthy to be repeated on this occasion,
namely, that we chuse our respective tribes,
able men, such as fear God, men of truth, and
hating covertousness. Which last character, must
at least, include in it, and invincibly detestation of all venality, in every shape, and a
hearty acquiscence in the maxim of truth, that
no man was born for himself. Accordingly, men
of such character, will be ready on all proper
occasions, to sacrifice this private interest
to the publick good; and will exert themselves
to promote the increase of trade and commerce,
in our maritime towns, and the most valuable
branches of husbandry, in our inland settlements.
In a word, let us chuse such gentlemen as are
of know, and unshaken loyalty to their king,
and of hearty disinterested affection to their
country: Gentlemen, who will Zealously maintain
the power and privileges of our General Court,
and support the dignity of our good and wholesome laws: Gentlemen who will not be warp'd from
their duty by either frowns, or smiles, but will
ever look, with a jealous eye, on the liberties
of the people; and be ready at all times, to
guard them against every bold and unjust encroachment.

  I have already observ'd in this letter, of
what great and interesting concernment it is to
this province, that able and suitable gentlemen
be elected to sit at the Council-Board: It is
indeed true, that such election of his Majesty's
Council, is the more immediate business of our
Representatives, yet, If I mistake not, we, may
without impropriety, be said to chuse them by
their bonds. But however this be, it is certain
that the freeholders and other inhabitants in
our respective towns, duly qualified to vote for
Representatives, have an undoubted right to give
them (when chose) a premonition relative to such
election; and to advise them to pass over such
gentlemen, as by experience have been found less

useful at the Council-Board, and such also, as by reason of divers great employments in the state, cannot so constantly attend their duty at the Board, without great inconvenience to his Majesty's subjects. Among the former, perhaps may be reckoned those gentlemen, who are oppress'd with the weight of years,* and bowing down under many infirmities. And with respect to the latter, I must beg leave to observe, that pluralities in the church, have been often long complained of; and perhaps they are no less to be avoided in the state: This one, being as detrimental to the civil interest of a community, as the other are to the ecclesiastical. It has been thought by many wise in the executive trust, can with no propriety act at all in a legislative capacity, because that many affairs that necessarily fall under their cognizance, oftentimes clash and interfere, when they exercise the different powers they are invested with. Instances of this, I believe are recent in our memory. And the great detriment arising from hence, which the King's subjects have suffered, has been long observ'd in our lower courts. This, it must be confess'd, in an evil not immediately in power of those whose chuse our Representatives to prevent; yet, it is obvious, they may redress the grievance, by drying up the first springs of it.

Thus I have given some important hints, relating to our choice of Representatives; which, if we wisely improve, will serve to secure our best temperal interest, and promote the welfare of our posterity.

By the favor of divine providence, we, in these parts, have now a recess from the hazards and toils of war; a prospect of beating our swords into plow-shares, and of making happy transition to enjoy fruits, and cultivate the arts of peace. The same good providence, which presides in the kingdoms of men, has lately placed on the British throne, a King, of great and promising hope; adorn'd with every princely virtue, and eminently form'd for empire. Let us all pray (as every good protestant will) that his reign may be long and glorious, and that his

illustrious house may be prospered with all
happiness. I hope I shall not be suspected of
flattery, if I add to this, that the representative of his Majesty's person in this province
is a gentleman of great abilities, of superior
talents for government, and heartily dispos'd
to promote the best interests of this people.
May we all in our respective stations, contribute every thing in our power, to render the administration easy and happy; especially, by
leading quiet and peaceful lives, and all godliness and honesty.
 I shall conclude this letter with the pertinent and emphatical words of a former writer,
on a like occasion.
 "May the Heads and Representatives of our
tribe, come together at the great anniversary
convention, inspir'd with all proper sentiments
on so great an occasion! And may the sreadily
pursue the best interests of this people thro'
the whole course of the Year! And in the whole
General Court, may there at all times subsist,
that harmony and union, which, as it is happy
cement that holds the civil frame from crumbling
into atoms, so, it will forever be the strength
and beauty, the sure basis, and firm support of
every Community." T. B.
Postscript.
 It will perhaps be no unprofitable innovation,
if any of our towns should cause the forgoing
Letter to be publickly read, immediately before
they proceed to the choice of their Representatives.
 * Of late years, several worthy gentlemen,
in their advanced age, have resign'd their seats
at the Council-Board, to their own lasting honour, and given laudable example to others.
 BOSTON April 27. All able bodied Seamen who
are inclined to serve His Majesty on board the
Ship King George (commanded by me the subscriber)
let them repair on board said Ship, now lying
in the Harbour of Boston, or my House in Hanover
Street, where they shall be kindly received and
entered into immediate Pay, at the rate of Fifteen Pounds Old Tenor per Month, and one Month's
Pay advanced before sailing. ——— over and

above a share of all Prizes that shall be taken by said Ship in the same proportion as Seamen share in his Majesty's Navy. ———

A few Landsmen will also be admitted.

Boston April 20,   Benj. Hallowell, jun.

NEW-YORK April 27. Two companies of the men raised in this province, for the ensuing campaign, viz. Capt Byrn's levyed in this city, and Capt. Walter's in Richmond and King's counties, where they got a considerable number of volunteers, more than their quota, are embarked on board Sloops, and will proceed directly to Albany: The quota of levies for the city and county of New-York likewise very near compleat.

CHARLESTOWN S. Carolina April 29. By letter from Capt. MacIntosh, commandant of Fort Prince George, we learn, that he had received about 20 more white prisoners from the Indians, and that the headmen of all the towns have come in, and brought strings of wampum.

Accounts are hourly expected of the Cherokees being come to camp to sue for peace.

The Cherokees are in great distress for provisions and other necessaries, 'tis said, that to prevent their planting this year, would totally ruin them.

A dispatch from Congarees, dated April 15. "On Wednesday last Colonel Grant arrived here with the regulars. We expect all the troops will be entirely gone from this place by Monday, or at the farthest Wednesday the 29th. Neither the number of regulars nor the provincials is so great as it is said in Charlestown."

On Friday sailed his Majesty's ship Greyhound for New-York with the transport under convoy having on board Captain Alexander Mackenzie and the Highlanders; with them was likewise Lieutenant Colquhaun of the 22d regiment who came here a volunteer with Colonel Grant, being recalled by the General to join his regiment, which is one of those destined for the Expedition.

PHILADELPHIA April 31. "The extraordinary account of the Loss of the Schooner Delight, John Byrne Master; at Egg Harbour, was false in every Circumstance except the lost of both Vessel and cargo. The Person who brought the Account first was one of the Villains who plundered that Vessel: in order to give some colour of the Justice to their proceedings, they alleged that she had been run away with, and on this precedence apprehended the Captain for Piracy, and the Murder of Captain Wallace (the Owner) who they said was real Master, and had been killed by the Mate, who with the People's Consent, assumed the Command. The Captain is now in Philadelphia with the Gentleman he was cosigned to, who desires this to be inserted in Justice to him."

MAY 1761

BOSTON May 4. To the Publisher of the Boston Evening Post,
Seeing in your last Monday's Paper some frank admonition to Electors in the choice of suitable Persons for Representatives, it brought to my Mind some Heads of Self-Examination, very proper to be used by every Elector, before he either gives or promises his Vote; which, by inserting, you will much oblige, Yours, &c. A. Candidate.

Have I thoroughly considered the privileges, which, as an Englishman, I have the right to enjoy?

Do I put a just value upon the right I have, by our excellent constitution, to assent to all those laws, by which I am to govern?

Have I reflected, that when I chuse a man to represent me, I convey to him, for the time of his representation, all my own share of the legislative power? That I am obliged to abide by his vote and decision, or by that decision of a majority, which his vote may contribute to make?

Ought not a man thus trusted, to be of known abilities, one whom I believe capable to distinguish what is for the good of his country, and ever look, with a jealous eye on the liberties of the people, and guard them against every bold and unjust encroachment.

What is in his general character in private life? Is he honest to his tradsmen, kind to his family, regular in his conduct, not addicted to any notorious vice?

Without these private good qualities, have I reason to think he will be faithful to his constituents, regardful of posterity, steady in his principles, frugal of the public treasure, resolute against the temptation of riches or honor?

How has he behaved in other offices? On what use has he made of his influence, on former occasions, among his neighbours and dependents?

Has he ever before had a seat and did he not fall? Was his steadfastness from a virtuous principle; or did he bargain and higgle in a manner to create suspicion?

Does he want to buy my suffrage, or bias me, by some favour or gratuity? if so, how do I know he would not sell my right and privileges, if any man should bargain for them upon the same principle?

Has he a fortune sufficient to keep him above corrupt dependency? Or his fortune already involved, and does he push for a seat, that the protection of it may be necessary to him?

Does not the well being of posterity, as well as the present age, depend upon what shall be done upon this important occasion? is not my part of this work, as an elector, equal to that of any other man in the same community? Have I any excuse therefore, can I have any, either to my country, or my conscience, for saying I am but me, and my vote can be of no great consequence among many?

May not my voice be decisive in the election of a Representative, as the voice of him thus elected, may be in a law to determine the weal and bane of this kingdom? If I gave it amiss therefore, either corruptly, or inconsiderately, am I not guilty of the highest public crime that can be thought of in civil society?

BOSTON May 4. Since our last we are favoured with the following particular account of Capt. John Frost's misfortune in losing his Schooner Old Monk, on their passage from Philadelphia to Picataqua, as extracted from the journal of Capt. Randell, who was a passenger on board said Schooner, which as it contains some singular providences, may be agreeable to relate.

"We sailed from Philadelphia the 2d of October last, and on the 7th we met with a violent gale of wind at N. N. E. and a heavy sea, which obliged us to throw over 80 barrels of flour

and above five tons of Iron: On the 8th the
storm increased, we then put before the wind,
and at 4 p. m. the sea struck our starboard
quarter, which broach'd herto, carried away our
bowsprit and boat, and one man overboard, but
soon recover'd him again, and hove the vessel
on her beam before the sea; but by lightning
the vessel the day before, the barrels shifted
in the hold, and stove all our water casks, and
lost all our water, excepting about four gallons. The 10th another sea struck us, and lifted
the quarter-deck. The 11th the storm continued.
The 13th the sea abated, wind N. W. we then
opened the hatches and threw over 40 barrels
more: From the 13th to the 19th we lay wreck,
having no command of the vessel, reduced to the
greatest extremity, oblig'd to drink our own
water to quench our thirst, being then in lat.
33 to N. & lomg. 68 12 W. (almost in dispair)
when to our unspeakable joy, we discovered a
sail, which bore directly towards us, and soon
came up with us. She proved to be French from
St. Domingo to Old France with 46 men, who
they hail'd us, and ask'd whether we would be
taken off, to which we consented: but as they
had lost their boat as well as we, and seeing
our great distress three of them jump'd overboard, and risqued their lives, swam towards us
tho' the sea ran very high, but could not get
aboard us, some were obliged to put back to
their vessel, having narrowly escaped drowning;
yet notwithstanding, after they had made a small
tack, they attempted again, and with an uncommon
resolution got on board us, by which means we
got a rope fastened to a small hawser on board
them and hove us near under their stern, whem
we all got safe in their vessel and left our
own, after taking only 8 barrels of flour out
of her. We then steer'd E. N. E. for Old France,
but unhappily on the 6th of December, we were
cast away in a terrible storm 45 miles to the
northward of Bayonne, and lost vessel and cargo,
and 7 Frenchmen were drowned in endeavouring to
get to shore. On the 6th we were taken up as
prisoners, and the 9th put into Bayonne Castle,
and were treated as well as we could expect,

all things considered. After which, we, with about 300 more prisoners, were put on board a cartel vessel bound for England. [but our informant left the vessel and got to Balboa, and came home via Salem, and supposes Capt Frost and his Son sail'd for England in the cartel soon after he left them.] We must must inevitably have perished in a day or two more, has we not been discover's by the above French snow Stork, formerly taken from the English, and the extraordinary kindness of the Frenchmen who thus risqued their lives to save ours."

BOSTON May 4. We hear from Hebron, in Connecticut, that on the 7th instant, Mr. Joseph Allen, of this place, being on horseback with a midwife who had attended his wife, he fell from his horse and expired. ——— It is remarkable he was telling the woman, that he had a calf died yesterday very stangely, by running round two or three times and then dying; upon his so saying, he fell from his horse and expired. A physician being near, he immediately attempted bleeding him, but in vein.

BOSTON May 4. Since our last we received the following account of Capt. Swatridge, who sail'd from hence last fall, in a large schooner with a very valuable cargo, for Quebec, viz. That on the 9th day of November last, being some 2 or 3 leagues to the eastward if the Isle of Beck, lying to, with the wind at E. N. E. blowing very hard, and a very thick snow, under a double reef'd foresail, about 2 in the afternoon discover'd the south shore; and at 4 o'clock wore, and laid the vessel to, with her head to the northward: About 7 saw breakers a-head, under the lee bow; upon which, directly put the helm hard at starboard, thinking to wear her; as soon as she got before the wind, she struck on a hard sand and some rocks, and the sea making a free passage over her; but no water till 2 or 3 in the morning, when the shipp'd a very heavy sea, which broke her back and bilg'd her, and was soon after full of water: It being ebb tide, and about two hours after the water being pretty smooth, they got out their boats and went to shore carrying some provisions with them. At low-water, being about 2 feet, they went along side the schooner, and found her so much damaged that the water run out of every seam of her bottom, and her sternpost very much shattered: It being very cold they were obliged to return and make a fire in the woods: The next day they went along side again, and found that she was sunk deep in the sand, and lying on her beam ends. ——— The day after, they took their boats and their provisions to seak Inhabitants; and on the 14th saw a canoe with two French men going to Isle Cordre, who told them they would keep by them; but on the 18th, the Frenchmen being a-head went off and left them; so that they were obliged to put ashore at that place where was nothing but rocks, and ice, and haul'd up the boat as far as the could; but the wind blowing hard in the night & the ice breaking, carried away the boat and almost all their cloaths, they afterward returned to their tents and their remained till the 14th of February, when a Lieutenant of the 35th regiment, who was at Tadousac, with a party of men, sent a man to guide them to that place. where they accordingly arrived the 28th of February. ——— Henry Edwards and George Lish, belonged to the schooner, both died: The rest were then well at Tadousac.

BOSTON May 4. The following lately arrived from London dated January 22, 1761.

"Early in the Spring, it is thought, General Amherst will undertake another expedition in America against Missisippi the only French settlement now left on the continent, the necessary preparations for such an undertaking are nearly finished; and it is said, that Admiral Saunders or Holmes, or both, will shortly sail with a squadron to the American Seas."

The Legislature of the Province of New-Hampshire Resolved to pay five Hundred & thirty four Men, Officers included to be employed in his Majesty's Service to the 15th Day of November next.

NEW-YORK May 4. The Men of War and Transports lately preparing here to assist in some important Expedition against our common Enemy the

French, fell down a few Days ago to Sandy-Hook, where they were left on Saturday last all well, waiting for a fair Wind to push out. As the Wind Tuesday Morning blew fresh from the Western board, no doubt they took advantage of it.

BOSTON May 11. We hear from East Hampton, that a few days ago, a lad about 12 years old, being with a cart passing over hilly ground, it suddenly turn'd over, and the wheel falling on him crush'd him to death.

Last Monday night, being very dark and stormy, a sea faring man fell into the town dock, near the vacancy, where the buildings belonging to the town were consumed by the late fire, and was drowned ——— Two other men also fell into the dock the same night, at a different hour and place, but by timely assistance their lives were preserved.

NEW-YORK May 11. We hear that the Connecticut provincials, ordered to be raised, viz. 2300 men, are nearly compleat.

On Sunday morning sailed from the Hook, with a fine Breeze at N. the fleet which has been for some time preparing here; viz. the Souterland, and Lizard, with several transports under their convoy, having on board three regiments of foot, viz. XXIId, commanded by Col. Vougham; but the destination of the fleet is yet a secret.

HALIFAX May 14. Last Sunday night, one of Major Gorham's rangers named John Tambrow, despairing of the mercy of God, and the Devil getting the predominant over him so as to persuade him to be accessory to his own death; which he effected in the following manner. By tying a small cord to the tricker of his firelock, with a loop at the other end which he put his foot, and putting the muzzle to the temple of his head, by movement of his foot pull'd the tricker, which in an instant put a period to his days.

BOSTON May 18. Thursday last Capt. Dejano arrived here in 14 Days from South Carolina: ——— Our accounts from thence are, That the Cherokees were in great distress for Provisions and other necessities.

We hear from New-London, that on the 3d Inst. Capt. Rogers sailed from that Port, with 137 Passengers going as settlers to Nova-Scotia.

ANNAPOLIS Maryland May 22. Both upper and Lower Creeks are at war with the Spaniards, they have killed some Spaniards, and carried others into their Nation.

The French came in and demanded the Prisoners but the Indians told them to go about their business, they did not know how soon they might serve them in the same Manner, for the many Lies they had told them.

BOSTON May 25. We hear from New-London that last Week arrived there a Schooner which belonged to that Place: She was bound from thence for the West Indies but taken by a French Frigate who put 12 Men on board, and ordered her for Mortineco: Six Englishmen being left on board, and not liking their new Masters, rose on the Frenchmen kill'd two of them, overcome the rest, and brought the vessel back as above.

Boston Evening Post

A letter from Hingham, dated May 15, 1761.

"On Tuesday the 12th instant, a Whale was discovered very near the shore, thought to be in pursuit of a Scool of Herrings; upon which four Men betook themselves to a Canoe with their arms and ammunition, and going without the Whale, did such Execution by their firing, that in a few Minutes the huge Animal was killed, and by an Easterly Breeze was cast ashore at the Southerly End of Hull Beech; where upon survey the enterprizing and lucky Captors found that they were possessed of a fish commonly known by the name of the Fin-Back whale, which measured 56 Feet and a half, in length, and it is thought will yield two tons of Oil.

NEW-YORK May 25. We hear from Montreal that the Vicar General of all Canada residing at Montreal has wrote a pressing Invitation to the Rev. Mr. Udang, Chaplain of a Regiment at Quebec, to return to the Romish Religion, with a promise of great Preferment in the Church; which Mr. Udang put into the Hands of General Murray, who sent it inclosed to General Gage, who upon the Receipt of it sent a Guard to take him into custody. What will be the Issue is not known.

BOSTON May 27. Province of Massachusetts-Bay.

The following Vote passed the Great and General Court at their Sessions began and held on the 27th of May 1761.

Voted, That all Persons belonging to this Province who have any Relations or Friends now remaining in the Hands of the French, or in captivity with the Indians in the Contries of Canada or Louisbourg, are hereby notified (if they have Cause) to return a List of the Names of such captives into the Secretary's Office on or before the first Day of September next, particularly setting forth in said lists, the Sex, Age, Time and Place of being captivated, and any other Circumstances, which they know relating to said Captive.   Attest. A. Oliver, Secr.

NEW-LONDON May 29. Extract of a Letter from Mr. Andrew Thompson late of this Town, to his Father here, dated London March 9, 1761.

"Four weeks after our departure from New-York, in the Brig Audre, Capt. Lawrence, we were taken by a privateer of 14 Guns. Our Captain and people were carried on board the privateer, leaving only myself, two seamen and a young lad, they put 12 Frenchmen on board us to carry the vessel to Bayonne. ——— After being in their possession 14 days, we fell upon them about 9 at night, with an Ax, two Adzes, and a Pistol; we soon gained the possession of the captain, leaving that of the deck to them, they barred us down all night, about 9 next morning, we put a brace of pistol balls through one of their principal seamen, on which they immediately called for quarters, which was granted; at the same time ordering them all up into the foretop, and so bound them one after another as we allowed them to come down. ——— After having them in possession 10 days, we, to our great joy; arrived safe at Plymouth. In this Action was killed 39 of the Frenchmen and wounded 6; some of us were hurt but myself, however, am in a manner recovered, except a cut over my left eye with a cutlass. ——— We bro't 9 Frenchmen to Plymouth, who are now in that goal. ——— When we were first taken the Frenchmen strip'd me of every thing, even to my shoe buckles, so have lost chest, money, cloaths, &c. as they were carried on board the privateer; however expect our loss will be made up, having already had the offer of a Lieutenancy, which thought proper to refuse."

Besides the above, a Gentleman from New-York writes, that the four were introduced to the Lord of the Admiralty, from whom the received thanks and a gold Medal, for their gallant behaviour. Likewise that the underwriters had made them a present of quarter part vessel and cargo.

QUEBEC May 1761. "Our winter has been tolerably agreeable, the cold not near so intense as the former; the snow began the latter end of October, and did not give us a sight of mother earth till the latter end of April; indeed it has not all yet disappeared; however, we have past the winter very agreeable. Our regiment exclusive of those in garrison, were cantoned in the country from this to Montreal; the men lived with the Inhabitants very quietly, and the Inhabitants well pleased on account of partaking in their salted provisions. ——— The gun was our excercise, and there was scarce a day so cold, but we could with the aid of a few furrs, go out with pleasure. The remaining of our little Army are very healthy; this climate is certainly very wholesome, and life may be well enjoyed here, with the company of a few friends and a moderate income.

The richer sort of the Canadians (particularly the Priests) live still in great luxury, whilst the poor, who had suffered by the calamity of the war, would certainly have perished in numbers this winter, had not a most humane act of British generosity been shewn them, by collecting about 400 pounds among us, and buying the necessaries of life for these these needy wretches. The Canadians have the least humanity for each other of all the people I ever saw; the parents care not if their children starve, provided they can be supplied themselves. They are however, very much attached to their clergy, and support them in the greatest profuseness; an instance I saw of it the other evening when supping at the priest's house, his table was served up with three different courses, of nine, seven and five dishes, with variety of wines, whilst numbers of his parishioners, to my knowledge, had scarce a mouthful of bread to eat but what we gave them.

   The Indians bring us a great quantity of Beaver, partriges, and begin to be very fond of British money. ——— They of this neighbourhood in every respect live like the Canadians, plow their ground, sow corn, &c. and are more industrious in the chace then they; they all speak French, and have a handsome church in their village of Leretto, where I have sometimes been to see their ceremonies and entertainments, which are curious enough."

JUNE 1761

BOSTON June 1. We have advice from Charlestown South-Carolina, that on the 4th of last month at half after 2 P. M. a most violent Whirlwind, as that kind usually known by the name of Typhones, passed down Ashley River and fell upon the shipping in Rebellion road with such fury and violence as to threaten the destruction of the whole fleet. This terrible phænomenon was first seen from the town coming down Wappoo-Creek, resembling a column of smoke and vapour, whose motion was very irregular and tumultious and came with great swiftness. The quantity of vapour which composed this impetuous column and its prodigious velocity, gave such a surprizing momentum as to plough Ashley River to the bottom and lay the Channel bare; this occasioned such a sudden flux and reflux as to float many boats, pettiaugers, and even sloops and schooners which were before lying at a distance from the tide. When it was coming down Ashley River it made a noise like constant thunder at that time was judged to be about 300 fathoms, and its height to be 35 degrees; it was met at White Point by another gust which came down Cooper's River, but it was not equal to the other; but upon this meeting together the tumultuous agitation of the air was much greater, insomuch that the froth and vapour seemed to be thrown up to the heights of 40 degrees, while the clouds that were driving in all directions to this place seemed to be precipitated and whirled round at the same time with the incredible velocity: Just after this it fell upon the shipping in the road, and was scarce three minutes in the passing thro' the distance was near two leagues; there was 45 sail on the road, five of which were sunk outright, and his Majesty's ship Dolphin with 11 others lost their masts, &c. The damage to the shipping, which is reckoned at 29,000 Pounds sterling was done almost instantaneously; and some of those that were sunk were buried in the water so suddenly as scarce to give time, those that were below to get upon deck: and 'tis remarkable that but 4 lives were lost in the road. The strong gust which came down Cooper's river checked the progress of that pillar of destruction from Wappoo-Creek, which had it kept its then direction must have driven the town of Charlestown before it like chaff. This tremendous column was first seen about noon, upward of 30 miles W. b S. from Charlestown, and had destroyed in the course several houses, negro hutts on the Plantations, and many both white people and negroes were killed or hurt, besides many cattle have also been found dead in the fields. In several parts of its course it left an avenue of great width, from which every tree and shrub was tore up, great quantities of branches and limbs of trees were seen furiously drivin about and agitated in the body of the column as it passed along. ──── The fleet lying in the road ready to sail for Europe was the largest and richest that ever cleared out from Charlestown. By 4 O'clock the wind was quite fallen, the sky clear and serene, so that 'twas scarce credible that such a dreadful scene had been so recently exhibited, were not the sinking and dismantled vessels so many striking and melancholy proof of it. ──── The sinking of 5 ships in the road was so sudden, that it was queried, whether it was done by the immense weight of this column pressing them instantaneously into the deep? or whether it was done by the water being forced suddenly from under them, and thereby leaving them sunk so low as to be immediately covered and ingulphed by the lateral mass of water? ──── Most of the disabled ships were towed up to town the next day, and Capt. Scott of the Scarborough is appointed to convoy those that are able to put to sea in the room of the Dolphin, disabled, and will be ready to sail by the 12th of May.

   The General Assembly of North Carolina have voted to raise 500 men, to be employed to next

December, according to General Amherst's Order.

BOSTON June 1. Any Person that has a Negro Fellow to dispose of, between 16 and 25 years of age, that is Sober, honest and healthy, and understands Farming Business, may bear a purchase that will give good Price for him, by inquiring of Isaac Royall, Esq; of Medford. ——— The said Royall wants, and will give the full price value for a Pair of Coach Horses, to match the Pair he already has: ——— N. B. They must be black, with a white Spot on their forehead, fifteen Hands high, trot all, not above six, nor less than four Years old. Said Royall wants a Coachman, that can be well recommended, and understands driving a Coach and Four; and if he understands something of Gardening, he shall have more wages.

Wanted, a Servant that understands taking Care of Horses, that can wait on tables, is perfectly sober, and can be recommended for his Honesty and Fidelity in his former Service; such a one may hear of a Place by enquiring of the Printer hereof.

Deserted last Friday Night from the Ship Bayard, Joseph Cheesman, Commander, a Seaman named Daniel Donele, about 35 Years old, speaks very broad Irish; had on a blue Cap, and a course blue Jacket. ——— Whoever will apprehend the said Deserter, so that he may be returned to his Duty on board the said ship, shall receive Ten Dollars Rewars, and all necessary Charges paid by Joseph Cheesman.   Boston June 1, 1761.

PHILADELPHIA June 4. Extract of a Letter from Winchester, May 6, 1761.

"We are now on the March to the Southward; but how far we shall proceed against the Cherokees is not known. They received a Stroke lately from the Northern Indians, within a Mile of Fort Chissel, our advanced Post. They attacked their Camp in the Night, killed six on the Spot, and wounded a great many. Next Morning the Cherokees delivered up their Women and wounded Men into the Hands of Major Lewis, and begged he would take care of them, until they should look who had hurt them."

BOSTON June 7. Monday last a Boy about 8 Years

of age being in a Distill House of this Town, accidentally fell into a Water Cistern, and was drowned before help could be obtained. ——————The Lad was Son of Ensign Hay, who at the siege of Fort Beausrjour (now Comberland) in Nova-Scotia was taken prisoner, but being in the Fort was killed with 4 French Officers, by a Bomb, which broke thro' one of their casemates, in the time of the Siege.

Deserted from the Ship Bayard, Joseph Cheesman, Master, the following Men, niz. John Alcock, John Gregson, Alias Kennedy, Charles Handgrave; and Edward Marsh Gunner of said Ship, has absented himself almost forty-eight Hours. If the above Men do not return to their Duty again on board the said Ship, in twenty four Hours from Date hereof, they shall be deem'd Deserters.

Boston June 7th, 1761.

BOSTON June 8. The Prince George left Portsmouth commanded by Capt. Blake, in Company with Capt. McTaggart and bound for this Place, and and other vessels under convoy of a Frigate bound to Newfoundland: She was taken on her passage by a French Privateer Ship after a running Fight 3 Glasses, whereby each Vessel received Damage: This Privateer ransomed the Ship for 9000 Pounds sterling, and took on board Capt. Blake and one of the passengers, viz. Edmond Quincy, tertius, of the Town, Merchant, as Ransomers, and carried them to Bayonne.

BOSTON June 9. Province of Massachusetts-Bay, His Excellency the Captain-General is informed, That some of the Officers who have received Beating-Orders have been very negligent in their Duty of Recruiting which he apprehends is on cause of the Levies being so backward: It is therefore His Excellency's positive Determination to suspend those Officers, if he finds any just Cause for such Complaints. And He expects that those Troops which are already raised for Col. Thuing's Regiment, proceed without any further Loss of Time to Castle William.

Thomas Goldthwait, Secr'y of War.

BOSTON June 10. Run away from the Ship Happy-Return, the following Seamen and Landsmen, viz. Thomas Ransom, Thomas Drew, William White, John

Philips, John Hamilton, Martin Allen, John Toole, Robert Murrell, John Harman, Andrew Grayham, William Hughes, Miles Regan, Benjamin Clough & William Breton.

This is to give Notice,

That if the above Persons do not return to their Duty on board said Ship, within forty-eight hours after this Date they will be deemed Deserters, according to the Act of Parliament.

Peter McTaggart.

BOSTON June 15. Last Tuesday Evening one Jeremiah Dexter of Walpole, a Trader was detected of offering false and counterfeit Dollars in this Town; and being apprehended and examined there were several upon him Five of them, cast in a Mould, they were made of pewter or some base Metal; & want near 3 penny weight, of the Weight of the genuine Ones. ——— He at first made very weak and evasive Answers to excuse himself; but being committed to Prison he confessed the next morning with tears, that they were of his own making, and that he had made no more than those Five; and then said he had no accomplices: Notwithstanding which, he has since accused one of being concerned with him, after, when a warrant for apprehending him was issued last Wednesday.

NEW-YORK June 15. On the 3d Inst. Capt. Chambers spoke with a Ship from Gorce, with about 50 Slaves on board, bound into Virginia, who informed him, that Capt. Nicoll, in a brig belonging to New-York, had been cut off on the Coast of Guinea, by the Slaves.

The Six Companies of the New-Jersey Regiment embarked the end of last Week, on board proper Vessels, and have since passed by the City, in their Way to Albany; it is said they are near complete.

Yesterday a Schooner with Connecticut Soldiers on board, passed by this City in her way to Albany.

Yesterday General Monckton arrived at his seat at Greewich, from Philadelphia.

CHARLESTOWN S. Carolina June 17. Col. Grant's Headquarters, near Fort Prince George, June 5.

"We arrived here the 27th ultimate from Fort

Ninety-six; nothing material happened on the March, but that on the 25th we were joined by 20 Chikesaws, and King Heigler, with 20 Catawbas. The Number of Indians we have amount to 90, which, with the white Volunteers, compose the Corps commanded by Capt. Quintyne Kennedy.

On the 29th Capt. Daniels arrived with the last of the Waggons from Ninety-six. About 50 or 60 Cherokee Indians, chiefly of the Lower Towns, have got themselves under our Protection, and a Piece of Ground, about a Quarter af a Mile from the Fort, on the side of the River is allotted to them to settle upon; some Bushels of Indian Corn, and a small Quantity of Pease, have been given to them by Col. Grant's Direction, in order that they may plant there; and for these few Days they have been that way employed: Misery is strongly painted in the figures of these poor Wretches. ——— The Effects of last Year's Campaign are best seen at present ——— They are destitute of every thing, and almost starved.

"We found Little Carpenter (Allakallakulla) at the Fort upon our arrival. He had set out from thence on his Return to the Nation, but on hearing the Troops were near, he came back on Purpose to see Col. Grant, and delivered him a Talk. He mentioned his constant Attachment to his Brother the English, was far from excusing the Behaviour of a great many People of his Nation, Whom he called Roques and wrong headed People; but was in hopes that things would soon be made, easy and pleasant, and begged with great Earnestness many different Times, that Col. Grant would not proceed any further with his Troops until he should return from the Nation: He received no Encouragement to think that his Request would be granted; on the Contrary he was a Eyewitness to the Expedition used in getting ready the Pack Saddles, &c. which he has sense enough to know the Meaning of. He was extremely much shocked at the behaviour of some People who fired at the Fort while he was there, before we arrived; he said he was certain that they would be put to Death by the Headmen of the Nation as soon as they came to the Knowledge of it. —— He set out for the Upper Towns on the 29 ult.

We shall march the 27th instant; the Number of our Packhorses will be pretty considerable; 630 will be loaded with Provisions; Ammunition and Stores, exclusive of the Officers Baggage Horses, &c. No more Advice from us may be expected till something is done in the Cherokee Country. —— The equipage of the Officers will consist chiefly be in a Bear Shin and a little Rum. We are allowed no tents."

Augusta May 22. Both Upper and Lower Creeks are at war with the Spaniards. They have killed some Spaniards, and carried other into their Nation.

The French came to demand the Prisoners, but the Indians told them "to go about their business, They did not know how soon they might serve them in the manner for the many lies they have told them."

BOSTON June 22. Deserted from the Ship Mercury, Charles Bolt, Commander the following Seamen, viz. Thomas Woodreck, Gunner, Thomas King, William Smith, Thomas Bigrey, Patrick Whaling, James Bruce, Edward Pearce, John Sutton, Sailors and Jack Hill and Joseph McClowing, Boys. If the above mentioned Seamen will return to their Duty on board said Ship within 48 Hours they shall be kindly received, otherwise deemed Deserters, and forfeit their Wages accordingly.

Boston June 22, 1761. Charles Ball.

From Marlborough, Dated June 11, 1761. "As two young Women (both belonging to this this Town) was riding in a Chair together, last Friday, unfortunately one of the Wheels pass'd suddenly over a Stone, by which Accident the Person that drove was suddenly thrown out; the other Person (named Morse) being much surprized cry'd for help, at which the Horse took fright and ran against a Stone Wall, and misfortune being on Mrs. Morse's side, she was flung out of the Chair, by which occurence both Bones of her Right Arm were broke below the Elbow, the left Shoulder badly dislocated, and her Skull fractured in a prodigious manner; but by timely Assistance of the Doctor, and the good hands of

Providence, she is in a fair way of Recovery."

BOSTON June 29. Extract of a Letter received from Philadelphia.

"A Person lately arrived here from Detroit or Fort St. Joseph, situated on the navigable Channel which unites the great Lake Huron and Erie; he informs, that at Detroit there is a Town of near 300 Houses, and a settled Country round of about 3000 Souls, and upward, of which we have no notion. —— What think you Men of Estate, some of whom keep Coaches, &c. at a Place 750 Miles behind us? The Lakes and Rivers open the Way to every remote Indian Nation, the Trade has enriched these People, who are 8 or 900 Miles from the Sea, in the Heart of North America. We have a Garrison ar Detroit, and a Vessel building to transport Necessaries over Lake Erie, (220 Miles long) to supply the Inhabitants, who are in want of Cloathing and other European Goods, &c. great Quantities have already been sent from hence. As soon as Peace, which they now enjoy, shall give them means and time to put their Farms in order, the Place will be able to import an army with Provisions."

HALIFAX June 30. On Wednesday the 25th inst, his Honor the Commander in Chief, assisted by his Majesty's Council, publickly received the Submissions of the Chiefs of the Mirimichi, Jediac, Poginouch, and Mickmack Tribes of Indians, Inhabiting the Districts, and entered into a Treaty of Peace and Friendship with them.

JULY 1761

HALIFAX July 2. In the beginning of last Week the first Battalion of the Royal Regiment, Montgomery's Highlanders, the Corps of Engineers, and Part of the Provincial Troops, lately arrived, encamped on the Common and the neighbouring Ground, to be at Hand for the Fortification Works.

Wednesday last arrived here a Sloop from Quebec, by the master of which we are informed that his Majesty's Troops are in a healthy Situation, and that there is Plenty of all Kinds of Provisions.

The same Day arrived here Capt. Doubleday from Louisbourgh, with Pickets for the Use of the Fortification.

We hear a great Number of French Prisoners arrived at Louisbourg, and are soon expected here.

CHARLESTOWN S. Carolina July 4. The Indians who came to town last Saturday are still here; they are Creeks, and there are twelve of them. For want of an Interpreter their business is not known.

No advice have been lately received from the army commanded by Col. Grant, but there are some letters this week from Fort Prince George, of the 12th, which mentions the whole crossing Keeohwee river, and marching forward, early in the morning of the 7th leaving there only 120 invalids, in lieu of the old garrison, with Capt. Campbell of the 22d, Lieut. Burton of the royals, and Dr. Johnston of Col. Burton's, since which no more intelligence had been received from or concerning them, than if there was no army in that country. altho' some Cherokees daily passed and repassed to and from the Fort, where Capt. Mackintosh still commands.

The Indians who surrendered themselves and obtained Col. Grant's permission to plant at Keeowee, remained quiet there; they exceeded 100, with very few men amongst them, but the Tale of Eftatowih was of the number.

Col. Byrd, with 1000 effective men besides officers, is said to have marched the 15th of May from Augusta County in Virginia, to meet Col. Grant in the Cherokee country.

We learn that some of the Chatahs Chiefs in the French interest have lately been at New-Orleans for the usual presents, but were disappointed and told, that it was owing to a large Spanish ship with Indians goods coming to them, having fallen into the hands of the English; that the French gave no ammunition to those of whose fidelity they suspected; and that they seemed to be in great confusion, and at work day and night in erecting many batteries.

CHARLESTOWN S. Carolina July 4. The late house of assembly of this province have passed a bill for laying an additional duty of 100 Pounds on Negroes imported.

Last Saturday afternoon sail'd from this bar for England, his Majesty's ship Dolphin, Capt. Marlowe with ten vessels that were to go under his convoy. He intended to wait off the bar till Monday evening for the rest of the vessels that were to go under his convoy, but a hard gale of wind at E. rising Sunday noon, and the weather appearing very wild, it became unsafe for the ships to lie there any longer, so that he was obliged to proceed with them.

The Elizabeth and Anne, Capt. Rippon, intended to go with the above convoy, but in attempting to get out unfortunately ran ashore up on the lower-middle bank, and tho' she was got off and brought up to town, she received so much damage, that she sunk as soon as she got to the wharf, so that her whole cargo, 1155 barrels will be lost.

We have advice from Maryland that Captain Norton, of his Majesty's ship Assistance has given notice, that he shall be ready in Hampton Road, to grant the benefit of his convoy to all such vessels as shall be bound for Europe, and join him there by the 20th of September next, on which day, wind and weather permitting, he will certainly sail. [This fleet last Year wanting Assistance, as they were almost all taken by the Enemy.]

BOSTON July 11. For the Compleating of the Provincial Regiments.

Notice is hereby given, that in pursuance to a Resolution of the General Court, whoever shall after this Day inlist into the Service of the Province in the present Expedition to complete the Number of Three Thousand Men, shall over and above what is already granted by way of Encouragement, be entitled to and receive six Weeks Pay, prior to the Dare of their respective Inlistments. And the several recruiting Officers are ordered to be careful in making frequent Returns of the Number they have inlisted, that a stop may be put to the inlistments as soon as the Regiment is full.

By Order of his Excellency

Tho. Goldthwait Sec'y of War.

BOSTON July 7 1761. By His Excellency Francis Bernard, Esq; Captain General and Governor in Chief, in and over His Majesty's Province of the Massachusetts-Bay in New-England, and Vice-Admiral of the Same,

A Proclamation.

Whereas certain Persons, who remain hitherto undiscovered, have of late committed great Disorder in the Night Time, within several Towns in this Province, and particularly have broke the Windows of some Meeting-Houses, and of the Dwelling Houses of several Persons, by flinging there into great Stones and Bricks, thereby endangering the Lives of the Inhabitants, as well as injuring their Houses, against the Peace of our Sovereign Lord King, and in Contempt of his Laws:

I have therefore thought fit, with the advice of his Majesty's Council, to issue this Proclamation, requiring all Justices of the Peace, Sheriffs, Constables, and all other Officers whom it may concern, and also recommending it to all other of his Majesty's good Subjects within this Province to use their utmost Endeavors for discovering and bringing to Justice all Persons concerned in such disorderly and riotous Practices.

And I hereby promise, whoever shall discover, and detect all or any of the Persons concerned therein, so that they or any of them, may be lawfully convicted of any such Offence, shall receive out of the Publick Treasury of the Province the Sum of Ten Pounds Lawful Money, as a Reward to be paid upon Conviction of such ofender or Offenders.

Given at the Council Chamber in Boston, the Seventh Day of July in the First Year of the Reign of the Sovereign Lord George the Third, by the Grace of God, of Great Britain, France and Ireland, King defender of the Faith, &c.

By his Excellency's Command,
A. Oliver, Secr'y.   Fra. Bernard.
GOD save the King.

ANNAPOLIS Maryland July 9. Some days ago the body of a lad about 15 years of age, was found in the crotch of a tree in Queen Anne's County: It is supposed that as he was getting sone arrows he fell, and was catched in the crotch of the tree between the head and shoulders, where he perished. His body was much eaten by turkey buzzards.

AUGUSTA July 10. Yesterday Mr. Cornal and Mr. Kidney, arrived from the upper Creek towns, and Mr. Brown from the Chikesaw nation. The Creeks are quiet and civil; the upper towns make no doubt of the satisfaction being demanded for the Murder of Mr. Thompson; and the Cowetas are determined to kill the murderer. Cæsar is return'd to the Cawata towns. He was one of the eight Creeks that were with the Cherokees, at their attack on Col. Grant, two of them were slain in the action, and another wounded; the rest, after they got back, honestly confess'd that the Cherokees were beat and forced to run; that a great number were killed and wounded, and made no doubt but that they have submitted before this Time to Col. Grant's terms, and are with goods as formerly. —— Mr. Brown saw the Mortar in the Creek nation, who has sent a short talk to out governor. The Chactaws are Desirous of Peace, and to have traders among them. One trader has been in their nation trading, has made a return to the Chickesaws country, and is gone again with a second cargo. A great King of the Chactaws has been killed by some of our nation, for giving our bad talks, and encouraging his men to steal the Chickasaws and the traders horses. On the whole, Mr. Brown is of opinion, that there is at present, the fairest prospect of establishing peace and friendship with the Chactaws. ——— The leaders of the Chickasaws has sent no talk of any consequence, but he and the nation are as well affected as ever.

"I have just learned for certain, that William Frazer, has been robbed of all his goods, by the fellow that murdered Thompson, and a party he had raised. Frazer was obliged to hide himself for the preservation of his Life: He will soon be here, when we shall have the particulars."

BOSTON July 11. Province of Massachusetts-Bay, Court of Vece Admiralty.

All Persons claiming Property in the Schooner called the Samuel, her Boats, Tackle, Apparel, Furniture, and Appurtenances, and also one hogshead and two Barrels of Beaver Skins, and other Furs, seized by James Cockle, Esq; Collector of his Majesty's Custom for the Ports of Salem and Marblehead, for breach of the Acts of Trade and illegal Importation, are hereby notified to appear at a Court of Vice Admiralty, to be holden at Boston for said Province on the 24th of July Instant, at ten o'Clock before Noon, to show Cause (if any they have) why said Schooner, Appurtenances and articles aforesaid, should not be adjudged to remain forfeited, pursuant to an information filed in said Court for that purpose.

Per Curiam,   William Story D. Reg.

CHARLESTOWN S. Carolina July 11. Just after the publication of last Saturday's Gazette, letters were received from Augusta dated the 30th ult. advising that most of the Chickasaws who went from thence in April and May last, to join the army commanded by Col. Grant on the present expedition against the Cherokees, had returned thither some days before, and brought in two Indian scalps, which they pretend to have got by surprizing a small town in the Cherokee nation: And that they reported as follows, "That on the 4th day of the army's march from Keeohwee (say 10th of June) they were attacked by the Cherokees, who fired upon them, unseen from morning till noon, killed 24 men and wounded 35 more; but that the Rangers being ordered to surround the place whence the smoke was perceived to issue, most of the Cherokees in that ambuscade were either cut to pieces by them, or trampled to death by the horses; that upon this the rest of the Cherokees fled, and were persued by Col. Grant who had burnt seven towns in the Middle Settlements, destroyed all the provisions he found, and turned the horses into the fields to eat up the growing corn; that they remained with the army three days after the Action, during which there had been no firing on the other side; and that Col. Grant was preparing to move forward."

Last Sunday morning an express arrived from Fort Prince George, with letters dated the 28th ultimo, confirming the accounts which had been received the day before from Augusta, with little variation. These mention 20 Chicasahs, and 2 Catawbas returning thither from the army on the 15th, and reporting there nearly to same as at Augusta, but observed, that the scalps they had were likely to be those of two Cherokees who had crossed Keeohwee river a few hours before they arrived and the way which they came.

At Prince George they had heard nothing of the Army since it moved from thence, but what these Indians reported: and from their reports it was supposed they had been some skirmish at the beginning of which these people ran away. The same letter assured, that Col. Grant had upward of 40 days provisions with him, for a greater number of Men than the army consisted of; and intimate, that no news from his head quarters was expected in less than 10 days, it is supposed, that after destroying the towns in the Middle Settlements, Col. Grant would proceed to the Valley and destroy the towns and provisions there.

NEW-YORK July 13. Monday arrived at the Hook

his Majesty's ship Assistance of 50 guns, William Norton, Esq; Commander: She sailed from Spithead the latter end of April, as convoy to the Maryland and Virginia shores, and having seen these safe into the Capes, she proceeded to Sandy Hook. We hear she has brought upwards of 30,000 Pounds Sterling, being part of Parliamentary grant for the Use of the Northern Colonies. It is said 25,000 of it is for this Government.

We hear that one of the Transports bound from hence to the West Indies, had been boarded by a French privateer, who had been obliged to sheer off, and leave most of her men behind, who were all cut to pieces, but with the loss of an English officer, and another man in the fray.

We hear from Poughkeepsi, that about a fortnight ago, one Hamilton, a silversmith, was commited to goal there on suspicion of making Spanish mill'd dollars; but a few days after, to save any further trouble, he hang'd himself with his own hankerchief.

We have Advice from several Parts of East New-Jersey that the late hot Weather has much blasted many Fields of Wheat, to the great Disappointment of the poor Farmers Hopes.

CHARLESTOWN S. Carolina July 15. Col. Grant's Head Quarters, near Fort Prince George, Friday July 10, 1761.

"On June the 7th, we marched from Fort Prince George, near 2600 men strong, including pack horsemen, who were mostly all armed, with a line of pack-horses, &c. amounting to upwards of 700. and with upwards of 400 head of cattle. The 8th and 9th we made force marches, to get thro' two dangerous passes, which was done without a shot being fired at us. The 10th, early in the morning, we moved from our encampment near Estatoe old town; and before the rear had got entirely off the ground, our cattle-guard was fired upon by a few Indians, who kept at a considerable distance, and did no hurt. About half after eight, our Indians discovered a body of the Enemy at our right flank, a good many shot were exchanged, and the Cherokees tho' numerous, gave way. An enemy Indian was killed and scalped, ours sustaining no loss at that time. The Indians hoop went directly after from front to rear in line of both flanks, and then the firing, which lasted till 12 o'clock became a little more serious. The Light infantry who were in front, received no hurt, except one man who was slightly wounded. The succeeding corps suffered more, and the heaviest fire seemed at last to fall upon our rear. The troops behaved with great spirit and coolness, and by their heavy fire dislodged the enemy, from the Posts they had taken possession of with considerable loss; popping shots continued till two o'clock, when the enemy thought proper to retire.

Considering the duration of the action, our loss is very inconsiderable, Ensign John Monro of the 22d, was dangerously wounded last year, with 10 privates were killed; Ensign Knight of the Royals, Lieut Barber, and Ensign Cambel of Col. Burton's, and Lieut. Terry of the Provincials, with 48 others are wounded; some horses were killed and we were obliged to throw some bags of flour into the river for want of horses to carry it up. At 3 o'clock our wounded men were dressed, and carriages provided for them, and the whole line marched on to Etchoey that night, 1000 men were left under Col. Middleton's command to take care of the sick and wounded, while Colonel Grant with the rest marched on to Noockasee and Tassee, in hopes of surprizing the Indians in those towns, but they were abandoned: Next day the whole joined at Noockasee, and since that time we have walk'd thro' every town in the Middle-Settlements, as well as outside towns which lie on the different branch of the Tennasee. All their towns, 15 in number have been burnt; upwards of 1400 acres of corn, according to a moderate computation, entirely destroyed, and near 5000 Cherokees, including men, women & children driven to the mountains to starve; their only subsistence for some time past, being horse flesh:

The officers and men are excessively Fatigued; no Body of troops was ever known to stay so long in an Indian country before; having been 33 days on this severe service, the troops having nothing better than bowers and bows to shelter them, and and much bad weather. We brought in upwards of 300 wounded, sick and lame, one half scarce able to march, their feet being mangled with the rocks, bryars, &c.

Name of the Towns in the Cherokee Middle and Back Settlements burnt by Colonel Grant's detachment.

Tassee, Noockasse, Noyowee, Canugo, Wattogee, Usanah, Cattoogee, Tomissee, Alajoy, Stecoe, Kittoweh, Tuckilegee, Burit Town."

We hear that it has been intimated to the Little Carpenter and other headmen of the Cherokees, that withstanding the superiority of his Majesty's Forces, if those Indians incline for Peace, they will be heard.

The Governor gave ten Guineas as a reward to Mr. Holmes, who brought his Honour the accounts fron Col. Grant of the good success of the army.

ANNAPOLIS Maryland July 14. One Day last Week as Mrs. Hearn, who lived in Worcester County, was standing near the Chimney of her House, in the Time of a Thunder Gust, making Punch for some Reapers, a Flash of Lightning came down the Chimney, and struck her instantly dead.

Last Wednesday the Ship Fishbourne, Captain Fahrington, lying at Patuxent, was struck with Lightning, three of the Men stunned but soon recovered.

BOSTON July 15. We hear from Halifax, that on the 22d & 23d of last Month, his Majesty's Forces in Garrison there with the Corps of Engineers, and that Part of the Provincial Troops lately arrived from Boston, encamped on the Common and the neighbouring Grounds, to be at Hand for proceeding on his Majesty's Works, &c.

BOSTON July 15. The General Assembly of the Colony of Rhode-Island have passed an act for inquiring into the rateable estates of the colony. ——— The valuation nearly to be taken in same manner as lately done in this province, with these differences. That every inhabitant is to give in account of all money they have by them, and all wrought plate; also the number of acres of unimproved land: ——— All vessels that are abroad only on third part of the number of tons, and one third part of their cargo to be given in.

To be sold a Healthy Negro Boy, about 14 or 15 Years of age, that can do any sort of business around the house, sold only for want of employment. Enquire of the Printer.

CHARLESTOWN S. Carolina July 15. Extract of a Letter from an Officer in the Expedition to the Cherokee Middle and Back Settlements, under the Command of Col. Grant, giving a particular Account of their proceedings in that country July 10

"The defile and Passes along War-Woman's Creek which we passed the 8th of June, in our Way to the Middle-Settlements, are horrid, and such, as, had the enemy disputed our passage, would have sorely grieved us. On one side high and rocky mountains hanging over our heads, the path rocky, and no wider than for a single pack horse; on the other side a great and deep precipice, at the bottom of which is the Creek, the path for several miles is little better.

On the 9th, we found on a tree, one of the Cherokees war-faces, it was nine Indians, running with their guns and tomahawks, and a white man prisoner, all done in red: A sure sign of war, which we were afterwards told by the prisoners was made by nine Creek Indians that were in the action of the 10th, where the place of attack was very advantageous. ———— Capt. Kennedy, with the Indian corps of about 140, first discovered and attacked the Cherokee on a high hill on the right, where they lay to attack us.

———— Under this hill the line was obliged to pass for a considerable way. Close on our left was the river, from the banks and savannah on the opposite side, they fired on us smartly. The line continued its march on the road, received the fire, and sent out parties up the hill on our right, to beat them off, which was done after some dispute. The line faced to the left and gave the enemy on that side their whole fire, which dispersed and drove them on the mountains, and they were no more troublesome from that quarter: They seemed to design a hard push at our cattle and flour in the rear. ————
After we had marched about two miles thro' this

defile and thro' the enemy's fire, we got into an open savannah. The hills on our left, out of gun-shot we sent out parties to take possession of. The picquet and cattle-gard of rangers had not yet got thro' the defiles and fire. Colonel Middleton received orders from Colonel Grant to send back some parties to support them; he accordingly sent two subalterns with 25 privates each of the provincials; presently Capt. Roberts with 60 provincials and 40 of the battalion corps, and immediately after one subaltern with 25 of the provincials. ——— This relief came very seasonably, the rear being hardly pressed, several baggage horses shot, bags of flour lying on the ground, and many provision horses standing without their leaders, who had run away into the front; all these would probably have been lost, the whole force of enemy being collected there; but Capt. Roberts and the others beat off the Indians, and put the flour bags on rangers horses, except a few that were thrown into the river, that they had not horses to carry off: They also sunk our killed, six in number to prevent the Indians getting their scalps; Such of the officers baggage as could not be bro't off was also sunk. During the action, some person among the Cherokee called out in French to Capt. Kennedy to come forward. We did not get to Etchoey with our wounded 'til midnight. We were first fired upon between 7 and 8 in the morning, and the enemy did not leave off till two in the afternoon: The firing was very heavy between 8 and 9 and did not abate till between 11 and 12. ——— The prisoners all agree that a great number of Cherokees were killed in the action, many of the headmen. They did not get one scalp from us; most of the bodies that were sunk in the river, were seen many days afterwards, and not scalped. The Prisoners which were took at different times say, that the Mortar and 100 Creeks are in the Upper-Towns; that the Young Warrior of Estatoey was wounded in the action; and that the Little-Carpenter, with some headmen of the Upper-Towns, was coming to meet Col. Grant, but hearing of the action, they all returned to their homes. The number of the enemy was not less than a thousand; the prisoners say, all the people of the Lower-Towns, Middle-Settlements and Valley were there, but none of the Upper-Towns.

From the 11th of June we were employed, without being molested, in burning the Indian towns, destroying their corn, beans, &c. to great amount. Colonel Grant always sent the Indian corps commanded by Capt. Kennedy forward to surprize and take any prisoners that might be in the towns, as well as to view the path, and to scout before the army.

On the 16th in the passage thro' Cowbee, Silver—heels the Mohawk, who seldom speaks, got on top of the Round-House, and with a loud voice, three times summoned all the Cherokees, from all their towns and mountains, to come & hear the news he had to tell them from the North, but they not appearing, he finished by tell them since they would not come and hear him, he must burn and destroy their towns. We had frequently heavy rains, and many men were unable to walk by the excessive fatigue. During the whole march we found no meat in the Indian houses but horse beef; their corn mortars seemed to have had no corn beat in them for some time. They appeared to have subsisted on horse flesh, and for some little time past on the stocks of young corn boiled. They have planted prodigious crop of corn this year in the settlements we saw.

Yesterday, July 9th we arrived at the river Keowee, but could not pass on account of the rains till sun-set, and got to our old encampment, where we now remain, having been 33 days on very severe service; the troops during the whole time, having nothing but bows to shelter them, and upward of 20 days on short allowance. but we are returned after having destroyed the whole towns, plantations, & of the Middle Settlements, and turned at least four thousand mischievous and perfidious animals to suffer miserably in the mountains; We have advanced our frontier at least 70 miles towards the enemy, by which means fort Prince George becomes a safe post; our back settlements easily defended by a small number of men, and not so readily hurt as formerly; and all this done at so cheap a rate as must reflect great honour on the commander for his steadiness, vigilance and unwearied care during the whole business; He took every method to hurt the enemy without too much exposing the troops in his charge. The whole loss to do this service is 10 killed, about 50 wounded, a few horses, and 50 bags of flour."

We hear that Colonel Grant is now repairing Fort Prince-George, where a new strong garrison is to be left, with 12 months provisions.

The Governor gave ten guineas as a reward to Mr. Holmes who brought his Honour the account fron Col. Grant of the good success of the army.

NEW-YORK July 20. Letters by the last Post from Albany, informs, that the Provincials continually pass forward through the City, to the several Posts where they are delivered; That Capt. Phodey's Company embarked on the 3d inst. from Oswago for Owagochee, where 'tis said he is to command: That General Gage's Light Infantry is to go to Detroit: That some few Indians at Niagara, appeared lately at a little refectory; and gave out Treats. &c.

BOSTON July 27. Extract of a Letter from Halifax, July 9. 1761.

"The first instant arrived here Capt. Doubleday from Louisbourg with pickets for the use of the fortification. A great Number of Prisoners are arrived at Louisbourg and are soon expected here' ——— Yesterday arrived here a sloop with French Prisoners, commanded by Capt. du Blanc, taken by the Norwich man of war off Louisbourg: Capt. du Blanc intended to sail for France. It's said his Majesty's Ship Greyhound will soon sail from this Place for New-York and from thence to the West Indies."

The Snow La Fortune, from Granades to Marseille, laden with sugar and coffee, has been taken by a New-York privateer.

Extract of a letter from Guadaloupe, June 7.

"The Troops sent to Dominica met with little opposition: The French were then retired to their Intrenchments near the Town, which were perfectly forced, and the Enemy obliged to surrender Prisoners of War. Our Loss was only 3 killed, and 6 or 7 wounded. Most of the Inhabitants that were in the Country, have since come in, and with those that were taken, have took the Oath of Fidelity or Allegiance; yet some remain in the Mountains. It is said, that though Lord Rollo refused to grant the inhabitants any Capitulation, yet he permitted them to carry on their Plantations, till his Majesty's Pleasuer should be known. ——— M. Lompré the French Governor, is sent to England in his Majesty's Ship Arundel, together whith his new Commision granted by M. Latouché, a Plan for the Island, and other useful Papers. All the remainder of the Fleet from New-York are now arrived here, with their Convoy, the Falkland, Sutherland, Lizard and Repulse, and are ready to join the Ships at Dominica from whence they will proceed to some other of the Islands. The Troops from New-York are the 22d Regiment of Montgomery's Highlanders which has been joined by Governor Melvill (who is second in Command and a Detachment from the Troops here. It is expected St. Vincent's will make a more obstinate resistance."

BOSTON July 27. From Augusta we have advice, that one William Thompson, a Trader, who set off from thence for the Creek nation, was found killed with a hatchet and a tomahawk on the road, which is the first blood that has been spilt on the Creek path since the commencement of the present trouble in those parts. ——— The Indians of the lower Creeks towns have always declared they would go to war against the Cherokees if they ever the path if their nation was spoiled. A messenger is accordingly sent up to acquaint them of this murder, and to see if they will be so good as their word.

NEW-YORK July 27. Thursday last Capt. Robert Rogers embarked for South Carolina, to take upon him the Command of Capt. Demere's company of Rangers.

The next day part of the 4th regiment came down from Albany and encamped on the East End of Staten Island. ——— As did also part of the first battalion of the Royal Americans. And on Saturday another body of his Majesty's forces came down and encamped at the same place.

We learn from Albany, that Sir William Johnson was to set out for Detroit about the first instant, the better to confirm the Indians there in his Britannick Majesty's Interest. By Capt. Lyell from the Coast of Africa, we have advice that Capt. Nicholl, of this Port was not off by the Negroes, as was some time ago published; but that he lost 40 of his slaves by an insurrection and saved his vessel.

On Monday Capt. Smith arrived here about four weeks from Quebec, with cloathing for General Amherst's regiment, By him we have account of three men of war and a tender cruizing at the mouth of the river.

CHARLESTOWN July 28. On Reading Mr. Wells's South Carolina Gazette, if the 15th instant I would not avoid taking notice of a part of one of extract letters inserted therein, to with.

——— That by the late successful campaign, our frontiers are advanced at least 70 miles towards the enemy; that great honour must be reflected on the command for steadiness, vigilance and unwearied care during the whole business; and that he took every method to hurt the enemy; and cannot agree with correspondent in every particular.

First, I cannot conceive, that an incursion into an enemy's country, burning their deserted town, and destroying their provisions, without leaving any force of fixing post in it, or even of dispossessing the enemy of the country, can with any propriety be said to be extending the frontier, it does not appear to me in that light; but as it may to others, who are fond of magnifying the exploits performed, I shall have such to enjoy the pleasing thought.

Secondly, by the steadiness of the commander I presume is meant, a steady adherence to the plans laid down by him, and the means he had resolved to use and exciting them; in which I will very readily agree with this correspondent; and I do acknowledge, that with the greatest steadiness imaginable, he did pursue his own plans, that he was, beyond comparison, steadily fond of his own opinion and self sufficiency, and that he very steadily adhered thereto; for which he ought doubtless, to be greatly applauded and highly honoured. But I cannot agree, with this letter-writer, that he has acquired great honour by his vigilance, and by his unwearied care of the troops; which did not appear, to leaving young troops, new raised regimented to sustain so long and heavy a fire from the enemy as they did; nor depending on such to support the picquet and cattle-guard on who firmness and good conduct depended the preservation of the whole stock of live provisions, where they might have supported by the slower troops, who were in the front of the line, had received less fire from the enemy, were halted and kept inactive, and had time and inclination, to return and fall upon the back of the enemy Indians while they were firing on the corps in the rear; this, and the disposal of the rangers upon every hill from which the front of the line could be fired on, prove indeed the care taken of those troops in general; and demonstrates.

Thirdly, That every method was not taken to hurt the enemy. A glorious opportunity of doing it was lost, by not sending troops from the front of the line, or at least a part of them, on the back of the enemy; and by not suffering our friendly Indians to take that advantage, who so plainly saw the fair occasion, that they several times applied and pressed for liberty to make use of it, but were denied.

As a farther proof that every method was not taken to hurt the enemy, I must acquaint you, that two squaws, taken at Stichowih on the 26th of June, informed that a party of Cherokees, men, women and children, were encamped at a few miles distance; and that our Indians applied for leave to go after them, which was refused, and that a man prisoner, taken at Ellajoy on the 28th of June gave information to Capt, Kennedy, that a Considerable number of women and children, with whom were only ten men, lay encamped a few miles off, and offered to conduct him to them; of which Capt. Kennedy immediately informed the commander, requesting that he might be suffered to go after them with his Indians who were extremely eager for this service, but was again refused permission.

These sir, are truths, And I can point out many other means thereby the enemy could have been very effectually chastised and hurt, which, when I have more leisure, perhaps I may do: and then also relate some other facts, although they should not be agreeable to certain set of men, who (right or wrong, and without knowing any thing of the matter) take flame, on the bare mention of any improper proceedings during the late campaign; because a party, and if, they dared, would take every man by the nose who will not implicitly agree with them, that it is impossible any wrong step could be taken, or that any thing has been omitted essential to the security and welfare of the good people of this province. Mr. Wells to get better information, and assuring him, that he is very wrong in asserting, that when the troops arrived at Keehowee, they had not one day of Provisions left.

PHILADELPHIA July 28. Saturday next we hear, his Honour the Governor sets out for Easton, in Order to hold a treaty with the Indians, where there are a great number of Onondagoes, Cayugas, Naticokes, Canoys, Tuteloes, Mohicons, Shawanese, and Delawares.

NEW PORT July 28. Extract of a letter from Antigua, dated June 25, 1761.

"The Cartel for exchange of prisoners at Martinico has been stopt for some time, by a difference between commodore Douglas and the General of that island, occasioned, as I am informed, by one of our men of war going there as a flag of truce for exchange of prisoners, when another of his Majesty's ships cruising at the same time in the Offing, retook a French prize, while the other ship's barge was ashore, this conduct so incens'd the French General, that he detained the barge and men; upon which commodore Douglas sent all the French prisoners in this port to England, in some merchantmen; the general of Martinico threatened that he would send the English prisoners likewise to old France:

However, he has permitted some New-England men to come to this island, in a small boat on their parole, in order to procure any French to return in the said boat, which if they could not obtain, they were to repair to Martinico again; this however they have had no occasion of performing, the difference in a great measure being accommodated, the General having restored the barge and crew.

Lord Rollo has publickly declared, that those inhabitants of Dominica who do not appear by the 24th instant, and take the oath of allegiance, will be treated as rebels and hang'd. The last account from that place mention, that the design of the English is, to take possession of all the other Neutral islands, but first to attack the Grenades, which is of the greatest strength, and when subdued, will render them a more easy conquest. This once effected, will be a great security to our navigation, as these islands are places of resort and refuge to the Martinico privateers. 'Tis the unanimous opinion of the gentlemen at Antigua, that so soon as the hurricane months are over, a body of 10,000 men from England will join the forces already here, and attempt the reduction of Martinico.

AUGUST 1761

BOSTON Aug. 1. Province of Massachusetts-Bay. The Officers recruiting for Col. Thwing's regiment are hereby notified to collect immediately, all the Men they have inlisted, and march them so as to be at Castle William by Saturday the 8th Currant, in Order to embark for Halifax.
By Order of his Excellency,
Tho. Goldthwait, Sec'y of War.
Whereas the Servant of me the Subscriber, by name of James Melvir, a young Boy about 8 years old, have by the Advice of some Person or Persons, been absent from my family since last Thursday the 30th of July; I do now by this publick Advertisement give Notice to all Persons who ever they are, that keeping him incog. that they may depend on the Laws having in Course with them. And any Person who will give me a true Information where he has been detained, shall have a reward that is Reasonable.
John Sterling.
CHARLESTOWN S. Carolina Aug.1. By an express from Fort Prince-George, we are advised, that the Mankiller and White-Owl of Keeohwee having been sent for on the 12th were dispatched on the 14th with messages to the headmen of the Valley and Overhill towns, in order to effect by negotiation, if possible, what has not been accomplished by the success of his Majesty's arms.
The General Assembly of this province have voted 3000 pounds for repairing the works at Fort-Johnson, and 1500 pounds for keeping in repair the fortifications about this town. They have likewise voted the sum of 200 pounds for the upper Chicasaws, who were of singular service in the late expedition under Col. Grant; and gratuity to Capt. Colbert their conductor, and 2000 pounds to the Mohawks, Catawbas, &c.

employed in the expedition.

'Tis impossible to ascertain the loss of the Cherokees in the action of the tenth of June; in which only one Indian was taken by the Catawbas, and immediately put to death. Two old women were taken on the 12th, who knew nothing of the matter, and were likewise put to death by the Catawbas. Two other women were taken on the 26th and a fellow, called the Yellow-Bird on the 28th; the three last did say they heard that some were killed of every town, but mentioned no number. The last prisoner was a stupid old fellow, who said he heard his town had lost 8.

CHARLESTOWN S. Carolina Aug. 1. Governor Wright of Georgia has sent an express here, to give an account of a small French privateer schooner, which has been in at Tybee, and taken four slaves belonging to Capt. Edward Tucker, having decoyed them by pretending to be a vessel bound in from Providence.

BOSTON Aug. 3. Friday last Capt. Cobb arrived here in 26 Days from Quebec, and informs, That some of our Whalemen here had great success in catching Whales in that River: At the Isle of Bic he met the Store Ship from England bound up.

We hear from Rochester, Barrington, and other Out-Towns in the Province of New-Hampshire, That above a fort'night ago the Woods above those Places were set on Fire by Lightning or otherwise, and had continued burning over since with great Violence, carrying every Thing before it, having reached 60 or 70 Miles from the Place where it first began, but cannot learn how far back. ——— it is to be feared much other Damage will be done by the Fire.

To be Sold, A Parcel of likely Negroes, imported from Africa, Cheap for Cash, or Credit with Interest; enquire of John Avery at his House, next Door to the White Horse, or at a Store adjoining to said Avery's Distill House, at the South End, near the South Market: ———
Also if any Persons have any Negroe Men, strong and healthy, tho' not of the best moral Character, which are proper subjects for Transportation, may have an Exchange for small Negroes.

Whereas Tabitha, Wife of me the Subscriber, on the Second Day of last September, left my House and Family in Boston, and has absented herself ever since, Contrary to her Duty and my Desire; These are therefore to warn all Persons not to harbour her or trust her for any Thing whatsoever, at their Peril, and no Debt which she has or may contract shall ever be paid by me.   Aug. 1, 1761.   Israel Hearsey.

Whereas Hanna, the Wife of me the Subscriber harh eloped from me ——— I hereby caution and forbid any Person whatsoever from trusting her on my Account. For I do hereby declare that I will not pay any debts she shall contract from the Date hereof. August 1, 1761.

                                          Nehemiah Edmunds.

BOSTON Aug. 3. The following Extract relative to the driving of Coaches and other Carriages thro' the Streets on the Lord's Day, and of Carts, Trucks, &c. on other Days, are from the By-Laws of the Town of Boston in Force, viz.

Great Dangers arising oftentimes from Coaches, Slays, and Chairs and other Carriages on the Lord's Day, as the People are going to, and coming from the several Churches in this Town being driven with great Rapidity, and the publick Worship being oftentimes much disturbed by such Carriages driving by the side of the Churches with great Force in Time thereof.

It is therefore Voted and Ordered, That no Coach, Slay, Chair, Chaise or other Carriages, shall at such Time be driven at a greater Rate than a foot Pace, on Penalty of the Sum of Ten Shillings, to be paid by the Person driving, or if he be a Servant or Slave by his Master or Mistress.

And its further Ordered. That henceforth no Cart, Dray, Truck or Sled drawn by Horse or Horses, Horse and Oxen, shall be suffered to pass through any of the Streets or Lanes of this Town, but with a sufficient Driver; who shall during such Passage keep with his said Cart, Dray, Truck or Sled, and carefully observe and attend such Methods as may best serve to keep said Horse or Horses or Oxen under command, and shall have the Thill Horse by the Head. And whatsoever Carter or others understanding to drive any Cart, Dray, Truck or Sled, shall during passing through the Streets or Lanes as aforesaid, either Ride in said Cart, Dray, Trucks or Sled, or otherwise neglect to observe and attend the Rules prescribed in this Order, such Carters, Driver or Owner of such Cart, Dray, Trucks or Sled, shall forfeit and pay the sum of eight Shillings for each Offence.

Publick Notice is hereby given that for the Protection of those Inconveniences in future, which have arisen from the Breach of the above Laws; suitable Persons are now appointed to Notice all such as do not conform themselves thereto, and all Offenders against the same may expect to be prosecuted for every such offence.

By Order of the Select-Men

William Cooper, Town Clerk.

BOSTON Aug. 3. Extract from Charlestown, South Carolina, dated July 9, 1761.

"We have just now imperfect unintelligible Accounts that our Forces under Col. Grant against the Cherokees, have burnt seven of their Towns, with the loss of two Officers and twenty Privates killed. Col. Grant wounded; but the account may not be depended upon.

NEW-YORK Aug. 3. Friday last eight transports under convoy of the ship Spry, of Philadelphia, arrived from Dominique with whom came Captain Ogden, and his company of Rangers belonging to the Jerseys, also Captain Hayt's of New-England. These ships sailed from hence last May, with the troops under Lord Rollo. By letters from the above Island we learn, that many of the Inhabitants continue obstinate, fled to the Mountains and would by no means swear allegiance to his Britannic Majesty.

The same Day arriv'd the snow Halifax Packet from Louisbourg, with the royal artillery on board.

HALIFAX Aug. 5. Deserted in the Night of the 3d Instant, from his Majesty's Royal Regiment of Artillery; and of Captain David Hay's Company, the following Persons. —— John Feavier, aged 26 Years, 5 Feet 8 Inches high, born in Switzerland, ruddy Complexion, chubtie Man with a broad Face, by Trade a Mason, went away in his Regimentals. —— Edward Smith, aged 29 Years, 5 Feet 8 Inches high, born in Wiltshire, brown Complexion, pitted with the Small-Pox and had a broad Flesh Mark on one Cheek, by Trade a Butcher, went off in a blue great Coat. —— John Turnbull. aged 26 Years, 5 Feet 9 Inches high, born in England, brown Complexion, pitted with the Small-Pox and has short Hair, and of a pleasant Countenance, by Trade a Carpenter, went off in his Regimentals. —— Whoever apprehends, and secures the said Deserters, in any of his Majesty's Goals, shall receive Four Dollars for each Deserter, by applying to Messiuers Joseph and David Waldo of Boston or Thomas Johnson Lieutenant of Artillery at Halifax.

N. B. All Masters of Vessels are forbid to take the above Deserters on board; and whoever is found to harbour or employ them, will be punished with the utmost Rigour of the Law.

CHARLESTOWN S. Carolina Aug. 8 our letters from North Carolina inform us, that the regiment of 500 men to be raised by that government was compleat, and would march to join the Virginians under Col. Byrd, as soon as they were provided with arms.

News may be hourly expected from Fort Prince George, as the Mankiller and White-Owl were to return the 29th, with answers to the message Col. Grant had sent to the Valley and Over-Hills; whereas, we hear, he told them, "That altho' it was as easy for him to destroy the rest of their towns, as those in the Middle-Settlements (which might have been spared, had not some of their rash young men been so mad as to fire upon the army on their way to Etchowih) yet, being unwilling to involve the innocent with the guilty, if they had any talks to send him, he would still hear them; but that if they did not, by the return of the said messengers, (in 15 days) sue for peace, then he would re-enter their country, and destroy all their towns, &c."

This now confidently said that Col. Grant will certainly make another incursion into Cherokee country, &c. it being apprehended that the destruction of the settlements and provisions in the Valley will so heighten their suffering, that they will soon after be reduced and glad to send talks that may be heard.

The Upper Creeks, according to the latest advice from their country were quiet, and had sent a talk to the Governor of Georgia.

BOSTON Aug. 10. The 29th of July, a Vessel arrived Express at New-York, dispatched by the Governor of South Carolina and Colonel Grant, to General Amherst, with Letters dated the 10th of the same Month, acquainting his Excellency, That the Army under the Command of Colonel Grant consisting of 2600 Men, including Pack horsemen, mostly armed, with a Line of Pack-horses, &c. amounting to 700 and upwards of 400 Head od Cattle, left Fort Prince William 7th of June. In their March they dispersed all the Cherokees that opposed them; burnt all their Towns, amounting to 15, many little Villages, and scattered Houses, destroyed upward of 1400 Acres of Corn, besides Beans, &c. kill'd a Number of them, and drove near 5000, including Men, Women, and Children to the Mountains to starve, their only Sustenance being Horse flesh, with the loss of ten killed, and not 50 wounded. The Particulars of this interesting Affair is so very lenghty, we are oblig'd to postpone them till our next.

BOSTON Aug. 10. By a letter from Rocky Point in Cape Fare, North Carolina, dated the 26th of May we are informed, "That they had the greatest rains ever known in those parts: Vessels of 120 and 200 tons, loaded, might have sailed over the fields: Many persons were obliged to swim their horses to return to their dwellings, and in great danger being drowned: ─── The people at Wilmington were obliged (many of them) to quit their houses by reason that the water flow'd therein several feet high: ─── Great damage has been sustained by this deluge: ─── The rain continued 40 days; in which time the Sun was not seen.

Wednesday last observed as a Day of Fasting by the Town of Medfield, on account of the Drought; in the Time of Service, a Barn belonging to Lieut. Morse of that Place was consumed by Fire, occasioned we hear by the burning of Brush, which communicated the Flames to the Barn.

About 20 Days ago, being a very dry Time, all the Grass, Hay and other Materials that would burn, on the Island, known by the Name of Tatcher's Island, lying off Cape Ann, were entirely consumed by Fire, occasioned, 'tis said, by the Mowers leaving Fire in their Pipes.

Monday last Capt. Duff, sailed from hence for Halifax, having on board 125 Provincials, under the Command of Capt. Edward Blake, of this Place.

NEW-YORK Aug. 10. Extract of a Letter from the Camp at Crown-Point, dated July 24, 1761.

"Our Employ her is working at the Fort: We have had the following Regiments. I give them as they arrived here from Canada, viz. the 40th, 42d, or Royal Highlanders, 2 Battalions, 15th, 35th, 28th, 48th, 43d, 3d Battalions of Royal Americans expected but not arrived; the 27th, who garrisoned here, and as far down as Lake-George. Each Regiment remain here about three Weeks or a Month. The 40th, 1st and 2d Battalion of Royal Highlanders and 15th have marched to New-York; the rest expected to follow successively. Provincial Regiments here are the two Connecticut complete, two Hundred New-Hampshire, and one Hundred of the Massachusetts, the remainder of the Troops raised in that Province, destined this Way, we hear are on the Road, and may be expected here in a few Days. ——— The Plan of the Fort so large that it can scarcely be compleated this Year."

SALEM Aug. 10. Broke out of the Newbury Goal on Sabbath Day the 9th Instant, Capt. Thomas Swett of Newbury, imprison'd for Debt, & one Thomas Butler, a Foreigner: Swett had on when he went away, a green Coat with a small yellow Cape, and about 25 Years old. Butler had on a blue Coat and a blue and white chints Jacket. Whoever takes up the said Prisoners and secures them in any of his Majesty's Goals, shall have as a Reward for Thomas Swett, Ten Dollars, and Five for Thomas Butler and all necessary Charges paid by me.   Robert Hale Sheriff.

NEW-YORK Aug. 10. We hear that a Commission

is come over in the Packet, appointing Cadwallader Colden, Esq; Lieutenant Governor of this Province in the Room of the Hon. James De Lancy, Esq; deceased.

CHARLESTOWN S. Carolina Aug. 12. Since our last a person arrived from Fort Prince George, which he left the 1st instant, a private letter by him to a Gentleman here, dated at the camp, July 31st says, "On the 21st Old Ceasar arrived here with a talk to Col. Grant from Oucanostata suing for peace; and on the 23d Ceasar set off with the Colonel's answer; he expected to be at Hiwasee in five days, where the head men and warriors were to meet him; they are allowed 13 days from the 23d to come down to settle preliminaries.

Old Ceasar informs us, that the Little Carpenter, Willanawaw, Oucanostata and himself, were coming down to Col. Grant, and were within 20 miles of the army when they heard of the action at Cowhowee, on which they all returned, and determined to remain quiet, and let the people of the middle settlements take the consequence of their folly. That the Inhabitants of the towns destroyed were in the utmost distress having scarce any thing to eat, but such roots as they could pick up in the mountains, the horse flesh they had to subsist on being mostly gone; many old people and children died and dying daily, and the young men and women that were strong and hearty much reduced and weakened; that Salloue was gone out with a party to hunt, but it was suspected to Skulk near the army to steal horses, or to try to take scalps, but, that the nation would kill him if he did the least mischief. That the white people were too strong for the Indians at the battle and forced them to run off; many Indians were killed, and many more were still missing. ——— We are employ'd on the fort which is just about half compleated."

"This afternoon came to the fort in 12 days from Col. Byrd's camp, two Cherokees, with letters from him to Col. Grant, by which it appears the warriors of the Overhills have been very solicitous with him for peace, but he told them it was not in his power, but they must come to Col. Grant with all expectation otherwise their whole nation would be destroyed. The two Indians paint their nation's distress in the most dismal colours; and say if we will not grant them peace they will be all ruined."

Salisbury (in Rowan County, North Carolina) about 260 miles N. W. from Charlestown, July 26.

"Col. Byrd with the Virginia forces, continue at the old camp on the waters of the great Kanawa. We hear his men have no plenty of provisions, & are ill supplied with carriages. Some gangs of cattle have been drove to them from this; the week before last one Montgomery arrived here from the Virginia camp, having contracted to supply them with some cattle, and about the beginning of August he will set out with 140 head. They gave from 25 to 30 pound currency a head."

NEW-LONDON Friday last was found lying in a desolate Bog Meadow, in the North Parish of this town the dead body of a person almost consumed; upon inquisition made, the jurors gave their verdict, that it was the body Dorothy Good, a transient vagrant person, that had wandered into that desolate place, and there Died. After their judgement was taken, as decent a burial was given her as the circumstances would admit.

PHILADELPHIA Aug. 16. Private Letters from London by the Packet, mention, That the French have agreed to cede all North-America and Guadaloupe to us, and to ratify the same at the Conclusion of the Treaty of Peace, without so much as making mention thereof at the ensuing Congress; only they want some Land North of the River St. Lawrence, to cure Fish on; but the English knowing them to be bad encroaching Neighbours, don't chuse they should have a Foot; and that Peace seems at a Distance.

BOSTON Aug. 17. Province of Massachusetts-Bay

The Officers recruiting for Col. Hoar's and Col. Saltonstall's Regiments are Hereby notified, to collect all the Men they have inlisted, and march them immediately to Springfield, where they will receive further Orders. Each Officer upon arrival there is to make a Return of his

Deserters to the Commanding Officer, giving as particular a Description of them as may be, that the same may be transmitted to the Secretary of War. By Order of his Excellency,

Tho. Goldthwait, Sec'y of War.

NEW-YORK Aug. 17. Last Week General Outway's Regiment came down from Albany, was landed at Staten Island.

We hear His Excellency General Amherst is expected in a few Days from Albany.

Last Week His Honour the Lieutenant-Governor was pleased to give Mr. Douglass Permission to build a Theatre, to perform in this City the ensuing Winter.

NEW-PORT Aug 18. Capt. Aldfield acquaints us, That at Wilmington in North Carolina, in the Month of May, it continued raining about 12 days, which rais'd the water 6 Feet higher at that place than a usual tide; at the head of the North West River, forty feet.

CHARLESTOWN S. Carolina Aug 19. Capt, Rogers is arrived at Cape Fear from New-York, and is daily expected here to take upon him the command of the independent company late Capt. Demere's to which he was sometime ago appointed by General Amherst.

On Thursday las quarter master Sylvester of Colonel Burton's regiment who arrived the evening before from New-York, set out for the army with General Amherst's dispatches to Colonel Grant: The Governor having ordered horses and a guide to be provided for him immediately on his arrival.

By letter from North-Carolina, of the 10th instant, we learn that Colonel Waddle was marched for fort Dobbs, with such part of his regiment as was provided with arms, in order to join the Virginia forces, as soon, and at such place, as should be ordered by Col. Byrd.

On Monday last week upwards of 300 cattle were to set out frome Ninety six to the army; 200 more were to follow in a few days, a number of waggons were expected at Ninety six, from the camp to carry flour.

BOSTON Aug. 24. By His Excellency Francis Bernard, Esq; Captain General and Governor in

Chief in and over the His Majesty's Province of the Massachusetts-Bay in New-England, and Vice Admiral of the same.

A PROCLAMATION.
For a Day of Publick Prayer.

It has pleased Almighty God to cause a severe and distressing Drought to prevail generally throughout the Province, thereby cutting short the Fruits of the Earth, occasioning destructive Fires to eage in the open Country, and threatening a very very great Scarcity, unless God should graciously interpose by sending Plenty of Rain;

I have therefore thought fit, by and with the Advice of His Majesty's Council, to appoint Thursday the Third Day of September next, to be a Day of publick Prayer throughout the Province, whereon we may humble ourselves before Almighty God; acknowledging our Unworthiness of the extraordinary Plenty we have enjoyed for some Years past, and confessing our many Sins whereby we have provoked Him to withhold the like Blessing this present Year; ---- And most humbly supplicate our heavenly Father, on whom we depend for our daily Bread, that he would visit us with such kind and refreshing Showers, as may still preserve the remaining Fruits of the Earth, and bring forward the withered Grass, that there may be Food for Man and Beast.

And as God hath in Judgement remembered Mercy and visited some Places, with Rain from Heaven, and may see fit before the Day herein Appointed to give us more effectual Relief we ought likewise to return our unfeigned Thanks for all the undeserving Mercies, while we humbly implore his further Favours.

And I do order the said Day to be observed as a Day set apart for Religion Worship, and that no servile Labour or Recreation be permitted thereon.

Given at the Council Chamber in Boston, the Twentieth Day of August, 1761, in the First Year of the Reign of our Sovereign Lord George the Third by the Grace of God, of Great Britain, France, and Ireland, King, defender of the Faith, &c.

By His Excellency's Command,
A. Oliver, Sect'y.   Fra. Bernard.
God Save the King,

BOSTON Aug. 24. On Wednesday the 6th of April was tried at Guildhall, London before Lord Mansfield Chief-Justice the cause of long depending between Samoel Blagden of Halifax, in Nova-Scotia, Plaintiff, and Capt. Gambier of his Majesty's Ship Burford, Defendant. The action was brought for damages the plaintiff sustained in Nova-Scotia, by the defendant's taking him by violence from his freehold there, burning his house, and detaining the plaintiff unjustly on board the Burford 125 days, when after a full hearing of three hours, a special jury of merchants gave the plaintiff eight hundred pounds damages, and cost of suit. ———

[this verdict must give great satisfaction to all his Majesty's subjects in America, and increase their esteem and affection for the mother country, whose excellent laws will not suffer any injury to the subject in the most remote part of the British dominions, to pass with impunity, and convince all military officers, that they are accountable, at home for every arbitrary act of power, even in the most distant parts of his Majesty's dominions.]

NEW-YORK Aug. 24. Extract of a Letter from Oswego, July 21, 1761.

"On Friday last Sir William Johnson arrived here in good Health; and this Day about four in the Afternoon, he embarked on board the Anson Schooner for Niagara; as did also Col. Eyre, Chief Engineer. Sir William I am inform'd, is taking a Tour quite round from Niagara to Fort Detroit, and round to Pittsburgh, we suppose to quiet the Indians, who seem uneasy by the persuasion of the French, that they, the Indians will all be either enslav'd, or cut off, if they suffer us to go on and make such a large conquest in their Country. ——— The greatest Part of Gage's Light Infantry, which arrived here last Week, with Major Gladwin, embarked this Morning by Sun rise, on board Battoes for Niagara: The Major went on board the Arson. A Party of Men are to follow Sir William to Detroit.

Besides the Anson we have another Schooner and Sloop belonging to the Garrison."

BOSTON Aug. 24. Wednesday last a Ship arrived at Marblehead from St. Kitts, which sailed from thence the 24th of July, with a fleet of upwards of 200 Sail of Merchantmen, under convoy, bound for Europe, and several Ports on the Continent.

List of Captures lately carried to Martinico.

Vessels,	Captain's Names,	where from,
Sloop,	Auldboy.	New-York.
Ditto,	Eddy,	Philadelphia.
Schooner,	Junkins,	Halifax.
Brig,	Lewis,	Boston.
Sloop,	Roach,	Cork.
Ditto,	Gules,	Philadelphia.
Brig,	Foster,	Cape Anne.
Ditto,	Crawford,	Maryland.
Ditto,	Jones,	Ditto.
Ditto,	————	Virginia.
Snow,	Ball,	Cape Fear.
Sloop,	Elliott,	Piscataqua.
Brig,	King,	Ditto.
Sloop,	Lafavour,	Guersey.
Sloop,	————	Londonderry.
Schooner,	Young,	Ditto.
Brig,	Niccoll,	Glasgow.
Ditto,	Turnwe,	Piscataqua.
Ditto,	Lovett,	Salem.
Ditto,	Hathorn,	Ditto.
Schooner,	Baffett,	Barbados.
Ditto,	Warren,	Ditto to Virginia.
Ditto,	Buck,	Newbury.
Sloop.	Saltonstall,	New-London.
Schooner,	Colefox,	Ditto.

Several others have also been lately taken, but the names not known.

A Description of several French Privateer which sailed from Martinico to cruize on the Northern Coasts.

A Brig with a Fiddle Head, 14 Guns, and two Sloops in Company of 10 Guns each.

A Sloop of 14 Guns, Yellow Bottom, a gilt Sun on her Stern, commanded by a Louisbourg Captain who was at Nantasket the beginning of the War, his Name Semins.

A Sloop of 12 Guns, one side Lamblack and

Tallow, the other side White Lead and Tallow looks like a Northern Sloop and sails fast.

A Schooner of 12 Guns, formerly a Marblehead Fisherman one side of her upper Works black, and the other Yellow and white Streaks; a Seahorse on her Hawse-holes, and looks very much like a Fisherman on the painted Side.

SEPTEMBER 1761

BOSTON Sept. 2. Port of Boston in New-England. We the Subscribers, Collectors, Comptrollers, and Surveyor of his Majesty's Customs for this Port, have received certain Information, that a Ship (whose Name and Master are known to us) having taken on board One hundred and twenty Chests of Tea, laden in Holland, under a Pretence of being bound to St. John's in the West Indies, hath landed, or is now hovering about the Coast of New-England, with design to land the said Tea: We therefore hereby promise to any Person who will inform us thereof, so that the said Vessel and Cargo may be siezed, and prosecuted to Condemnation, One Thousand Pounds Sterling; and so in Proportion for any Part of said Cargo, which shall be seized and prosecuted as afore said.
George Cradock,
Robert Temple,
Charles Paxton.

PHILADELPHIA Sept. 3. By advices from Detroit, we learn that the Indians in those parts, countenanced by the Seneca tribe, had designed an attempt on Fort Sandusky, where a considerable quantity of ammunition was lodged under a slender guard, and then to make themselves masters of Detroit, &c. This was to have been executed early in July, but being discovered, the stores were removed, and the confederacy broken. Sir William Johnson is gone in those parts, accompanied by Major Gladwin, an engineer and 350 Men. It is expected that such a respectable force will over awe the savages who are very numerous, and therefore despise our slender Garrison. We hear that this Detachment is ordered to penetrate into the country, as far as the season will permit, in order to procure as much acquaintance with the inland seas of North

America as possible.

PHILADELPHIA Sept. 3. Friday last Capt. Bowies arrived here from Fyall, whith whom came one of the hands late belonging to the ship Granby, Capt. Appowin, of this port, bound to Jamaica, and informs us as follows, viz. That the said ship, on the 6th of July, two days after she left our capes, was taken by a French 74 gun ship, from Hispaniola, with two frigates in company: That soon after a Vessel from Virginia for Glasgow was taken by the same ship and ransomed; on board which vessel this person. with some others of Capt. Appowin's hands, were put, to help to carry her home, but that he jump'd from the Glasgow man and with great difficulty got on board Capt. Bowies, on hearing he was bound here. A sloop from Maryland for Providence was likewise taken by these vessels.

ANNAPOLIS Maryland Sept. 3. On Monday last an Express went from hence by Water for Hampton with a Petition sign'd by Twenty-nine Masters of Tobacco Ships, to Capt. Norton, of the Assistance, to put off his Sailing as Convoy to the 10th of October: The Time being so short this Year, but few could get loaded in Time. And we hear an Express of the like Nature, was sent from Fredericksburg.

HALIFAX Sept. 5. Tuesday last one Fleming, a Dyer, was found in a sump leading towards the north west arm, with his throat and wrist cut in a most shocking manner, supposed to have murdered himself, his penknife being found close by him; The Doctor sewed in the wounds and he soon after expired in the utmost agony. ——— What could be the instigation is uncertain.

Monday last arrived here Capt. Denke, in the Snow Bristol, in six Weeks from Cork, and by him we are informed, that there was a report that a treaty was on foot, and that the preliminaries were signed, between England and France.

CHARLESTOWN S. Carolina Sept. 5. Col. Grant's head-quarters, near Fort Prince George, August 18, 1761.

"Since our arrival at this camp from the middle settlements, several Cherokees have come in, some with talks from Ouccanostato, and the

Standing Turkey, others with messages from the towns and particular headmen, they all tender to the same purpose, and they appear to beg for peace with great sincerity.

On the 9th inst. Tiftoe and the Slave-catcher brother to the Little Carpenter, came in with a flag: They were carried to Col. Grant's tent, but gave a very short talk; they told him they were sent down with a message from their nation desiring peace, but did not then enter into Particulars. They said 'it was with difficulty that any person could be prevailed upon trust himself in our lands, that fear had kept their people and us so long separated, but that their present necessities and their desire of peace had determined them to make an attempt.' They were assured of protection, were civilly treated, and were conducted that evening into the Fort, where they were offered an apartment for the night; they both decline staying there, and they seemed uneasy while they remained within the gate; Tiftoe in particular pointing to the guard-room, said he had reason to remember the house, that he had been there loaded with irons, which the great Warrior, meaning Col. Grant, had ordered to be taken off when he came there. They petitioned to be allowed to go to the other side of the river to sleep, for they had left their horses there in charge of another Indian. Next day they delivered their talk in form and presented a string of white beads, from Ouccanostato, who, in name of the whole nation, begged they might have peace, and enjoy the benefits of trade with the white people as formerly; They also brought in a string of beads, a pipe ornamented with white beads and white feathers, and some tobacco, which was sent as a present to Col. Grant, from the headman of Neeyowee in the valley, who desired he might accept of these as a token of his sincerity and desire of peace, in behalf of his people. They again assured the Colonel, that their people were afraid to come in and begged that he would allow Capt. Watts to return with them, as it would undoubtedly free them any apprehension and be the means of bringing the headmen of the nation. Capt. Watts seemed to approve of the proposal, and told Col. Grant that if he had no objection that he was very willing to go; the Colonel's answer was, that he should not desire him to go but if Capt. Watts chose it, he should certainly give his leave. The Indians finding he had obtained leave to accompany them back to the nation, discovered the greatest joy and satisfaction, particularly the Slave-catcher, and promised that no harm should befall him, and that they would be punctual to any reasonable time that should be fixed for their return; they were accordingly desired to be here again after the twelfth sleep; to which they agreed, and on Monday night they all set out together.

Some Indians, said to be the Young Warrior's party, have stolen a number of our horses at different times; but as they have nothing else to live upon that piece of hostility is thought the more pardonable."

"The Little Carpenter and some other headmen have been with Col. Byrd; letters have been received from him the 19th past from Stalnakers, which is considerably nearer the Cherokee country than where he was last year; he had been informed, by the Indians themselves, of our operation, and, he says they are much alarmed and distressed; he prevail with two of them to bring his letters to Col. Grant, which they did in 12 days, but were almost starved when they arrived. Col. Grant kept them two days, fed them well, but told them he would give them no presents till a peace was concluded, which he would only grant to save their nation, for that we were not afraid to make war with them; One of them made answer that they were now convinced of that, and that all their people were turned good, and would gladly join us against the Creeks, who were the cause of all the mischief. These two Indians carry a talk from Col. Byrd to the head warriors, desiring to come and treat with Col. Grant."

The famous major (now Captain) Rogers, arrived in town on Friday last: He was received and entertained in the greatest manner by the Governor and the principal inhabitants, and on Monday set out to join the troops commanded by Colonel Grant.

BOSTON Sept. 7. For the benefit of Trade.

Extract of a letter from Commodore James Douglass, to his Excellency Governor Wentwort, at Portsmouth, dated on board the Dublin, Antigua, July 7, 1761.

"By his Majesty's ship Doblin, I take to opportunity to acquaint you, that I have ordered her to Halifax to carren and refit again for the Sea with all possible Expedition, and to be ready to proceed again to the West Indies by the Middle, or at shortest, the latter end of September; And as the Vessels from North-America, have been particularly unfortunate in falling into the Hands of the Enemy, to the great Detriment of the Colonies, I am to desire your Excellency will be pleased to give timely Notice on the Trade at different Ports within the Limits of your Commonwealth, That if they proceed to Halifax by the Time before mentioned, Captain Gascoign of the Dublin, will take them under Care and Protection, and give them safe Convoy to the Island of Barbados, and I shall order one of his Majesty's Ships to see them in safely from thence to the different Islands they may be bound to within the Limits of my Command.

I am, Sir, with great regards, Your Excellency's most obedient humble Servant.

James Douglass."

BOSTON Sept. 13. Tuesday last Capt. Delap in a small Schooner sail'd from hence for Halifax, but after being out a few Hours, his Vessel sprung a Leak, and the Water gained upon them so fast they were obliged to throw all the Cattle off the Deck, and part of the Cargo in the Hold, in order to preserve the Vessel from sinking, and the next Day they got safe back again.

——— Capt. Shiverick coming from Philadelphia, took up two of the Cattle alive after they had been in the Water a considerable time, and bro't them with him.

NEW-YORK Sept. 7. From Charlestown in South Carolina, we have public papers to the 20th ult. but nothing material in them. ——— It is said, that the loss of the Cherokees at Cowowee, the

10th or June, was not less than 200 men, and that Col. Grant would certainly make another incursion into their country, the more readily to make them sue for peace, they being in great distress for want of provisions: That Col. Byrd, with the Virginia forces, was at his old camp, on the waters of the Great Kanawa, with to great plenty of provisions, and but ill supply'd with carriages; but that the North Carolina regiment of 500 men was compleat, and would march to join him as soon as they could be supplied with arms; That the Creeks were under apprehensions of a body of Spaniards being sent against them from St. Augustine, to revenge some mischief received from them: And that the enemy's privateers have been very troublesome on the coast; but that the Captains Campbell and Greenwood, in two of his Majesty's Ships, were to go on a cruize against them.

PHILADELPHIA Sept. 10. On Friday last was brought in here by Capt. John Blair, a retaken schooner, late Capt. Davidson, bound to Quebec, to the eastward of Bermuda, was taken by a French privateer sloop of 12 carriage guns, belonging to Martinico. Next day the said privateer fell in with the ship Sarah, Capt. Katter of this place, bound to St. Christophers, when a smart engagement ensued, which lasted 4 glasses; and after the first glass the Frenchman hung up his bloody flag, on which Capt. Katter's men agreed to stand by the ship to the last, and accordingly plied the enemy so warmly, that he thought proper to sheer off, in a shattered condition, after having made several attemptd to board the Sarah. None of Capt. Katter's people received any hurt; the lose of the privateer not known, but it was thought a principal officer and several of her hands were killed. On the 15th of August Capt. Katter about 75 leagues S. E. of Bermuda, re-took and sent in the above vessel, her lading molasses, rum, &c.

NEW PORT Sept. 10. "As the Opposition and Clamour against the Play House erected here, it was much too vehement to continue, and, like Snow and Hail of Midsummer, melted gradually away. The House was open'd on the second of the

Month with the Fair Penitent, and Etop in the Shade: and I cannot think you ever saw the Royal House of Drury and Covent Garden fuller (without being crowded) or any Audience the more deeply attentive or better pleased. On the Evening of the fourth Jane Shore with The Toy Shop were performed to the highest Satisfaction of a very full House. On Monday and Friday last the Provok'd Husband with the Miller of Manfield were perform'd with the greatest Applause, Last Evening George Barnswell with the mock Doctor were exhibited before a great many of our General Assembly, and as many others as they could be admitted, and I can assure you that the audience were greatly mov'd and affected with the Distress and Fate of the unhappy Hero of that very moral and virtuous Entertainment.

Upon the whole I not only invite you here on this Occasion, but encourage you to give all your Friends ample Assurance that the Company of Comedians here, more than verify their just Letters of Credence from Virginia, and are indeed capable of entertaining a very polite and sensible Audience.

I am yours, &c.

CHARLESTOWN S. Carolina Sept. 12. Camp near Fort Prince-George, Aug. 17, 1761.

On the 28th arrived Capt. Watts, with the Little Carpenter; Wilanawah, his brother; Harry, Old Hopp's son; the Mankiller, Half breed Will, and the Raven of Naucasih and the Raven and old Cæsar of Hywassih: These are all the Indians that are pretended to be of any note; 17 others of inferior rank came down with them. On the 29th they waited on Col. Grant and being all seated in order, in a spacious bower prepar'd for their reception, the Colonel asked Little Carpenter, "if they came to sue for peace?" he answer'd Yes. The Colonel then asked, "if they had power from the whole nation?" To which he answered, "That they all came down for that purpose, and that they would stand to whatever he agreed to." Then the Cherokee orator went on: and having delivered his talk, Col. Grant told them he would give them his answer the next day; accordingly on the 30th, the Indians attended, and Col. Grant acquainted them, that as their suffering were great, in consequence of their folly and madness in breaking with us, he would now tell them on what terms they should have peace, in the words of the following articles,

Art. I. Four Cherokee Indians shall be delivered up to be put to death in the front of the camp; or four green scalps bro't in 12 nights from this day.

Art. II. Fort Loudoun with all its cannon, &c. shall be delivered up to whatever garrison the English shall think proper to send thither, from Virginia or Carolina.

Art. III. All prisoners, horses, &c. taken from us, shall be delivered up as soon as possible.

Art. IV. The English shall be at liberty to build forts in any part of the Cherokee country they shall think proper, for the protection of their traders; and have as much land about such forts, for planting and pasturage as the garrison shall think necessary; which land shall not be trespass'd on by the Indians.

Art. V. If a Cherokee kills a white man, the headman of the town to which he belongs shall put the murderer to death as soon as he is found: If a white man kills an Indian, they shall not take satisfaction themselves, but deliver him down to Charlestown; and if condemned, some of the Cherokees may see him executed, if they please.

Art. VI. No Frenchman shall be suffered to come into the Cherokee country: If any should come, the Indians are to assist, or at least not prevent, our taking him.

Art. VII. The traders shall not be molested. If the Indians receive any injuries from them, they are to lay their complaints before the governor of Carolina, who will redress their grievances.

Art. VIII. The Chicasaw and Catawba Indians are to be considered as white men, and included in these articles accordingly.

Art. IX. As soon as these articles shall be finally concluded and ratified by the governor at Charlestown, all the Cherokee prisoners in our possession shall be brought to Keeohwee and delivered up; and traders shall be set up with goods to supply the wants of the needy and necessitous Cherokees, which they will exchange for skins, furs, &c.

The eight last articles agreed to, but the first, the Little Carpenter objected; upon which Col. Grant gave him till the next day to consider it.

The particulars of the reply of the Little Carpenter and the other Indian Chiefs, and the conferences with Colonel Grant, are too long to admit of a place in this paper, but the most material circumstances are. That the Little Carpenter still objected to the severity of the first article, and Col. Grant insisting on that article as well as the rest, the Little Carpenter said he had not power to agree to it himself, but would return and consult his people, promising to be back in 10 nights; meanwhile, Col. Grant promised that all the Indians that remained should be safe till the Little Carpenter's return, who thereupon promised to set out immediately for Charlestown: but the next night they all went privately off, except the Little Carpenter, and a fellow of no note; The Little Carpenter says in consequence of a report of M'Cunningham, that Col. Grant only wanted them to go to Charlestown to catch a disorder that kills all who were seized with it. Some think this only an excuse, but M'Cunningham was put in irons, and the Little Carpenter satisfied the report false.

BOSTON Sept. 14. All Persons licensed to retail Wine and strong Liquors within the Town of Boston, are hereby notified, That proper persons are appointed to make Strict Enquiry into any breaches of the Laws respecting licensed Persons. ——— Such as suffering any Person or Person to sit Drinking or Tipling in their Houses, Cellars, or within any of the Dependencies of such Houses. ——— or selling any other sort of Drink than what they have license for, ——— or of delivering any of the Strong Drink to Negro or Molatto Servants without special Order or Allowance of their respective Masters. ———

All other Offenders of this Sort may depend upon their not being approbated as a fit Person to be licensed for the future, as well as upon their being prosecuted according to the rigor of the Law. By Order of the Select-Men, William Cooper, Town-Clerk.

NEW-YORK Sept. 14. To the Printer.

Sir,

As the Curiosity of the Publick is very much raised to know the Destination of our Forces. I have made it my Business to get the best Intelligence I possibly could from those who are acquainted with the Secret in the Camp; And as a Result of my Inquiries, I send you for your Paper, "a whole Packet of News, as follows; in the first Place I inquired when the Forces were to proceed on the Expedition? They told me they were perfectly strangers to that Matter. Secondly, I asked when they were to embark? They answered and said they never heard. Thirdly, I inquired the Number of Troops? They replies it was more than they knew. Fourthly, I demanded the Name of the Officer who was to command in the Expedition? Their Answer was they could not tell. Fifthly, I asked to what Place they were bound? they said they were ignorant of that. Lastly, I desired them to tell me whether there was to be any Expedition at all or not? They replied they knew nothing of the Matter. And this is all the Material Information that could be obtained by,

Your humble Servant, A. B.

PORTSMOUTH New-Hampshire Sept. 18. A melancholy accident happened at the time of Capt. Simpson's endeavouring to turn into this harbour last Friday night; after many fruitless attempts to get in the wind being easterly, he was obliged to come to anchor off Rye, a sail boat was immediately sent to his assistance, and they had not been long on board before the cable parted; upon which they came under sail, and put a hand, Mr. Samuel Barnes of this place into the sail boat to steer her, and most unfortunately entangled the tow-rope round her mast, which immediately overset, and tho' all means were used to preserve the said Barne's life he drowned.

What added greatly to the distress of those on board was, after she overset he caught hold of the tow-rope and was getting up by it, when it suddenly broke and was lost with a valuable boat, a great sea ran all the time, altho' the ship's boat was soon twisted out, and sought for him.

HALIFAX Sept. 19. One Day last Week, a Seafaring Man suppos'd to be Deserter from one of the Men of War in this Harbour, was found kill'd and scalp'd at a place called Ketch Harbour; but by whom or what Tribe we have not yet heard.

BOSTON Sept. 21. Extract of a Letter from Quebec.

"About a fortnight ago the British Merchants of this Place presented a Memorial to the Governor, complaining of the Hardships laid upon them in particular, as well as upon the Nation in general, by the 26th, 37th, and 48th Articles of the Capitulation of Canada. By these Articles the French have Liberty to export to France whatever Peltries they may have without being confined to any particular Time or Quantity, to which Purpose they are, moreover to be found with Britiah Vessels at any Time. By this Means the French have got Possession of the Furr Trade as fully as before the Conquest of Canada, and run no other Risque than that of the Sea in fencing it home; the Circumstances of which is, that the French Merchants being better acquainted with the Country than the British. the former ingross all the Furr Trade, and even import goods of the Manufacture of France, by way of Geurnsey, and Jersey, by which means they will always be enable to engross the Furr Trade and laugh at all the Efforts of the British Merchants to share with them; To that if a Stop is not put to the French Exportation of Furrs and the Importation of French Goods by way of Geurnsey and Jersey, adieu to the British Trade in Canada: it will be in vain to import any Thing more than the trickle that may be wanting for the use of the Troops."

BOSTON Sept. 21. Ran away from his Master Obadiah Sprague, of Providence on the 30th Day of August last past, a Negro Man, named Cumber, about 35 Years of Age, of a middling stature, has a pretty old Look, had on when he run away a bluish colour'd Cap, a woolen Jacket of a grayish Colour, short linnen Breeches, and a Pair of old Shoes, has a small Bunch on the left Side of his Face, near his Ear, and speaks very bad English. ——— Whoever shall apprehend the said Negroe, and convey him to his said Master in Providence, or give Intelligence where he may be had, shall have Four Dollars Reward, and all necessary Charges paid by   Obadiah Sprangue.

CHARLESEOWN S. Carolina Sept. 23. "This day Attakullakulla had his last public Audience, when he signed the terms of peace, and received an authenticated copy under the Great Seal and signed by the Governor. He earnestly requested that Capt. John Stuart might be made chief Whiteman in their nation; he said all the Indians love him, and there would never be any uneasiness if he were there: He promised to return in six Weeks, with other headmen. This faithful Indian afterwards dined with his Honor the Governor, and Tomorrow sets out for his own country. He has received several presents, as a mark of the regard this government has for him in particular, for his unaltered fidelity and attachment: The other Indians received only some necessary cloathing for themselves, of which they were in great want."

CHARLESTOWN S. Carolina Sept. 23. On the 15th Instant the General Assembly of the Province met at Ashley Ferry, agreeable to Proclamation, when the Governor opened the Session with the following Message to both Houses, viz.

Mr. Speaker and Gentlemen,

Although the making of the War and Peace are the most undoubted prerogative of the crowd; yet as the exercise of their prerogative is intended for the benefit is most likely to be secured by taking their advice in it.

Attakullakulla, commonly called the Little-Carpenter, has applied to Col. Grant in the name of the Cherokee nation for peace, and has been referr'd by Col. Grant to me; I have given him audience on the subject this morning, and a copy of the conference is herewith sent you, as I think this matter of the greatest consequence in the honour, interest, and future security of this province, I desire your advice therein, and for better information. I lay before you a copy of a letter I wrote to Col. Grant the 14th of April last and also Col. Grant's letter to me of the 18th instant, after confering with the Little-Carpenter and several other headmen on the subject matter of peace and likewise a letter from Col. Byrd dated the 26th of July last.

Being sensible of the inconveniencies that must attend many of you whilst the General Assembly sits at Ashley-Ferry, I have declined the method of opening the business to you by a speech, as ceremonies of that occasion might be attended with some delay.

  Sept. 15th, 1761.   William Bull.

On the 19th inst. the following Meeting was presented to his Honour the Lieutenant Governor by the Common House of Assembly, in answer to the Honour's message of the 25th instant.

May it please you Honour,

Your message of the 15th instant, with the important papers accompanying it, give us the highest proof of your warmest intentions for the welfare of the province; and the present instance of your Honour's condescension, in advising with this house in matters relating to war and peace, the undoubted prerogative of the crown, we shall always remember with the greatest satisfaction.

We are sorry to find ourselves obliged, by the necessities and particular, circumstances of the province, to advise your Honour to recede from the first, and what you considered as the grand article, that must be insisted on the satisfy our honour, and shew to the world an evident acknowledgement of our superiority in arms, and at the same time revenge the blood of our fellow subjects the late unhappy garrison of Fort Loudoun.

We flatter ourselves we do not err, when we think, that no province in America can have exerted themselves more vigorously than we have done this year; and with the assistance his Majesty has been graciously pleased to afford us, we had the greatest reason to hope, a solid and lasting peace would have been the happy conclusion of the campaigns; especially as the commanding officer had declared, that "he would not agree to any terms till he was in the center of the Cherokee nation, and that no preliminaries should ever be signed by him but in one of their Town-Houses." Had this been done by a speedy, and, we may say, generally expected, march to the Valley, since the army's return to Keeowee, we flatter ourselves we should not be reduced to this disagreeable necessity, of advising your honour to accept a peace, upon terms so precarious, and less honourable than we had reason to expect: But notwithstanding these expectations, we have foundation to think, by Col. Byrd's letter to your Honour dated only several days after Col. Grant's return to Keeowee, that a peace was determined upon: for Col. Byrd says "my orders were to co-operate with and assist Colonel Grant. That gentleman writes me, he has compleated his work already; so that, could I proceed I should not answer that end." We dread the unhappy consequences that may attend Colonel Grant's depending too much on the importance of destroying the Middle-Towns; a thing he made light of last year, for in the letter your Honour then laid before the house, dated 3d July 1760, he says "destroying an Indian town may be creditable; but, in fact, 'tis a matter of no consequence, when the savages have time to carry off their effects." Again, "we could have gone to any town in the nation; but, we should have had a brush to get at it, and then we should have found it, or rather them all abandoned," which was the case this year. We conceived that the only thing in the Cherokee war, that will have any effect to bring those savages to a firm and lasting peace, is to destroy as many of their people as we can, and when an opportunity offers so to do, to miss it by no means, which, we fear, has been too much the case of the late expedition and defensive action; and we are not without our apprehensions, that your Honour's information, that their young men entertain no very respectable opinion of dread of the English manner of fighting Indians, though our numbers are formidable," may be too well grounded. From these reasons, as the province is already greatly loaded with taxes, and as we have little prospects of war being carried on in a different and what we conceive, more effectual, manner, that hitherto has been done; or, that the Colonel of the provincial regiment, thought of great influence, merit, and abilities, and well acquainted with the interest of the province, and the proper manner of treating the Cherokees, will ever be consulted; we are reduced to the necessity of advising your Honour, to agree to a peace, upon the terms propose by your Honour, in your letter to Colonel Grant of the 14th of April last, except as the first and ninth article, adding in the second article, after the word prisoners, the word "negroes;" leaving out in the third article the words "for the protection of our traders there," and adding at the latter part of the article, "and that the head or scalp of the murderer be bro't to the commander of the next English fort." And we beg leave to recommend to your Honour another article to the following effect. ———

"That to prevent, as much as may be, any disturbances that may arise between the Cherokees and the white people on back settlements, no Cherokee Indian shall come down into this province, within the limits of six mile river, or any pretence, whatsoever, without some white person in company; or unless by order or permission of this government; and that all white men whether French or English, who have been amongst the Cherokees, and have aided and assisted them during the last war, shall be delivered up"

This House has resolved to make provisions for the pay of four companies of rangers, upon present establishments, with a major-commander, until the first day of January next if their service should be thought so long necessary; but we beg leave to inform your Honour, that we will not make any provisions for garrisoning of fort Loudoun, in case it should be delivered up by the Indians.

By order of the House,
Benjamin Smith, Speaker.

The Conference between his Honour the Lieutenant Governor and the Little Carpenter.

Lieut. Governor. "I am glad to see you the Little Carpenter, as you have always been a good friend to the English: I have now shook hands not only, with you, but with those with you also, as a pledge for their security whilst under my protection.

Col. Grant has acquainted me that you the Little Carpenter have applied to him for peace: He has sent you to me; you are now come, and I met with my beloved men to hear what you have to say, and my ears are open for that purpose."

The Little Carpenter thereupon called for fire to light his pipe, which being brought, he then smoked; then delivered the pipe to his honour the Lieutenant Governor and the council, who smoked also; then gave it to one of his warriors, who handed it to all the gentlemen present, who smoked likewise.

The Little Carpenter then spoke as follows: "I am come to see you, as a messenger from the whole nation: I have now seen you, smoked with you, and am glad, and hope we shall live as Brothers together; and I expect you and all the gentlemen present will consider us as brothers; and I do leave this pipe as a token of our friendship ——— I came down to Keeowee to Col. Grant, who desired me to come to you; I come accordingly, and am now to begin my talk." Then he delivered to his Honour a string of wampum and said. "You live at the waterside, and are in light; we are in darkness, but hope all will yet be clear with us; I have been constantly going about to do good, and tho' I am tired, yet am come here to see what can be done for my people, who are in great distress." Here he produced several strings of white wampum, and taking one in his hand, said. "This I had from the town Chorih, from whom I am a messenger, and denote their earnest desire for peace; and they hope and desire the path may be made as strait and clear as formerly." Then he took another string, and said, "This was given to me by

Settico, with whom it has been dark, but they hope the same as Chorih," in the like manner he proceeded with several other strings from different towns, from whom he came as a messenger, an all whom he said were desirous of peace. He then took another string, and said, "This concerns what I told Col. Grant at Keeowee, viz. that our women and children are in great distress, and dying on account of their towns and corn being destroyed."

"It is a great while since I saw your Honour last; but I always speak one way, and am not doubleminded. I am glad to see all the beloved gentlemen now present. As to what has happened, I believe has been ordered by our Father above. We are of different colour from the white people; they are superior to us; but one God is father of all, and we hope what is past will be forgiven. God almighty made all people, and there is not a day but some are coming into, and others going out of the world.

"Im sent a messenger from the whole nation, and hope the path (as the great King told me) will never be crooked, but strait and open for every one to pass and repass." Here he delivered his Honour a string of wampum and said, "I hope as we all live on one land, we shall all live as one people.

"When I was at Keeowee, Col. Grant desired me to come to you for a peace; I am come accordingly, and my people will be anxious to know what answer I shall receive from you."

Lieut. Governor. "I have heard what you have said; before I give an answer will consider of it: I have but tongue, and what I say to you may depend upon: I have always heard of the good behaviour of you the Little Carpenter, during the war; therefore have given orders for your being well taken care of." ——— The Indians hereupon shook hands and withdrew.

On Monday last Attakullakulla, had another publick audience of the Governor in council, when the following articles were propose and agreed to.

The Terms of Peace to be granted to the
Cherokee Indians.

Whereas war has subsisted for some time past between the Cherokee Indians and his Majesty's subject's, particularly of the Province of Virginia, North and South Carolina: And Whereas the said Cherokee Indians have applied to me for peace, by Attakullakulla, one of their principal headmen specially deported and authorized for that purpose, and they having by their said deputy expressed their earnest desire that an end may be put to the war and peace restored; which application I have duly considered, and being desirous to deliver the said Indians from the hardships and distresses the said war has brought upon them, as well as to remove the inconveniences which attend his Majesty's subjects, whilst they are engaged in such a war; I have therefore thought proper to grant them peace on the conditions contained in the several articles hereafter set down.

And It is hereby stipulated by me the Honourable William Bull, Esq; Lieutenant Governor and commander and chief of the province of South Carolina, on behalf of his Majesty, and the said Attakullakulla, on behalf of the Cherokee Indians, that peace may be restored, confirmed and established between his Majesty's subjects and the Cherokee Indians ——— which peace, it is intended, shall endore as long as the sun shall shine, & rivers continue to run into the sea.

ARTICLE 1.

All English prisoners, negroes, horses and cattles, in, their possession, to be delivered up immediately to Colonel Grant.

II. Fort Loudoun and the cannon belonging there now lying at Chote, to be delivered up to any persons sent to take the charge of them; and any forts shall be built hereafter, in the Cherokee nation, when the same shall be thought necessary by the English.

III. The Cherokees shall not admit any Frenchmen into their nation, and if any come, the Cherokees shall assist us, at least shall not pretend to interpose their protection, to prevent us, when we think proper, to apprehend the Frenchmen.

IV. Any Indian, who murders any of his Majesty's

subjects, shall be immediately put to death by the Cherokees, as soon as the murderer and murderers are known in the Cherokee nation, and that the head scalp of the murderer be brought to the commander of the next English fort.

V. The Cherokees shall not hunt to the eastward of twenty-six mile river, nor the English to the westward of it, to prevent any quarrels or mischief that may be occasioned from hunting parties meeting in the woods;

VI. That to prevent as much as may be, any disturbances that may arise between the Cherokees and the white people on the back settlements, no Cherokee Indian shall come down into the province, within the limits of twenty-six mile river, on any pretence whatsoever, without some white person in company, or unless by the order or permission of the government; and that all white men, whether French or English, who have been amonst the Cherokees, and have aided and assisted them during the late war, shall be delivered up.

VII. The Cherokees shall not molest the creatures belonging to, nor trespass on grounds necessary for planting and pasturing for the use of the garrison of forts built, or to be built, in their nation.

VIII. The Catawba and Chicesaws to be comprehended in this place.

IX. That all the Cherokee prisoners we have taken shall be restored.

X. Our friendship shall be granted to them; a firm peace shall be made and firmly ratified at Charlestown, trade shall be renewed and plenty of goods sent up to be exchanged for their skins, to supply their wants.

XI. And an equal justice is the surest foundation of a lasting peace, it shall be agreed, that when an Englishman murders a Cherokee, the Cherokees shall not put him to death, but shall be delivered to the officer of the fort, sent to Charlestown, and there tried according to our laws, and if found guilty, to be executed in presence of some Cherokees, if they desire to be present; and when the Cherokees think they are injured by the English in their nation, they are not to take revenge themselves, but shall make complaints to the commander of the next English fort, to be from thence, transmitted to the English governor who will right them therein, according to our laws; and when the Cherokees injure any English among them, on complaint thereof, the Cherokees shall right the injured; thus the guilty will only be punished on both sides; thus friendship. peace, and trade will be preserved: but when they cease to observe this treaty, friendship, peace and trade will also cease.

XII. That Attakullakulla communicate these stipulations to the nation on his return, and acquaint them, that in order to have these articles of peace finally ratified and confirmed, so that out old friendship may be renewed, and last as long as the sun shines and the rivers run, some of the headmen from the Upper, the Valley, the Middle and Lower Settlements shall come down to Charlestown, and confirm these stipulations, and then settle such matters, as concern the trade to be carried on with their nation.

In testimony whereas both parties have hereunto interchangeably set their hands; and I the said William Bull have caused the great seal of this his Majesty's province to be hereunto affixed, this twenty-third day of September, in the year of our Lord one thousand seven hundred and sixty one, and in the first year of his Majesty's reign,

William Bull.

I Arrakullakulla do accept the foregoing terms of Peace, on behalf of the Cherokee nation

his
Attakil☐lakulla
mark

On Tuesday the 15th the Little Carpenter had a Conference with the Governor, where he produced his full Powers from the different Towns, which, as the Indians have not the use of letters, consisted of belts of wampum: and yesterday he had his last public audience of the Governor and Council, which was as follow:

His Honour acquainted the Little Carpenter and

the other Cherokee Indians who lately came hither, to attend in order to communicate to the Little Carpenter such terms of peace between the English and Cherokees, as had been thought proper by the legislature.

The Little Carpenter and seven other Cherokees attended, they were called in, when they shook hands, and being seated, his Honour desired the interpreter to interpret to the Little Carpenter as follows.

Lieutenant Governor, "When you were here last, you brought with you a pipe ornamented with white feathers, some of which are consumed and gone as you may observe [here the pipe was produced.] This pipe you brought in time of peace; after smoking with your friends the English, you left it as a token of friendship. There has been war since, But, my beloved men, after a great deal of talk; and having duly considered your earnest request made to me, at the desire and in behalf of all the Cherokees, for peace being restored them, you being authorized by them for that purpose, have advised me to grant peace to the Cherokees: This being agreed to, I will again smoak with you out of your own pipe." [here the pipe was lighted and his Honour, all the Council, and the Indians smoaked.] His Honour then acquainted the Little Carpenter, that the several articles upon which a peace was to be granted and made should be read to him: and a copy thereof should be prepared and delivered to him, in order to be carried into, and truly interpreted to all the headmen in the nation: And that they might be throughly satisfied of the truth of every thing therein contained, the Great King's Seal should be affixed to the same, which seal was never affixed to any thing but truth. The articles were interpreted to him accordingly. [see above.]

"This said articles being distinctly and fully interpreted, his Honour observed to the Little Carpenter, that the terms mentioned in the said articles had been thought not only reasonable, but necessary for a long and lasting peace, that most of them had been communicated to him by Col. Grant, before he left the nation, and agreed to; that there was one article in those communications by Col. Grant. (to wit) four Cherokees were to be put to death,* but by the advice of his beloved men, he had agreed to leave out and not insist upon the article; therefore expect that as the Cherokees had been so favourably dealt with on that head, they would be faithful and punctual in the performance of all the other articles. His Honour further said, "You said, "You, the Little Carpenter, have been sent messenger by the nation to me to sue for peace, my talk is directed to you only; I know your heart is straight. I have taken you by the hand as an old acquaintance, as well as on account of the errand you now come upon; after you have advised my talk to the nation, and they being satisfied therewith (for my satisfaction of their sincerity) Expect and desire some headmen from several settlements to come immediately to Charlestown, in order to confirm all the matters now agreed to; every thing shall then be written on paper, to which I and they will set our hands and seal for final ratification thereof; and at the same time; all matters shall be settled in regard to the trade; and tho' you have had a great deal of trouble, yet I hope you will accompany these principal headmen to Charlestown. I have done my talk, and am ready to hear what you have to say."

Little Carpenter. "I am extremely well satisfied with every thing your Honour has proposed and said."

Lieutenant Governour. "I have written to col. Grant that I have agreed to give you peace upon the terms, which have been communicated to you. Here I must observe to you, that when people make peace and are friends, the enemies of one are always considered as the enemies of both. My intention of mentioning this to you at present is to acquaint you that some of the Creeks have, at the instigation of the Indians called the Coppers, who live near the Halbama fort, killed some of the Chickesaws; therefore as peace now to take place, and the Chikesaws being being friends to the English, the Cherokees must not join the Creeks against the Chickesaws nor

130

make war upon them."

Little Carpenter. "I have heard every thing with attention your Honour has said, ——— I approve of it; as I am messenger, I am desirous to be gone, and to report the same to the nation."

*see Charlestown the 12 of September, for this article proposed by Col. Grant.

BOSTON Sept. 28. The following published in the publick print, dated London June 13, 1761.

It hath been alledg'd, North American Continent Colonies being situated on the widely extended coast of a vast continent, and chiefly in temperate climates, without any one powerful enemy on the same land, they cannot be prevented from rising into independency and empire. But the vast and connected American territory of Spain and Portugal, which are as securely possessed now, as they were at their first peopeling by Europeans, are proof that large territories may be preserved on the continent of America, even by weak European states; whose policy will naturally never let their colonies keep up a military, or establish marine forces. So that while we have British governors, civil offices, garrisons, and ships of war there to secure our power, there can be no reasonable apprehension of a revolt of our North Americans, were that country better peopled then it can possibly be for five hundred years to come. Besides, many of the states of North America have very little intercourse with, and less friendship for one another: Which hereditary rivalries and dislikes will be preventing of a general combination for revolt, and any partial endeavour will be sure to prove unsuccessful. The point therefore to be considered is, whether we ought to trust to our own Colonist always, considering their true interests, and consulting their own welfare; or whether, with an eternal scene of pillaging, butchering, and contention, we should place our security in a French neighbourhood on that continent, which we know will be always pushing at our entire extirpation; and whether we had not better hazard that country's becoming entirely independent of all

European powers, than that it should fall in the hands of the French. As in the first case we shall always preserve our national trade with it, which would certainly be very great; and in the latter case, we should not only lose that vast advantage but also have the sovereignty of the ocean thrown with it into the hands of our natural rivals and enemies, which would be sure to being on our ruin more effectually, than the loss would of all America, if it ever should become an independent country.

Nor can I see how South America sugar-islands can be more secure against combination than the several states of North America, as we can be no otherwise secure of them than by a very good government, and by being the strongest power at sea. But the truth of the matter is, that the possession of North America will always have the command of the sugar-islands of South America, as well from its own power and commodities and from the power of the sea which is secured to its holder. For great Britain, and North America together, can starve, take, or disable, when they please, any island in South America. A Circumstance that may be made in future to give more weight to Great Britain, than any other whatsoever, as no country that has islands there, will dare wantonly to provoke her.

It hath been farther alledged, that the North Americans are continually building ships, and sell many of them to foreigners, thereby taking much employment from the ship-builders, shipping, seamen, &c. of Great Britain, and augment the naval power and commerce of other nations.
———— But I believe there is no other colony than that of New-England, which build any quantity of shipping; and that article and the fishery are its greatest branches of trade. Besides the shipping of Old and New-England do not at all interfere with one another, for that of the latter rather interferes with the ship building of Venice, Genoa, Spain, Portugal, Holland, Denmark and Sweden, some of whom have a great trade in building shipping cheap for sale, which they can do on better terms than we; and others are prevented from building ordinary ships,

because they can buy New-England ones cheaper. Thus it is a branch of trade that serves England and only interferes with her rivals. Ship-building with us is too dear for sale for ordinary uses, and therefore if New-England did not supply the demand other nations would: And as for augmenting the naval power and commerce of other nations, it certainly does neither, because seamen are not sold with the ships; as for the vessels if they had them not of New-England, they would buy them off other nations, or else build them themselves; for every country that has ports are builders, more or less, of ships, and have mercantile navigation, though some of them have no navy. All, therefore, that have been advanced, is but a mere flourish of words, or a misrepresentation of the matter; for even most of the trade of North America is carried on with British-built ships, and many more of them are employed in it than in the South American trade.

BOSTON Sept. 28. At the meetings of the freeholders and other Inhabitants of the Town of Boston, legally qualified and warned in Public Town-Meeting assembled, at the Town-House on Tuesday rgw 12th Day of May, A. D. 1761.

Voted that the Assessors be, and they hereby are directed not to abate any Part of the Tax of the inhabitants as do not give or send in to them a List or Valuation of their rateable Estates, within the Time said Assessors shall fix for bringing in the same, except such of the Inhabitants as were not in the Province within the time limited by the Notification of the Assessors for doing it. Provided however, That this Order or Vote shall not be construed to extend in such a Manner as to abridge the Power the Assessors have by the standing Law of the Province for relieving of poor Persons in their Taxes.

   Attest.   William Cooper, Town Clerk.

These are to notify the Inhabitants of the Town of Boston, to bring in true and perfect Lists of their Polls and rateable Estates as the Law directs, to the assessors of said Town; who will attend to receive the same at the Chamber in the Town-House, on any Day from the Twelfth to the Thirtieth of October inclusive, (Lord's Day and Saturdays excepted) between the Hours of Ten and One of the Clock, and Three to Five of the Clock on each Day.

Boston September 22d, 1761.

Public Notice is hereby given, That the President and Tutors, of Harvard-College, will, for the future, strictly examine Candidates for Admission into the College, as to their Skill in Verse, or at least in the Rules of Prosodia.

Edw. Holeyoke, President.
Cambridge, September25, 1761.

OCTOBER 1761

BOSTON Oct. 5. We have received some long accounts from Carolina, via New-York as usual; but the whole may be reduced to this, ——— That the Great Warrior, &c. were certainly to be at Fort Prince George on the 23d of August to settle with Col. Grant the preliminaries of a lasting peace; so that the next express boat will undoubtedly bring on the article agreed on. In consequence which intelligence it was expected at Charlestown that the King's troops would be at Ninety-six before the 15th of September, on their way down to re-embark.

BOSTON Oct. 5. Ran-away from me the Subscriber at Boston, the 7th Day of November last, John Aitkens, an indented Servant, aged 30 Years, 5 Feet 5 Inches high, born in Scotland, of a brown Complexion, pitted with the Small Pox, by trade a Cabinet-Maker, but for 3 Years past has followed the peddling, he's now in Gloucester it the County of Essex, and has been ever since he went away. Whoever will apprehend and secure the said Runaway in any of His Majesty's Goals, shall receive Three Guineas as Reward, and all necessary Charges paid by   Andrew Ritchie.

N. B. All Masters of Vessels and others, are hereby caution'd against habouring, concealing, entertaining, or carrying off said Servant on penalty of the Law.

BOSTON Oct. 6. Ran-away on the 5th Instant, from John Lloyd of Stanford in the colony of Connecticut, a negro man servant named Cyrus, about 5 Feet 9 Inches high, well built, but is rather slim waisted, legs and feet somewhat large has lost one or more of his fore teeth, about 30 or 32 years of age, long visag'd, very black, active and ingenious in all sorts of country business, and is a good butcher, bred in the country, and speaks good English and a little French, but stammers when frighted or confus'd. Had on when he went off, an iron collar rivited round his neck, and a chain fastened to it; carried with him a red cloth jacket, and another of brown frize, both considerably worn, black everlasting breeches, almost new, tow shirt, 'tis not unlikely he may consort with any deserter or other straggling fellow he may meet with, as about two years ago he ran off with two deserters, and was taken up at Philadelphia. Whoever takes up said Negro is desired not to trust him a moment till he is put in irons and secur'd in some of his Majesty's Goals, otherwise (his crime being great) he will certainly give them the slip; and upon sending me word, so that I may have him again, such person shall have Five Pounds New York money reward, and reasonable Charges paid by

        October 6, 1761.   John Lloyd.

N. B. As inserting the Advertisement in the several News Papers is judged the most expeditious method of spreading them far and near, if any Gentleman will be so good, when they have read their paper, to cut out the Advertisement and set it up to the most public Place, it will be esteemed as a Favour.

All Masters of Vessels and others, are cautioned against habouring, or carrying him off, as they will answer it at their Peril.

BOSTON Oct. 12. Last Week a French Flag of Truce, with a Number of English Masters of Vessels belonging to different Parts of the Continent arrived a Plymouth from Martineco —— Two of the Captains, who had taken the small Pox whilst they were confined in Goal, died of the Distemper on the Passage, but the Vessel was clear from the Infection several Days before she got in; one of the Masters who died belonged to Newbury and the other 'tis said belonged to Casco.

Capt. John Stevens of this Town came in the above Vessel, and informs, that while he was at Martineco, which was 29 Days, 62 Prizes was brought in there, 8 into Grenedes, 2 into St. Cruz, a large ship of 700 hogsheads of Sugar from Jamaica, was sent to France; 15 Ransomers were also brought there, and two Vessels were taken by our Ships of War; during his stay on the Island there was an Exchange of Prisoners by the Raisonable Man of War, of 100 Men: and that about 200 others remained in that Island confined as Prisoners of War.

BOSTON Oct. 12. On Thursday Evening last were committed to his Majesty's Goal in Boston, Seth Hudson and Joshua How, being charg'd with forging Treasury Notes; and on Saturday last were apprehended in the County of Worcester, Jacob Stevens and Banjamine Fiske, who were charg'd with being concern'd in the same and are this Day expected in Town, several forged Notes have been put off in this Town to the Amount of about 800 Pounds. To prevent further Impositions of this Kind, the following Account of said Notes is inserted: All forged Notes which have yet appear'd are every Way like true Notes, save that the written Part is badly done; the Treasurer's Name appears at first glance to be genuine; but upon Examination, is apparently laboured, being executed by laying a true Note over the forged one, and making out the Name with some sharp pointed Instrument, so as to leave the Impression on the forged Note, and then filling up the Impressions with Ink; and in some of the said Notes, it is very distinguishable that the whole of the written Part is traced out in the same Manner.

Extract of a Letter from New-York, Oct. 5.

" Governor Hardy, Lord Sterling and Mr. Temple, who is appointed Lieut. Governor of New-Hampshire, are on board the Alcide, and I am told the Ship is on the outside of the Hook. It is said our Expedition to the West Indies is certainly to go on, that four Regiments more are ordered from above, who commands I know not."

Last Thursday Evening, as two Lads belonging to Charlestown, were returning home with a Gun which they had loaded to kill Birds, and a Negro in company belonging to Mr. Celeb Call, of the same place, one of them imprudently pointed the Gun at the Negro, not minding it was cock'd;

when it went off and killed him on the spot.

NEW-YORK Oct. 12. It is conjectur'd that the Transports expected in, from England, are intended to carry Troops from hence to Dominique, where 'tis said they are to be joined by Two Thousand Forces from England, and to be under the Command of General Monckton, who will from thence proceed to the Attack of Martineco, and probably thence to Louisiana, should not the French (no doubt made sensible the English will not be amused out of the Advantage they have bargained) prevent those Operations by hastening a Place.

BOSTON Oct. 14. The Navigation of the Coast of North and South Carolina being very dangerous on account of all the many bars, Shoals, Sandbanks, Rocks, &c. The late Donald Dunbibin, Esq; of North Carolina has at a very great Expence and Labour, draughted the Sea Coast on both the Provinces in a large whole sheet Chart of 33 inches by 23; together with all the Rivers, Bays, Inlets, Islands, Brooks, Bars, Shoals, Rocks, Soundings, Current, &c. with necessary Directions to render the Navigation both easy and safe, and are much esteem'd by most Pilots: —— A few of the Draughts may be had of the Subscriber if applied directly.

       Edmund Quincy Jr. Broker.

HALIFAX Oct. 15. Last Friday arrived here the ship Hopewell, of Londonderry, by whom came upwards of 200 Persons, for the Settlements of this Province, with Col. Alexander McNutt, who are informed has contracted for 10,000 Tons of shipping, 5,000 bushels of Wheat, 5,000 bushels of Barley, 5,000 bushels of Potatoes, 3,000 bushels of Flax seed, 300 Bushels of Hemp seed; with other seeds in proportion, for the use of the Irish settlers of Nova-Scotia the ensuing Spring.

The Passengers arrived in good Health, and a considerable number of them will proceed tomorrow with Col. McNutt to view and examine the Country.

CHARLESTOWN S. Carolina Oct. 17. Letters from the camp near Fort Prince George, dated the 6th instant, received last Saturday, advise, that the regiment of provincial rangers had been reduced to four companies, viz. Major Thompson's, Captain Thomas Bosher's, Captain Charles Russells,s and Captain Deagan's: That the provincial regiment of foot had been paid off to that day: That no Indians of any note had been in the camp since our former account, nor has any material advices been received from their country: That it was still doubted whether the Great Warrior, &c. would make Col. Grant a visit notwithstanding the repeated invitations they had had to come down: That the distress and necessities of the Cherokees were certainly very great, and must soon increase, as the Middle-Settlements people were to numerous to be supported during the winter season by the other parts of the nation: That the price of rum and wine in camp was 6 pounds per gallon, loaf suger 20s. per lb. brown sugar 12s. 6d. Biscuit 10s. to 15s. Butter and cheese 12s. bacon 16s. salt 25s. per quart, and other articles in proportion: And that it was expected the camp would break up in a week.

All the Lower Creek towns, except one or two continue to war hotly against the Spaniards.

BOSTON Oct. 19. About a Fortnight ago a melancholy Affair happened at the Eastward: ——— Mr. Small, an ingenious and improv'd Surveyor, being employed by the Government to reconnoitre and explore that Part of the Country which lies between Fort Halifax and Kennebec River, and the River Chaudre so on the Quebec: he was attended by Capt. Howard and a party of 9 Men, and had set out from the Fort upon that business; but when they had got about 120 Miles Distance, one Day about Twelve o'Clock, Mr. Small being within some bushes taking an Observation, one of the Men perceived a rustling and something moved apprehended it to be some wild Beast, unhappily fired, and shot him dead upon the spot.

NEW-YORK Oct. 19. Monday Morning Capt. Hunter of this Port arrived in 11 Days from St. John's in Newfoundland: By him we have Advice of a great Scarcity of fish, and Plenty of all kinds of Provisions at that Place, that the Labradore

Indians have lately killed several English Fishermen that were employed in curing Fish at a small Island in the Streights of Bellisle; and that some of the people that escaped from the Indians, were arrived at St. John's with Indian Arrows flicking in their Bodies, as they could not extract them without the help of a Surgeon.

Yesterday 7 Sloops arrived with Troops from Albany and immediately embarked on board Transports.

CHARLESTOWN S. Carolina Oct. 21. On Thursday the 8th instant died, at Mar's Bluff in Craven County, the Hon. Edmond Atkin, Esq; his Majesty's superintendent of Indian affairs in the southern department of North America.

According to Letters from the Camp near fort Prince George, dated the 24th and 27th ult. nothing of much consequence had happened except "That on the 20th, two Indians arrived there from the Over-Hills, with a talk from the Great Warrior, &c. to Col. Grant, requesting and confirming what was before delivered by the Little Carpenter, viz. "That they had buried the hatchet, were desirous to be and continue at peace with us, and renew friendship; and that Occunastotah, the rest of the headmen together with the whole nation, were resolved to abide by whatever should be stipulated and agreed to between Col. Grant and Attakullakulla." Col. Grant asked these messengers many questions, among others "Why the Great Warrior, Standing Turkey, and other headmen had not come down to see him?" telling them at the same time, "That he would be glad to see all the Warriors; that they might be sure he would not hurt one of them, but permit them to go away when they please. Why they did not bring in the prisoners that were still among them? Where was the Young-Warrior, who he heard was coming down with some of the horses, &c." Adding, "that if they brought down the prisoners, he should look upon it as good, and then believe that they really desired to be at peace with us; that he had heard there were three Frenchmen in their nation; that he would take it well if they would bring them down to him, and he would then believe they did not love the French, who were nothing, and would soon be rooted out by the English." The Indians listened with great attention, to all that was said to them, and answer'd, "That the Young-Warrior was at Nottelih, but they did not know he intended to bring any horses down; and that none of the Over-Hills people were concerned in the stealing of horses: That it was true they were three Frenchmen at Cotih, and they would endeavour to bring them down, but hoped he would not kill them (the Colonel answer'd he should not hurt them) That the Great-Warrior would come down, but was afraid: And that if Capt. Watts was permitted, or would go up again he would still come as he would then believe that we were really friends."

That was the substance of what passed after which Col. Grant gave them a talk to the Great Warrior and all the headmen, and dismissed them. That the Indians were daily coming to the camp and fort, but none of any consideration. That notwithstanding all their promises and Col. Grant's menaces, not a single horse or bullock had yet been brought in; on the contrary, they continued stealing them, and had lately got two of Colonel's own horses. That there had been great destruction from Col. Middleton's regiment, which had lost upwards of 170 men since the detachment's return from the Middle Settlements, looking upon themselves as naturally discharged after twelve months service. That Fort Prince George and every thing about it was completely finished, and is a good piece of work. That about 500 of the troops in different corps were already at Ninety-six. That the provincials expected to march downward by the 8th inst. And that Col. Grant's remaining so long a Keehowee must have the best effect on the Indians, and has prevented their committing one single act of hostility since the destruction of their towns and provisions, which would not have been the case had the forces been obliged to return so hastily as they did last year.

CHARLESTOWN S. Carolina Oct. 21. Last Saturday Evening we received the following particulars of the late hurricane on the coast of North

Carolina, viz. That it began on the 24th of last month in the evening, and continued without abating till the 24th, in which time it blew down many houses, tore up abundance of trees, destroyed the greatest part of the crops, and drove all the vessels in Cape Fear river ashore, except a Snow which cut away her masts and a Sloop for Philadelphia that rode it out at Fort Johnson: That when it began the wind was at S. E. which shifted continually during the whole time, but was severest and did the most mischief on the 22d: That about 4 miles below, and nearly opposite the Brunswick, the sea forced a passage thro' a neck of land called Bald-Head, and formed a channel half a mile wide, and fourteen feet deep at low Water, and which continued to deepen, as was observed upon sounding on different days; so that the navigation of Cape Fear river, from being the most difficult, is changed to the easiest and fastest on that part of the continent, the Frying-pan, the Bar, and other shoals, all being avoided by vessels falling in to the N. E. and the passage much shorter to Brunswick: That on other parts of the coast, more new inlets are made; some above a league in width; one in particular, about 14 miles from Wilmington, which is three miles wide, and 9 feet deep at low Water. Doubtless several vessels must have perished in the terrible tempest; but as yet we have only heard of a snow of and for New-York, from Jamaica, Christopher Miller master, which was beat to pieces, about 9 leagues N. E. of the Frying-pan, whose crew and part of the rigging were saved. Ever since the hurricane, we hear, the flood tide makes three hours later on Cape Fear Bar than formerly.

We have the pleasure to acquaint our readers from the best authority, that this town is now entirely free from the yellow fever, or any other distemper, many families, who went out of town, are already returned convinced that there is no danger receiving any injections.

BOSTON Oct. 26. Friday Evening last between 8 and 9 o'Clock, came on the severest N. E. storm of wind and rain, that has been known here for 30 years past, and continued till between 2 and

3 o'Clock the next morning; in which time a hemp house improved by Messirs. Box and Austin, the old wind-mill on the neck, and several chimnies were blown down, besides tops of chimnies, turrets on houses, fences, trees, &c. The Shipping in the harbour also received considerable damage, particularly Captain Phipps's schooner, which arrived the day before in three days from Halifax, and another schooner belonging to Situate, who had their sterns beat in and filled with water; many other vessels were damaged, and damage 'tis tho't would have been greater to the vessels at the wharfs, had it not been near low water at the height of the Gale: ——— The province ship King George, Capt. Hallowell, we hear, parted a 15 inch cable. His Excellency our Governor having dined on board the ship that day, very providentially tarried the night, for the chimney at the Castle fell in by the violence of the gale, and carried the bed to the ground in which his Excellency was to have lodged that night: ——— Two barns were blown down at Lynn, and a cow killed; and a barn in Chelsea, and two horses killed. ——— Five or six vessels were drove ashore at Providence in Rhode-Island Government, and greatly damaged; and it being high water there, it got into the Stores, and damaged Sugar &c. to the amount of 12 or 15,000 pounds their currency; it also carried away the Great Bridge at that place. ——— On both roads E. & W. so far as we have heard, the roofs of houses, tops of barns, and fences, have been blown down; and it is said thousands of trees have been torn up the roots by the violence of the above gale.

BOSTON Oct. 26. Last Monday se'nnight, as Mr. Edward Weld of Roxbury, was returning Home with a Cart, his Oxen took fright, and he falling off, one of the Wheels went over his neck and breast, and the Wheel being new, the Nails of the tier bruis'd him to such a Manner that he expired the next day.

And on Friday last, as one Mrs. Williams an ancient Woman of the same Place, was turning a corner in a Chaise, it struck a Post with such force that it threw her out, and struck her head against a Stone, which fractured her Scull to the degree that she expired immediately.

On Monday last a Boy about 9 Years of Age, named Belcher, belonging to Braintree, riding on the tongue of a Cart the Oxen took fright, and he fell off, when one of the Wheels pass'd over his Body, and so much bruised him that he died the same Day

Last Wednesday Night the Dwelling House of Capt. Solomon Davis of this Town was broke open and several things stolen out of it, the thief being closely pursued, he was on Friday apprehended at Roxbury, and some of the Goods being found upon him, he was committed to our Goal. It is said his Name is Robinson, and suspected to have been an old Offender, and that his being confined in a Goal will be no new Thing to him.

Our advice from South-Carolina, are the 23d of September which import, That on the 22d of Sept. the famous friendly Cherokee Indian to the English, had a public audience of Governor Bull in council, where he produced his full power from the different towns, which, as the Indians have not the use of letters, consisted of belts of wampum: ——— That after some Time's conference the pipe was lighted, and his honour, the Council, and the Indians smoked, in token of friendship and desire of peace being restored: ——— That on the 23, Attakullakulla or the Little Carpenter, had another public audience, when the terms of peace to be granted to the Cherokee Indians, were agreed to by him on behalf of the Cherokee Indians and interchangeably signed by the Governor and himself; which he much approved of, and seemed desirous to be gone, to report the same to his Nation.

One of the Officers who fought a Duel about 10 Days ago near this City, is since dead of his Wounds; but before he died, acknowledged himself the Aggressor.

NOVEMBER 1761

BOSTON Nov. 2. Last Thursday Night as Mr. George Moody, his Wife and three Children were going from Portsmouth to Kinery, the Boat was forced by the strength of the Tide across a Sloop's Hawse, which lay moor'd off, and overset, by which means Mrs. Moody was drowned, but the others were taken up..

Last Night, a little before Eight o'Clock, a small Shock of Earthquake was sensibly felt in this Town, attended with a loud rumbling Noise.

NEW-YORK Nov. 2. On Monday last the commission from his Majesty, appointing his Excellency Major General Robert Monckton Captain General and Governor in Chief in and over the Province of New-York, and territories thereof depending in America, was published at the City Hall, with the usual solemnity; on which occasion his Excellency was attended by the Lieutenant Governor, His Majesty's Council, the Gentlemen of the Clergy, the Gentlemen of the Corporation, the Sheriff with his proper Officers, and the City Militia under arms. A considerable number of Officers of the Army and other Gentlemen of distinction accompanied the procession; at night the City was handsomely illuminated.

CHARLESTOWN S. Carolina Nov. 7. The camp near Fort Prince George broke up the 16th ult. Col. Grant marched all the troops for Ninety-six, where the arrived the 25th: He left a garrison of Fort Prince George (consisting of above 100 independents, under the command of Captain Mackintosh and Ensign Cameron) well supplied with every thing ——— The 28th all the privates of Col Middleton's regiment, to about 200 who continue in the service, were paid off and discharged ——— The 29th Lieut. Parker arrived in camp express from New-York, and next day the four companies of the 17th and regiments, commanded by Capt John Campbell, Sir Henry Seton, Christopher French, and Quintin Kennedy, likewise marched for Congarees: They may be expected in town on Wednesday next: The transports in which they are to embark are ready.

Capt. Napier of Col. Burton's regiment, with about 300 men, is also come to Congarees: The rest of the troops, 'tis said, will remain at Ninety-six, till the Little Carpenter returns from the nation, who is expected there about the 9th instant.

CHARLESTOWN S. Carolina Nov. 11. We hear his Excellency Gen. Amherst has been pleased to order away immediately from this province, all the regular troops except three independent companies.

CHARLESTOWN S. Carolina Nov. 14. We hear that the Young Warrior of Estatoe has declared, that the peace between the Cherokees and us is so agreeable to him, that altho' he must and will have provisions for his people from our settlements, yet he will not hurt any of our people if they do not oppose him.

Yesterday arrived off the Bar with dispatches from New-York, his Majesty's ship Dover, Capt. Percival, of 44 guns. This Ship it is said is come to convoy the four companies of the Royal and Burton's regiments on the intended expedition, as soon as they can arrive in town and embark, which may be in about 3 weeks. This ship draws no more water than some 20 gun frigates.

Last Tuesday arrived here Capt. Curtis, in a Snow from Quebec who was taken about 60 leagues from this bar, by a privateer Snow of Martenico commanded by the Chevalier Aguste de Megederne, and ransomed for 200 pounds Ster. They plundered her of every thing, even the Captain's and crew's bedding. While he was on board the privateer he heard they would proceed to cruize off New-York and Philadelphia, but by the course she steered after she left him, he imagined her station to be near Bermuda.

CHARLESTOWN S. Carolina Nov. 14. Besides about four months provisions left by Col. Grant at Fort Prince George, a large supply of flour with

80 fine late hogs are set out from Ninety-six for the use of that garrison, who, when the receive them, will have 12 months provisions. —— It is said, that an express from the fort had come up with the army on the 24th ult. at Coronacre, with advice, that the Indians has stollen 13 out of 23 head of black cattle left there; which shews that they were very hungry, tho' it is by no means a proof of their keeping the late treaty of peace inviolably.

NEW-York Nov. 16. Since our last the Troops that were encamped an Staten Island, consisting of eleven regiments, have struck their tents and embarked; and the fleet of near one hundred sail fell down to the Hook; and Yesterday his Excellency the Honorable Robert Monckton, Governor and Commander in Chief of the Province, and Major General of his Majesty's Forces, embarked to take upon him the command of the Expedition. He was saluted on going off by a discharge of the Cannon of Fort George, and welcomed by a discharge of the ships guns when he got on board.

We have reason to hope that these brave troops, with their experience commander, who have had so great a share of the conquest of Canada, will acquire fresh glory in this Expedition; which we hope will be crown with success, and complete their military service, by reducing our enemies to an incapacity of supporting the war, and the necessary of accepting reasonable terms for peace.

NEWPORT Rhode Island Nov. 17. Extract of a Letter from New-York, Nov. 9, 1761.

"The Expedition you may depend is getting on: and I am informed, that last Night a Man of War arrived at the Hook, Express from Guadeloupe to the General, acquainting him, that Sir Edward Hawke was arrived there with 15 Sail of the Line: This is reported as Truth, and I believe it to be so, for last Night at 11 o'Clock the Forces began to embark, and the Ships ordered down; but wether they are determined to Martenico or Missisippi, remains a Secret."

PHILADELPHIA Nov. 19. Last night came to town some seamen belonging to the Ship Royal Ann,

Capt. Smith, bound from this port to Guadeloupe, who informs, that near Bermuda, in a violent gale of wind, the ship overset and lost all her masts, and that the next day, we was taken by two French Privateers, and sent to Martinico. That soon after they took a brig Capt. Pearce from Madeira for this port, and after taking out some wine, gave her to the prisoners, in which they arrived at Maryland.

By a vessel from Providence we learn, that on the 5th of October put in there, Capt. Dickenson, in a sloop from New-London for Barbados, who had in a gale of wind lost his mast and all his horses, being 28.

BOSTON Nov. 23. Wednesday last, a Hearing was held before the Hon. the Superior Court of Judicature then sitting in this County, upon the Petition of the Officers of the Customs for a writ of Assistance ——— As this was a Matter in which the Liberty of the People was most nearly interested, the whole Day and Evening was spent in the argument. The Gentlemen in Favor of the Petition alledged, that such Writs by Law issued from the Court of Exchecquer at home; and that by an Act of this Province, the Superior Court is vested with the whole Power and Jurisdiction of the Exchecquer; and from thence it was inferr'ed, that the Superior Court might lawfully grant the Petition.

The Argument on the other Side were enforced with such Strength of Reason, as did great Honour to the Gentlemen concerned; and nothing could have induced one to believe they were not conclusive, but the Judgement of the Court immediately given in Favour of the Petition.

It is probable that very urgent Necessity for this Writ was set forth in the Petition as some private Hints had been given, that the King's Officers were set at Defiance ——— An Assertion which no unbiassed man will believe to be true, who is either acquainted with the Character of the Body of the Merchants in this Town or knows the powerful Influence under which the King's Officers are protected.

It is worth observing, that the Power of the Exchecquer had never been exercised by the

Superior Court, for near Sixty Years after the Act of this Province investing them with such Power had been in Force. ——— The Writ, which was the Instance of their exercising that Power now granted, was never asked for, or if asked, was certainly deni'd for this long course of Years, until Charles Paxton, Esq; whose regard for the Liberty and Property of the subject, as well as the Revenue of the King, is well known, apply'd for in 1754 ——— It was granted by the Court in 1756, sub. filentie, and continued till the demise of the late King ——— Upon the new Application, it is now reviewed, and no doubt will be of eminent Use to the present Generation at least; otherwise it is nor to be presumed the Court would have allowed it ——— it will never be look'd upon in an indifferent Light; and therefore if it lives to posterity, it will afford to them one striking Characteristic, at least of the Effects of it to be, when it may arrive to more perfect maturity, whether good or bad.

BOSTON Nov. 23. Last Evening between 7 and 8 o'Clock, the following sorrowful Accident happened at the South Part of the Town, viz. as one Mr. Stephen Holman of Sutton, and another Person with him had just gone thro' the Fortification with a Team partly loaded, and three Persons coming through on Foot at the same Time it being very dark, and they not observing each other till the Horses had just got upon them, which being on the Trot started aside, and unhappily threw him off, and the Wheel going immediately over his body bruis'd him to such a degree that he died on Thursday Morning following. We hear he has left a Widow and four Children.

NEW-YORK Nov. 23. On Thursday morning the 19th inst. the fleet of men of war and transports mentioned in our last, weighed anchor and put to sea, having an extraordinary fine leading gale, which, by twelve o'clock at noon carried them clear of the Hook; and its continuance almost ever since, give us hopes of their having a good offing, and in a prosperous way of arriving at their destined port. ———

The following is a list of all the principal

Officers and the Regiments embark'd at New-York on the present expedition. —— [besides which, there are forces at Antigua, Guadeloupe, and Dominica, which, we hear are to join in the West Indies.]

His Excellency the Hon. Maj. Gen. Monckton, Commander and Chief.

As Brigadier Generals, Col. Haviland, Lieut. Col. Grant, Lieut. Col. Welch. Adjutant Gen. Lieut. Col. Darby. Quarter Master Gen. Major Montgomery.

Regiments.

15th, Sir Jeffery Amherst's. 17th, Hon, Gen. Monckton. 27th, (late Lord Blackeney's.) 28th, Hon. Gen. Townshend's. 38th, Lieut. Gen. Otway's. 40th, Col. Armiger's. 42d, Or Royal Highlanders, 2 Bats. Ld. Murray's. 43d. (late Gen. Kennedy's) 48th, Maj. Gen. Webb's. 3d Battalion of Royal Americans.

In all eleven Battalions.

BOSTON Nov. 23. From a London Publick Print, Dated September 22.

Extract of a Letter from an Officer at Quebec.

"Since my last Letter to you, from Montreal, our public Affairs here amount to very little. This Winter and Spring has passed away in the most profound Peace and Tranquility; whereas the last afforded nothing but continued Skirmishes and alarms, the consequence of which was, that the Country for 20 Miles round the Capital was destroyed by turns, both by the French and ours, which reduced the inhabitants to the greatest degree of Misery and Distress. Their Situation was deplorable, that it caused a Subscription to be made in the Town by the officers and others 500 pounds which was laid out for Bread, &c. and distributed by the Curets of the different Parishes and to the most indigent Families.

The Example of the Charity was followed by the Regiment in the Country, who all made handsome Collections, which was applied in the same Manner; and that the common Soldiers should not be behind in so commendable a Spirit, they have given a Day's provisions each Month, which has kept Thousands from starving. Thus you see Works of Love and Charity have succeeded War and Devastation. The Canadians are surprised to experience such Instances of Humanity in Hereticks, a little while ago their Enemy, which has contributed a good deal to undeceive them of the opinion they had formed of us."

CHARLESTOWN S. Carolina Nov. 25. Several Indians who come under the direction of Tiscoey, and are settled almost under the guns of Fort Prince George, another numerous party are come down and settling Toxowee, one of the Lower Towns.

On Thursday a runner arrived at Ninety-six from Fort Prince George, with an account that Attakullakulla or the Little Carpenter, the Prince of Chote, and several other headmen, with a numerous retinue of men and women, were arrived there; and would be at Ninety-six about Sunday last.

Several of the Cherokee Indians that came down to re-settle the Lower Towns on the news of peace, left their baggage with Capt. McIntosh and went out to hunt for subsistence: Some parties of them were met by the white people, and they behaved on all such occasions as friends.

The Nightingale and the transports have made several attempts to get out, but are still detained by contrary winds.

NEW-YORK Nov. 30. Besides what was mentioned in our last, with regard to the store's ship'd, &c. on board the expedition fleet which lately sailed from this port. ——— we are assured there were 15 officers, and 184 men of the Royal regiment of artillery, with a large battering train also embarked, under the command of Gen. Monckton.

'Tis said that the Royal Scotch and Montgomery's Highlanders, who have been at Halifax for some time, are to embark from thence to join the fleet gone to the southward.

Some say this fleet are to rondezvous at Barbados, others at Guadeloupe, &c. ——— Be that as it will, the whole affords great grounds to believe we shall soon see the finishing stroke given to the French power both in North and South America.

Next Tuesday his Excellency Thomas Boone, Esq; embarks on board the Edward, Capt. Davis, in order to proceed to his Government at South Carolina.

NEW-YORK Nov. 30. Sir William Johnson safely returned about the beginning of November, to his seat at Mount-Johnson, from his journey among the Indians to the Westward, having we are told, proceeded as far as Mishilimacinac on Lake Huron, and found the different Tribes in very good Humour.

We further learn from S. Carolina of Oct. 28, That the four Companies of the 17th and 22d regiment, then at Ninety-six and commanded by capts. John Campbell, and Christopher French, sir Harry Seton, and Quintin Kennedy, were to march down the country immediately, and to embark on board the transport ship Amity's-Assistance, and Brotherly-Love, and proceed for Domineco, Guadwloup, or Barbadoes, under convoy of his Majesty's ship Nightingale, James Campbell Esq; commander. Major Alexander Monypenny of the 22d regiment, they say, will embark with those four companies.

DECEMBER 1761

ANNAPOLIS Maryland Dec. 3. By a letter from Frederick-Town we are informed, that vast quantity of rain fell in and about Winchester, about the 20th of October, that in some places there was six feet of water on the level land, not near any creek or river; and in the town the water run out of some of the cellar windows. Many farmers have lost the greatest part of their crops by this uncommon fall of rain.

On Sunday last week, as a shallop was going up Delaware to Philadelphia, with 5 people on board, she unfortunately overset near Chester, and three of the people, who were in the Cabbin were drowned.

CHARLESTOWN S. Carolina Dec. 4. We hear the march of the King's Troops under Gen. Grant, from Ninety-six downward, depends upon the coming in of the Cherokee headmen, to ratify the treaty concluded between the government and Attakullakulla. That Cappy (old Hop's son) and some headmen, with a great number of baggarly attendants have been some time at Fort Prince George, and may be here in about 8 days: But Occunnastota (the great warrior) the Standing Turkey and Judd's Friend, still avoid coming in, and are either out hunting, or gone to some of the French forts. 'Tis said these leading men of the Cherokee nation are afraid to venture among us, lest they should be imprison'd or put to death, but most solemn assurance have been given them that they should not be hurt, notwithstanding their inhumane conduct to fort Loudoun garrison, &c.

On Thursday last sailed for the West Indies, the Nightingale man of war, with the transports under her convoy, having on board the four companies of the 17th and 27th regiments, commanded by Major Alex. Moneypenny. Silver Heels, the Mohawk Indian, who came hither from the Northward, is gone with Capt. Kennedy of the 17th, being determined to have another brush at the Great King's enemies.

The Assembly met here on the 3d inst. when, the Governor returned them the thanks of Gen. Amherst for the provisions they made for the wives and children of the soldiers employed in the Expedition. He acquainted them that he expected the Little Carpenter in a few days, and some headmen of each of the 4 Cherokee settlements, to ratify the peace. That he had disbanded the provincial regiment, except the troops of rangers, which were necessary, especially as the treaty with the Indians was not yet fully concluded; and he congratulated them on the appointment of his successor, his Excellency Governor Boone.

The two houses of assembly return'd some very obliging answers, approving what he had done, and given very honourable testimony on his administration.

BOSTON Dec. 7. Messieurs Edes and Gill of the Boston Gazette.

The People of this Province very justly bear the Character of Loyal Subjects: We have always given the fullnest Proof of it, and therefore whatever Representations have been made to the contrary, are groundless and injurious. We hope the other Colonies are as Loyal as we, and there is no Reason that I know of to believe they are not: We do not pretend to any Superiority over them in this Regard; and while we affirm against Gainsayers, that we never have been, and I hope never shall be, behind any of his Majesty's good Subjects in Point of Loyalty; we are not sullicitous of being represented in higher Colours, lest we should be abnoxious either to Envy of Contempt.

If then we are in all Respects as loyal as our Neighbours —— if we are equally dispos'd to pay all Regards to the Laws of the Mother Country, and stand just in the same relative Circumstances with them, would it not be unreasonable that we should be made subject to severer

Laws than they? Should it be said, this is not the Case —— I grant it; but if those Laws which were intended to bind us all, are vigorously executed here, while in the other Governments they are at loose, and the Breaches of them even connived at, I pray, does it not amount to the same Thing?

It is not notorious that the Acts of Trade are no way executed with Rigor but in this Province? What other Reason can be assigned for it, upon a Supposition that the Officers of the Customs in every Province are honest Men, but because they have different Apprehensions of the Importance of these Laws? —— Perhaps some of the Persons might account for it in some other Way —— This is the most candid Reason I can at present think of; and it is not a Grievance that we should be subject to Laws, the necessity and Importance of which is so differently conceived by those whose Office it is to execute them, in different Places indeed, Tho' under the same Circumstances?

We are watched with the utmost Severity —— private informers, the disgrace of Civil Society; are multiplied and well paid at our own Costs —— Uncustomed Goods, when found, are seized to the utmost Farthing —— if not found, the Person suspected to have imported them is served with a Writ, as having sold them, and the Money is attached in his Hands —— Nay, he is further to be prosecuted for aiding in an illegal Importation, for which he is to pay treble Damage —— Writs of Assistance are now established and granted to the Officers of the Customs, who were tho't by many Persons, to have had full Power enough over us before —— If it be said that all this is no more than Law prescribeds, I again ask, Whither the Law is carried to these Extremities in any other Province? if not, is it not an unreasonable Hardship upon us, that we only should be so rigorously dealth with? We ask no favor —— we complain of Inequality, and we have a Right to complain —— We do but mention our Grievances, and I hope they will be repeatedly mentioned till they are redress'd —— We form no Combinations, tho' it had been said to the contrary ——— We engage in no private Parties, tho' we have been charged with it ——— we offer no Violence, and yet it has been hinted, even to those, who it is presumed, pay no Regard to any private information, which are not supported by the best Evidence, "That the King's Officers have been set at Defiance" ——— Let us be upon an equal Footing with our Neighbours ——— Let no Indulgencies be given any where, and we are content without them ——— We want nothing but to be free as others are, or that others should be restrained as well as we ——— This is reasonable.

  We have a Right to Claim It.

          A Fair Trader.

BOSTON Dec. 7. Extract of a Letter from St. Kitts, Oct. 14, 1761.

"We learn that the French at Martineco, are in daily Expectation of being attacked; They give out that they have five thousand regular forces on the Island, but those well acquainted therewith, say, they have not more than Fifteen Hundred, ot two thousand at most. Their chief strength consist in Militia white and black."

 On Saturday Evening last a Schooner from North Carolina belonging to New-York, John Atkins, Master, in coming into this Port, was driven by the high Gales of Wind we then had on a Place called Egg-Rock, near the Light-House: the Master kept on the Wreck, and the Men on the Rock, till the next Morning, when they were taken off by the Pilot Boat. The Vessel was stove to Pieces and her Cargo lost.

 Extract of a Letter from Capt. John Thompson, to his owner at Newport, Nov. 15, 1761.

"Ten Days after I sailed from Newport, in Lat. 32. Long. 77. I met with the snow Olive Branch, Capt. Fowler, bound from Cape Fear to New-York, in distress, having 7 feet Water in her Hold, and both Pumps continuously going. At Capt. Fowler's request I lay to and took him and his people on board, being 13 in Number. They had but just time to save a few Cloaths, when the Snow went to the Bottom. The Captain and people were carried in a Pilot Boat to South Carolina."

We hear that a Sloop of about 80 or 90 Tons is ashore on Nantasket Bar, and bilg'd, but none of but no Hands on board: By her Papers and cargo 'twas judged she was bound from North Carolina to this Place, commanded by one Monro; and that the People from Nantasket were using their Endeavours to save the Vessel and Cargo, but that it was feared the former with a great Part of the latter would be lost.

NEW-YORK Dec. 7. Extract of a Letter from Capt. Basset, late Master of a Brig belonging to this Port, Dated Cape Francis, October 31, 1761.

"My last informed you of my being taken by the Defiance man of war, on my voyage from Jamaica to the Mount, the 11th inst. On the 17th he put his first Lieutenant on board with 50 hands, and sent us in company with Capt. Little in quest of a number of Dutch armed sloops, who before been obliged to quit. The 18th we saw 13 of them coming out of Port Paix, and stood for us, and in the afternoon they began to fire at us, and we seeing such a number, fired a gun to the leeward, and hoisted our jack; they still continued firing, we immediately struck, but the constant fire, which made us imagine they'd give us no quarters. At 5 we were boarded by four Dutch Sloops, and a little after by two others. The usage we met with from these villains, is imposible for tongue to express, or pen to describe; they just left me with what I had on my back; They killed my Boatswain, after we struck: Poor Capt. Little was cruelly butchered in cold Blood."

The Boatswain's name was Ross Barbeit. The Commodore's Name was Kunche, who was the chief Instigation of this Cruelty. Besides which we are informed, that three of the Men put on board Capt. Basset's brig by the man of war, were butchered in a cruel manner, by the Dutch Sailors, several hours after they had possession of the vessel.

NEW-YORK Dec. 7. The fleet that sail'd from hence to the Southward, was spoke with a few days ago all well.

The sloop Love and Ann, Robert Cobham, master from Jamaica for Philadelphia, on the 29th of

Sept. was taken by a French frigate, off the N. W. end of Cuba; but being left on board with five Frenchmen, himself alone an opportunity to dispatch one with a brace of balls, and to oblige the other four to jump into the boat, and so retook the vessel. He was ten days turning to the windward before he met with relief when he met a brig bound to Scotland, which had been taken and ransomed who spared him one hand. On the 16th of October the sloop sprung a leak, which continually got the better of the pumps, when on the 18th they happily met with the ship Antelope. Capt. Farrel, bound to this port, when they got on board of, leaving the sloop with 3 feet of water in her hold.

BOSTON Dec. 14. Monday Capt. Frost arrived at Portsmouth in a Flag of Truce from Montineco, where he had been to redeem three Hostages, for three several Vessels belonging to Piscatagua, taken and ransomed. By him we have the following Intelligence; that he left Martineco the 5th of November, where the French were making great preparations to receive the English forces who they expected every moment would pay them a visit, and had encamp'd their Women and Children in the Country: ——— That Captain McPherson in a Privateer from Philadelphia had taken two French Privateer Sloops of 10 Guns each, and carried them to Antigua: ——— That his Majesty's ship Griffin, Capt. Taylor, was cast away on Barbados, and the ship lost, but most of the Crew saved: ——— That Com. Douglas, has by Proclamation, given great Encouragement to the English Privateers, that they shall have all the plunder they can get in Martineco, in consequence of which, near 100 sails of English privateers were cruising in those seas; ——— That he left the following Hostages at Martineco, for vessels taken and ransomed by the enemy, who were enduring the most extreme Hardships on that Account, viz.

Schooner Dispatch, of Maryland, Job Warren, Hostage taken and ransomed for 30,000 Livres.

Snow Peggy, of Maryland, John Tardy, Mate and Hostage, ransomed for 12,000 Livres.

Sloop Fanny, of Norfolk in Virginia, Thomas

Sampson, Mate and Hostage, ransomed for 7,500 Livres.

Schooner Sally, of Virginia, John Brigs, jun. Mate and Hostage, ransomed for 4,000 Dollars.

Sloop Neptune, of Boston, John Taber, Captain and Hostage, dead, ransomed for 500 Dollars.

Sloop Mary Flower, of Nantucket, John Jones and Daniel Hussey Hostages, ransomed for 2,000 Dollars. Hussey has been put on an English sloop taken after the ransom and since retaken; Jones is dead.

Brig Ranger of Salem, Joseph James, Hostage, ransomed for 2,300 Dollars.

Brig Three Friends, of North Carolina, Peter Clear, Mate and Hostage, ransomed for 800 Dollars.

Sloop ———, Plymouth or Falmouth, Samuel Arwood, Hostage, ransomed for 50,000 Livres.

Schooner Revenge, of Marblehead, Martin Walker Mate and Hostage, dead, ransomed for 12,000 Livres.

Schooner Dolphin, of Providence Gidion Whiple, Hostage ransomed for 3,000 Livres.

Snow Hopson, of Halifax, Richard Frayne, Mate and Hostage, ransomed for 20,000 Dollars.

Sloop Careful, of Boston, John Beney, Mate and Hostage, ransomed for 1,800 Dollars.

Capt. Frost begs leave in behalf of the Hostages, to remonstrate against the Cruelty of keeping so many innocent Men in the greatest Distress; he forbears to accuse any particular Person of Blame; but that they should be relieved, Humanty, Generosity, and Gratitude call loudly of the Owners or Masters of such ransomed Vessels, to spend their Fortunes, and even to risque their lives, rather than let them remain in such a condition as may be better conceived than express'd, in the present Circumstances of Affairs in Martineco.

The Captains King and Bullfinch, from Picatagua, was lately taken and carried into Martineco.

NEW-YORK Dec. 24. Our Accounts from Charlestown, South Carolina, are to the 5th of December, according to which it appears that some of the Headmen of the Cherokees had not come to ratify the Treaty made with them lately; but

they had quarreled with Attakullakulla or Little Carpenter, and left him at Fort Prince George:
——— That Col. Grant will not march his Troops down at present, but had sent an Express to Ninety-six, to be informed whether the Indians intend to come and ratify the Treaty, or not.

BOSTON Dec. 28. Tuesday last Capt. Bass in a Transport Vessel arrived here from Halifax. He sailed from thence a Week ago in Company with several others bound to this Place, having on board a Number of our Provincial Troops who have been employed in his Majesty's Service in Nova Scotia: a Detachment of about 300 of our Troops are to continue in his Majesty's Service there this winter. There is also a Detachment of about 300 provincial Troops that were in his Majesty's Service at the Westward, to be continued at Crown-Point this winter: The others are returned.

BOSTON Dec. 31. On this Day the Governor gave a public Audience in the Council-Chamber to Hougougsaniyonde, otherwise Thomas, King of the Oneidas, one of the six united Indian Nations. The Indian Chief in a Speech addresses to the Governor, expressed a great Regard his Nation had for the People of this Province, and the earnest Desire he had had to visit them, especially since the Appointment of the present Governor. He complimented the Governor and the Province upon the interesting Events of last Year; and concluded with wishes that the Country conquered from the French, might never be given back again. He confirmed what he said with a Belt and two Strings.

His Excellency taking up the Belt and Strings, repeated, as usual, what was said with them, and returned proper Answers to the several Particulars. And then, informing the Indian Chief, that what he was going to say was addressed to the united Nations, to be communicated to them in their General Council, spoke in the following Words:

Brethren the Chiefs of the united Indian Nations, commonly called the Six Nations.

"I take this opportunity to let you know, that the distance between us hath not made us unmindful of you: We still Remember and Regard you as our good Friends and Brethren.

"Since we last met together, the Almighty hath done great Things for us; He hath made our enemies to fall before us; and hath planted the Tree of Peace in the midst of it. Let us make a good Use of these Blessings; let us Water this tree, and defend it from the Storms and Blasts, that the Branches may overspread the Land: and we may all live Happily under the shade of it, as Children of one Father. This confirms what I say.

A String of white Wampum with a few black Beads intermixed.

"Brethren,
The late great King George the Second lived to receive Advice from this Country being entirely subjected to him: He seemed to be reserved for this completion of his Glory; for in a few Days after he died full of Years and Honours, without sorrow or Pain. The loss of so good and so kind a Father must certainly grieve you. With this String I console with you, and wipe the Tears from your Eyes.

A String of black Wampum with 77 single white Beads.

"Upon his Death, his Grandson our present gracious King succeeded to the Throne; a Prince, young in Age, but old in Wisdom; graceful in Person, lovely in Manners, and Virtuous in Mind: who, in the short time he hath reigned over us, hath given the fullest Assurance that it is his firm Intention to defend and maintain all his Subjects in the fullest free Enjoyment of Their Rights and Privileges. Happy are the People who have such a King placed over them! You my Brethren, will partake with us in the Blessing of his Reign. I Hereby congratulate you thereupon.

A String of white Wampum with 24 single white Beads each between two black.

"Brethren,
The Chain that holds you and us together is now become a long and weighty Chain: And we should all exert ourselves to hold it up, that it may not fall to the Ground, nor contract any Rust, be you strong and hold fast your end; We will support the other: and let this help to

brighten the Chain."

    A Belt of white Wampum adorn with Diamonds of black.

The Indian Chief took up the Strings and belt one by one, and repeated what was said with with them, and promised to deliver the whole to the united Nations in their general Council. He then returned Thanks for the kind Treatment he had received since he came to Town: And upon the whole conducted himself with surprizing Dignity.

JANUARY 1762

BOSTON Jan. 1. By His Excellency Francis Bernard, Esq; Captain-General and Governor in Chief in and over His Majesty's Province of Massachusetts-Bay in New England, Vice Admiral of the same, &c.
The Right Honorable the Lords Commissioners of His Majesty's Treasury having been pleased to appoint the Honorable John Temple Esq; to be Surveyor General of Customs in the Northern District of America. And the Surveyor General having requested me to grant unto him and the Officers of the King's Customs under his Direction, such Aid and Assistance of the Acts of Parliament made in behalf, and in Obedience to his Majesty's Royal Instructions, order and enjoin all Justices, Sheriffs, Constables, and other Civil Magistrates and Officers, and all Officers belonging to the Admiralty, and Commanders of Ships and Ports, and all other the King's Officers and Subjects who it may concern within the Province of the Massachusetts-Bay, and the Territories thereof, and the Rivers, Waters, and Seas thereof belonging, that they and every one of them be aiding and assisting to the said Surveyor General, and to the Officers of the King's Customs, acting under his Direction of Authority, in the Execution of the Laws of Trade and Navigation according to the true intent and meaning thereof.
Given at Boston under my Hand, and Seal at Arms, the First Day of January, in the Year of our Lord, One Thousand Seven Hundred and Sixty-two.
By His Excellency's Command.
    A. Oliver, Secr'y   Fra. Bernard.
MONTREAL Jan. 1. To the Honourable Major General Thomas Gage, Governor of Montreal and the

Dependencies, &c.

The Humble Address of the Trading People of the City and Government of Montreal.

We His Majesty's most dutiful and loyal Subjects, and Trading People of the City of Montreal, inspired with sentiments of the most affectionate loyalty to the best of Sovereigns, beg Leave upon the Commencement of the Year, to present our mostly seigned Tribute of Duty and Respect to you, His Majesty's Representative in this Government.

With Hearts full off the most sincere Joy we congratulate your Excellency, upon the rapid and uninterrupted Series of Victories and Successes which under the Divine Blessings, have attended His Majesty's Arms by Sea and Land, during the present War; and offer up our most ardent Vows, and Prayers, to the Supreme Director of the Universe, for a Continuance of the same.

We beg leave to assure you, that we are unable —— extremely unable to express the grateful Sense we have, of the Moderation and Justice of your Administration; and the great Encouragement and Protection you have, upon all Occasions, given to Trade and Commerce; the Business of Access to your Person; the polite and condescending Manner with which we are received; the expeditious Administration of Justice, and the late Appointments of an English Council to hear and redress Complaints of His Majesty's Subjects, are convincing Proof, that you have the highest Sense of, and strictest Regard to, the Liberties and Privileges, of a British Subject. And it gives us infinite Pleasure, that we can, with strict Regard to Truth say, That we find ourselves in the full and free Enjoyment of those inestimable Privileges; which, as Subjects of one of the best Governments in the World, we are intituled to. No Encroachments upon our Properties, or Insults upon our Persons, but what are redressed, with the utmost Justice and Humanity.

From the great Benevolence and Candor, which, among the many other Virtues that constitutes your Character, we promise ourselves the fullest Security of our Rights and Liberties. And we humbly hope, that whilst we continue to Manifest the sincerest Loyalty and Attachment to our most gracious Sovereign, and chearful Obedience to the Government of his Representative, we shall not fail the Continuance of your Excellency's Countenance and Protection.

We therefore with Sentiments of the most dutiful Respect, and cordial Esteem, do unanimously wish your Excellency a happy Year, in the most extensive Sense of that Expression, by the Accession of every Thing that can any Ways contribute to the Happiness of Yourself and Family.

We are, May it please your Excellency,
Most respectfully,
Your Dutiful and Obedient Servants,
The Trading People of the City and Government of Montreal. Montreal, Jan. 1, 1762.

To which His Excellency was pleased to give the following Answer.

To the Trading People of the City of Montreal,
Gentlemen,

I Thank you for your very kind Address; and heartily rejoice with you, in the signal success of his Majesty's Arms, during the Course of this War. I flatter myself that the new Branch of Commerce opened to his Majesty's Subjects, by Conquest of this Country, will, thro' your Integrity, Care and Industry, be improved to the highest Advantage.

You will find a Readiness in me to encourage your Endeavours, and second your Attempts; and will ever meet with the Protection, for your Person and Properties, which every Person born under the benign Influence of a British Government, has a Right to expect and demand.

I am Gentlemen your most Obedient Servant,
Thomas Gage.

BOSTON Jan. 4. In the blustering Weather we have lately had, we hear that four Vessels were cast ashore at or near Cape Cod, Viz. a Schooner from Sheepscut, Benja, Chapman, loaded with Lumber; the Vessel like to be got off. ——— A Schooner from Newfoundland, laded with Fish, Clark Master, bound to this Place; The Vessel and most of the Cargo 'tis said are like to be saved, but the season was so severe, that the

Mate, named Lynch, was so wet and benumb'd with the Cold, that he died soon after he got ashore. ——— A Schooner from Halifax, Glover, Master, was drove ashore at some distant from the other, and the Vessel said to be stove to Pieces. ——— Another Schooner is also said to be ashore, and her Bottom beat out, but have not yet learnt who she is. Some of the People belonging to the above mentioned Vessels are come round by Land.

NORWALK Connecticut Jan. 4. By the Honourable Thomas Fitch, Esq; Governor of the Colony of Connecticut in New-England, in America.

Whereas the Commissioners of the Customs have, pursuant to a Warrant from the Treasury, issued their Deputation to the Honourable John Temple, Esq; to the Surveyor-General of His Majesty's Customs for the Northern District of America: And whereas they, as also the Lords Commissioners for Trade and Plantations, have respectively signified their Desire, that I should afford him such Assistance, Support, Protection and Countenance as he may have occasion to apply for in the Execution of his Office, and as it due to the Character and the Important Trust conferred upon him.

I Do therefore, on applications of the said John Temple Esq; hereby Order and Direct all Officers and all other of His Majesty's good Subjects throughout the Colony of Connecticut to be aiding and assisting to the said Surveyor General: And the Officers of the Customs, under, or authorized and directed by him within this Government, as Occasions may require, for putting in Execution the Laws, relating to Trade and Navigation, whereof they are not to sail, on the Penalties of the Laws in such Cases provided.

Given under my Hand on Norwalk in said Colony, the 4th of January, in the Second Year of the Reign of Our Sovereign Lord George the Third, of Great Britain, France and Ireland, King, Defender of the Faith &c. Annoque Dommini, 1762.

           Tho's Fitch.

HALIFAX Jan. 7. By reports from Fort Cumberland on Sunday last, we learn, that the Ship Halron, Capt. Benjamin Hollowell, belonging to

Hull, but freighted from London for Quebec, was lost in a Storm on Monday, the 16th of November last, on a Sandy Island at the Mouth of the River Marimichi in the gulph of St. Lawrence; The Captain and all the Crew, excepting the Mate, were unfortunately lost, Providentially for the Mate there were some French People, who had stopt by the badness of the Weather, relieved him; he was just gone, when they picked him up, but is now in a fair way of recovery.

Tuesday last arrived here Capt. Phips in 3 Days Passage from Louisbourg by whom we have an Account of a Cartel Ship being lost near Cape Nore, bound from Quebec to old France with 120 Men on board, of which only the Captain and 6 Frenchmen were saved.

BOSTON Jan. 11. An Account of the Burrials in the Town of Boston, and the Baptisms in the several Churches in Town, for Seven Years past.

Year	Burials			Baptized
	Whites	Blacks	Total	Total
1755	419	65	484	442
1756	461	69	526	441
1757	361	73	526	415
1758	476	57	533	423
1759	565	54	619	376
1760	508	68	576	430
1761	448	83	531	412

Observations on the Use of the Bills of Mortality, with a Computation of the Numbers of People in the known Part of the Globe.

If a common observation derived from pursuing a series of Bill bills of mortality, that in every kingdom more persons are born than die; and consequently that the human species are continually increasing. Among all the obstacles that hinder the increase of mankind, the pestilence is the greatest; next to this are war, famine, and celabacy. The effects of the latter are chiefly felt in Roman catholic communities, occasioned by their great number of nunneries and convents. All populous towns in which the births and deaths are at least equal, suffer greatly from the irregular lives of the inhabitants, together with their unhealthy Situation, and other circumstances often attending them.

It is agreed by all writers that the earth is capable of subsisting three thousand million of the human species, but a third part of what number never actually existed at one time. Perhaps the following Scheme, which has been calculated with considerable attention, nearly exhibits the number of mankind now on the surface of the globe,

Great Britain	7500000.	Austria and Netherlands	1500000.
Ireland	2600000.	Switzerland and Geneva	3100000.
France	18400000.	Sweden	3300000.
Spain	7400000.	Norway	1600000.
Portugal	3600000.	Russia	17000000.
Italy	4100000.	Hungary	5000000.
Islands in Mediterranean	2700000.	Poland	3200000.
Germany	20600000.	Turkey Europe	18400000.
Republic of U. Provinces	3200000.		

Thus contains Europe 125300000.
Asia 460000000.
Africa 150000000.
America <u>160000000.</u>
895300000.

If we reckon with the antients that a generation last thirty years, in the space 895300000 of men will be born and die, consequently 81762 will die every day.

The lists of Christening plainly proves that there are more males born than females, the ratio between them being as 21 to 20; but wars and other casualties reduce them to an equality. So that the proportion between the sexes is an unanswerable argument against polygamy.

The increase and decrease of the inhabitants of a country or town, is evident from the lists of Burials: and by these the number of the living may also be nearly computed; for, in large and populous cities, we may reckon 25 or 28 living persons for every one that dies, including cities as Copenhagen, Berlin, Boston, &c. 29 or 30, but in the country 40 or 50. Whereof some reckon, that in the towns and villages of the country, takes the gross, one out of 40 dies annually; but in London and Paris, one nearly dies out of 20.

BOSTON Jan. 11. A Few weeks ago and English 64 Gun Ship took out of a Fishing Schooner belonging to Salem a Pilot, to bring her in here; but as she did not arrive we had no Intelligence what Ship it was till by the last Vessel from Halifax we have an Account of its being His Majesty's Ship Intrepid, which sailed in August last from England, Convoy to the Virginia Fleet; from hence she was bound to Halifax, but having met with some Damage in the bad Weather on this Coast the beginning of November, intended to put into this Port for repairs, but a strong North West Wind came up, she stood away for Halifax where she arrived in 14 Days.

NEW-YORK Jan 11. A few days ago, a new born Male infant was found dead behind some wood in a garret in this city. ——— The coroner's inquest found, upon examination, that one Magarete Berbury Dagbrien, a servant in the house, was delivered alone of the said child, an immediatly wrapped it up in a sheet; that she kept it in bed with her two or three days; and that she then got it into the above place, where it was discovered: So that the verdict was bro't in Murder in the Mother.

On Monday Morning last was found the body one Mary Obrien, near Fresh Water, the coroner's inquest being summoned, returned their verdict, that the said Mary Obrien, was dragged out of the house of one Mary Lyhin, who goes by the name of Moll White, by her the said Mary Lyhin, and two fellows. The the said Mary Obrien, being in Liquor, that she was beat and abused by the said Mary Lyhin, alias Moll White, and two fellows, where she perished by the weather.

The Severity of the weather about ten days ago, occasioned such great quantities of ice to be driving in our harbour and bay, as to give great interruption to the navigation. His Majesty's ship the Rochester, Capt. Burnet, was in danger being driven about two miles, but being well provided, received little or no damage ——— Wednesday, Thursday, Friday and Saturday last, the weather was very warm, close and foggy, attended with rain, sleet and snow, at times, which in great part removed the interruption, so that we hope the Rochester, who now lays near Staten Island, waiting for a fair wind to sail for the West-Indies, with nine sail of transports loaded with provisions, and one ordinance ship, will soon depart.

Early Yesterday morning, the wind began to blow very hard from the N. N. E. which, and the moon fulling about two o'clock, occasioned for a great tide, as to overflow most of the wharves; we might have visited our neighbours by Water. ——— It did great damage to the sugars, &c. in stores along the docks; ——— and we are in great anxiety of hearing of much damage done at sea, and on the coast, by the violence of the wind.

BOSTON Jan. 18. Wednesday the Great and General Court of this Province met here, and His Excellency the Governor was pleased to make the following Speech to both Houses, viz.

Gentlemen of the Council, and Gentlemen of the House of Representatives,

You are now met together at this Time of the Year most suitable for the general Business of this Court: And as I have no Orders from His Majesty's Ministers to communicate to you, your Attention will be wholly confined to your own Province; within which Range you will find Business well deserving your best Consideration. I shall have no Occasion at present to lay before you any fresh Matters; as here are Recommendations from me to the Council and House of Representatives of Business of great Importance now lying unredressed and unanswered: To these I must now refer, and must particularly desire, that all Business then depending in the General Court, you will now take these matters into your Consideration as freely as if they were now first laid before you: Or if you do not recollect any Thing passed, let it be only with intent to avoid as much as possible such disputative Points as may tend to prevent you forming good Conclusions.

Gentlemen of the House of Representatives,

His Excellency Sir Jeffrey Amherst has dismissed all our Troops excepting two parties amounting to less than Three Hundred Men each at Halifax and Crown Point, As the Rolls are now preparing for the payment of the whole Regiments to the Time of the making the Detachments, you will take Care that the Treasury be properly Supplied: For which propose the Treasurer shall lay a State of it before you.

Gentlemen of the Council, and Gentlemen of the House of Representatives,

It will always become me to recommend to you to cultivate a Harmony among your selves and between the several Branches of the Legislature. Unanimity is the Life of Business; and an Examination to it, even where it is last necessary, will always be well received. ———— But I have said enough on this Subject: I shall only add that a Reflection upon your own Importance, and the Trust committed to you, will be sufficient to direct your Deliberations to their true Object, the general Weal; and will make you superior to private views and partial Prejudices, if ever they should attempt to influence your Councils. ———— On the other Hand, I trust that my sense of my Duty, and my form Resolution not to deviate from it, will make me equally attentive to the true and real Interest of the good People of the Province.

Council-Chamber, January 13th 1762.

Fra. Bernard.

NEW-YORK Jan. 18. Monday last near 30 Sail of Vessels that had been detained here by the Ice left this Port, with a fair Wind, and several of them we hear got to Sea that Night.

BOSTON Jan. 25. We hear from Marlborough, that last Week one Mrs. Allen of that Town, who for some Time past has been disordered in her Senses, and confined in a Cage, and lay on Straw, which was scattered about the Room, which by some Accident took Fire and communicated the Flames to her Cage, her son soon after returning from the Barn, attempted to enter the Room to recover his Mother, when the Smoak beat him back in such a Manner when he opened the Door that he was stunn'd with the fall, but immediately recovered and made a second Attempt, and drew her out by her Legs, though very much burnt, her Ear and Tongue almost to a Coal and her

Ribbs so they appeared quite plain, and in this condition she lived a Day or two and then expired raving mad.

BOSTON Jan. 25. Ran-away from Salem-Village on the first Instant, from William Boynton, a Negro Man belonging to Joseph Cottle of Newbury, named Daniel, a sturdy thick set Fellow, about 28 Years of Age: Had on when he went away a check Shirt, brown Coat and Jacket, and 'tis suppos'd he has changed his Cloaths: He has been gone from said Cottle about three Months.

Whoever will apprehend said Negro shall have Two Dollars Reward, and all necessary Charges paid. And all Persons are cautioned against entertaining, harbouring, concealing or carrying off said Negro, as they would await the Penalty of the Law.

Salem-Village, Jan. 7 1762. William Baynton.

N. B. Said Boynton took him out of Charlestown Goal, and was carrying him Home to his Master when he run away from him at Salem-Village, as above.

NEW-YORK Jan. 25. A Schooner belonging to this port, Lewis, master, was lately cut off by the Negroes on the Coast of Africa. Capt. Lewis is arriv'd at St. Kitts, in a sloop lately commanded by Capt. Handy, of this place, who with all his crew, died on that coast some time since.

PHILADELPHIA Jan. 28. We have advice from Pittsbourgh that the late freshet have done Damage there, that to the amount of several Thousand Pounds, the Rise of the River being about 40 feet higher than usual, by which some Houses, Stores, &c. were carried away.

CHARLESTOWN So. Carolina Jan. 31. A late letter from the West-Indies, says, ──── "Our Fleet is before Martineco. ──── The French Inhabitants are entrenching themselves in the mountains and others most inaccesible places. Every thing has been done by them to make the siege a long one; but we know all their motions, by the canal of St. Eustatius, &c. ──── "

FEBRUARY 1762

Boston Feb. 1. Last Week Capt. Webb arrived at Salem in 21 Days from the West-Indies, by whom we have Advice, that the Men of War and Transports, with the Troops from Belleisie, South Carolina, New-York, &c. destined for the Reduction of Martineco, were arrived and assembled at Barbados; and it was not doubted but that it would be accomplished very soon. ———
We hear further, that 70 or 80 English Privateers were out on the Cruize; but scarce a French Vessel to be seen.

Last Tuesday was committed to his Majesty's Goal John Welch, Charles Lane, and John Berry, for a very uncommon Piece of Forgery, viz. they each of them presented an Order in the following tenor.

Sir Please to let John Welch have to the value of Sixteen Dollars, he being a Soldier in my Company, and when the Muster Roll is made up I will account with you for the same. Your humble Servant,
To Mr. Sam. Parkman.   James Gray.

After taking to the value of their Order, they went peddling thro' the Country at 20 per Cent Loss upon their Goods till they were apprehended. Note. They had other Orders in their Pockets, therefore such Shopkeepers as are fond of intercepting the Soldiers Money by trading off their Goods, will do well to be on their Guard.

At the Superior Court of Charlestown last Week, Joshua How of a Place called Westmorland, in the Province of New-Hampshire, was convicted of procuring and keeping in his possession sundry Tools for counterfeiting Dollars with an intent to use them for that end, and for soliciting and tempting divers Persons to be concerned with him therein. And in counterfeiting the Province

Treasurer's Notes, &c. was sentenced to set in the Pillory one Hour, to be whipped 20 Stripes, and pay a fine of 20 Pounds.

And upon another indictment against him for counterfeiting Dollars, (of which Crime he was some Years ago convicted) he was sentenced to be committed to the House of Correction, and there kept to hard Labour for the Term of 20 Years.

His Excellency the Governor has been pleas'd very much to the Satisfaction of the Inhabitants of this Province to give an Assent to a Bill directing and impowering the Treasurer to borrow a Sum of Money and issue his Notes payable in Gold and Silver, ——— And we have a greater Reason to believe that another Bill which has pass'd both Houses, declaring Gold to be a Tender, will meet with the same Reception.

BOSTON Feb. 1. Greenwich, January the 22d A. d. 1762.

These are to certify, That I Isaac White of Greenwich, am desirous that my Wife Elizabeth White, should for sundry Causes be posted in a public Paper, to prevent her from running me in Debt any more after this Date: And I aver, that I won't pay any debts contracted by her after this Time, and forbid any Person from harbouring or trading with her,

As Witness my Hand   Isaac White.
in presence of Test. James Swain, Joseph Lark.

Braintree, November 23, 1761.
Whereas I the Subscriber have been exposed, and apprehend myself still to be exposed, to the Payment of Debts contracted in my Name, without my Knowledge and Consent. These are therefore to give public Notice. That after the Date hereof, no Debts contracted will be paid by me,

Benjamin Beale.

NEW-YORK Feb. 1. Col. Grant was on board his Majesty's Ship Dover, of 44 Guns, the 10th of January last, with the Troops under his Command in six Transports, crossing the Bar of South Carolina for the West-Indies.

ANNAPOLIS Maryland Feb. 4. On Friday Night in a very high Wind and Storm of Snow, a Boat with 6 or 8 People in her going down the Bay, was drove ashore on the Cliffs and 5 or 6 of them were drowned. It is supposed to be a Boat from this Place, which went away the beginning of the Week, having a Man and his Family on Board, who went off in a private Manner, without taking leave of his Acquaintance.

We hear from St. Mary's that a Man and Negro Woman are in Goal there for the cruel Murder of a Child 3 Years of Age. It is said the Child was the Man's own, which he had by a neighbouring Woman before his Marriage and to whom he used to pay a Quantity of Tobacco to keep it secret; but on his Marriage to another, and withholding the usual Payment, the Mother of the Child brought it to, and left it at, the Father's; who ordered his Negro Woman to carry it back and throw it into a Corn Field near the Mother's Dwelling, where the poor little Innocent was the next Day found dead.

We hear from Richland, in Bucks, that on the 29th ult. a Man went to a Distiller's, about 3 Miles from his House, for a Keg of Whisky, of which drinking too freely, and the Weather being very severe, he died in the Night on the Road. He has left a Wife and eight Children.

BOSTON Feb. 8. Miscellaneous Thoughts extracted from some of the most celebrated Writers, ancient and modern.

Dignified Persons from the Elevation of their Rank, are necessarily subjected to public Observation and Remarks.

Envy which is natural in Mankind, induces them to watch their Superiors with an Eye of Censure.

The Interest which every Individual has in the Conduct of Men in Office, engages the whole Community to survey their Actions with jealous Scrutiny.

The Author whose Writings tend to abridge the Authority of an imperious Dictator, a mere Leviathan in power, by promoting Liberty of Thoughts and uncontracted Enquiry, will unavoidably be the Object of furious Malediction, as well as of Praise and Commendation.

There are some pitiful Animals, who being themselves inured to Clinging and Abasement, imagine the human Race created for beast of Burden; and a few divinely commissions to mount, to spur, to whip and gallop them.

The original Equality by some as mere Chimera in Politicks.

If one was to endeavour to draw the lovely Features of Liberty, and the hideous Deformity of Vassalage, some dirty Slave or other would immediately appear stupid Advocate of despotic Rule.

Insidious and indirect Practices to surpress the Truth, and prevent Animadversion, are a melancholly Omen of the Declaration of public Spirit, and a most flagicious Encroachment on the Rights of the People.

His Honor the Li--t----t G------r has an undoubted Right to appear, when he pleases, with his Name in full Length, in every News Paper on the Continent; and so has Mr. Otis; and so has his honest Neighbour Mr. Cooke the Cobler; and so have all Mankind.

An Evolution of the little Arts practiced by Politicians Trimmers to gain Popularity, would greatly surprise Men of Honest Minds unacquainted with public Affairs.

Public Proposals are not always examined by the Reason of the Thing, but by the Person who made them.

In democratical Governments things are often determin'd rather by number than weight.

A Man of a generous, independent Spirit, is often frowned upon, and ill-treated; while a Flatterer, an Minion, a Sycophant, is caressed and loaded with Favours.

When private Views of Ambition, and a lust for Power, shuts the Eyes of Men's Understanding to every Object that has not Charm to captivate those prevailing Passions, the Soul is lost to every generous and diffusive Sentiment.

A Man may in general account himself happy in Proportion as he has given Reason to hate him, who hates their Country.

The Clamor of People are often by crafty Seducers kept for a Governor's Knowledge! and while Men of Candor and Sincerity, by being misrepresented, decried, and traduced, and kept at a Distance from him, he is sometimes murmur'd at for Measures, which he believes to be popular.

No wise Ruler, in the next Government, would chuse to be unacquainted with the Inclination of his Inferiors: or the Principles and Motives, that actuate contending Parties.

When the People have no Right to inspect into, or animadvert upon, the Actions of their Superiors, is a Doctrine, fit only for a Tyrant to enjoin, and Slave to obey.

The Coward, the Flatterer, the Wretch whose sordid Soul pays obedience to the splendid Insolence of Power and Fortune, can never feel the generous Warmth of honest Patriotism.

Such is the trancendent Dignity that beams from Patriotism and public-Spirit, that the Trophies thence acquired, will triumph over all the Monuments erected to exterior and adventitious Grandeur.

The Influence of many Men is founded on the Stupidity of their Admirers.

The Duration of some Men's Importance, like his Commencement, demands implicit Faith and ready Acquiescence.

If some Men could hold their Places for Life, they would not be afraid of offending every low lived Fellow among his Constituants.

To those who are come to take things upon Trusts, Thoughts and Reflections are useful and Laborious.

When two Zealots of different Sects damn one another, neither of them abounds with Christian Charity.

When a certain King was cannonized, there was an extraordinary Scarcity of Martyrs.

A Man should prize as a Treasure inestimable, the Consolation arising from the Testimony of a good Conscience; which are not only able to support, but solance and delight, amidst the vilest Defamations and the rankest Ingratitude.

BOSTON Feb. 8. We hear from Portsmouth, that on Tuesday last his Excellency Governor Wentworth was pleased to appoint Theodore Atkinson Jun. Esq; Secretary New-Hampshire, in the room of Theodore Atkinson, Esq; who has resigned.

Capt. Dixey who sail'd from Annapolis Royal in Nova Scotia the 3d of last Month, for Fort Cumberland with Provisions for that Garrison, arrived here last Tuesday, having been out a Month; he had very severe Gales almost the whole time, and we hear his Cargo is much damaged.

On Tuesday last Joshua How received 20 Stripes, and stood in the Pillory one Hour, at Charlestown, agreeable to that part of his Sentence mentioned in our last Monday Papers.

BOSTON Feb. 8. By a Letter from an Officer at Crown-Point dated January 4th, we have an Account that the Weather has beem extremely cold there; and that a Party of 40 Men which had been out, were much frost bitten but had got better: the Garrison were in good Health, excepting those which had been froze. ——— The Garrison is well supplied with Provisions. ——— A Serjeant in the 55th Regiment was found froze to Death.

BOSTON Feb. 15. An ancient and well attested Register, which may be depended on, gives us the following very mortifying Instances of the brevity of Human Life, of a hundred Persons who were born at the same Time:

At the End of 6 Years there remained only 64
At the End of 16 Years ——— ——— ——— 46
At the End of 26 Years ——— ——— ——— 26
At the End of 36 Years ——— ——— ——— 16
At the End of 46 Years ——— ——— ——— 10
At the End of 56 Years ——— ——— ——— 6
At the End of 66 Years ——— ——— ——— 3
At the End of 76 Years ——— ——— ——— 1

Add to this Account the many thousands that perish every Years by War by frequent Attendant Famine, and by Pestilence. For some Years past to the great scandal of our holy Religion and its Author (which breathe nothing but Peace and Unanimity) those who call themselves Christians have Slaughtered one another in Germany and in other Parts of the World, with all the fell range of wild Barbarians, while the more virtuous Deciples of Mahamet live in Peace and Unity among themselves, and with their Neighbours. And all this waste of Blood and Treasure, is not for any important point of Religion or Civil Liberty, but merely to extend the Territories of the Contending Princes ——— It is amazing, that the Populace should be such Bubbles to the fantastic Ambitions of their Rulers, as to cut one another's Throats for six Pence a Day, when their own Circumstances will not be at all improved which every Party prevails: ———

The taunting Speech of Caled, General of the Saracen Army, to the Christian Chief in the siege of Damascus, is justly applicable to the present age.

——————————————— Your numerous vices,
Your clashing sects, your mutual rage and strife,
Have driven religion and her Angel-guards
Like out-casts from among you. In her stead
Usurping Superstition bear the sway,
And Reigns in mimic state 'midst idol show;
And Peagentry of Pow'r. Who does not mark
Your lives! rebellious to your own great prophet
Who mildly taught you.

BOSTON Feb. 15. Thursday last Colonel Thwing, Commander of the Regiment of the Provincials employed in His Majesty's Service last Year at Nova Scotia, arrived here from Halifax.

A Healthy young Woman, with a good Breast of Milk, would go into a Family to suckle; enquire at Printer hereof.

A Likely Negro Child to be given away; inquire of Edes and Gill.

NEW-YORK Feb. 22. On Wednesday Night last about 8 o'clock a Fire broke out in a Stable full of Hay belonging to Mr. Duane, which opens on King street, it was not discovered till rising to a great Height to be extinguished. Many Houses were in danger and some took fire, but as there was little wind and the Night rainy, by timely Assistance the Fire was prevented from spreading to any other Buildings.

Letters dated Cape-Francois, Nov. 9, 1761, from Mr. John Robinson, of this Place, late Mate of the Sloop Friendship, Capt. Robert Hutchins, belonging to Jamaica informs. ——— That the said Sloop was taken about seventeen Months ago, and ransomed for Four Hundred Pistoles: ———
That Robinson went as a Hostage; and altho' the Owners at Jamaica (Richard Pellamy, and others) were frequently applied to for the Hostage Money they very inhumanly suffered him to be kept in Goal at the Cape, notwithstanding there were

several opportunities offer'd for them to have sent the Money: ——— That at the time Mr. Robinson wrote, he had been confined near fourteen Months; and had no Prospect of being relieved: ——— That he had been reduced to a great distress while under Confinement; and, That had it not been for the Assistance of one or two English Gentlemen who happily were at that Place he must have died for the Want if necessaries of Life.

NEW-YORK Feb. 22. 'Twas the sentiment of one of the most sensible Men that France ever produced that there were no Kind of reading more generally advantageous than the reading the
NEWS-PAPER.

He said, and he said truly, that it diffuses the knowledge of Geography, History, Mechanics, and indeed the principle of every Species of useful Science, thro' the whole Mass of the Nation; The Truth of this will be evident if we consider that News Papers are common only in polite Nations; and that amongst stupod and barborous People, there are no such things.

But besides those general Uses they have another; which is to fill greater Consequences to a free Country: They afford an Opportunity of bringing all Causes before the impartial Tribunal of the Publick; which in all Cases will bear and in some manner redress, the Grievances, which no Law can reach. For this Reason there never was a Man an Enemy to the Press, who was not secretly, and in his Heart an Enemy to all Liberty.

It is to this bringing Grievances before the Tribunal of the Publick that we owe every good Law that has been passed within our Memory; and though it may be true that there are many Grievances still unredresses, against which long Complaints have been often made: yet this is no just objection: for tho' they are not yet redressed, they may and will be in Time; for Circumstances will, at one Season or other, promote what hitherto they have disappointed. But there is another very good Effect, which may be looked upon as certain though we can afford no proof of it; it is this, that many more Grievances we shall have, if ever it is taken from us; which under the English Constitution can fear nothing from it.

PHILADELPHIA Feb. 18. On Thursday last Capt. Phoenix arrived here from Antigua, by whom we learn that the Governor of Martineco was summoned the Seventh of January, to Surrender up that Island to his Britannic Majesty's Arms, but returned for Answer, that he would defend it to the last Extremity: That our Army landed the next Day, with very little Loss, and soon got Possession of the Forts Royal, St. Pierre, &c. And that the Enemy (supposed to be about 20,000, white and black, among them 2,000 Regulars) had retired in the Country, carrying their Cannon with them.

PHILADELPHIA Feb. 25. By Capt. White from Barbados, we have the following Advices relating to our Army at Martineco, &c.

Extract of a Letter from Barbados, dated Jan. 25, 1762.

"Our Troops attacked Martineco the 7th Current, and landed 2,000 Men the 9th which afterwards took off, and made Point Negro the landing Place for our Troops, which was effectually executed, tho' not without Opposition, which was soon Stop'd and their Batteries and Fortifications silenced. ——— Our Troops consisting of 14,000 brave Men, landed safe without the loss of a Man. ——— Our Ships had about 20 killed and wounded. ——— On the 19th Instant our Troops were got to Capuchin-Hill, where a large Body of French Troops were entrenched, and whom they intended to attack the next Morning: If this succeeds of which we have no doubt, our Troops will soon be Masters of Fort Royal."

A Letter from Barbadoes Jan. 28, 1762.

"Just now arrived a Packet from Martineco, which gives us an Account, that on Sunday the 24th Instant, our Army forc'd and took Possession of all the Enemy's Redoubts on Mount Fortoseng so that they now commanded Fort Royal within a Cannon Shot."

Extract of a Letter from Barbados, Jan. 29,

"In regard to Martineco, we had an Express form thence last Night, which left it on Sunday Evening, and brought the following Intelligence, viz. That Col. Haviland was ordered with 4,000 Men to attack Capichin-Hill where there was a French Camp, in which it was tho't there was half of the French Army; That they began the Attack about 11 o'Clock, on Sunday the 24th Instant, and took five of the Redoubts with little or no loss; but on attacking the sixth Redoubt, in which the Regulars were, the engagement was so obstinate, that Col. Haviland was obliged to send for a Reinforcement, and as soon as they came, he attacked them Sword in Hand, killed a Number of them, made 1300 Prisoners, and the rest fled. Among the Prisoners is the French General's Brother, and several Officers of Distinction. They are now in Possession of Capuchin-Hill, about a Mile from Fort Royal, which the Generals expects to have in a few Days, it is tho't we lost a great Many at the taking of the last Redoubt."

Our Army we learn, is very Healthy, and in high Spirits, and it is said did not lose a man in Landing; but the Ships had about 20 killed and wounded.

The brave General Monckton, we hear, was so well pleased with the Behaviour of his gallant Men, in attacking and carrying the Redoubts above mentioned, (in which there was seemingly insurmountable Difficulties) that he wrote to Admiral Rodney, that none but British Troops could have taken, nor none of the Frenchmen would have left, such a strong Posts.

The following Captains were taken and carried to Martineco, from the 31st of October, to the 7th of December, viz.

Captain Mathews from Liverpool. Jones from Havredegrace. Fergurson from Belfast. Merchant from Quebec. Lavecompt from Jersey. Letchers from Guernsey. McTagget from Antigua. Phillips and Ashley from Virginia. Bullfinch from Piscatagua. Tucker from Cape Ann. Civan, Watner and Collins from New-London. Harley and White from Rhode-Island. Varnett from Esquebo. Ramsey from New-York. And Capts. Craig Tull & Scot from Philadelphia.

NEW-YORK Feb. 22. Friday last John Higgins alias Blair, and John Anderson were executed here; the former for altering and passing the Paper currency of this Province, knowing it to be counterfeit; and the latter for Burglary.

Higgins was born in Alexandria in Virginia, of respectable Parents, was about 30 Years old; and made no other Speech at the Gallows, than saying he was Innocent of the Crime for which he suffered.

Anderson was born in New-York, was about 24 Years of age, made no Speech at the Gallows, and died vastly unconcerned; he confessed his fate to be just, and that he had deserved it much before.

NEWPORT Rhode Island Feb. 23. On Friday Night last, about Ten o'Clock, the Inhabitants of this Town were alarmed by the cry of Fire, which proved to be in in Store on the Long-Wharf, in which, and three Stores Adjoining, were deposited a Quantity of West India and other Goods, to the Amount of Eight Thousand Pounds Lawful Money: These, before the Fire could be extinguished, were all consumed. Two Brigs would have probably shared the same Fate, had not their Masts been immediately cut away. It Happened providentially, that all the Houses were covered with Snow or otherwise the whole Place might had been laid to ashes as the Wind was Westerly, which blew directly upon the Town, and carried with it large Flakes of Fire, which flew to a great Distance. This was no Accident; but perpetrated by an abandoned Negro, who is now confined in His Majesty's Goal in this Town waiting the Demerits of his Crime.

BOSTON Feb. 27. Notice is hereby given that upon Act of Incorporation for the Purpose of "Propagating Christian Knowledge among the Indians of "North America," a Bill was allowed to be brought in and an Act accordingly passed the Great and General Court in their present Session for the Purpose aforesaid; by which Act it was provided ——— "That the Society shall meet at some convenient Place in the Town of Boston, in this Province, on the fourth Day of next, and there choose a President, Vice President, Treasurer and Secretary, and such other Officers as they shall judge proper, and may also elect new Members, and may make by-Laws and Orders for the Regulation of the said Society, provided such Laws be not repugnant to the Laws of England or the Laws of this Province, and act upon all Matters which they shall apprehend needed to promote the End of their Institution."

The Subscribers are therefore desired to meet at the Manufactory Hall in Boston on Tuesday the 4th Day of March next, at Three o,Clock Afternoon, than and there to act upon the Matters aforesaid.

MARCH 1762

BOSTON March 1. Last Friday Afternoon at the Superior Court held here came on the Trial of the noted Dr. Seth Hudson, and John How for counterfeiting the Province Treasurer's Notes, which Facts was proved so plain against them by the Testimony of the Evidences, that the Jury, without going out of Court, bro't them both in Guilty: several other indictments were found against the said Hudson for Crimes of the like Nature for which we hear he is to be tried this Week: ——— The Court House being so small for the concourse of people that came to hear the above Trial, that Court was adjourned to one of the largest Meeting-Houses in this Town, where the greatest Number of People attended that was ever known at any Trial in this Place before.

We hear that orders are come over to the several Governors of the Continent for raising the like Number of Men raised by them last Year and under the like Encouragement of a Compensation. Which Men are to serve under His Majesty's General and Commander and Chief here, while the Regular Troops are employed in some important Service abroad.

All able-bodied fit Men, who have an Inclination to serve his Majesty George the Third, in the Corp of Rangers commanded by Joseph Gorham, Esq; Major Commandant, now in the Province of Nova Scotia. by applying to Lieut. William Willoughby Shipton's Quarters at Mrs. Wethered's in Long Lane, or Lieut, Stephen Holland at Londondarry, will hear good Encouragement and many Advantages accruing to a Soldier in the Course of his Duty, in that Service; and may depend on being discharged at the Expiration of the time enter'd for, and to have every other Engagement punctually complied with.   W. W. Shipton.

NEW-YORK March 4. Thursday last, John Likens and Mary his wife, with Elizabeth Ridgeway, were committed to goal, for attempting to rob a man the night before. The two women cut the man in several places with knives, he having knock'd down Likens and another of their associates, as soon as they attempted to rob hin.

And on Saturday, Samuel Playford, received 39 lashes at the whipping post, for making free with a piece of handkerchief from a shop of Dr. Milligan, a few days before: He arrived here from London with his wife only 4 weeks ago.

The Severe cold we have had for above a week past, has filled the harbour with ice, and prevented several outward bound vessels from sailing ——— Wood is risen to the high price of 3 Pounds 10 Shillings per Cord. ——— [Almost nine Dollars.]

We are credibly informed, that a smart shock of an earthquake, was felt about 4 o'clock in the morning on the 21st of last month at Middletown, Woodbridge (New Jersey) and other parts adjacent.

BOSTON March 8. We hear from a Town North of Worcester, That a single Woman was suspected to be with Child, on being interrogated owed the same, and laid it to a married Man, whose wife was greatly disturbed at it; but after the Birth of the Child, she went to see it to satisfy herself, upon undressing the Child and viewing its Back she determined that it was not her Husband's for she said she had prayed that if it was, there might be two first letters of his Name; but finding nothing of this Appearance, went away well satisfied that it was not his, Tho' he had given bond for its support. This account is said to be a Fact.

If Martin Huber, Native of Bazil in Switzerland, who has been absent from his Family about 10 or 12 Years, and thought to be in America; will apply to William Bayard, and Company, in New-York, he may hear of something very considerable to his Advantage.

N. B. He set out from Bazil for America and enter'd as a Soldier, but was afterwards dischared. Any Person who give intelligence of him, whether dead or alive, will be thankfully rewarded.

NEW-HAVEN March 13. The General Assembly at the present Sessions, have Ordered 2,300 Men to be raised for his Majesty's Service, the ensuing Campaign: The Field-Officers appointed to command them, are the same that commanded the, last Campaign.

They have also Ordered the Sum of Sixty five Thousand Pounds Lawful Money to be emitted.

Wednesday, the 7th of April next is appointed by Authority, to be observed as a Day of Fasting and Prayer throughout this Colony.

BOSTON March 15. By his Excellency Francis Bernard, Esq; Captain-General and Governor in Chief, in and over His Majesty's Province of the Massachusetts-Bay in New-England, and Vice-Admiral of the same.

A PROCLAMATION

Whereas the General Court, in Obedience to His Majesty's Commands, signified by His Secretary of State, hath provided for the immediate Raising Two Thousand Men (in addition to the Forces now in the King's Service, and in the Pay of the Province) to be formed into Two Regiments, under the Command of Gentlemen of this Province, to be commissioned for that Purpose; which 2,000 Men together with such Forces as this Province hath already in its Pay, and shall hereafter raised for the same Purpose, are to be put under the supreme Command of Sir Jeffry Amherst, Commander in Chief of all his Majesty's Forces in North America, to serve only within the Northern District of North America:

I have thought fit to issue this Proclamation, to invite His Majesty's good Subjects to inlist in such Service on the Terms following: They are to serve only until the last Day of October next, and will be discharged sooner if a Peace should intervene. They are to enter into immediate Pay, and to receive Seven Pounds each, as a Bounty besides a Blanket, and they will have Six Dollars per Month; and be provided with Victuals, Tents, Camp Equipage, and all other Accommodations, in the same Manner as last Year. And they may be in general depend upon serving under the Officers with whom they inlist.

Given under my Hand at Boston, the Fourth Day of March, in the Year of our Lord 1762, and in the Second Year of His Majesty's Reign.

Fra. Bernard.

By His Excellency's Command,
   Tho. Goldthwait, Sec, of War.
        God Save the King.

BOSTON March 15. At the Superiour Court held here last Week, the Noted Seth Hudson, having been convicted on four several Indictments of counterfeiting the Province Treasurer's Notes, was sentenced to be set in the Pillory one hour, to be Whip'd 20 Stripes, to suffer one Year's Imprisonment, and to pay 100 Pounds as a fine to the King, upon each Conviction: The corporal Punishment to be inflicted four Times also. ——— His Confederate John How, who was convicted of the like Crime on two Indictments, was sentenced to stand in the Pillory one Hour, to suffer one Years Imprisonment, to be whip'd 29 Stripes, and to pay 100 Pounds on each Conviction.

John Welch, Charles Lane, and John Berry, who were convicted of forging Notes on some Shops in this Town, was sentenced as follows, viz. The said Welch to be whip'd 20 Stripes, to be imprisoned 12 Months, and to pay 10 Pounds fine, he being convicted on two Indictments. Barry to be imprisoned 3 Months and to pay fine of 40 Shillings.

One James Dow, who was convicted of breaking into a House at Roxbury, and stealing from thence, was sentenced to be whip'd 20 Stripes, to be imprisoned six Months, and pay treble Damages, &c.

Also John Terrell who was convicted of breaking into a Shop in this Town and stealing from thence, was sentenced to be imprisoned six Months, to pay a fine of 10 Pounds, and to pay treble damages,&c.

We hear from Providence, that on Friday last William Ratcliff, as he call'd himself was whip'd there for Stealing: ——— It appeared when he was stript, that he hed been used to Whipping, his Back being full of Marks, and some very fresh. ——— He is a stout resolute Fellow, and has but one Hand, We imagine him to be the same Fellow that was branded in New-York last Month for the like Crime; and that he and another may come this way upon the bad Design ——— Therefore we give this public Notice that People may be on Guard.

PORTSMOUTH New-Hampshire March 15. As this Province was never more in distressed Circumstances then at present, on Account of the Necessaries of Life, both for Mankind and Beast, we hope our Southern Brethren, by this Information, will incline to send several Vessels of Provisions, particularly Wheat, Flour, Corn, Rye, Oats, Brand, Cheese, Hay, &c. this Way.

Boston Capt. Benson who arrived at Marblehead from Barbados, we have the following Authentic Advices of the Operations of the British Troops at Martineco.

Extract of a Letter from an Officer in the Expedition, to a Gentleman in Boston.

Camp near Fort Royal, on the Island of Martinique, 29th January, 1762.

"We landed in Cassis Navires Bay on the 15th Instant, the Ships of War having previously silenced many Batteries along Shore. The Enemy with their whole Strength collected had possession of two remarkable strong Hills called Montes Fortenson and Granier, with many strong Redoubts mounted with Cannon, Batteries, Breastworks, &c. On the 24th our Troops crossed a very deep and almost impassable Riviere, and that in the Face of the Enemy, to the Attack of their Works, on the Monte Fortenson so impregnably posted as the Enemy seemed to be. It was really amazing to see the Ardor with which our brave Men advanced, they drove them out of one Work, and the another, and in a few Hours we took possession of all their Works, consisting of no less then ten Redoubts with Cannon, strong and most advantageously situated, the Enemy retired in the utmost Confusion to the Monte Granier which commanded the Ground we had got Possession of, and where they had also Redoubts mounted with Cannon, and a deep Riviere or Gully between us.

The 25th and 26th we were annoyed a good deal

with Cannon and Shells from Fort Royal and Monte Granier.

The 27th in the Afternoon the Enemy had the Temerity (inspired with a good Quantity of L'eau de Vin) to Attack with about 3000 Men, and under cover of an new-erected Battery, The Brigade of the Army on the Left: They were received properly and instantly repulsed, and the happy Consequence was that our Troops pursued them, passed the Riviere, and got Possession of Monte Granier, where two Brigades, the Light Infantry and Grenadiers took Post that Night, in order to attack the strong Works on the Morrow, but the Trouble was saved, by the Enemy evacuating them in the Night, so that we are now in Possession of the Ground on which the Safety of Fort Royal depended. ——— It must immediately fall when our Batteries get off against it, which will be to-morrow Morning.

The General is perfectly well.

In our different Actions we have not had more than 400 killed and wounded, and but two Officers killed on the Spot. Capt. Cockburn of the 42d and Lieut. Jermin of the 22d.

We have killed Numbers of the Enemy, and have more Prisoners than we know what to do with, several Croix of Distinction.

As the Enemy have been defeated in their very strongest Post, and where they had collected almost all their Forces, we may expect that the future business in the Reduction of the Island will be easy, ——— although by Nature the most undesireable Country to attack that ever was seen: The whole Island is nothing but deep Gullies and high Mountains.

There cannot be enough said about in Honour of our brave Troops; they really surmounted more Difficulties that could have been expected from Men.

We yet a very healthy notwithstanding the necessary Hardships and Fatigues they had been exposed to, laying upon their Arms without any Cover for above a Week together." ———

Extract of a Letter from a Gentleman in Barbados to one in Marblehead, dated Feb. 7, 1762.

I have the Pleasure to tell you, that although

the French tho't themselves so well secured and intrencched, that we must have re-embarked our Troops again, that upon the first Attack on Mount Fortenson they were then convinced of their Mistake. ——— Our Grenadiers were ordered to attack them in their intrenchments and Redoubts, which they marched up to, with Bayonets fixed, in the Face of the whole Fire of the Enemy, which so amazed them that they gave up and retired from Redoubts to Redoubts, until we drove them out of the whole. ——— Mount Grenier was also very strong, but we have got possession of that before now, I am pretty sure, we are now in Possession of Fort Royal. Deputies have been with Terms of Surrender, but they were rejected ——— as we shall not receive that Island upon the same Terms of Guadeloupe."

Postscript of another Letter from Barbados, dated February 7, 1762.

Yesterday our Packet arrived from Martineco, which she left Tuesday the 2d Inst. ——— Our Forces were then in Possession of Capuchin Hill (which is near Fort Royal) there were then erecting more and heavier Cannon to play on the Fort; several of our Batteries being then employed in that Work, and that the Fire from Fort Royal was so slow, that we have reason to think the chief the French had deserted it. ——— Mons. Latouch the French General, it is said, can't be found, ——— it is the general opinion that we are Masters of the whole by this Time. ——— It is said the new French Governor of Martineco arrived there before our Troops landed, but seemed not much pleased with the state wherein he found the Island, notwithstanding the gasconading Accounts published by the French of their Preparation against an Attack.

Extract of a Letter from Antigua, dated January 27, 1762.

"The French General at Martinico has given a Reward of two Moidores for every Leg, Arm, and Head brought into his Camp, which has exasperated our Soldiers and Indians so much, that they have sent in a Number of the French Negroes scalped to the General.

BOSTON March 22. Tuesday last a Provincial

Soldier Came to Town from Crown-Point which Place he left the 6th Inst. He came to Albany in a Sleigh, from thence travelled on Foot. —— We learn that several of the Men in the garrison there had been Frost bitten in the late severe Weather. —— That they had buried 8 or 9 Men this Winter. —— That the Troops doing Duty there were in general healthy and well —— That a Number of Sleighs with fresh Supplies were gone up to Albany, for the Use of the Garrison —— We don't learn that there were any particular late Advices from Montreal or Quebec. Considerable of Merchandize, &c. in Sleighs, were at Crown-Point, on their way to those Places.

We hear from Newport, Rhode Island, that John Shearman, convicted of Burglary, and Fortune, a Negro Slave, of setting Fire to Warehouse on the Long-Wharf; are to be executed on Wednesday the 14th of next Month. And William Lawton, who was convicted of Perjury, is sentenced to Stand in the Pillory two Hours, to suffer one Month's Imprisonment, and pay a Fine to the King of 500 Pounds.

NEW-YORK March 22. On Monday Morning last the Fire Engine house belonging to Schuyler's Copper mines, in New-Jersey, took fire and was burnt to the ground, and the works belonging to the engine, which is said cost near ten Thousand Pounds, were destroyed. It is conjectured to have been set on fire by the carelessness of one of the workmen, who was the only person in the house. The fire began below, where he acknowledges he lighted a candle when he went to bed in the upper room, where he was waked by the fire, and ran down to the lower floor which fell in with him, into the flames below, but by some means, which he doth not at all remember, he got out, but is terribly burnt. —— It's said that above 2000 cord of wood was also consumed.

Accounts of the Proceedings at Martinico, from the Sixth of January to the Eighteenth, viz.

6th. Made the land at Martinico and lay to all night.

7th. Made sail and anchored that night in St. Ann's Bay, at 4 o'clock the Raisonable ran ashore.

8th. Made sail further into the bay. At 4 o'clock the Rainsonable's crew went ashore, Attacked a small village, set two houses on fire, and put the enemy to flight.

9th. Major Skeen ordered the second brigade to land under a brisk fire of 5 of our ships; and half an hour after their landing English colours were flying on a battery. The rangers and light infantry scoured the wood, and took a French officer, and some negroes.

10th. Commodores Swanton and Douglass sailed round to Pigeon island. ——— This night all but a battalion embarked.

13th. Made sail for Pegion island, and came to at Grand Ance bay, where was a fort of 17 guns, taken by our ships and in possession of the marines ——— This evening Col. Scott with his rangers and infantry came in from scouting the woods, where they met with a party of about 200 French grenadiers, whom they attacked, and killed and wounded the greatest part of them, with only the loss of Lieut. Barclay.

17th. Sailed for Port Royal, with the whole fleet and Army. At. 8 A. M. came in sight of it, and three ships drew in shore, and began to fire against the redoubts on the hills; upon which the enemy's camp, at 2 o'clock P. M. gave way, and people left their houses and plantations; The Carolina Indians, amounting to 150, were then landed among whom was Silver Heels; who immediately took to the woods, and cleared them.

18th. All the Troops were landed: those that landed first had a skirmish with the enemy, in which they made several prisoners, and killed and wounded many, among the killed an officer, who appeared to be of distinction, one of the soldiers too his gold watch and another cut off one of his fingers, for the sake of a Diamond ring. By the several prisoners taken we cannot learn that the French have above 800 Regulars. They were much surprised to see such a fleet & army.

BOSTON March 22. Notice to the Publick is hereby given, that James Lee, of Pomfret, proposes to ride as a News-Carrier from Boston to

Windham in Connecticut, to set out every Monday from the First Day of April and to perform once a Week during the Summer Season. —— He goes thro' the following Towns, viz. Roxbury, Dedham, Medfield, Holston, Bellingham, Mendon, Uxbridge, Douglass, Killingsly, Woodstock, Pomfret, Canterbury, and Windham, and will carry the News-Papers, to every of the above Places, also Bundles, &c. and may be spoke with at Green and Russell's Printing Office every Monday till Twelve o'Clock at Noon.

BOSTON March 24. Province of Massachusetts-Bay.

The Officers recruiting for His Majesty's Provincial Service are hereby Notified, That the Time appointed for making the first Returns of the Men which they have inlisted and are passed Muster, is the 30th of March Instant: and it is expected that they punctually observe to make them at that Time.

By Order of his Excellency,
Tho. Goldthwait, Secr'y of War.

BOSTON March 29. Extract of a Letter from Montreal, dated March 3, 1762.

"This Town is in the greatest Tribulation on Account of the loss of a Cartel Ship that sailed from hence in November, and was soon after cast away, and of 120 Souls, on board, only six were saved; among the six, is the Captain, four others and M. Luke, the latter is arrived after suffering much with Cold, Hunger, and immense Fatigue: He has lost a Brother two Sons, two Nephews, and several Relations and Friends. There were on board the Ship 14 Officers, 10 Ladies, and 14 young Men, all of Fashion, in short, scarce any Body here, but what has lost some Relations, Friends, Child, Husband, or Wifes."

We learn from Connecticut, that the General Assembly, besides the 2300 men Voted to be raised for the Service of the ensuing Year, have also ordered that they raise for his Majesty's Service 500 Men to be under the Command of regular Officers, and to have a Bounty of Five Pounds.

We hear the General Assembly of New-Hampshire have voted to raise 534 Men for the ensuing Campain.

APRIL 1762

BOSTON April 5. Since our last several Vessels have arrived here from the West Indies, by whom we have the following Advices of the Success of our Forces at Martineco, viz.

Fleet at Martineco, Feb. 8, 1762.

Dear sir,

"I have the pleasure to advise you of our arrival here the 3d inst. and had the satisfaction to see the surrender of Fort Royal on the 5th. It happened on the 4th that one of the Royals being a little drunk, strolled to nigh the centry at the gate of the fort, and was apprehended. By him the French understood we were to storm on the next day. A lucky gasconade indeed! they immediately sent out a truce at midnight to propose a capitulation, which being agreed on, the next day out troops marched in, and took possession at 5 o'clock P. M. This was a scene well worth seeing, for which we arrived very opportunely; the like mayn't be met with in the course of my life. The taking of Fort Royal with 300 men by intercepting its communication with the fort, and 6000, they say, were put to flight; on which we obtained the town and a great part of the country round. The pannick was great, and I hope it's not over. Monsieur Latouche, walked off into the mountain called La Montaine, with a number of men, and did not give any orders at Fort Royal for 6 days before the surrender: The language in general is, That they ought to be hanged for giving up so strong a place.

It is true they were well plied with shot from our batteries; but had they kept close, hauled in their guns, and only guarded against a storm, it might have been a long time before we could have taken it, it is surprizing to see its strength, which is beyond expectation ——— The men of war did very right in not attacking it, as they must inevitably have been drub'd.

It would amaze you to trace the march of our troops from first landing (a kind of protecting providence at least must be acknowledges) against most advantageous redoubts.

The French Governor of Guadeloupe came in some time since, and seems to be well pleased at his lodging in the head quarters.

An old priest, or frier, who lodges at the same place, makes this remark: If the Governor deserv'd hanging for giving up that in three months, what will Monsieur Latouche merit for that of Martineco, or Fort Royal? A Rack.

The 6th instant I had the singular pleasure to accompany my namesake into the fort, who, as Commissary of Artillery surveyed the lines and found the following ordinances.

Iron guns mounted			Mortars	
14	42	Pounders	3	13 inch & half.
9	32	ditto	1	7 ditto
23	26	ditto		
4	24	ditto		
26	18	ditto		
1	12	ditto brass.		
77				

Powder, 650 barrels, shells about 575 of 13 inches and a half bore, and 22 ditto of 10 inch; besides a great number of cannon at our forts.

Yesterday I went with him in his cutter above three leagues above Fort Royal, to a bay where six sloops were sunk. I landed, and traversed a spacious house, commodious garden, and fine potters work, with tile sugar pots, &c. and must confess it often touch'd me, the reflection of flying one's own habitation, where, by appearance of furniture &c. they lived in splendor.

Oh the devastation of war! its enough to make one tremble at the thoughts, yet could not but with eager curiosity pursue the search of ruin upon ruins.

We met a canoe with sundry French Gentlemen, who told us they were going to propose a capitulation (whether for themselves, or any body of inhabitants I can't tell)

As to the surrender of Fort Royal, the number of men that marched out was 800, and those of sick & wounded left about 400.

The Terms of capitulation is not known, except what was ocular, namely, about 530 regulars & militia march out with arms, ammunition, colours, and baggage, preceeded by two brass six pounders, to the head of the harbour, where the flat bottomed boats were ready to carry them on board the transports.

After this about 270 privateer gentry march'd out, grounded their arms, and were conducted on board.

These terms at present bespeak that honour and humanity of British subjects.

The capitulation relates only to Fort Royal, and not any other part of the island.

About 250 English prisoners were found in the fort.

As to the description of their town, with a most comfortable and elegant hospital, you have many about you to be informed of.

This place is of little trade, being told it chiefly centered at St. Pierre so that there's no merchandize as yet to be bought."

  I am sir your's &c.   Britannicus.

We learn by a letter from the West Indies, That the inhabitants of St. Eustatia were almost certain the English could not reduce the Island of Martineco. ——— Our man there, on the 7th of February, held Stakes for fourteen Thousand four hundred Pieces of Eight, that the Island would not surrender in 9 Months. ——— The French gasconaded most scandalously on the appearance of our Forces; and contemptuously called those brave Troops who had conquered Quebec and Belleisle, Women in Soldiers Cloaths; but an univerasal Gloom was soon spread on that whole French Corp at St. Eustatia. When the General retired, he gave leave to the Privateers to quit the Island, and escape in the best manner they could: A Number of Pettiaugers got to Eustatia with Women, Children, Negroes and Effects from Martineco. ——— The Flower and Glory of the Island fell the same Day that Grenier fell: a select body of 100 Men were entirely

cut to pieces, except 39, with (as the French say) 1500 more of less note in all: A dreadful Carnage! and that executed in a very short Time.
—— It's tho't some of the Noblesse of Guadaloupe will forfeit their estates and be hanged, as it appears plainly by the merchants books, that they were concerned in the privateering business.

BOSTON April 5. Extract of a Letter from the West Indies, dated March 4, 1762.

"Martineco surrendered to the British Troops the 12th of February, upon such terms as the English thought fit to allow them: —— All the Windward Islands are intirely in Possession of the English.

NEW-YORK April 5. By a Gentlemen from Montreal we hear they enjoy health, peace and plenty, at that place. They are well supplied with goods of all sort, and provisions is good and cheap.
—— On Friday sev'night 300 Sleighs came to that town. —— The following accident happened there, on M. St. Lukebycorn having with his wife and sister drank some coffee, they were suddenly taken ill; his wife died in 5 hours, and his sister's life is dispair'd of. It is imagined this accident was occasioned by Ratsbane, which had been used in poisoning Rats.

In Capt. Nichoson from Martineco, came passenger Mrs. Shute, a Woman of this place, widow of Serjeant Shute of the 3d battalion of R. Americans. When our forces landed at Martineco, the Woman not being allowed to go on shore, she dressed herself in men's cloaths and accompanied her husband, who was killed by her side.

Last Thursday one Mr. Lefyear of Hakinsack, in New-Jersey, happening to have some high words with his Wife, went out of the house in a passion, shot himself thro' the body, of which wound he instantly died.

On the 26th of March, Capt. Gardner spoke with the ship St. Andrew, Capt. William Price, bound from Boston to Virginia, who had been out nine weeks, and had been drove to the eastward of the banks of Newfoundland, and was much damag'd by the bad weather she had met with.

BOSTON April 9. Public Notice is now given,

that Joseph Goldthwait, of Boston, Gentleman Sealer of Wood in the said town of Boston has filed an Information in the inferior Court of Common Pleas, setting forth, that on the sixteenth of March last he seiz'd on Campbell's & Cockran's Wharf, in said Boston, about twenty eight Cords of Cord Wood as forfeited, not being four feet in length, and praying the same Wood may be adjudged to remain forfeited, two Third Parts to the use of the Poor of the Town of Boston, and the other Third Part to the use of him Joseph: All Persons claiming Property in the same Wood are hereby notified to appear before the said Inferior Court on Monday the 20th of April current at Ten o'Clock in the forenoon, to show Cause (if any they have) why said Wood should not be adjudged to remain forfeited as prayed of.

April 9, 1762. by Order of the Court,
Ezekiel Goldthwait Clerk.

CHARLESTOWN S. Carolina April 10. We hear that a Sloop from St. Augustine, for the Havanna, with a passenger (among others) of some note on board, about 7 weeks ago calling at some of the Florida keys, a party of Creek Indians being there, fired upon the boat, killed some of the people, and took the gentleman prisoner, for whom a ransom of 10,000 dollars has been offered.

We hear also that the Governor of St. Augustine has applied to Governor Wright of Georgia, that he would interpose his good offices to accommodate matters between the Creek Indians and the Spaniards.

His Excellency the Governor has inpower'd proper persons to recruit the 268 men required by General Amherst from this province. Major Rogers is gone on the same service.

BOSTON April 12. Extract of Two Letters from an Officer at Martineco, to a Gentleman in this Town, dated the 10th and 13th of February 1762.

"I have the pleasure to acquaint you, that we are in Possession of the whole Island, ——— 'tis a glorious act, and worth the trouble of taking it, ——— On the 16th of last Month at 4 o'Clock Afternoon we landed without the loss of a Man, the Ships having first destroyed the Enemy

Batteries near the Shore, we immediately took possession of the rising Grounds about the Place where we landed, far as it was late in the Day when we got on Shore we had not Time to push any farther for that Night, but got our Field Artillery landed directly, and lay upon our Arms till next Morning, when we advanced towards the Enemy, who skirmished with our Light Infantry, but never stood near enough to make a serious Affair of it; when we came near enough we found the Enemy posted as strongly as you can imagine on the Monte Fortenson. General Monckton went in Person to reconnoitre their Situation, and upon finding that they were intrenched to their Chins, that their Intrenchments were amply provided with Artillery, and that they had several Redoubts with many Pieces of Cannon in each, all of which could play upon the Troops as they advanced to the Attack, he prudently deffered it till he could get up his heavy Artillery, and raise some Batteries to annoy the Enemy, while we advanced to charge them: their Situation was thus, they had a very deep Gully in their Front, upon the side of which they threw up an Intrenchment, from whence they could keep a most furious Fire of Musquetry upon us while we were passing it, which we must absolutely have done before we could come to an Engagement with them: Beyond this Intrenchment they had another amply provided with Artillery to play upon any Body of the Troops that should advance to attack them; on the Flanks of the second Intrenchment they had two Redoubts, one on the Right the other on the Left, which were provided with Cannon to rake the Troops as they came up; beyond this they had other Redoubts and Intrenchments and beyond them again others all the Way to the Town, which was about two Miles: This you will say was being strongly posted; but British Grenadiers inoured to War, and used to conquer, surmount all Difficulties. —— We got our Batteries perfected by the 23d at Night, when the General gave Orders for the Grenadiers of the Army to be in Readiness to storm the Enemy's Intrenchments at Day Light the next Morning, supported by the fourth Brigade; while the other Brigades of the Army made other Attacks in different Places: ——— Accordingly the Moment Day began to appear, Brigadier Grant, at the Head of Twenty-two Companies of Grenadiers, advanced toward the Enemy, when the Grenadiers began to enter the Gully the French directly perceived us and began a brisk Fire upon us, which we were obliged to suffer for about twenty Minutes, as the Gully took us that Time to pass it, however we pushed on, and as soon as we got to the other Side we forced them from their Intrenchment and they retired to the other; from whence as soon as we shewed our Heads above the side of the Hill they began a most furious Fire of small Arms and Artillery, loaded with Grape shot, which killed and wounded many Officers and Men, but not a Man of our Grenadiers Attempted to give Way: nay on the contrary charged the Enemy with the more Fury and carry'd this their chief Intrenchment with both their Redoubts in a very few Minutes; from this Monsieurs retreated into the Sugar House which they had fortified and prepared for that Purpose, behind which they had another Redoubt with Cannon, which play upon us, and did us great Damage; here they made their chiefest & last resolute Stand: but we forced them to abandon these Fortifications, not without Loss on both Sides, after this we drove them from Intrenchment and Redoubt, and from Redoubt to Intrenchment till we drove them into Town; whither it was impossible to follow them on Account of the Fort: Some of us pursued so far as to pass the Bridge at the Grand Hospital, but were ordered to retire. ——— Our chief loss fell upon the Grenadiers, 300 of whom were killed and wounded besides a Number of Officers, and the 1st Battalion of Royal Highlanders likewise suffered greatly. ——— The Action was over by Nine o'Clock in the Morning to the Honour and Satisfaction of the General and the whole Army. ——— The Enemy being now drove from their darling Spots, took Post on Mount Grenier (a high Hill which commands Fort Royal, and which is the strongest Post I ever saw, with Batteries of 24 Pieces of fine heavy Cannon and two 13 Inch Mortars) this the General was resolved to drive them from, and accordingly detached Brigadier Haviland and Walth with their Brigades, and all the Light Infantry to go on every Side of it, to get Possession of Mount Grenier; but from the Strength of the Place it was not possible to attack it but by a regular Siege: which would have employed us a long Time; but the Enemy took it in their Heads on the 27th to come down and attack, the Brigade and Light Infantry, and whom were so well received that they were totally routed in five Minutes Time with great Loss, and we pursued them so fast up the Hill, that they abandoned all their strong Works, and ran down the other Side in the greatest Panick, leaving us to take Possession of a Vast Quantity of Artillery, and indeed every Thing they had there, nay they did not even spike up a Gun, Redoubt here was as strong as Nature and Art could make it, and which would have cost us many Lives had they staid to defend it: We began about 2 o'Clock in the Afternoon and pursued them till 11 o'Clock at night. —— The next Day we began to fire in the Fort with their own Cannon and Ammunition; and the Day following our Batteries began to play upon the Fort from Monte Fortenson, we continued battering the Fort with Shot and Shells till the 5th of February at Night when they sent out a Flag of Truce and Surrendered upon being allowed the Honors of War; and glad we were to give them any Terms for they might have defended it a Month longer: It is Prodigious strong, and very little damaged: The Inhabitants immediately came in and surrendered themselves. The 13th Mr. Larouche capitulated for the whole Island. I have not heard upon what Terms; but believe much the same that was given to Guadaloupe —— The Grenadiers of the whole Army and the second Brigade have receiv'd Orders to embark early in the Morning for St. Pierre's where Mr. Latouche has agreed to lay down his Arms, and surrender —— That I have endeavoured to give you the best Account I could of this great Conquest: Never was an Army more happy under the Command of any General than we are under the worthy Mr. Monckton; his whole Steady is to serve his King and

Country and to make every one under him happy; but I must drop the Subject for I am not able to express his worth; and a General so beloved will ever have success."

Boston April 12, By the Honourable Jonathan Belcher, Esquire, Lieutenant Governor and Commander in Chief in and over His Majesty's Province of Nova-Scotia, or Acadia, &c. &c. &c.

A PROCLAMATION

Whereas may Rights have become vacant in several of the Townships in the Province, viz. Sackville, Amherst, Berrington, Onslow, Granville, Yarmouth, New Dublin, Chester.

By failure of the Grantees of Performance of the required Conditions of settling with their Families within a limited Time.

I have therefore thought fit, by and with the Advice and Consent of his Majesty's Council for the said Province, to publish this Proclamation, giving Notice. That all Persons who shall come as Settlers to any of the above mentioned Townships, with their Families and Stock, on or before the Fifteenth Day of September next, shall be intitles to Shares according to the Number in proportion to the Grants heretofore made, until the Number in each Township shall be compleated.

Given at the Council Chamber at Halifax, this twenty fifth Day of March, 1762.   J. Belcher.

By Command of the Luiet. Governor, with the Advice and consent of
his Majesty's Council   Rich. Bulkeley.

A True Copy. Rich. Bulkeley, Secr'y.

N. B. All persons inclined to be settlers agreeable to the aforesaid Proclamation, are desired to send the lists of their Families and Stock, included in Letters directed to his Excellency the Governor of Halifax, and left with the Hon. Thomas Hancock, Esq; to be transmitted to Nova-Scotia.

BOSTON April 12. We hear from Charlestown, in South Carolina, that Major Robert Rogers has publised proposals for printing by Subscription in four Vulumes Octavo. A Journal of the Different Excursions made by him against the Enemy, since the Commencement of the present War; with the Letters and Orders of the several Generals and Officers under whom he had acted since the year 1755, for carrying the same into Execution and the answers thereto. A Description of the Soil, Produce and extent of the several British Colonies in America; the Number of Inhabitants in each of them, the different Forms of Government, &c. A brief Account of Canada, and a true Description of that important Conquest; the Inhabitants thereof, in Soil, Produce and Extent. An Account of the different nations of Indians that have any Commerce with the English; their Customs, Manners, Habits, religious ceremonies, Methods of proclaiming and carrying out War, and their policy in Treaty and making Peace. Some reflections on the great Advantages that would accrue in regulating a proper Trade with them, and the great Value of the interior Country of Ohio, and betwixt the Country and the Illinois, and Great Lakes northward to Hudson's Bay; and some proposals for the Discovery of the North-West Passage by Land. The Price to Subscribe to be one Pound Sterling, sewed in Blue Paper.

BOSTON April 12. His Excellency having received his Majesty's Declaration of War of the 2d of January last against the King of Spain, with Orders to proclaim the same in this Province; has appointed Wednesday the 14th Instant at 12 o'Clock, for the Solemnity.

Among the many English Captains of Vessels that we found at Martineco when it surrendered, were the following belonging to North America, viz, Capt. Ramley of New-York; Tull of Philadelphia; Ballard Phillipson of Boston; Foster of Cape Cod; Bruce of Virginia; and Collins and Johnson of Connecticut.

Extract of a Letter from So. Carolina, dated March 6, 1762.

"This Evening arrived here Capt. Morton from New Providence, after an excessive bad passage of 17 Days. The Sloop Rising Sun, Daniel Buckler, Master of Providence in Rhode Island Colony sailed 3 Days before him, but he fears she is lost, as he saw some dead Bodies at Sea, which by the red Jackets they had on he judg'd to belong to her; he likewise say a Boat and some

Pieces of a Wreck. ——— A Sloop from New-York, expected here some Time past, one Francis Browne, Master, and the Sloop Betsey. Capt. Martin, not having been heard of here, are supposed to be Lost."

BOSTON April 14. His Excellency General Amherst Commander in Chief of his Majesty's Forces in North America, &c. &c. having ordered a Number of Transports Vessels to be taken into his Majesty's Service at Boston:

This gives Notice to all such as has good double Deck'd Ships, Snows, or Brigs suitable for Transports, that they may apply to Mr. Hancock, who will acquaint them the Terms on which they are to be taken in said Service, and that they will be put into Pay as soon as they are fit for the Sea.

PROVIDENCE April 15. Bound on a Cruizing Voyage against His Majesty's Enemies, the Privateer Sloop Revenge, Caleb Granston Commander, mounts 10 Carriage and 12 Swivel Guns, will carry 50 Men, is a prime Sailor, and will be compleatly fitted for the Sea in 15 Days. All Gentlemen Sailors that have a Mind to make their Fortune by entering Volunteers on board said Sloop, are desired to repair to Mr. James Mitchels in Providence, where the Rendezvous is kept.

CHARLESTOWN S. Carolina April 17. For this past week a very suspicious vessel has been several Times seen both to the Northward and the Southward of this bar, supposed to be A Spanish privateer; She is a brig of 12 or 14 guns, few of which she shews, black sides, boot top'd, and a horse head painted white. Thursday she chased a pilot boat a great part of the day, after being so near that one of the pilots in her was going to board, and only prevented by discovering her deck to be full of men laying on their bellies; when the pilots hailed her, they answer'd in broken English, that they came from Providantia. When she gave over the chase, she stood off the S. E. the wind then blowing at E. by N.

Besides two Schooners to be fitting out as privateers, viz. Major Rojers, Capt. Rogers, commander, and 6 carriage and 12 swivel guns, and 50 men; and the Schooner Halequin, Capt. Wm. Lyford, commander of 8 carriage and 12 swivel guns with 70 men; there is also fitting out, with the greatest expedition a fine Brig, Called Charlestown mounting 14 double fortified 6 pounders, 20 swivels, and carry 120 men. There is talk of more privateers to be fitted out here.

BOSTON April 19. On Thursday the 1st Instant, His Majesty's Ship Enterprize, commanded by John Holton, Esq; arrived at New-York from England, with Dispatches to his Excellency General Amherst, and to several Governors of this Continent: On Friday the 8th those for his Excellency our Governor arrived in Town by Express as also His Majesty's Declaration of War on the 2d of January last, against the King of Spain, with orders to publish the same in this Province: whereupon his Excellency appointed Wednesday the 14th current for that Solemnity: Accordingly in the forenoon His Excellency's Troops of Guards, commanded by the Honourable Brigadier Royall, the Regiment of Militia in this Town, commanded by Colonel Phillips and his Excellency's Company's Company of Cadets, commanded by Colonel Jarvis, were mustered in King-Street: At Noon his Excellency the Governor, his Honor the Lieutenant Governor, the Members of the Honourable His Majesty's Council, and House of Representatives, and a Number of other Gentlemen attended at the Council-chamber, when his Majesty's Declaration of War against the King of Spain was published from the Court-House: The Guns of Castle Williams were immediately fired, and also those at the Batteries in this Town, and on board the Province Ship of War King George: three Vollies were then fired by the Troops, the Militia, and Company of Cadets. The whole was carried on with the greatest Solemnity and good order.

The same Day, being the Time to which the Great and General Court or Assembly of this Province was prorogued, the said Court accordingly met; and in the Afternoon his Excellency was pleased to make the following Speech to both Houses, viz.

Gentlemen of the Council, and Gentlemen of the House of Representatives,

The Hopes which flattered you last Session, that the Difficulties which prevented the Conclusion of Peace might be over, are now vanished: and we are not only assured of the continuance of the War, but find we have a new Enemy to contend with. Nevertheless, we have no Reason to despair: We may well expect that as the Justice of our Cause is still prevalent, the same steady Council will direct, and the same vigorous Arms will enforce the wise Measures which his Majesty, with the Divine Assistance, shall pursue for the general Defence and Security of His People.

But although I would not have you despond, I must caution you against being to secure or indifferent. You must not think that if the War does not rage in your own Doors, you may therefor be unconcerned Spectators of it. Your Interest is at the bottom of this Contest; and wherever the Battle is fought, the Prize lies in this Country. The Negotiations for Peace were interrupted by the Spaniard demanding a Right of Fishing on the Banks of Newfoundland, and he was also avowed that the Concessions of the French were too advantageous for the British Nation: Whereas the Cession of Canada is the only one that can be said to be greatly advantageous to Great-Britain. The North American Fishing therefore, and the Possession of Canada, are at Stake for which the Game now begun to be played.

In this Time of Danger, in which not only the Character of this Province, but the very being of its Possessions and Rights may be determined, I call upon you to exert the best of your Powers to assist the King in working out your own Preservation. Whatever other Times may have been, This, I am sure, is a critical one. The Events of War are in the Hands of God, and, whatever they are, you must submit to them. But it is your own Power to secure to yourselves the Credit of having assisted the King's Arms with all that was required of you, and to avoid the Imputation of having by your Deficiency or your Example occasioned the Defeat of his great Purposes of establishing this Country in perpetual

Peace and Security.

Gentlemen of the House of Representatives,

I must again recommend to your Consideration the Subject of the Letter of the Secretary of State, which I communicated to you last Session, and desire that you would proceed thereon, and compleat what remains to be done. The Assurance you gave me at the End of last Session leave me no room to doubt that you will do this in a Manner effectual to the Service, and credible to yourselves. As nothing more is required of you than your Proportion, so I hope that, at this Time, you will offer nothing less. What that Proportion will be easily estimated: According to the Calculation, which is made by Comparison only, it so little exceeds what you voted last Year, that it is not worth while for so small a Difference, to leave it in the Power of any one to say that you have not contributed your full share to the common Cause.

I must also inform you, that I have received another Letter from his Majesty's Secretary of State, conceived in the most forcible Terms, to induce you to assist the recruiting His Majesty's Regular Forces as such Conditions as in such a Manner as Sir Jeffrey Amherst shall Propose: That his Excellency the General has explained, by desiring that you would grant the same Bounty as you gave the Provincial Recruits for raising what is considerable one from His Majesty. This Requisition is considered by the Secretary of State as an Equivalent for third Part of your former Quota of Men, which His Majesty has now remitted, tho' it makes but a small part of the Expence of such third; and as the whole Requisition is reduced to an inconsiderable Sum of Money only, and the Demand hath been complied with by the Neighbouring Provinces, I persuade myself that it will not meet with any Difficulty on your Part.

Gentleman of the Council and Gentlemen of the House of Representatives,

After what I had said before, it will be needless to add any Thing more to persuade you to a chearful and ready Compliance with what is required of you. Upon this and all other Occasions,

I shall constantly lay before you such information and Observations as I shall think will continue to your judging and determining for the best. But I shall not dictate to you: I shall leave you to deliberate for Yourselves. As I desire not to rob you of the Merit of them.

All I have to ask is, that you will consider what your own Interest, your own Honour require you, and act accordingly, Such a Procedure must include all the Requisitions of his Majesty.

Council-Chamber April 12, 1762.

Fra. Bernard.

New-York April 22. Yesterday arrived the Sloop Robert, Capt. _____, from Barbados, By a Letter from thence, dated the 28th March, we are informed that Admiral Rodney with all the ships of War except three were gone from Matineco to Jamaica. That the Frigate from England touched there and went after them: That a Vessel from Bristol in 7 Weeks was arrived, and brought Advice, That Admiral Pocock with 5 Sail of the Line, and Lord Albemarle with 6000 Troops were immediately to proceed to Martineco, and with the Forces there, attack the Havannah (Capital of Cuba).

PHILADELPHIA April 22. On Friday last Captain Taylor arrived here from Martinico and confirms the account of the Inhabitants of St. Lucia and St. Vincents, &c. surrendered to General Monckton. He likewise informs us, That Admiral Rodney, with eight sail of the Line, was gone to Jamaica: That the French Regulars that belonged to Martinico had sailed for Old France: That the late French Governor of Guadaloupe was gone to England: and that Mr. De la Touche was to sail for France.

CHARLESTOWN S. Carolina April 22. Captain Joliss, in the Ship Tartar, arrived this day. He sailed from Portsmouth, February 24th, with a large Fleet for the West-Indies, under convoy of his Majesty's ship Oxford, of 70 Guns, Capt. Arbutnot, and the Edgar, of 60 Guns. On the 9th of March they saw four sail standing to the Westward, which the Edgar chased, and about 12 o'clock at night returned with one of them as a prize which proved to be a French transport with

200 troops on board for Louisiana, then with three others that escaped, five days from Rochfort. The number of Troops on board the four transports was 800, all destine for Louisiana, and without convoy. The commander in chief of the French troops, and a great many officers, were on board the prize, which Capt, Arbutnot arrived along with him.

Annapolis Maryland April 22. On Tuesday last week just after sun set, as Uriah Wirt, an elderly man of 65 years of age, and his son were travelling from Virginia to Fredericks Town, in Frederick County, about 6 miles from the town, they were attack'd by a man on horseback, who demanded their money, and almost at the same instant, fired his pistol at the old man; the bullet went in at his shoulder, and into his breast, of which he died in about two hours; the murderer who went by the name of Crosby, made off, but is since taken and confined in goal.

BOSTON April 23. For recruiting his Majesty's Forces in America.

All able-bodied Volunteers above the age of Eighteen and under Forty Years, who are willing to engage in his Majesty's Regiments in America, to serve during the present War, or until the said Regiments shall return to Europe, shall receive the Province Bounty of Seven Pounds, Lawful Money, and also his Majesty's Bounty of Five Pounds, New-York Currency, equal to three pounds Fifteen Shillings Lawful Money. Amounting to Ten Pounds Fifteen Shillings Lawful Money; and immediately after entering upon such Service will be compleatly cloathed.

All those who are willing to take the Benefit of those advantageous Terms may apply to the Provincial Officers who are or shall be employed to recruit for this Service, or repair to Castle William, where they will be well received and immediately provided for according to the Proposal. By Order of his Excellency,

Tho. Goldthwait Sec'r at War.

BOSTON April 26. By his Excellency Francis Bernard, Esq; Captain-General and Governor in Chief, in and over His Majesty's Province of Massachusetts-Bay in New-England, Vice Admiral of the same.

A PROCLAMATION

Whereas there is undoubted Proof that the Enemy hath hether to been supplied with Provisions from Divers Parts on North-America, which infamous Practice if suffered to be continued, must contribute very much to prolong a War, already carried to a great Length. And whereas it is probable that the Intentions of the French and Spaniards, in large armaments which they are making in the West-Indies, will be defeated if British Provisions can be with held from them: for which purpose an Embargo upon Provisions hath already been laid in Great-Britain and in Ireland: and his Excellency the Commander in Chief of his Majesty's Forces in North-America, hath requested that I would effectually prohibit the Exportation of Provisions from the Ports in this Province. And whereas there is great Reason to believe that the Enemy has been furnished with Gun Powder and Ammunition from some Parts in North-America in Defiance of the Laws:

I have thought fit to, and I do by and with the advice of his Majesty's Council, lay Embargo upon all Ships and Vessels within the Ports of this Province, which are or shall laden with Provisions of any Kind, excepting such, as so much as shall be necessary for the subsistence of the several Crews of such Ships or Vessels, according to a bill to be allowed and signed by the Collector of Chief Officer of the Customs, and also upon all Gun Powder, Ammunition and Warlike Stores, excepting nevertheless what shall be permitted by me upon a Certificate of the intended Use or Destination thereof. And I strictly order and enjoin all Officers of the Customs and Naval Officers, and all others whom it may concern, that they take Care that this Order be carried out into Execution. And All Magistrates and Civil Officers, are hereby required to be aiding and assisting to them in so doing.

Given at the Council Chamber in Boston, the Twenty-sixth Day of April 1762, in the Second Year of the Reign of our Sovereign Lord george the Third, by the Grace of God, of Great Britain, France and Ireland, King, Defender of the Faith, &c. Fra. Bernard.

By His Excellency's Command, A. Oliver, Secr'y.

BOSTON Aptil 26. By the Hartford Post which came on Wednesday last, we are informed, that on Friday Night, a House at Windsor, on the West Side of Connecticut River, was consumed by Fire, with all Goods that were therein, it was occasioned by a young Man's leaving a Candle burning near his Bed, which catch'd the Cloaths on Fire while he was asleep, and almost suffocated him before he awaked: He immediately called up the Family: A young Woman lodging in one of the Chambers not awaking, he ran up to save her; but the Fire got to such a Height before they could return, that they both perished in the Flames.

Capt. Chambers in a Schooner from the West-Indies for this Place was cast away on the Caucases's, and Vessel and Cargo lost; the People were taken up and carried to Philadelphia, from which Place they came in a Sloop that arrived here last Week from thence.

We hear that the Sloop Olive, Capt. Cushing, from this Place, is arrived at Maryland after a tedious passage of 53 Days.

We learn from Halifax, that Captain Abbot in a Sloop belonging to Salem, bound for the West-Indies, was cast away on Cape Sable, but that most of the Cargo was saved; 'tis said one Man was froze to Death.

NEW-YORK April 26. Friday being the Anniversary of St. George, his Excellency Sir Jeffrey Amherst gave a Ball to the Ladies and Gentlemen, all very richly dressed; and 'tis said the Entertainment was the most elegant ever seen in America.

We can assure the Publick, That above a Month ago 8 Sail of small Privateers, lay ready to put out from the Havannah, in order to cruise on the Coast of America, as soon as War was declared against England; The Reason of it's not being declared was, the Spanish Packet from Old Spain fell into the Hands of the English with the Dispatches on board for S. America, &c.

MAY 1762

BOSTON May 2. Received from New-York the following Advices, dated April 26, 1762.

By Captain Marshall, arrived here from Barbados, we received a Copy of the Articles of Capitulation for the Island of Martineco in French; of which the following is an exact translation.

Artiles of Capitulation, for the Island of Martineco, Between their Excellencies Admiral Rodney, and General Monckton, and his Excellency Monsieure La Vassor La Touche, Commandant General for the Most Christian Majesty, in the Windward Islands in America.

Preliminary Articles.

A Suspention of Arms shall be agreed on for fifteen Days; at the Expiration of which the following Capitulation shall take Place, If no Succours arrive.

Answer. Twenty four Hours shall be granted the General to accede to the Terms offered him, to be computed from the Time of Monsieurs De Bouran and De la Touche's arrival at St. Pierre; and if he accepts of them, the Troops of his Britannic Majesty shall immediately take Possession of all the Forts and Posts which their General shall judge proper to occupy.

ARTICLE I.

All the Forts and Posts of the Island of Martineco shall be evacuated by his Most Christian Majesty's Troops whether Regular or Militia: They shall march out with four Field Pieces, their Arms, two Charges each, Drums beating, Colours flying, and all the Honours of War; after which his Britannic Majesty's Troops shall take Possession of the same Forts and Posts.

Answer. The Troops and the Inhabitants shall march out of their Garrisons and Posts with their Arms, Drums beating, and Colours Flying:

four Pieces of Cannon, with 2 Charges to each, and two Charges per Man shall be allowed to the Troops, provided the Inhabitants immediately lay down their Arms, and that all the Forts, Garrisons, Posts, and Batteries of Cannon or Mortars, with all Arms and Ammunition, and Utensils of War, shall be delivered to Persons appointed to receive them.

Art. III. A sufficient Number of Vessels and Provisions shall be furnished at the Expence of his Brittanic Majesty, to carry the regular Troops aforesaid, with their Officers, Arms, and four Field Pieces, Baggage, and Effects to the Island of Granada.

Answer. Granted to be carried to France only.

Art. III. Mr. Rouille Governor, and Monsieurs the Lieutenant Governor, of the King in the Island of Matineco, the General Officers, and the Engineers, shall be conveyed to France in Vessels, provided at the Expence of his Britannic Majesty.

Answer. Granted.

Art. IV. A Vessel, and all the necessary Provisions, shall also be provided at the Expence of his Britannic Majesty, to convoy M. De la Touche Commandant General of his Most Christian Majesty's Windward Islands in America, together with his Lady and Family, and all their Effects to the Island of Granada.

Answer. Granted to be carried to France, the Granades being actually blocked up.

Art. V. Mr. DeRochemore, Inspector of the Artillery in this Island, shall likewise be conveyed to Granada in same Vessel, with all the Persons dependent on him in the King's Service, their Domestics and Effects.

Answer, Granted to be carried to France.

Art. VI. Two Commissaries shall be appointed, one of each Nation, to make an exact Inventory of all Effects belonging to his Most Christian Majesty, in the Arsenals, Magazines, and on the Batteries, and in general of all the arms, utensils and ammunitions of War, to be delivered into the Hands of his Britannic Majesty's Commanding Officer.

Answer. Granred.

Art. VII. The Merchandize, except Arms and Ammunition of War, found in the said Inventory for any other purpose than to be restored to their proper Owners.

Answer. All Utensils of War, and other Things used as such, shall belong to his Britannic Majesty.

Art. VIII. All Prisoners made during the Seige or at Sea before the Siege, of what Nation or Quality soever, shall be mutually restored; and these made in the Citadel, if Troops, shall have the same Terms granted to the other Troops; and, if Militia, the same Terms with the other Militia.

Answer. These Troops shall have the same Terms granted to the others, and the Militia shall be set at Liberty, after the Capitulation is signed.

Art. IX. All Free Negroes and Mulattoes, made Prisoners of War, shall be treated as such, and restored to their Liberties as other Prisoners are.

Answer. All Negroes taken with Arms in their Hands, shall be reported Slaves ——— The rest is Granted.

Art. X. The Sieur Nadau Du Tiel, De la Pottorie and Cornette, State Prisoners, shall also be carried to the Granades in Vessels, at the Expence of his Brittanic Majesty, in order to be delivered up to Mr. Le Vessor De la Touche.

Answer. Messieurs De la Pottorie and Cornette shall be delivered up, if they fall into our Hands; but Nadau having our Promise, when he was made Prisoner, to procure him a Passage to France, and to grant him a convenient Time to regulate his Affairs; we accordingly grant him three Months for the Purpose, from the Date of these present.

Art. XI. The Island of Matineco shall remain in His Britannic Majesty's Possession until its Fate shall be determined by a Treaty made between the two Powers, without the Inhabitants being obliged in any Case, to take up Arms against the King of France, his Allies, or any other Power.

Answer. They become Subjects of Great-Britain

and shall take the Oath of Allegiance; but they shall not be obliged to take up Arms against his Most Christian Majesty until, by Treaty or Peace, the Fate of the Island shall be determined.

Art. XII. All the Inhabitants of Martineco whether present or absent, even those that are in the Service of his Most Christian Majesty; and also all Religious Houses and Communities, shall be maintained and protected in the Possession of their Goods and Property, whether moveable or fixed, and all their Negroes and Vessels, and in general all their Effects; whether the said Goods, Moveables and Effects, are found in Martineco, or in any other Island; and the Slaves which have been taken from them during the Siege, shall be restored.

Answer. The Inhabitants, as well as the Religious Orders, shall be protected in the Possession of their Goods; and as they become subjects of Great Britain, they will enjoy all the Privileges which the Inhabitants of the Leeward Islands Enjoy; what relates to the Slaves, is answered in the ninth Article.

Art. XIII. The Vessels, of what sort, belonging to Martineco, which are actually at Sea, or in neutral Ports, whether they be armed or otherwise, shall have Liberty to return into the Ports and Roads of this Island, upon a Declaration to be made by their Owners, that they will order them to return, and shall give Security that they shall not take any Attempt upon any English Vessel; and that upon such Declaration Passports shall be issued for their safe return.

Answer. Refused, foreign to the Capitulation; but all Remonstrances that may be made to us on that Head hereafter, shall be regulated agreeable to Equity, and the Laws of War.

Art. XIV. The Inhabitants of Martineco shall enjoy the same and public Exercise of their Religion; the Priests and Religious of both the Sexes shall be protected in their public Exercise of their Functions, and in the Possessions of their Prerogatives, and Exemptions.

Answer. Granted.

Art. XV. The Judges, as well superior as

inferior, shall also be protected in their Functions, Privileges and Prerogatives; and they shall continue to distribute Justice to the Inhabitants of this Island, according to the Laws, Ordinances, Customs and Usages hitherto observed. No Stranger shall be permitted to sit in the Council as a Judge; but if any Place in the Magistracy becomes vacant the Superior Council of Martineco only shall fill it up: and that he, that they shall chuse, shall exercise that Function, until it shall be otherwise ordered by one of the two Courts, after they have fixed the State of the Island by a Treaty.

Answer. They become Subjects of Great Britain; but they shall be governed by their Laws, until his Brittanic Majesty's Pleasure is known.

Art. XVI. Mr. Le Baron De Huart, Commander of the Militia of this Island, and also Mr. de Bouran, Major General, shall be transported to the Island of Granada, in the same Vessel in which the Royal Grenadiers are embarked, together with their Domestics, Effects, and all the Officers of these Troops. The said Officers shall be permitted to collect their Effects that are in the different Parts of the Island, and sufficient Time allowed them for that Purpose; the Inhabitants shall be ordered to pay these Officers what they owe them, and the Officers shall do likewise be obliged to discharge the Debts they have contracted in the Island.

Answer. They shall be sent to France the rest granted.

Art. XVII. All the Land and Sea Officers that are in this Island, whether in actual Service, or by Permission, shall have the Terms of one Year to regulate their affairs.

Answer. A convenient Time shall be allowed to these who have Settlements in this Island, which the usual restrictions, and they shall obtain of Mr. Du la Touche, their Governor General their Discharge.

Art. XVIII. The Noblesse shall continue to enjoy all Privileges and Exemptions they have always had.

Answer. Granted, provided it is not incompatible with the Laws of Great Britain.

Art. XIX. The Slaves who have been enfranchised during the Siege, or to whom their Freedom hath been promised, being reported and declared free, shall peaceably enjoy their Liberty.

Answer. Granted.

Art. XX. The Poll-Tax, and Duties on Imports and Exports, and in general all the Duties established in this Island shall continue to be paid for the future, on the same Footing as Heretofore.

Answer. Answered in the Fifteenth Article.

Art. XXI. As the Glory and Interest of every Prince requires him to Honour in the most public Manner, with his special Protection, all those whose Characters are conspicuous for Zeal. Love and Fidelity to their King; it is therefore but just, that all the Materials furnished by the Colony, both before and during the Siege, for the Support thereof, should still be considered to be as much the Debts of the Colony, as they would, or ought to have been, had it remained in its former Condition; and consequently, that the Price of the Materials shall not cease to be reputed Debts which this Colony ought to discharge, into whose Hands soever it passes by the Fortune of War; and for the Dignity of his Britannic Majesty to grant them Protection in order to their being paid out of the first Funds raised, as well by the Poll-Tax as from the Duties on the Exports and Imports; for which Purpose, the State of these Debts shall be adjusted by Mr. De la Riviere, Intendant of the Windward Islands in America.

Answer. It shall be regulated by the Generals of both Powers, being a Matter foreign to the Capitulation.

Art. XXII. Upon the same principle and considering the Necessity this Colony is under of a speedy Supply of Provisions, it hath been likewise judged reasonable, that those Merchants of the Town of St. Pierre who, in Persuance of the Intendant Mr. De la Riviere's Orders, had entered into the necessary Measures and Engagements for importing Provisions from Neutral Islands, shall be permitted to fulfil their Engagements, as well to prevent the Damage they would suffer, as to procure, without Loss of Time, Supplies for this Island; and therefore two Months shall be granted them, for the Signing presents, to fulfil their Contracts: ——— But, to prevent Abuse in this Respect, M. De la Riviere shall give Certificates of the Nature and Quantity of the Provisions which he ordered to be provided in the Neutral Ports; and as he promised and granted, that the said Importation should be exempted from all the Duties, that said Exemption shall take Place agreeable to his Promise, being equally for the advantage of the Colony and the Merchant.

Answer. All the Provisions which Neutrals engaged to import, to supply the troops of his Most Christian Majesty and the Colony, shall be deemed good Prizes, if they fall into the Power of his Britannic's Vessels; and all Contracts made with Neutrals before the Reduction of the Island being void, no Commerce shall be carried on for the Future but in English Vessels.

Art. XXIII. Mr. La Vassor De la Touche shall be permitted to put five Inhabitants on board the same Vessels that carry his Most Christian Majesty's Troops. His reason for demanding this is, that it is for the Interest of all the Powers to grant no Protection to such as violate the Obedience and Fidelity they owe their King.

Answer. It cannot be granted, since they are already under the Protection of his Britannic Majesty.

Art. XXIV. Sufficient Time shall be granted to Mr. De la Riviere, Intendant, and Mr. Guinard, Commissary-Comptroller of the Marines in this Island; to adjust every Branch of their respective Business, and to do what may be Absolutely necessary in that Respect. A Vessel and Provisions shall be afterward furnished at the Expence of his Britannic Majesty, to carry to the Island of Granada the said Sieur Intendant, his Lady, Children, Secretaries, Domestics and all their Effects that said Sieur Commissary Comptroller of the Marine shall pass in the same Vessel to the same Place.

Answer. Granted; & to be Afterwards sent to France.

Art. XXV. The Persons employed in the Management and administration of the Domain of the Marine, and Receiver of the Revenue, who incline to go to France shall be transported with their Effects in Vessels; at the Expence of his Britannic Majesty.

Answer. Granted.

Art. XXVI. The Records shall immediately be replaced in their proper Repositories, and his Majesty's Governor shall grant the necessary Protection for that Purpose.

Answer. They shall be delivered to Persons appointed by the General to receive them.

Art. XXVII. As to the Books of the accounts they shall be put into the Hands of the Accountants, that they may be able to draw out their accounts, and have them proved and discharged.

Answer. Granted.

Art. XXVIII. The Inhabitants, Merchants, and others, shall be permitted to transport themselves, Negroes and Effects to St. Domingo or Louisiana, at their own Expence.

Answer. Granted.

Art. XXIX. If any Grenadiers should attempt to remain an the Island or to make their Escape, the necessary Protection and assistance shall be given, to prevent their deserting & to embark them completely.

Answer. Granted; except in particular Cases.

Art. XXX. Vessels of Trade belonging to French Merchants in Europe, which are actually in the Ports and Roads of this Island, shall be reserved for the proper Owners with Liberty either to sell them, or send them to France in their Ballast.

Answer. Refused, for all Privateers, and all Vessels trading to distant Ports; Granted for all Vessels trading in the different Ports of this Island.

Given at Martineco, the 12th of February, 1762.
(Signed) La Vassor De la Touche.
G. B. Rodney Robert Monckton.

BOSTON May 3. The General Assembly of the Province of New-Jersey, in their last Session agreed to raise a Provincial Regiment of six hundred and sixty-six Men only; but the Scarcity of Men among them, they say, laid them under a necessity of not complying with his Majesty's Requisition for Recruiting the Regular Forces.

In Weatherfield a Child rocking an Infant about 3 Months old, overset the Cradle and turned the Child into a Fire, by which it was so much burnt that it died in a few Hours.

From London, John Leach, School-Master, at the North End of Boston, Teaches Arithmetic both Vulgar and Decimal, Geometry, Trigonometry, Menserations of Superficies, solids, Heights and Distance, both accessible & inaccessible, Surveying, Gauging, Navigation, &c. &c. ⸺ The Use of the Globes and Charts, with the Description, Use, & Construction of the several instruments used in the above Branches; also Drawing as for as it is useful and necessary for a compleat Sea Artist, in taking Prospects of Land and Surveying Harbours; from several Years Experience to his Majesty's Navy, and 3 Voyages in the Honourable East-India Company's Employ.

N. B. Said Leach Surveys Lots both in Town and Country, and Draws Plans: ⸺ He whole performs in the same familiar concise and practicle Method as taught in the City of London, & as cheap as by any Teacher in North America.

NEW-YORK May 3. The Schooner Garland, Capt. Symmes, from Barbados to Maryland, was taken on the Virginia coast, by a privateer Brig and Sloop from Cape Francis, and ransomed for 1000 Dollars, but was afterwards lost about ten leagues to the southward of Virginia.

At the Supreme Court last week, John Lickens and Mary White, on indictment for street-robbery were convicted, and sentenced to be executed on Friday the 14th instant.

BOSTON May 5. Province of Massachusetts-Bay. The Officers belonging to Colonel Saltinstall's and Colonel Ingersol's Regiments are notified to march immediately all the Men they have inlisted, that are passed Muster, and received their Bounty: ⸺ Those whose residence to the Eastward of Worcester or near Worcester, are to Rendezvous at Worcester on Friday the 14th current, those to the Westward of Worcester and all the Residence of said Regiment to Rendezvous at Springfield on Tuesday the 18th Corrent. The Officers are desired to let no Time be lost in getting their Men to the said Places of Rendezvous. By Order of His Excellency,

                Tho. Goldthwait, Sec. at War.

NEW-HAVEN May 9. Last Monday a very unhappy Accident happened at the Muster of the Militia in North Haven. After the Arms and Accoutriments of the Military Company in that Place were view'd by the Officers for the sake of Meriment, it was agreed to have a Mock Indian Fight, and a Part of the Company dress'd in an Indian Dress, and encounter'd the other part of the Company; when one Enoch Ivea, a young Man about 18 who was one of the Indian Party, had his Windpipe, Jugular Vein, and Throat tore in such a Manner by the Discharge of a Gun, that was close by him, that he expir'd in an instant.

The same Day, a Man at Ripten had the Calf shot off one of his Legs, in a Frolic of the same kind.

BOSTON May 10. Monday last a Detachment of 500 Men, belonging to Colonel Hoar's Regiment embarked from Castle William on board a Number of Transports and sail'd for Nova-Scotia; the Remainder of said Regiment will soon proceed for the same Place; the two other Provincial Regiments are destined to the Westward, one of them commanded by Col. Saltinstall, the other by col. Ingersol. The whole of his Majesty's Requisition for the Provincial Service was compleated by the first of May, and his Excellency's Orders were immediately issued for inlisting Recruits for his Majesty's Regular Regiments in North-America, agreeable to his Majesty's Requisition for that Purpose.

BOSTON May 10. By Capt. Lander, who arrived at Salem last Wednesday in 27 Days from Martinico, who have Advice, That a Number of British Troops were embarking on board Transports there destined for some Expedition: Admiral Rodney with his Fleet were at Antigua: Col. Murray, and several other Officers died there lately.

——— A Number of French Privateers were cruizing between Martinico & the Granades and had taken 7 or 8 Vessels a few Days before Captain

Lander sailed.

We hear from Martha's Vineyard that on the 27th of last Month, the House of Mr. John Baxter, Tavernkeeper of Home's Hole, was consumed by Fire, with most of the Household Furniture and Goods that was therein. ⸺ It was occasioned by a Defect in the Chimney; the whole was consumed in about 8 Minutes.

Hollister in Middlesex County, April 7th 1762.

Whereas my Wife Phebe that had sometime ago eloped from me, and contracts Cost against me contrary to my Knowledge and Consent; and has done so since her Return; Therefore I warn and forbid every Man or Person, that they do not trade with her. This is done with Continuance of the former Crying-down and Warning set up. I will not pay them.   Abraham Cozens.

NEW-YORK May 10. The Regular Forces are daily arriving here from Quebec, Montreal, &c. and encamping on Governor's or Nutten Island, near which the Transports are Rendezvousing for the ready reception if the Troops.

Early on Sunday morning the 2d inst. a fire broke out in the store of Capt. Lewis at Huntington, which entirely destroyed it, and the dwelling houses adjoining, together with all the goods, household furniture, &c. to the amount of about 1800 Pounds. In the store were a quantity of spirituous liquors, and several casks of gun-powder, which increased the flames so violent that render'd it impossible to be extinguished; and the people in the house escaped with utmost difficulty, some of them being much burnt.

Having mentioned in a former Paper the foundering of Capt. Pearne of Portsmouth, at Sea, the following Particulars are extracted from his Journal of that Misfortune, viz.

"On the 14th of January last, we sail'd from Portsmouth in New-Hampshire, bound for Barbados, and had fine weather till the 21st, at night, when a hard gale of wind at S. W. split our foresail to pieces, after which the wind veered to the W. and then at N. W. we run under our reefed square sail most of the time till the 25th. In the morning the wind being S. W. we

ship'd a large sea, which threw the vessel almost on her beam ends, washed over part of the deck load, and made her so leaky, that we could not keep her free with one pump, and the other we could not work, which obliged us to throw overboard the Lumber on deck; yet notwithstanding on the 27th in the morning she sunk all under except the quarterdeck and part of her bows, being then in lat. 35 40. long. 56. We saved about three pounds of bread, 25 pounds of flour, with 60 gallons of water, with beef, pork and salt fish, enough, but 3 Days after had 40 gallons of water wash'd overboard which obliged us to come to the short allowance of half a pint a day, having 5 men besides myself on board. We endeavoured to keep her head before the wind, which continued to the westward 14 or 15 days and most of the time had gales; we had not two gallons of water on board at this time, and we were bro't to the yet smaller allowance of six spoonsful, and about one ounce and a half of flour for 24 hours. Three days after was a very hard rain, when we procured 16 gallons of water, which was the chief means of preserving our lives. —— In this condition we remain'd till the 20th of February, when my people all gave out, the sea constantly breaking over us, and washing overboard almost every thing we had saved. —— We saw plenty of fish, but could catch none till the 24th, when we catch'd two fine dolphins. The same day we saw a vessel, which made towards us, and on coming up, proved to be the Enterprize man of war, who took us all on board we being almost spent, and but one gallon of water and three pounds of flour left. myself and two men having bad fevers. —— Capt. Houlston and all the officers on board treated us in the most kind and friendly manner possible, and we are now in a fair way of recovery, tho' low in flesh."   William Pearne.
  BOSTON May 17. Province of Massachusetts-Bay.
  All Soldiers belonging to His Majesty's Provincial Forces, who have not joined their Regiments, are required to proceed immediately to Springfield, otherwise they will be deem'd Deserters and prosecuted against as such.

By Order od his Excellency
Tho. Goldthwait Sec. of War.

NEW-YORK May 17. Last Wednesday night one William Conberford, a Provincial soldier, jump'd from one of the Transports into the river and was drowned.

NEW-YORK May 20. Yesterday arrived here the Charming Betsey, Capt. Richardson, in 23 Days from Jamaica, by whom we hear, that his Majesty's Ship the Fowey, having about 100 Men on board, had had a very smart Engagement with a Spanish Frigate of near 300 Men, which at last was taken and brought to Jamaica. Commodore Douglass was there with 11 Or 12 Sail of the Line, besides Frigates, &c. but our Forces were not arrive from Martinico.

HALIFAX May 20. At One o'Clock on Tuesday morning a Fire broke out in the House of Mr. Thomas Day in Hollis Street, and before it could be stop'd consumed four other Houses in the same Row, the fire had got such a Head before it was discovered, that an Apprentice Girl about 15 Years and a Boy about 9 Years old, both perish'd in the flames, and it was with great difficulty that Mr. and Mrs Day saved their Lives; it is imagined this unhappy accident was occasioned either by a Squib or Wad of a Gun, falling into the Yard among the shavings, which communicated to the kitchen.

New-London May 21. Capt. Burnham arrived here on Monday last, in 30 Days from Barbados, he informs that two large French Transport Ships bound from Bourdeaux to the Missisippi laden with Warlike Stores and Men, were lately taken by the Acteon Frigate, and sent to Barbados: They sailed from Bourdeaux in Company with two other Ships bound for the same Place, the whole having upwards of a Thousand Soldiers on board. Two Spanish Ships have also been lately taken by our Cruisers, and carried into the before said Place, which were Condemned.

BOSTON May 24. To the Printer of the Boston Evening Post.

As the Spaniards have thought proper to force us into a war with them, it behoves us to prosecute it to all points to our greatest Advantage.

Now the main points that I think we ought to have in view, are the compleating and securing our Empire in North America.

The Empire will be compleat and entirely secured by our acquisition of Spanish Florida, and French Louisiana: And there is little more necessary for the getting those two provinces into our possessions, than the taking of New-Orleans, and what other French settlements may be near the mouth of the Missisippi, and of St. Augustine on the promontory of Florida. The Possession of the shores of the two provinces must soon make us masters of the interior countries, which are but thinly inhabited, and if once in our possession, I do not think it can be possible for the French and Spaniards together ever to retake them from us; so, by our persisting in retaining them at all event for ever, we shall complete our empire in North America; and fix its security on a firm basis.

These conquest being made and possessed, they will remain a large and secure barrier of Indian nations between the Compleat body of British settlements in North America, and the great Spanish Empire in Mexico; and such a distribution of territory, with the total exclusion of the French, we will be the only means likely to procure a lasting peace on that continent, as well as for securing the prosperity and power of this Kingdom, and for enabling it to discharge its public Debts, and thereby secure its great commerce throughout the worlds.

Whatever views besides may be entertained by our ministry, I cannot help thinking this ought to be their primary object; as what all the pursuits will be the most important to obtain: because it will fix our colony security beyond the reach of rival States in future times to endanger; and add such a strength in numbers of people, in trade and in navigation, will establish our power uncontroulable on the Ocean. The great game of policy I shall therefore think is now fairly in our hands, and, if played with true wisdom, it will infallibly become our own. We shall rise up with the whole stake for which we have, with our worst enemy, so long contended.

By this Secondary conquest, Canada only can become valuable; and, if it is atchieved the glories of the present Administration will exceed those of the past, for they will not only add to our possessions a much larger extent of Territory but also give security to the whole, and such advantages to their country as it never before received.

BOSTON May 24. The Regiments of Provincial Troops under Col. Hoar, destined for his Majesty's Service at Nova Scotia, are sailed for Halifax: Colonel Saltonstall and Colonel Ingersol's Regiments are on the Road to Albany, destined also for his Majesty's Service at the Westward. ——— Besides these Troops which have been raised and compleated some Time here are a Number of Recruits for his Majesty's Regular Regiments in the Province who are embarked in a few Days from Castle William for New-York.

Tuesday last just before dark, a Boy about 4 Years of Age, fell from a Wharf at the North End, into the Dock, and was drowned.

To be sold a Parcel of likely healthy Negroes, both Male and Female from Ten years of age to Twenty; Imported the last Week from Africa. Enquire of Capt. Wickham on board the Sloop Diamond, now lying at the Wharf adjoining to John Avery's Distilling-House, near the White Horse.

Boston May 24. [The Advices from South-Carolina, of the 28th of April last relating to the Indian Affairs, are; ——— That all the Lower Towns which were destroyed are again settled, and the Indians have been obliged to eat Horseflesh for some time. ——— That this is the firmest Peace that ever was made with the Cherokees, the Chain is bright, the Path is Strait, the Talk is good, the Hatchet is buried and the Sun shines."]

NEW-YORK May 24. Saturday last Capt. Williams arrived here in 20 days from St. Croux, about 10 leagues off Spanish Town, ne was chaced by three sloops one of which came up with him, and a smart engagement ensued, when Capt. Williams gave him a broadside within pistol-shot, then tack'd and gave him a second, which put the Dons in such confusion, that after giving Captain Williams on broadside, and several vollies of small arms, with many showers of arrows, they tho't proper to leave him. Capt. Williams had only 8 guns and 9 men, one of which, his mate, having receiv'd a mortal wound by an arrow near 6 feet long, died in 5 days. The privateer mounted 12 guns and 160 men.

The 19th of May, Capt. Williams in Lon. 71, 24. Lat. 37, 17., saw 17 sail standing to the eastward, and on the 20th, in 20 fathom water, fell in with King George of Boston, Captain Hallowell.

CHARLESTOWN S. Carolina May 29. The Cherokee continue to make excuses to void delivering up their English prisoners, according to treaty, and notwithstanding their profession of friendship, there is reason to suppose that they have been endeavouring to renew their treaty with the French at New Orleans. That already they have gone beyond the limits on the hunting ground, and have intimated that they shall not be satisfied unless their prisoners are restored, and a trade granted them.

By Capt. Young, arrived last night from St. Christophers, we are informed, that Sir George Pococke, with 12 ships of the line, and 12,000 land forces, from Martinico, called at that Island the 8th instant for the Cock and London fleets for Jamaica, and sailed with them the same day, on the intended expedition. He likewise informs us, that a Spanish privateer from Porto-Rico was taken and carried to St. Christophers, and that they have 36 out from the same place, most of whose crew are French. One of them chased Capt. Young into Anguilla.

M. Blenac's squadron lay at the Cape with their yards and top mast struck, their seamen having deserted almost as soon as they got in. They were in great want of masts, naval stores and other necessaries.

BOSTON May 31. Thursday last His Excellency the Governor was pleased to open the present Session, with the following Speech, viz.

Gentlemen of the Council, and Gentlemen of the House of Representatives.

You are met together at a very interesting Time, when probably by Events even now issuing from the Womb of Fate, the future Fortune of this Country will be finally fixed. In this state of Uncertainty we can still resort to the comfortable reflection, that, as the same steadyness which has hitherto directed his Majesty's Councils, and the same Vigor which has conducted his Arms still prevail, they still continue to produce the same Effects.

The King's paternal Care for the Preservation of the Rights and immunities of his People, seems still to be favoured by the King of Kings, who if he hath permitted new Enemies to rise up against Us, hath also turned the Hearts of other Princes, whose Power has been hitherto inimical to our Causes. Tho' by the Intrigues of our Enemies the seat of the War may be changed, there is now doubt but we shall still maintain our superiority; and we may promise ourselves that His Majesty will yet be enabled (perhaps at no great Distance in Time) to establish Peace upon Terms equally advantageous and permanent.

But whatever shall be the Event of the War, it must be no small Satisfaction to us that this Province hath contributed no small share to the Support of it. Every Thing that has been required of it hath been and readily complied with: And the Execution of the Powers committed to me for raising the Provincial Troops hath been as full and compleat as the Grant of them was. Never before were the Regiments so easily levied, so well composed, and so early in the Field as they have been this Year. The common People seemed to be animated with the spirit of the General Court, and to vie with them in the Readiness to serve their King.

Gentlemen of the House of Representatives,

The ample Provisions which has been already made, leave me nothing to ask you for the immediate Service of the King. It is probable that some Occasion may occur, or some Disapointment may happen, which may require a further Provision. But even these do not appear at present; if they should, I shall no doubt on your ready Compliance with what I shall have occasion to ask you.

Gentlemen of the Council, and Gentlemen of the House of Representatives.

The Business of this Session will be confined chiefly to the domestic Concerns of this Province; and these alone will afford you an ample Field. Each Matters as shall more immediately belong to me. I shall from Time to time advertise you of. But I cannot now excuse myself, at this your first Meeting, proposing some general Principles, which at all Times, it will become to recommend to you to attend to. Let your council be founded in Loyalty and Public Spirit, and conducted by moderation and Impartiality; Unanimity and Expedition will necessarily follow; and the general Welfare and your particular order will be the Fruit of the whole.

    Council Chamber,
    May 27, 1762.   Fra. Bernard.

BOSTON May 31. Last Friday one Mr. Pearce of Dorchester fell from the Scaffold of a House which he was shingling, and broke one of his Legs, and otherwise bruised him, so that his Life is Despaired of.

Last Friday Evening, as Mr. William Jackson, Son of Colonel Joseph Jackson, of this Town, was going thro' the Street to his Father's House he fell down in a Fit, and notwithstanding all possible Means were used to save his Life, he expir'd in about 4 hours, to the great Grief of the Family, and all his Acquaintance. ——— He was in his Sixteenth Year of Age; a young man of very promising Genius, and a natural Sweetness of Disposition, which rendered him agreeable to all who knew him.

The same Night a valuable Negro Servant in the same Family was seized with a Convulsion Fit, and expired Yesterday morning.

JUNE 1762

Crown-Point June 3. The following Speech was made by Captain Nixon, to the Massachusetts Troops at this Place.

Fellow Soldiers,

As the Province of Massachusetts-Bay has voted a Number of Troops for his Majesty's Service this Year, in which Number you are included, and has directed me to assure an Encouragement of three Pounds ten Shillings to those here, who will re inlist and continue in the Service with the New-Levies till the last of October next, then be discharged.

Agreeable to this Direction I shall just mention the Advantages you have more than those who have or may inlist at Home.

And first consider, ——— The Fatigue and Hazard of your Health, in hot sultry Weather, by so long and tedious a March, you happily escape, by being on the Spot where you are to remain during the Term above mentioned.

And, The Season when your Time is expired much pleasanter and safer for your Health to return Home than in the Heat of Summer.

And further consider, That so long and tedious a March is very expensive especially, when the Weather won't allow any marching far in a Day: Even the most Frugal that will only purchase bare necessities, will find his Pockets well drained of his Bounty before he reaches this Place; And rightly to consider the whole you will find that the Difference of Bounty between you here, and those at home, will turn out I am Perswaded to your Advantage.

If you return home in July, you are very sensible that the Season is past, either to improve your own Farms, or to be imployed by others.

And as I intend to tarry my self, I should

rejoice to have you all remain with me. ⸺ I could with one Mind, possess you all. ⸺ If this was the Case how pleasing to your Country and Friends it would be for you to set so laudable an Example to your Fellow Soldiers. ⸺ And so soon as his Excellency Governor Bernard receives my Return of the Number that will engage, an Officer will be appointed and sent forward to pay you your Bounty here in Cash.

Boston June 7. By Capt. Bradford, who arrived here last Friday from Martinico, we learn, That on the 6th last, Admiral Pocock with his whole Fleet, consisting of upwards of 20 Sail of the Line and Frigates, and 180 Transports, with about 16,000 Land Forces, took their Departure from that Island, and 'twas supposed were destined for the Havannah; that it was said the Admiral gave the Captains of Transports and other Vessels belonging to the Fleet, particular instructions to be vigilant in observing Signals, for that they had a narrow Passage to go thro'; that only two Men of War and three Regiments of healty Troops were left at Martinico; that 1300 sick and wounded were soon to embark for New-York; and that his Excellency Brigadier General Manckton sailed from Martinico for this Government, the 9th Instant, in a Frigate, but intended to touch at Antigua, Guadaloupe, &c. in his way hither.

The following Affair which lately happened at Danvers in the County of Essex, is related as a Fact: ⸺ As three Children were sitting at a Door of a House an Adder came from a Pond that was about 20 Rods distant, and seized the Hand of one of the Children about two Years old, and swallowed it as far as the Wrist, and immediately twisted it's tail round the Child's Legs; upon which the other Children ran into the House affrighted, where were 2 or 3 Women who ran to the Door and discovered the Child in the above Condition, when one of the Women squeez'd the Throat of the Adder, by which the Child was cleared: The Woman carried the Child into the House, when the Adder chaced her round the Room several Times, but being disappointed of it's Food turned about and bitting itself, swelled to a considerable degree, and died. The Child was not poisoned, nor did it receive any harm.

NEW-YORK June 7. Since our last fell down to Sandy-Hook, his Majesty's ships the Intripid, Chesterfield, and Porcupine sloop, with 13 Transports, having on board his Majesty's 46th regiment, four independent companies, and about 1000 Provincial Troops; and we hear they are to sail from thence this Day for their farther destination, under the command of Col. Burton.

Capt. Scaile, of his Majesty's ship Chesterfield, has informed his Excellency Governor Sharpe, of Maryland, that notwithstanding what he wrote in his letter of the first instant, of being detained at New-York, on particular service, that he is to be dismissed from that service time enough to be in Hampton road in Virginia by the latter end of June, to take under convoy all ships then ready to sail for England.

CHARLESTON S. Carolina June 9. Major Rogers, who has been on the recruiting Service is returned, having enlisted upwards of 100 men for recruiting his Majesty's regular forces.

The Standing Turkey, Judd's Friend, with several other Cherokee Indians, were lately at Williamsburg in Virginia, to confirm the peace and get a trade ——— Judd's Friend is gone to England in the Squarrel man of war to see the great King George, and to brighten the chain of peace and friendship.

The last letters from fort Prince George advise, that the Cherokees behave in the most friendly manner, all their white prisoners, about 20 in number, mostly children, had liberty to go where their pleased but they were not able to procure provisions, nor had the Indians any to give them, nor were they able to travel far.

——— Great numbers of people came daily from the northward, and settled on Broad Turkey Creek and other frontier places contiguous to the Cherokees.

ANNAPOLIS Maryland June 10. On Tuesday last one William Wright, an old Man, about 75 years of age, attempting to swim across Magothy river, to fetch a canoe, which some ill natured Boys refused to bring over to him, sunk, and was drowned, when he had got almost over. He told the people whom he left on shore, that tho' he had not swam for thirty years, they should see that he could swim yet. His body was taken up soon after.

On Wednesday the 26th ult. Richard Crosby, alias Dew, was executed at Frederick Town for the murder of Mr. Wirt on the road.

BOSTON June 14. Last Friday morning about One o'Clock, a Fire broke out at the Bake House of Mr. George Bray, at the upper End of William's Court, in Cornhill, which had got to such a Head before it was discovered, that the same together with his Dwelling House, all the Furniture, Bedding, Cloaths, &c. with about 150 Barrels of Flour were wholly consumed; The Family having but just Time to save themselves. ―――― the Fire being communicated to most of the Dwelling Houses Barns and out Houses in said Court with other Buildings contiguous they were soon in Flames: ―――― the Place where the Fire began was confined and difficult of Access, but the Engines of the Town together with those of Charlestown and Castle William, which kindly assisted, being in excellent order for playing, and the Fire Officers and Inhabitants encouraged by the presence of his Excellency the Governor, exerting themselves to a great degree, a Stop was put, thro' the Favour of Divine Providence, to the Progress of the devouring Flames much sooner that our Fears suggested: as it is much Substance has been lost, and several Families were turned out of their Dwelling, but no Lives were lost. ―――― It is melancholy to observe what a considerable Part of the Metropolis has been destroyed, and how many new Object of Charity have been created by these repeated disasters; this being the third considerable Fire, besides the great one, which has happened in the Town within the short space of three Years.

The following Families who lived in the Court are by this terrible Accident now burnt out viz. Mr. George Bray. Mr. John Popkins. Widow Slaten. Mrs. Jane Day. Capt. Arthur Noble. Mr. Samuel Holbrook. Mr. Eph. Copeland, Jun. Mr. Jacob Tayer. Mr. Benjamin Loring. Widow Gould.

Mr. John Barker.

Last Friday Noon a young Child tied up in a Handkerchief, was found in a Dock at the North Part of the Town, supposed to have been murdered.

BOSTON June 14. Friday and Saturday two Persons from Connecticut, who stile themselves Baptist Quakers, one a man with a white hat, a noted Person of that Sect went about the Streets vending some Pamphlets, tending to persuade People that the first Day of the Week is a pretended Sabbath, and that it ought not be kept Holy, and that we please God by Working on that Day, with several other dangerous Tenets, which is a reproach to any People. It is hop'd the Town will take no other Notice of them than to order them out of it. But such Books may have bad Effects on the Minds of some younger Persons, we doubt not the pernicious Principles will be expos'd by these whose Province it is on that Holy Day.

BOSTON June 14. Whereas the good Design of having Rows of Elm on the Sides of Boston-Neck has been repeatedly frustrated by some evilminded Persons breaking and otherwise destroying these Trees, and Damage likewise done to Trees on the Common: ———— The Select-Men in order to bring such base Offenders to Justice, and to present Abuses of this kind in the future hereby offer to any Person who shall inform them of those who have thus injured the Publick, so as they may be brought to Justice, Five Dollars Reward for each Person convicted.

Boston June 10th, By order of the Select-Men.
William Cooper, Town Clerk.

New-York June 14. The Fleet at Sandy-Hook got underway last Thursday morning; but were obliged to come too again, his Majesty's ship Intripid having struck on the middle ground; and they were obliged to start fifty tons of her water before she could get off; But they again put to sea on Friday evening.

Last Saturday afternoon, his Majesty's Ship Lizard, Capt Banks, arrived here from Antigua in 14 days passage, on board whom returned his Excellency the Hon. Robert Monchton, our Governor and Commander in Chief, and Major General of his Majesty's forces; from his successful expedition against the Island of Martinico. His Excellency landed at Whitehall stairs where he was received by his Honor Lieut. Governor Cclden, and a great number of other Gentlemen, under the discharge of the cannon at Fort George; his Excellency's sudden (tho' not unexpected) arrival affording no time for the militia, who were under orders, to appear for his more general welcome reception.

The Lizard had under Convoy, a Schooner which had on board Governor Monckton's baggage, and five of his domesticks; but the third day after they sailed, they were espy'd by two large ships, who giving chace came up with the Schooner, and detained her; from which conjectur'd they were enemy's ships. It is said one of the appeared to be a double decker, the other a frigate. The Schooner has not been heard of since, and 'tis feared is made a capture of.

Saturday se'nnight two young men at Haddam in Connecticut, wrestled for a wager, when one of them falling on his head, broke his neck and expired.

CHARLESTOWN S. Carolina June 16. We hear all the white prisoners are now delivered up by the Cherokee Indians, and we most heartily congratulate all friends in their Country on the suspicious event. The number of those prisoners, not amount to 20, and they are mostly children, between 5 and 12 years old; they have entirely lost their English Tongue, and can speak nothing but Indian; they are the prettiest creatures you can ever behold, and wild as if they were in heather. Tistoe says they often ran away from him at the beginning of his journey downward, and he had to hunt for them among the Woods as if they had been so many rabbits, or Sqirrels; he kept them together in the latter part of the journey by constantly watching them night and day. ———

The Young Warrior is just arrived, and delivered his prisoners a Dutch woman to Capt, Mackintosh, she with others, are going with Capt. Mackintosh to Ninety-six.

In consequence of the prisoners being delivered

up by the Cherokees, a trade is to be opened with these Indians by this Province, in Terms of the late Act of Assembly.

BOSTON June 17. Province of Massachusetts-Bay. Deserted from Castle William, the five following Soldiers, who lately inlisted in this Province, as Recruits for his Majesty's Regular Regiment in North America.

Ebenezer Nightingale, of Stoughton, aged 39 Years, by Trade a Farmer, fairish Complexion, well set, has brown Hair, blue Eyes, has sore Eyes, he is 5 Feet 6 Inches High. —— Ebenezer Allen of Stoughton born in Newton, aged 23 Years by Trade a Husbandman, a dark Complexion, has dark Eyes, and black Hair, he is 5 Feet 5 Inches High. —— Lemuel Kingman, born in Bridgewater, aged 29 Years, by Trade a Farmer, brown Complexion, black Eyes, dark brown Hair, 5 Feet 9 Inches high, and slim. —— John Bushington of Dighton, born in Kellingsly, by Trade a Fisherman, dark Eyes, dark Hair, 5 Feet 7 Inches high. —— John Young, by Trade a Barber, dark Complexion, with Green Eyes, and has a Cast in his left Eye, black Hair, 5 Feet 6 Inches high.

N. B. Ebenezer Nightingale and Lemuel Kingsman has been heard of in Johnston-Town Rhode Island Government, where they were suspected of stealing, and got away into Scituate in the same Government, and said to be at the House of one James Perrigreen, they left Perrigreen's House and went into the Parish of Norwich in the Connecticut Government early in this Month, and has since been heard of returning from Norwich to the said Perrigreen's. The said Nightingale calls himself John Spear, and the said Kingsman goes by the name of James Loring.

Whoever, apprehends any of the said Deserters and will deliver them to the Commanding Officer of the Troops on Castle Island, or to Lieut. Elloitt at Mrs. Allen's near the Town-House in Boston, or secure them in any of his Majesty's Goals, shall receive Six Pounds, Lawful Money, Reward, for each Man.

NEW-YORK June 21. Yesterday arrived here after a fine Passage of 19 Days from Martinico, 11 Transports viz. The Lion, armed Transport Ship;

the True Briton; Black Prince; Elizabeth and Mary; Mary the Second; Two Brothers; Rachel; Ship James; Brig James; Hope; and the Fanny:

On board these Vessels came all the sich and wounded Officers and Soldiers from Martinico, amounting to between 800 and 1000; The commanding Officer Major Curry and his Lady came in the Hope.

By Letters from South Carolina, we learn, that 30 Days ago, War was not declared at Augustine against England; altho' they were busy in fitting out Privateers to cruize against the English, no less than one Polacca, 3 Sloops and 2 Schooners being almost ready for the Sea; and that 2 Sloops and 3 Men of War, having 3000 Land Forces on board, lately arrived there from the Havanna's.

NEW-YORK June 21. We hear that Magaret Davies, formerly a Servant in the King's Arms, in this City, has lately been left, by an old Aunt, who died some time ago in England, the Sum of 2000 Pounds Sterling per Annum.

The Intripid, Chesterfield, and Porcupine Men of War, with 13 Transports under convoy, having on board the 40th Regiment, 4 Independent Companies, and near 1000 Provincials: sailed from Sandy-Hook on Friday the 11th Instant. Another Fleet of Men of War and Transports are preparing to follow, the Men embarking as fast as possible, but were bound is not yet publickly known.

Thursday Night last Capt. Mitchell arrived here from Jamaica: 27 Days before he came in he met with off Baracoa, the Fleet under the Command of Admiral Pocock, who a few Days before was joined by that under the Command of Sir James Douglass, from Jamaica, having on board 2000 Negro Soldiers; and for the Course they Steered he was pretty certain they were bound to the Havannah, from which Place, when he left them, he supposed them to be about 15 Leagues.

CHARLESTOWN S. Carolina June 23. The Northward Indians have lately killed some of the Chikesaws, and a party of them also came upon and surprised a camp, where were 15 Cherokees, all of whom they put to death, except one who they sent to the Cherokee nation to tell them who had killed their companions.

'Tis said the Creek Indians are now actually meditating something of importance; a great many of them have been in the Cherokee nation, and because they did not satisfy them in all Points, they robbed a Georgia trader of most of his goods and horses.

BOSTON June 24. For a Cruize of Six Months, against his Majesty's Enemies, the Billander Tartan, a private Vessel of War. (a noted sailor) William Augustus Peck, Commander: Mounts 14 six pounders, 20 Cohorns, and to carry 120 Men, will sail in 15 Days, as many has already engag'd.

All Gentlemen Seamen and able-bodied Landsmen that are inclined to take a Cruize in said Vessel, by applying to the King's Head Tavern, at the North End, may see the Articles, which are more advantageous, to the Mariners than any other offered.

PHILADELPHIA June 24. Yesterday launched by Monsieurs Tho. & James Penrose, the privateer ship Hero, 95 feet keel, and 32 feet beam, she mounts 24 9 pounders on one deck, on the stocks only 73 days, and is reckoned the finest vessel for that purpose ever built in America.

CHARLESTOWN S. Carolina June 26. Two talks and a string of white beads are brought down from the Lower Towns. The Cherokees beg most earnestly for peace, and also for the speedy restoration of the prisoners we have here; that when these are obtained, no one shall dare to give a bad talk talk in the nation; and express great desire to see the Governor, if his Excellency will permit them to come to Charlestown. Some Measures are accordingly taking to send up the Cherokee Prisoners from this town to ninety-six as soon as possible, of which Notice is already sent to the Indians; and a Trade is to be forthwith open with them, not by private persons but of the government, agreeable to a late Act of assembly.

From the Creek Nation we have a certain account of the arrival of some troops from France at New-Orleans with a ship of war, and two store ships. Our advices add, that those were the only ships that arrived there directly from France for five years past; that a boat load of these goods brought in said store ships was on its way to Albahma Fort, the whole whereof; was provided to be distributed amongst the Creek Indians; and that the Creeks had received an invitation from the Spaniards to go to Pensacola, to receive presents from them likewise.

BOSTON June 28. I Would inform the Public, that I have bought Ephran Goss out of Prison; and that he hath deserted my Service from under Col. White of Leominster about the 26th of May: Said Goss is a short well-set Fellow, with black hair & Eyes; his Cloathing when he went to Col. White, was a brown Jacket, a check Woolen shirt, old Leather Breeches, and hath been seen with red Breeches, and white Waistcoat. If any Person shall take up said Goss, and convey him to me the Subscriber, shall receive Two Dollars Reward and all necessary Charges paid. And all Persons are forbid harbouring him, or trading with him, on Penalty of Suffering the Law provided in such Case.   Benjamin Marble.
Boston June 15, 1762.

Whereas Mary, the Wife of me the Subscriber, hath elope from me, and trades so as to run me in debt: These are to caution and warn all Persons against trusting her, for I will pay none of her Debts. Weston June 26, 1762.

his
John + Willington.
mark

Boston June 28. Province of Massachusetts-Bay Court of Vice Admiralty , Boston June 18, 1762.

All Persons claiming Property in the Schooner Barcelona, Apparel, Furniture, and Appurtenances, seized by James Cockle, Esq; Collector of his Majesty's Customs for the Port of Salem, for breach of the Act of Trade; are hereby notified to appear at a Court of Vice Admiralty, to be holden at Boston, for the said Province, on the 29th of June Instant, at Nine o'Clock before Noon show cause, if any they have, why the said Schooner and Appurtenances shou'd not be adjudged to remain Forfeited, pursuant to an Information filed in said Court for that purpose.

per Corium,   Wm. Story D. Reg.

NEW-YORK June 28. The unanimous Address of the Merchants and Traders of the City of New-York, to his Excellency the Honourable Robert Monckton, Captain General and Governor and Chief in and over the Province of New-York, and the territories depending thereto in America, Vice Admiral of the same, and Major General of his Majesty's Forces.

May it please your Excellency,

We his Majesty's most loyal subjects, the Merchants and Traders of the City of New-York, beg leave to express our congratulations to your Excellency on your safe arrival in the Province from a dangerous climate and a hazardous campaign.

The conquest of Martinico and its dependences, which has, thro' Divine Providence, been achieved under your command. cannot but reflect the greatest honour on your Excellency, place your character in the highest military light, and render you the darling of a grateful people.

To the best of Sovereign we owe the obligation of yor Excellency's presiding over us; and from a knowledge of his good qualities we have reason, to expect, that his power has been delegated where his virtues were conspicuous so that we have the strongest hope that under your government we shall enjoy every blessing of a free people.

We confide in your Excellency's protection of the trade of this province; and beg leave to assure you, that we will respectively contribute as much as possible to the observance of the laws, and to the alleviating the fatugue and burden of government.

That your Excellency's administration over us may be long and happy, is the ardent prayer of.

      May it Please your Excellency

Your Excellency's most obedient Humble

      June 18, 1762.   Servants.

      His Excellency's Answer.

Gentlemen,

It is with pleasure I receive your congratulations, You may be assuere of my care and attention to promote the commerce of this province.

and protect the merchants in their just rights and immunities.

NEW-YORK June 28. Wednesday last arrived here in 27 days from Jamaica, the Captains Goodwin, Webb, Kerstead, and Dobson: They came under convoy of the Britannia privateer, Capt. M'Pherson of Philadelphia, who has taken two large Dutch Sloops loaded with sugar and indigo, from Port au Prince, which he has taken with him to Philadelphia. Capt. Goodwin spoke with the Deptford man of war off Nichola, about the 3d Inst. who informed him of the junction and destination of the two fleets under Sir George Pocock and Sir James Douglass, which united make 211 sail, of which 29 were are ships of the line, and 15 frigates, having on board 12,000 regular forces; Commodore Douglass also carried with him 2500 Slaves, and 150 free Negroes, as bush cutters, rangers, &c. the whole bound to the Havannah; an English cutter was stationed in the old straits, where she is to ply, and advise the Admiral if any fletts appear.

We have now a fitting out of this harbour the six following privateers, viz. ——— Brig Mars, Capt. M'Gillicuddy, of 18 guns ——— Brig Mockton, Capt. Sennet, of 14 guns ——— Schooner Harlequin, Capt. Wright, of 14 guns ——— Schooner Polly and Sally, Capt Thurston, of 8 guns ——— Sloop Dolphin, Capt. _____, of 10 guns ——— Schooner New Harlequin, Capt. Brereton, of 8 guns.

JULY 1762

BOSTON July 5. We hear from Rhode Island, that last Friday se'nnight, as a Number of Persons were mowing Grass in the Town of Portsmouth on that Island a Thunder Shower came up, whereupon they betook themselves to a Tree for shelter, and one of them hung a Scythe on a Limb over his Head: Soon after a Stream of Lightning came down the Tree, took its Course along the Blade of the Scythe, and from thence went off the Point on the Heads of Mr. Fish, and a Lad named Murphy, and kill'd them both instantaneously. ——— The other Persons that stood under the Tree received no hurt. We hope some observations will be made of this Occurrence, and the Nature and Utility of Electrical Points: In the mean Time it may not be amiss to re-print the following.

Extract from Mr. B. Franklin's Letter on Electricity. ———

"As electrical Clouds (says he) pass over the Country, high hills and high Trees, lofty Towers Mast of Ships, Chimneys, &c. as so many Prominences draw the Electric Fire, and the whole Cloud discharges there: dangerous it is to take shelter under a Tree during a Thunder Gust; it has been fatal to many both Men and Beasts. It is safer to be in the open Field for another Reason: When the Cloaths are wet, if a Flash in its way to the Ground should strike your Head, it would run in the Water over the surface of your Body, whereas if the Cloaths are dry, it would go thro' your Body. Hence a wet Rat cannot be killed by the exploding electric Bottle, when a dry one may."

BOSTON July 5. From Weston, dated July 1, 1762.
Misters Fleets,
I find in your last Mondays Paper, that my Husband has informed the Publick, That I have eloped

────── and that I run him in Debt, and has given a caution not to Trust me on his Account. Altho' I am very sensible that neither him or I are of much Importance to the Publick, for he has not an Estate to entitle one of any Credit on his Account; yet I desire you to be so kind to me, as to let the Publick know, That I never run him in Debt one Farthing in my Life, nor ever eloped, unless it was to Day Labour, to support me and the Children, which I am of necessity obliged to do; and shall be ever glad to do my duty to him, and wish he would for the future behave to me in such a manner, that I may do it with more ease than heretofore.

        her
     Mary § Willington.
        mark

NEW-YORK July 5. Wednesday evening last sail'd from Sandy Hook, his Majesty's ship Enterprize, the Lizard frigate, and Porcupine sloop, with 8 transports, laving on board his Majesty's 58th regiment 4 companies of Major Gorham's rangers. and about 500 provincials; their destination we leave our readers to find out.

Last Saturday three weeks, on John Woodsides, a pedler, was robbed by two men on horseback, near Andover Iron Works in New-Jersey, of cash and goods to the amount of 160 Pounds currency. As soon as the villains approached Woodsides, one of them discharged a pistol at him not more than 7 Yards distant, but missed him; he then drew his pistol and fired it at the Highwayman, but without effect also: This conduct of Woodsides so enraged the rogues, that one of them run at him with a hanger, and intended to have killed him, but after he had received a terrible wound, in his side and a large cut on his shoulder, he took to his heels and escaped.

NEW-YORK July 8. Last Tuesday arrived here the Brig Boon, Captain Munds, in 6 Days from South Carolina, and on his Passage from thence spoke with a Vessel from Jamaica, who informed him that a few Days before she took a small Vessel from the Havannah; and that about five leagues from the Havannah, he heard a heavy firing, but as it is surrounded by Mountains he could not discern any Ships, but supposed that it was the English besieging it; whom God grant Success to in all their undertaking.

Early Thursday Evening las a Fire broke out in the upper Appartment of a Dwelling House of Mr. Samuel Farley, of this City, Printer, on the new Dock; which did great Damage to that and the House adjoining (in Possession of the Widow Vernon's Tavenkeeper) before it could be extinguished, notwithstanding the quick attendance of the Inhabitants, and the Advantage of the river being close at Hand.

Friday Evening the Sloop Stanford, Capt, Wimble, arrived here from Boston (which Place he left Saturday before) with recruits for the different Regiments of Regulars on the Continent; which Recruits, with those brought from Virginia by Capt. Rolles, are we hear, to sail this Day for Quebec.

NEW-YORK July 8. Yesterday between 3 and 4 o'Clock in the Afternoon cane up a violent Gust of Wind and Rain, accompanied with uncommon Thunder and Lightning, during which the Steeple of the Trinity Church in the City was struck with the Lightning and took Fire, but was by timely and usual Vigilance of the Inhabitants happily extinguished, with little Damage. The Steeple was under Repair and one of the Gentlemen who had the care if it, being bellow, was, (together with two of his Lads) struck down, but received no Hurt, otherwise than remaining feeble for a short space. Mr. Calloe's House in Wall Street, was struck much about the same Time, but sustain'd little Damage, unless be the Shivering of a Sette, &c. 'Tis said that the Mast of a Boat in the Harbour was shiver'd by the Lightning and several Creatures in the Hold kill'd, but no Person hurt. We also learn from Hushwike, on Long Island, that a Barn was burnt there by the Lightning, its fear'd that we shall receive similar Accounts from the adjacent Parts.

PHILADELPHIA July 8. On Tuesday Night last 6th Instant, arrived here the brig Susanna, Capt. Sutton, in 25 Days from Jamaica. He informs, That he sailed under Convoy of two Men of

War who was convoying the Negroes raised in Jamaica to the Army at Cuba; That he came through the Gulph, and on the 25th of June was off the Havannah about four Leagues distance, where he lay becalmed all the Afternoon and Night, and could see the Smoak and hear the Report of the Guns of the Arm and Enemy, firing at one another. ——— That on the 26th he spoke with the Harlequin Privateer of South Carolina, who had seen Capt. Rivers of this Place, and by him was informed, That our Army commanded by the Earl Albemarle had landed safely at the Havannah, and were in Possession of a high Hill (which commands the Moore Castle and City of Havannah) on which they had erected their Batteries, and began to play on the Place the 15th of June. Capt. Sutton did not see our Fleet. ——— The Number of Spanish Ships of War at the Havannah, said to be 20, 14 of which of the line.

   Come to New York Thursday Night last, Mr. William Johnson, arrived here from Eastern, New-Jersey, where he was at a Treaty with the Heads of several Tribes of Indians.

   BOSTON July 12. A Master of a Fishing Vessel arrived Yesterday from Cape-Ann, who says, That on the 27th of June, on the Bank Vert, in Lat. 46. he spoke with a Brig in Company of another Brig and a Schooner, all full of Men, Women, and Children, who said that on the 24th the had been drove off their Settlement in the Bay of Bulls, near St. John's in Newfoundland, by three Spanish Men of War of the Line, from 80 to 60 Guns, and one Frigate, who landed and destroyed their Castle; that they escaped in another Harbour, and got on board those Vessels. That the Spanish Ships had drove on Shore a Brig from Ireland, with about 100 Soldiers, who got to Land; but the Brig was taken. That a fishing Vessel had got to St. John's, who said he saw the Spaniards sink 10 Fishing Vessels on the Great Bank. That they were other Spanish Ships of Force on the Banks besides the forementioned Vessels. That they expected to be attacked at St. John's.

   Samuel Dogget, of the Sloop Swallow, arrived here Yesterday in 8 Days from Halifax, who says,

That on the 27th of June he heard that the Syrene Frigate was arrived there, with Advice that a Fishing Schooner had come into St. John's who said that on the Banks he met with 5 large Ships, and 2 Frigates, who fired 100 shot at him, and several Vollies of small Arms, but escaped in a fog.

BOSTON July 12. By a Letter from Paris we are informed that on the Arrival of the Marquis de Vaudreuil in France, from his late Government in Canada, he was sent for immediately to Court, in order to give an Account of his Conduct in that Department, when several Officers appearing against him with bad Management, &c. in his Proceeding against the English, he was committed Prisoner to the Bastile, where he now lies. The Bishop d'Autun, First Almoner to the King, interceded for him, and spoke very strongly in his Favour, saying, that he had acted with Spirit in the Service of his Country; and, if it did not meet with the Success he meant, it was not his Fault: Adding that the Marquis had Enemies, who were much more deserving of being sent to the Bastile. This Freedom however was so far from being of Service to the Marquis, that, according to these Letters, the good Bishop himself got severely reprimanded, and has been ordered to quit the Court, and confine himself entirely to his own Diocese.

BOSTON July 12. Yesterday Morning between 3 and 4 o'Clock, a Fire broke out in the Cabin of a Sloop belonging to Mr. Vans, of this Town, and commanded by Capt. Harlow, lying at a Wharf at the North End, which having communicated to about half a Barrel of Powder before it was discovered, it blew up with a loud Noise and immediately set all the After Parts of the Vessel in Flames, almost the whole of which, together with the underside of the Main Deck, and some of the Lading were burnt; and they were obliged to sink the Vessel before the Fire could be extinguished, the rest of the Cargo will be greatly damaged, she being fully loaded and ready to sail for the West. Indies: —— The Fire did also considerable Damage to the Wharf, and a large Parcel of Pine Boards that lay on it. 'Tis not known how the Fire happened, but supposed to be occasioned by the Fireplace in the Steerage.

NEW-YORK July 12. Friday evening Capt. Rolles arrived here from Virginia with 130 recruits for his Majesty's Royal American regiment. —— Capt. Rolles says, that the Day he left Hampton, a sloop arrived there from South Carolina, the Master whereof said, that a sloop had got in from Jamaica, who in the Gulph had been met with by an English frigate, the commander whereof acquainted him, that the army under the command of Earl of Albemarle, was safely landed at the Havannah, on the island of Cuba.

NEW-YORK July 15. On Tuesday last arrived here the Sloop Alice, Capt. Tosh, in 30 Days from Jamaica; but last from the Havannah in 15 Days. By him we learn, That 17 Days ago, 3 Leagues off the Havannah, he was boarded by an English Officer of his Majesty's ship Alcide, who informed him that the Troops under the command of the Earl of Albemarle, landed at the Havannah without Opposition; but that the Spaniards gave them a warm reception as soon as they made their Approach; that they had sunk three of their Ships, in the Entrance of the Harbour to prevent the English Fleet from getting in, that a party of Sailors belonging to an English Frigate going on Shore in Search of Fresh Provisions were surrounded by the Enemy, and 13 of them cut to Pieces, in a very unhuman Manner; and that a Lieutenant of the Rangers has his Nose and Ears cut off, and was otherwise used very ungenteely by the Spaniards, and sent to the English Camp by way of Derision, which Intelligence Incessed the Earl of Albemarle so much, that he sent Word to the Governor of the Havannah, that he should neither give nor take Quarters and desired him to kill every English Prisoner he should take, for he would do the same by all the Spaniards he met with.

BOSTON July 17. Notice hereby given, by the Field Officers of the Regiment of Militia in the Town of Boston, to every Person on the Alarm, and Training, Band Lists, that on Friday next the 23d Instant, there will be a strict View of their Arms and Ammunition; and whoever is deficient in any Article requir'd by Law, may expect to be prosecuted. July 17, 1762.

The following Extract from the Province Law is order'd to be inserted for the Information of the Inhabitants that none may plead Ignorance Viz.

"That every listed Soldier and other house-
"holders except Troopers shall be always prov-
"vided with a well fixed Firelock, Musket, of
"Musket or Ball to Musket bore, the Barrel not
"less than three Foot and a half long; or other
"good Fire Arm to the Satisfaction of the Com-
"mission Officers of the Company: a napsack, a
"Collar with twelve Bandeliers, or Carchouch
"Box: one Pound of good Powder, twenty Bullets
"fit his Gun; and twelve Flints; a good Sword
"or Cutlass, a Worm or Firing Wire fit for his
"Gun: On Penalty of Six Shillings, for the want
"of such Arms as it hereby required and Two
"Shillings for each other Defects, and the like
"sum for every four Weeks he shall remain un-
"provided: The Fines to be paid by Parents for
"the Sons under Age, and under their Command;
"and by Masters of Head of Families, for their
"Servants other than Servants upon Wages."

PHILADELPHIA July 17. Extract of a Letter from Providence, June 29, 1762.

Since my last a small Prize has been sent here, that was taken by one of our Privateers off the Havannah. The Substance the Prize Master's Account as follows, viz. That the Fleet and transports arrived 12 or 14 Days ago off that Place and landed 20,000 Soldiers on a Bay about 3 Miles to the Windward of the Havannah, after knocking down a small Fort or Battery that was there: That the English Men of War have battered the Moore Castle very considerably; indeed the Prize Master says so much, that the Castle did not return one Gun for some Time before the English desisted: That the Night after our Army landed, the Spanish Army was divided into two Bodies, with an intention of placing the English between the two Fires, and that by some Mistake, in the night time, the two Divisions of the Spanish Army fell foul of one another, each taking the other for English and killed many on both Sides, before they found their Mistake: That our Bombs have sunk four Spanish Men of War in the Harbour: That the English Army is at the Back of Havannah bombarding it: And that the Admiral declared, he expected the Place would surrender in less then ten Days after the Vessel sailed from thence. ──── The Prize master also brings an Account, that one of our Frigates in company with the Port Antonio Sloop of War, had taken two Spanish Frigates."

BOSTON July 19, Extract of a Letter from Halifax July 3, 1762.

"Two Days past Capt. Douglass arrived here in the Serene Ship of War from Newfoundland, who come to give some Advice to Lord Colvill of 5 or 6 Sail of Spanish Ships, which were said to be seen by a Schooner upon the Banks of Newfoundland. ──── This News came in the Morning, and put many people into a Consternation, but upon enquiring more minutely into the Circumstances of it, it all appeared to be a Mistake of a Timorous Fisherman, ──── Lord Colvill was preparing to sail with the Northumberland (the only Ship in the Harbour) but has since that laid the thought aside for the present. ──── The Syrene sail'd this Morning for Newfoundland."

Wednesday arrived here the Schooner Hope, Edmond Freeman, Master, in 17 Days from Quebec. The Captain informs, That on the 5th Instant he say 5 Sails of Ships off Cape Rosier, bound up to Quebec, supposed to be Merchantmen from England: That on the 9th he spoke with a Brig belonging to this Place, William Cockran Master, who informed him, that he had been 5 Days from Newfoundland, and was bound for Halifax, being then about 12 Leagues S. E. of that Place; there were a considerable Number of People on board the Brig, who informed him, that two Ships of the Line and three Frigates both French and Spanish, had taken Bay of Bulls, Ferriland and St. Johns. Capt. Freeman also spoke with a Schooner that Day before, who had given him the same Account. The Wind blew hard when out Informant spoke with the Brig, and it is not certain whether it was said they were 5 or 9 Days from Newfoundland.

And on Friday last arrived here the Schooner Dolphin, Capt. Silas Atkins, in 17 Days from Newfoundland, who hath the following Declaration, Viz.

That he left the Harbour Grace in Newfoundland the 27th of last Month, and that before he sail'd from thence Advice came that there was about 3000 French Troops landed on the 24th at the Bay of Bulls, who march'd in two Days to St. John's, and laid siege to that place, which it was suppos'd would be taken, but that a great firing was heard that Day at St. John's: ——— That the French force in the Bay of Bulls consisted of 3 Ships of about 70 Guns, one Frigate of 40, and a Bomb, and that there was out at Sea, off the Bay of Bulls, 5 more Ships of the Enemy, some of which were 70 Guns, but how many he could not say:

The French General had published a Manifesto, a Copy of which he had procured and compared with the Original: ——— That many boats came into the Harbour Grace with Inhabitants many of whom he knew, and has but bro't about 20 with him. ——— That he believed many had returned to their Habitations in Consequence of the French General's Manifesto: That they seemed disposed to preserve the Place and keep it: And that he could not learn they had done any Mischief upon the Banks.

The next Day arrived here Capt. Phillips in 19 Days from Trinity-Bay in Newfoundland, and informs, that the Inhabitants there, as well as other Harbours in the Island, were in the utmost Distress and Confusion, on Account of the unwelcome Visit paid by the French Fleet: ——— That a Shallop which escap'd from St. John's Habour, had come into Trinity, and bro't advice that St. John's has certainly surrendered to the French Troops, said to be about 1500, on Sunday the 27th of June, at Noon, having made little or no Opposition; firing, 'twas said only one Gun, tho' the Place of considerable Strength, having upwards of 60 Cannon mounted, but was very poorly garrisoned; ——— That the Gramont Frigate, with a Number of the Ships that lately arrived from England, were in the Harbour of

St. John's and must (if the Place is taken) fall into the Hands of the Enemy, none of the Vessels being suffered to leave the Harbour after Advice came of the French landing at the Bay of Bulls: —— And that it was the general Opinion there that it was the Enemy's Fleet from the West-Indies, as the Ships appeared to be very foul.

The same Day another Vessel here from Harbour Grace, which they left the Day after Captain Atkins, have bro't several Families from thence with some of their Effects.

The following is an Exact Copy of the Manifesto published by the French General.

"We Count De Hosson Ville, French General, do Declare to all the Inhabitants of the Island of Newfoundland, That French Grenadiers landed on said Island, we shall not do then any Harm, but shall protect them if they do not take up Arms, if they give necessary Succours; we bound them expresly, as well as those Justices of the Peace and principal Planters, do not leave their Houses or Settlements, neither to defend themselves: if they do any thing against the said Declaration they shall be treated accordingly to the Laws of War.

    Saturday June 26, 1762.
      (Sign'd)   Le Compte DeHosson Wille."

We hear that upon Advice being received at St. John's of the Enemy's Ships being at the Bay of Bulls, one or two Vessels were immediately dispatched from thence to England with with an Account of it.

And on receiving the above Advices here, his Majesty's Council were immediately called together, and several Expresses were dispatch'd and two Vessels hired by the Government as Packet Boats to proceed immediately to Admiral Pocock in the West Indies.

BOSTON July 19. Capt. Searle, in the Ship True-Blue belonging to this Place, which has been employed as a Transport in his Majesty's Service for 4 Years past, arrived here on Tuesday last from New-York, having some French Prisoners in order to go on board the Lauceston Man of War which convoys the Mast-Ships to England from whence they are to be transported to France

According to capitulation. ——— They belonged to the last Division of the Garrison of Fort Detroit and Michilimakinak, brought to New-York last year by Major Rogers.

Charlestown S. Carolina July 24. Letters from Savannah Georgia dated the 16th inst. advise, that some deserters from St. Augustine had lately came there (first two, then four) said more would follow, and that hard duty, bad pay, and the want for provisions, &c. forced them to it.

——— The same letters mention the Georgia scout boat, commanded by Capt. Braddock, being sent to seize a Vessel which information has been was taking in cargo of hogs and other provisions at Talbot Island near St. Juan's river, for the Spaniards at St. Augustine.

Near 40 Creek Indians left Savannah about 10 days ago in good humour; and every thing seemed quiet in that nation, according to the last advices from thence; but as those Indians were returned who lately went from St. Mark's and Pensacola, by invitation to receive presents, and had brought 150 Kegs of rum with them, it was apprehended while the rum lasted, the traders in the nation would have a troublesome time.

CHARLESTOWN S. Carolina July 24. We hear by the measures taken by his Excellency General Amherst, Augustine is reduced to great distress from want of Provisions; they had little bread and flour, but no meat of any kind.

Letters from Capt. Walter Kerr of the Brig Diana (which sailed from this Port for Jamaica the 26th of May) dated the 26th of June, mentions the loss of said vessel with cargo, on the 9th of the same month, on a reef of rocks 3 leagues N. W. of Crooked Island, which he never saw laid down in any chart. At 7 in the morning of the 10th, he and the crew got to Bird Key in their boat, where they met with two privateers belonging to New Providence, commanded by Capt. Palmer and Broughton, who directly desired Capt. Kerr to go to the wreck with them, which he did. and saved some cloaths and books; after these were got on board Palmer's Palmer's vessel, Capt. Kerr was again put on shore at Bird Key, and the privateers promised not to meddle with the wreck till they had consulted him next morning, but at day-light he observed that his vessel had been plunder'd and stripped of all her sails, rigging, anchors, cable, masts, yards, &c. Which the privateers denied to have taken. He was 8 days after this on Board Palmer's vessel, during which time he expressed the greatest joy, when he could get out of her into a brig, bound to Jamaica, which they met with.

BOSTON July 26. Since our last arrived here Capt. Lillie, from Newfoundland and informs, that he left Harbour Grace the 29th of June, before which Time they had received certain advice, that the French Forces landed at the Bay of Bulls and marched across the Land to St. John's; that the English Forces there were out to meet them, but upon seeing the great inequality returned to the Garrison: That upon Sunday the 27th about 2 o'Clock P. M. French Colours appeared to be hoisted at the Garrison, and that they fired a Shot at the South Battery to make them haul down their English Colours: That the French Fleet which came into the Bay of Bulls, consisted of a 74, a 64, a 40, and a Bomb: That he spoke with Capt. Lawrence in a Brig, in Lat. 47. and told him there were 4 more French Men of War at Placentia, and had taken it: That that there were not 40 Families in the Southern Parts of Newfoundland, but what were gone: That the Man of War in St. John's, of 20 Guns, before the Garrison surrendered flung her Guns overboard, and run the Ship ashore: That it was reported and generally believed, that the Fleet was the same that sailed from Brest for Martinico, and that they had orders, in case they failed there, to infest the Coast of North America: That in general they have behaved very well to the Inhabitants and profess'd to pay for what they took: That they said they came for the Ransom Money of St. John's when it was taken in Queen Anne's War which had never been paid.

Wednesday last arrived here a Schooner from St. John's in Newfoundland, the master of which informs, that he left the Place the 27th of June in the Morning, in company with a Brigantine, who were permitted to sail with the Women and

Children of the principal Families of the Place, when it was invested by the French Troops, which he heard consisted of 4000, that marched from Bay of Bulls by land: ——— The Brig was bound for Halifax: ——— In the Schooner came the Family of _____ Thomas Esq; Mr. Thomas and the other Gentlemen of the Place were detained to assist in the Garrison. ——— A few Hours after the Schooner came out she was becalmed and the Master says he saw the French Flag hoisted on the Walls of St. John's and a Shallop passed by him in the Afternoon which told him that it was surrendered to the French. ——— The whole number of Vessels in the Harbour consisted of between 20 and 30 Sail including the Gramont Frigate with part of the Cork Fleet. ——— None of the French Men of War were there, being all at the Bay of Bulls, which he heard were 7, and a Bomb Ketch. ——— The following is a Copy of the Manifesto sent to the Inhabitants of St. John's the Morning the above Schooner sailed from thence.

"We Compte De Hosson Ville, General Commander of all the French Army, composed of Grenadiers and Packets of the Regiment of Marines, Mount Revel, Beausolois, Pentbere, Royal Artillery, Gunners, and Royal Marines, Summons and gives Notice to all Inhabitants of the Island of Newfoundland, not to go out of Town, either to go into the Woods, nor at Sea, under penalty that is inflicted by the Laws of War.

We promise and assure all the Inhabitants that if they surrender themselves without Arms, we will use them as Frenchmen, and we shall not do them the least Molestation, but to the contrary we shall protect them. Given at the Camp before St. John's." On Sunday the 27th of June 1762.

Charlestown S. Carolina July 27. The Measures for some time past persued by his Excellency Jeffery Amherst, in regard to the exportation of provisions, &c. from the Northern Colonies have had the best effects; for, at Hispaniola and other places, the French are now reduced to such straits, that they can hardly subsist themselves. and are almost disable from fitting out their Merchantmen, much more whole Fleets of

Privateers as heretofore. The same measure too may be said to contribute to the more easy of early reduction of the Havannah; and would certainly have prevented our trade being annoyed by privateers from St. Augustine, had orders been there in due time to grant commissions.

NEW-LONDON July 29. Saturday last two young men named George and Charles Hall, brothers, being in the Mill-Pond at the North Parish of Town washing themselves were both unfortunately drowned; their bodies taken up the next day and buried.

The same Evening two Women were killed by the Lightning at Preston, one the Wife of John Kennedy, the other named Keturah Tracy, a single Woman.

Friday Night last the Custom House in this Place was broken open, and Joseph Hull, Esq; robbed of about 150 pounds currency.

Saturday last arrived here the Brig Britania, Capt. Dudley Saltonstall, from St. Martin; In lat. 23. she was attacked by an enemy's privateer, who engaged her three glasses, but was beat off. Capt. Saltonstall bro't about 10 passengers, among whom are several Captains whose vessels have been taken.

AUGUST 1762

BOSTON Aug. 2. Extract of a Letter from Halifax, July 15, 1762.

"Marshal Law is published here, ——— A Company of Militia mount Guard every Day: ——— an Embargo is laid on all Shipping for about 10 Days. We are putting this Town in the best posture of Defence that is possible; and, should the French pay us a visit, we shall be in a conditiom to give them a very warm and suitable Reception. ——— This comes by Capt. Church, who is permitted to sail, by Reason of his carrying some public Letters. ——— Our Harbour is filled with topsail Vessels and Schooners from Newfoundland; but no Advice is received from Authority of the Particulars of St. John's being taken; but in general 'tis said, that the Inhabitants had 8 or 9 Days allowed them to settle, and dispose of their Effects to the best Advantage they could."

Extracy of a Letter from Halifax.

"I Herewith inclose you a Notification, which was sent to the Inhabitants of Bay of Bulls, Newfoundland, viz.

We, the Commander of his Most Christian Majesty's Fleet in Bay Bulls, make it known to all the Inhabitants of the said Place, that they may come to their Habitation without being Molested.

Aboard of his Majesty's Ship the Robusle, the 24th of June 1762.

(Signed) Lt. Ch. de Turnay."

The Antelope of 50 Guns, with the Convoy from England, and thought to be upon the coast of Newfoundland at this Time: but hope they will receive some advice of the sad Affair, before they get too near and are taken by the Enemy."

By several Vessels arrived here from Newfoundland since our last, we have the following further Accounts from thence, the Master of one of them informs, that he left Ferriland the 1st of July, that he was at Halifax on the 14th, and was informed by a Gentleman who left Ferriland in the Afternoon of the 1st of July, that he saw on the said Day, four French Men of War come out of the Bay of Bulls, and steer as he judged for St. John's. that two of the Ships were of 74 Guns one of 40 Guns, and a Frigate; and it was generally thought there were no other French Ships on that Coast; but that the other four supposed French Ships which had been seen off was now judged to be English Ships bound up the River St. Lawrence: It was said the French landed 1500 Men; 1000 of which disembarked from the two large Ships, and the Remainder from the other two Ships, there being no Transport Ships in Company with them.

We have advice from Halifax, that Capt. James Brooks, Master of one of the Vessels that were taken at Bay of Bulls, which he left on the Appearance of the Enemy's Ships, has deposed that having got to Ferriland, on the 30th of June last, a Man came there and declared to him, that he was in the Fort of St. John's when it surrendered on the 27th; that he left the Fort that Day; That the Number of the Enemy who invested the Fort was said to be 12 to 1500 Men; that they march'd by Land to St. John's from the Bay of Bulls, where the Ships lay: That they brought no Cannon with them against said Fort; and that they had not at the Time of his Departure destroyed any of the Houses at St. John's; but knew not any of the Particulars of the Capitulation.

And last Evening arrived here Capt. Cockran in a Brig from Newfoundland, but last from Halifax in 6 Days, in whom came Passenger the Master of a Vessel who was taken at St. John's and made his Escape from thence the 4th of July, 6 Days after the Place surrendered, who informs, that the French Forces which march'd from the BaY OF Bulls, to St. John's consisted of 1600 fine Troops, and that the Garrison submitted without making any Opposition or any articles of Capitulation, That the French were erecting new Fortifications at St. John's, and were determined to keep the Place, that they had also fitted out 14 sails of Privateers, which were all sail'd on a Cruize before he got from Thence; that they had destroyed the Bay of Bulls, but done no Damage to St. John's. The Inhabitants remaining in quite Possession of their Houses; but that a Guard of French Soldiers were placed at all the Stores; That the French Fleet consisted of 2 Ships of 74 Guns, one of 44, and 2 Frigates, the latter which kept constantly by cruizing off the Mouth of the Harbour; and that they all came from Old France.

The following is a Paragraph from M. d'Arc of the Commerce of Navigation of the Amirauté; which no doubt the French would be glad to put in Execution. ——— "We must attack the English colonies, for all the strength of our enemies live there. I shall keep to this point, and shew the means of putting it into Execution. A superior fleet will cut off the English commerce enterely. The opulence of their colonies consists in, and arise from, their connection with the Mother country. We must cut off this connection by our fleet, and then they will dwindle away and become our prey."

BOSTON Aug. 2. Several Accounts agree that the Enemy had destroyed the Vessels at Bay of Bulls and burnt the houses there, a great Smoak being seen over the Place on the 29th of June; that they destroyed all the Vessels they took, and that the Enemy declared they intend to destroy every thing on the Coast. ——— That the Enemy marched across Country 25 Miles from the Bay of Bulls to St. John's; after they had taken this place they gave the Inhabitants nine Days to sell their Effects, after that, what remained undisposed of, was all to become the Enemy's Property.

BOSTON Aug. 2. By His Excellency the Captain-General.

Whereas I have ordered the Recruiting Officers to apprehend and bring to Justice all such Perons as have deserted from the Provincial Service during the present War, and have never maded Satisfaction for the injury done to the Province, either by repaying the Bounty by them received, or by engaging in other Service, in lieu of that from which they Deserted; I do hereby command and enjoin all Magistrates and Officers, Civil and Military, and all other Persons whom it may concern to be aiding & assisting to such Officers in apprehending and bringing to Justice such Deserters.

And I do hereby give Notice, that if any of the said Deserters shall, voluntarily appear and surrender themselves to Thomas Goldthwait, Esq; Secretary of War at Boston, and repay the Bounty before received, and all other Charges which the Province hath been put to on their Account, or engage to discharge the said Bounty by further Service, which Persons will be excused the Penalties which they have incurred by such Desertion.

And if any Person shall secure or harbour any such Deserters, they may be assured that they will be prosecuted for the same, and have the Penalty of Five Pounds levied upon them, upon due Conviction thereof, according to the Laws made on that behalf.

Given at Boston under my Hand, the second Day of August, in the Year of our Lord 1762.

By His Excellency's Command.   Fra. Bernard.
Thomas Goldthwait, Sec'ry at War.

NEW-YORK Aug. 2. Wednesday night last about 11 o'clock a gentleman was stopped in the Broadway, by a single Foot-Pad, and ordered to stand and deliver; but the gentleman not willing to comply, disputed the point with him, and would have overcome him, but seeing two other rogues coming to his assistance of their companion, the gentleman made the best of his way, and got off from them.

ANNAPOLIS Maryland Aug. 5. On the 26th ult. about 8 miles from Frederick-Town, Mr. George Jacob Poe, was shot at his own House, by a Dutch servant man of his, with two bullets and 5 Swan shots, thro' the body just below the navel, of which he instantly died, and has left a widow and several children to lament him. The Villain who shot him is confin'd in irons in Frederick county goal.

CHARLESTOWN S. Carolina Aug. 4. Letters from

Marinico advise, that the Commanding officers in the expedition were well informed of the strength of the Spaniards in Cuba, and the conditions of the fortresses of that island, before they left Montinico; and that they did not expect to finish the conquest before the month of August. The same letters say, that the Grenades which surrendered on the same terms of Martinico, is a very fine island, and has great plenty of every thing. That the French had taken pains to fortify the hills, which were strong by nature as they commanded both the town and fort; had they taken the same pain to defend them, the conquest of that island would have been harder than that of Martinico, for it may be defended by two thousand men against sixteen thousand. To form some idea of the difficulty of getting to those works, the chief engineer told some of our officers, that to get up one of the guns, a 24 pounder, with the carriage, was a task for 3000 negroes for a whole day.

BOSTON Aug. 9. On Thursday last arrived here the Sloop from Newfoundland with about 50 Men Passengers, sixteen whom made their Escape from St. John's in a Boat a Fortnight after the Place surrendered to the French; they inform that the Enemy had already erected three new Fortifications there, and had also greatly strengthened the old Fort on the Land side: ——— That they had sent to England in two small Vessels, the English Garrison which they took there, consisting of about 80 Soldiers; and that other Vessels were preparing to carry home the Merchants and Seamen: ——— That they were fitting the Cramont Frigate for the Sea; and that no English Vessel had come into the Harbour since the French had Possession of it; ——— That the Antelope Man of War having received Intelligence of St. John's being in the Hands of the Enemy, landed Her Marines on the Isle of Bowy, at Ferriland, where there is a Fort, and the only Place that held out when the Island was taken by the French in the Queen Ann's War; and that the Antelope afterwards went to St. Mary's Bay: That the had fitted out no Privateers of any Consequence, but only a few small Crafts, which were gone to the Northward and had destroyed the Settlement at Conception-Bay, and were proceeding to Trinity to do the same there; both of which Places the Inhabitants had deserted with most of their Effects: ——— That the French General had issued a Manifesto signifying that such of the Inhabitants who did not come in and submit themselves before the 25th day of July, should if taken be treated with great severity: ——— That the French gave out they expected to be joined by 6 or 8 Spanish Men of War, and also a Number more from France, and that they totally determined to keep Possession of the Place.

Extract of a Letter from Louisbourg July 30.

"This Moment we have, had a Cartel arrived with two Officers and a Number of Men from St. John's and are bound to England; they put in here for want of Provisions having only enough for 12 Days; but they are to proceed from here to Halifax, we have only sufficient for ourselves: These Officers inform us that the French have 2 Ships of the Line and 2 Frigates, and 1600 Grenadiers, very fine Troops, they having pick'd them out of 20 Regiments, they ar busily employ'd in fortifying the Place, which they say will be compleatly done; and that there is 500 Men to Garrison this Winter & they have no thoughts of proceeding any further, and the remainder are to return from whence they came: ——— They oblige the Inhabitants at St. John's to work and pay them nothing for it; and they are greatly afraid the Fleet soon coming to them, they having constantly Reports of that Kind. ——— One of the Gentlemen told me, that they spoke with a Fishing Schooner who inform'd them that he saw 4 English Men of War, who spoke to him and told him that they were going to block up St. John's Harbour: ——— The French treat the Prisoners very ill, putting them on board with stinking Provisions, and Blubber Casks filled with Water: this is all I can learn at present."

We hear at Louisbourg they are preparing to prevent the French getting Possession there, if they should attempt it from Newfoundland.

PHILADELPHIA Aug. 12. The following is the substance of a letter wrote by a Person at Snow

Hill dated the 31st of last Month.

"That he had just parted with three Men who had been taken in Chesopeak Bay at the mouth of the York river, on their way from Norfolk to some river in Maryland: That in the schooner were Goods to the value of 6000 guineas: That the vessel that took them was a sloop of 8 carriage and 12 swivel guns, and 75 men, from Cape Francois, commanded by Don Pedro Ordogriez: That the Captain informed them, a few days before the sloop attacked a letter of Marque brig from Philadelphia, off the capes of Delaware, but was obliged to leave her, with the loss of her first Captain a Frenchman, who had a French commission, tho' the chief of the crew were Spaniards, as the above-named Captain. That afterward they took Captain Baird, from Wilmington to Sinepuxent, whose vessel they scuttl'd and endeavoured to sink her, but she ran ashore on Asiatongue beach: That they gave a small schooner they took in the bay to the prisoners, who got into Sinepuxent inlet: That there was on board the privateer an Englishman, born on the eastern shore of Maryland, who was well acquainted with the bays and shores and had agreed with the enemy to plunder and destroy the plantations &c. And accordingly they had landed 23 men, in order to carry off some negroes from a vessel just arrived; but the Captain having notice of their design, got his men together and stood on his defence; upon which the privateer's men went on board again."

One of our Pilots, who was on board the boat they gave the prisoners, informs, that the sloop had also taken two other vessels off Carolina.

Extract of a letter from an officer on board his Majesty's ship Centurion off Cape-Florida July 21.

"I left the army and fleet going on very well in the siege of the Havannah. ——— The troops from New-York are much wanted.——— I doubt not but by this time the Moore castle is ours, as they expected it to surrender, or to take it by storm, by the twenty-second. It has made a very obstinate defence."

PORTSMOUTH New-Hampshire Aug. 13. We have

certain Intelligence from Brintwood about 20 Miles from this Town, that the reason of the present dry Season, large Fires have been burning for above a Week there, several Houses and Barns have been already destroyed, and others in the utmost Danger. It has run over two or three Thousand Acres of Land, with to greatest Rapidity, destroying all the Corn and Fences: some Farms are burnt to the degree, that there's scarcely any Thing either green or dry to be seen except Rubbish and Ashes. Above 200 persons are constantly employed Night and Day in watching its progress, and striving to keep it from the Buildings, being no Prospect at present of it stopping. ——— It proceeded first from Brintwood to Epping, but upon the Wind shifting, it returned with great Fury on Monday last, and it burnt within half a Mile of Brintwood Meeting-House. The Woods in many Places in the Country are on Fire, which makes vast Destruction amongst the Pines, so that the Prospect at present is dismal, having no Hopes of it's abating, but rather increasing, unless we should be favoured with great rains.

BOSTON Aug. 16. Yesterday arrived in Nantasket Road a Brig from St. John's in Newfoundland in 20 Days; She was bound to Virginia and had on board about 90 Passengers, among whom are several Masters of Vessels and others who had refused to take the Oath of Allegiance to the French: They confirm the accounts of the French having strengthened the Place, and that they were to leave a garrison of 600 Men during the Winter: That Capt. Ross, the late commanding Officer there, and the Capt of the Gramont were gone to England, and that a cartel was soon to sail for New-York with a number more of the Inhabitants, who are not allowed to carry off any Effects: The French Troops are all fine pick'd Men, and had recruited about 200 since they had Possession there; but that the Fleet, consisting of only two Ships of the Line a Frigate and a Store Ship were poorly manned: That the Antelope Man of War of 50 Guns, and the Surene Frigate were in daily expectation of an English Fleet from the Continent. ——— That the above mentioned Brig was one of the Fleet from Ireland with Provisions, and arrived at St. John's after that Place had surrendered, and was afterwards made a Present of the Gentleman who commands her together with most of the Cargo, but for what Reason may perhaps hereafter appear.

BOSTON Aug. 16. We hear there is no Truth in an Account from Sheffield of the Onondago Indians having fallen upon German Flats, and killing 40 of the Inhabitants; the Story having arisen from a Drunken Frolick among some of the People there, but no Blood shed.

We hear from Douglass in Worcester County, that two Children of Ensign Chaberland of that Town being left at home, got a Pair of Shears to play with, the Point whereof accidentally struck one of the children (about 10 Years old) under his Pap, whereby she bled to Death in 5 minutes.

NEW-YORK Aug. 16. By a vessel arrived at Wilmington from Martinico we learn, that on the 19th ult. about 70 leagues E. S. E. of the Nantucket Shouls, he was chaced by two vessels, one a 50 gun dhip, the other a small frigate; and on the 22d saw a brigantine ashore between Little Egg-Horbour and Barney's Gut.

WILLIAMSBURG Aug. 16. A letter from a gentleman to his friend in Norfolk, dated Maryland, Oxford, August 4, 1762.

"This will inform you of a French privateer being in the bay. Mr. Glassel and Mr. Mackie, who went up in Capt. Goodrich's schooner, were taken the night they left Hampton road, by a sloop of 8 carriage and 12 swivel guns, called La Marian, a French commander, but all the rest Spaniards. The present Captain's name Don Pedro Ordogriez, and behav'd very well, but could not influence his people to do the same, for they stripp'd them of every thing. --- This happened the 27th of last month. On taking the vessel they refused to ransom at any rate; but carried her off Cape Charles, where they came to anchor, and landed on the island with 26 men arm'd, in order to attack a Guineaman brig, that was driven ashore there: But the Captain, with 16 hands, and the negroes, stood on the defensive, and made them lay all attempts there. They then went to sea, and about 4 leagues off gave the prisoners a pilot-boat they had before taken, and put them all into her, among whom was one John Baird, who commanded a small sloop belonging to Wilminton in Pennsylvania, which they had taken and sunk: This Scoundrel behaved worse to Mr. Glassel and Mackie, than the Spaniards; he obliged them to row, and gave them no victuals; also extorted a promise that they should not mention any thing concerning his vessel being taken for some time, that he might make much insurance on her. I forgot to tell you she belong'd to the Cape, was short of provisions, and went off the land after taking this schooner. --- Some time ago they had an engagement with a brig bound to Philadelphia: The first broadside the Captain of the privateer and 4 men were killed, and the mast damaged, when they quitted the brig. It is to be added that this Baird would not suffer Mr. Glassel to speak with a ship they saw in the night, with a light on her mizzen-peak, and two vessels under convoy: He was afraid of a man of war and the press. Could they had spoken to her, Mr. Glassel says could have directed them exactly to her, as they had left her but a few hours."

BOSTON Aug. 23. Some additional Accounts from Newfoundland.

The Brigantine that arrived from Newfoundland on condition of his carrying from St. John's 92 English ——— Men, Women and Children to Maryland; he landed 17 of them at their desire at Louisbourg in Nova-Scotia, the rest he brought to this Port. ——— Some of the principal Persons who came in her, are, William Thomas, Esq; a Merchant of St. John's whose Family arrived here some time before; Capt. Shepherd of this Town, whose vessel was taken there; Capt. Kesley of Rhode Island; Capt. John Johnson of New-York, and John Lewis, of London: ——— The French as soon as they got Possession of St. John's immediately set about fortifying the Place & have made a Tier of Ramparts all around, and mounted them with Guns taken from the different ships, and have also built a new Battery on the

Southward of that called Fort William, or the South Battery: The Captain of the French Storeship who is an Irishman named Sutton, but calls himself Clanard, has Inlisted about 200 of his Countrymen, who were at work every Day and seem'd to be very fond of their new Masters: The French have laid a Boom across the mouth of the Harbour of St. John's, with Masts fastened together with banking Chains: It is the opinion of several Persons who have seen the Fortifications, that they could make but little resistance if a regular Force came against them; for tho' the troops are the best of their kind, yet the Seamen are so very bad that they are not able to fight their Ships: The Ships in the harbour have their Yards and Top-masts down and Sails unbent, designing to stay till the latter end of September; but notwithstanding their seeming Resolution they are constantly alarmed with the Expectation of English Men of War: The Enemy are determined to remove all the English from St. John's, and leaving only those who would engage on the side of the French King, for which Purpose the Inhabitants were all ordered on board the respective Vessels provided for them, with very little Allowance of Provisions, and permitting only to take a bed and blanket, not more being granted even to those who had Possessions of great Value there: But it is said that this was contrary to the Disposition of the Marquis de Hossonville, Commander of the Land Forces; Whose behaviour to the English was very humane and generous: Tho' it could not be extended far, as he was under the Command of Commodore de Tournay, who commander and Chief of the whole Land and Sea Forces, and whose cruel Disposition would not allow the least Favour to be granted the Inhabitants; which M. Hossonville has given out that he will represent to the Court on his return to France: He gave Liberty to some principal Persons that came here in Capt. Hearn, to take some of their own Stock of Poultry for their Voyage, but before they got out of the Harbour the Commedore ordered most of them to be taken away: He is so severe as to threaten with Death any Englishman that only kills a Hog.

After the above Brig came out of St. John's, they saw a Sloop standing in, supposed to be from New-York, as such one was expected. ———
The Brig also met a Shallop, off Cape Race, and sent Word by her to the Commanders of the Antelope and Syrene Men of War, who were at Placentia, of the Design of the French in sending out 8 or 10 Fishing Vessels with 30 or 40 Troops on board of each, with Muskets, Swivels Guns, and some Carriage Guns to destroy the Fishery in the several adjacent Harbours to the Northward of St. John's as far as Trinity.

It is said the Irish at Ferriland, in Expectation of the French coming there, while the Inhabitants were in Confusion, broke open many Stores, and pillaged great quantities of Goods.

BOSTON Aug. 23. We have no Accounts from the Havannah of a later Date than those which have been already published: 'Tis said our Forces had possession of all the Neck of Land to the Westward of the Entrance of the Harbour (except the Puntal, some Batteries along the shore, and a Castle call'd the Governor's, lately built upon a Hill which commands the Town and other Forts, and mounting three field Cannon) and also the River Lagida, wherefrom the besieged were usually supplied with Water thro' Pipes; and that the Spanish Governor had sent a Flag of Truce with a Message to Lord Albemarle exclaiming against the Measures of cutting off the Water from the Inhabitants, as contrary to the Rules of War among civilized Nations: That the Spaniards were said to have 1870 Pieces of Cannon at the Havanna, mostly on the Forts and Batteries which faced the Entrance of the Harbour: That the Men of War sunk at the Mouth of the Harbour, were buoyed up so that their upper Decks appear'd above Water: That Admiral Pocock's Squadron lay at Anchor all along the Shore both to the Leeward and Windward of the Harbour, just out of Gun-shot, with Winter Top-masts up and no Top-gallant-masts; and we make no doubt that by the first Vessel from thence we shall have Advice of the Place being in the Possession of the English.

BOSTON Aug. 23. Thursday last was committed

to Goal at Salem, one Ellingwood of Beverly, for the Murder of Mr. Poland of the same Town, having run him thro' the neck with a sword, in a Fray which happened between them, of which wound he instantly died.

Friday last a Vessel arrived here in 10 Days from Halifax; she sail'd from thence in Company with Lord Colvill in the Northumberland of 74 Guns; the Gosport, Capt. Jarvis, of 40, and the Massachusetts Province Ship King George, Capt. Hallowell of 24 Guns, bound to Newfoundland where they were to be joined by the Antelope of 50 Guns, and Syrene of 24, in order to block up the French Fleet at St. John's till Assistance arrive from Europe.

We also learn, that all the Remaining French Neutrals at Nova-Scotia, amounting to between 300 & 400, were ship'd on board several Vessels and were to sail the first fair Wind for ????, and that their Wives and Children were not permitted to embark with them, but ship'd on board other vessels to be transported to the same Place.

BOSTON Aug. 23. Wheras great Complaints are made that many Hucksters in this Town are guilty of forestalling the Market, notwithstanding the Law which orders, "That no Hucksters shall before one o'Clock in the Afternoon in any Part of Town, buy any Provisions brought to Town by Land or over the Ferries for sale, with intent to sell the same again, under Penalty of Twenty Shillings for each offence." ——— They are therefore to acquaint those Offenders, that proper Persons being now appointed to take Notice of such Offences, they may depend on being prosecuted for the same accordingly to Law.

By Order of the Select-Men.

William Cooper, Town-Clerk.

BOSTON Aug. 30. A Late Author, in his Book entitled The Importance of Canada considered, has the following Speech of an Indian Sachem, which shews the Consequence of the Possession of Niagara to the English.

"My name id Waybukcumigut, I am Chief and Captain of the Messasagas, a nation that has ever been at war with the English. I confess we had laid your fairest provinces to waste, that we have slaughtered your men and your women, and your children we have made captive. But do not attribute this to any particular antipathy we have to you, or any partiality and attachment to the french. If you would search for the real cause of our proceedings, cast your eyes on the map; you will there see that whoever is in possession of this strong Castle of Niagra must effectually command the Messasagas, and may dictate them what measures they think proper. From hence we are supplied with the very means of our subsistance; for we have now been so long diffused to bows and arrows, the weapons of our ancestors, that without ammunition we cannot subsist.

The French were sensible of this our state of dependency, accordingly they treated us as if the Great Spirit had not created us of the same species with themselves; we groaned under their Yoke, but had only this alternative to chuse, either implicitly to obey their commands, or to perish through famine with our wives and children: We have now changed our masters, for our masters we must acknowledge you to be, and we believe you to be a better and more generous people than they are: we hope we shall find you so; on our part we promise that you shall experience in us most faithful and obedient subjects; no danger shall approach you from any quarter, but we will give you timely notice, that you may avoid it; and the fears which we have raised in your eyes we will wash away with blood of your perfidious enemies that should the French be ever restored to the possession of this Castle and you shall hear that the Messasagas have resumed the war hatchet against you, do not accuse them of persuading us, lay the blame on your own folly and stupidity."

Boston Aug. 30. The following lately happened at Carpoon, a small Island at the entrance of the strait of bellisle and the most northern part of our Fisheries at Newfoundland.

The Indians comes from the Main once a year (the strait being very narrow) to trade with the Europeans, and if to rob them if they can. These

Indians, who are a tribe of the Eskimaux, coming over with their whalebone traded two days with our fishermen, but the 3d day observing them to be off their guard, their firearms at some distance, and that they were a good way from the blockhouse, these savages thought it a good opportunity to attack our people especially as it was Sunday, which is a sort of holiday with the fishermen, when every one's curiosity or avarice prompted them to run and meet the Indians, the two preceeding days having been spent principally about the fish. —— The Indians mixing with our people, traded with each particular man for his knife, or whatever cutting instrument he had, almost at the same moment: Whilst others brought bows and arrows from their canoes, and distributed them among their own people; This being done, they instantly, with one consent, fell upon the fishermen and stabbed many with their own knives, which they had parted with but the moment before.

They killed 11 on the spot, and wounded 16 or 17; whereupon all our people that could, fled to their boats, and got on board a sloop that lay in the road (4 or 5 however, having a little less fear than the rest, got into the blockhouse, and bro't off most of the arms, killing one Indian who was more foreward than the rest) They then weigh'd one anchor, cut the cable of another, and came away as fast as possible, leaving their whole season's fish, furniture, trade, whalebone, and every thing behind. our Countrymen were 50 at first, 11 were killed outright, 17 or 18 got off wounded, and of these two died in a few days. The Indians were so prudent as to single out and make fire of the principal people, killing two masters of vessels (one of whom commanded the sloop, and the other took care of the fishery ashore) and the mate, and slew or wounded every boatmaster, splitter, and master-voyager, who are the chief people among the fishermen and shoremen.

These Eskimaux are a faithless cruel tribe, and have often surprized the French in the same manner, and are notwithstanding so terrified at fire-arms that a dozen resolute men, armed, would have destroy'd every one of those wretches, had they been 500, as they were on an island; and had five of our men kept themselves armed, they would never had been attacked at all.

BOSTON Aug. 30. We hear that a French Priest has been among the Neutrals at Nova-Scotia ever since last Spring, who of late have behav'd a very insolent Manner, giving out on hearing the success of the French at Newfoundland, that they should soon have Possession of their Land again, when they would cut all the Englishmen's throats. A Number of Indians has also been among them.

Wednesday last nine sail of Vessel arrived here from Halifax, having on board upwards of 700 French Neutrals (so called) that were collected from several Parts of Nova-Scotia, and sent here.

Last Thursday Night arrived here a Brig in 21 Days from St. John's in Newfoundland, having on board a Number of Men, Women, and Children, late Inhabitants of that Place, together with about 50 Regulars belonging to the Garrison, but no Officers of any Note. ——— This Vessel was sent from St. John's in order to proceed for England, and was commanded by Frenchmen, but not having Provisions for such a Voyage, they confined the Captain and Mate, and bro't the Vessel to this Port, and when they got in here they had expended all their Provisions, except Bread and Water: ——— By this Brig we learn, that the French are still fortifying the Place, and even oblige the English People to Work daily on the Fort, one of which refusing, was instantly shot dead on the Spot by a Frenchman.

BOSTON Aug. 30. Moore-Castle.
[The following Fortress at the Havannah] Taken by the English.

This Evening arrived from Havannah, which he left the 7th instant, by whom we have the following Account:

Letter from the Havannah, July 12, 1762.

"The Siege of the Havannah began 40 days ago, and has been ever since continued very warm: The Spaniards behaved with the greatest bravery and resolution: The Moore Castle is almost beat to rubbish; and most of the batteries are greatly damaged, and it is computed that they have lost 100 men every day since the siege commenced.

—— Yesterday morning the Spaniards sallied out among our batteries with about 2000 men, who were in the space of two hours repulsed with the loss of 1200 men killed and prisoners; the Spaniards afterwards sent a flag of truce to Lord Albemarle and Sir George Pocock, who offered them a capitulation, which the Spaniards refused, declaring they would be buried in the ruins before they would accept such terms, upon which our batteries were opened and now playing like thunder. Our troops got possession of the glacis some days ago, and have sent about 40 miners into the ditch, who have already dug about 10 feet under the wall of the Castle, and now filling it with powder, so that very soon we expect to see their strong Castle blown up, and then our troops are to storm, and put every man to the sword."

Capt. McAuley informs us, that on the 28th of July our troops sprung two mines under Moore-Castle, which destroyed great part of the walls, and at 12 o'clock at noon the same day stormed the Castle and carried it with the loss of about 50 men, the number the Spaniards then killed were about 1500: As soon as we got possession of the Castle, the Spaniards began firing from all their forts at the parts that remained standing, and when McAuley left it the whole was a heap of rubish.

From the 28th of July out troops began erecting batteries opposite the town, and on the 10th of August they were to be opened, and 8 sail of the line were to enter the harbour and make a general attack, and all were sure we should take the whole in a short time.

Col. Howe was burning all the villages, which Capt. Capt. McCauley says looks as if the whole country was on fire.

Many of our troops were sick, owing to the fatigues and dews, but few died, and even those that were taken down soon recovered. The first division of troops from New-York in going thro' the old Streights lost 5 of the Transport ships, and a 40 gun ship, the people were all landed safe at the Havannah. Four of the second division was taken by some French men of war, viz. The Britannia, Smith; the Pretty Sally, McLeland; and the Polly, Davidson, from this port; and a Brig belonging to New-York; the names of the 5 vessels lost, we have not been able to learn.

[On receiving the above joyful News on Thursday Morning last, the Cannon belonging to the Artillery Company of this Town, were immediately drawn out and discharged, and about Noon, a Number of the Guns at Castle-William, were also discharged on the same Occasion.]

NEW-YORK Aog. 30. [The following Letters we believe, will be thought to give the best general Accounts of affairs from the Havannah.]

On Board the Briton, off the Havannah in Cuba, July 28, 1762.

"We left Martinico the 6th of May and arrived here the 7th of June, and immediately landed our troops and took possession of several Spanish out-posts, with very little loss or opposition from the enemy. A history of whose proceedings since our being here, I imagine will not be disagreeable to you; therefore I'll proceed from our landing on the 7th of June, which was, immediately to take possession, and maintain ourselves masters of all the heights and advantageous grounds near the Moor-Castle, and encamp'd our troops on different heights all round the town, in order to observe the enemy's motions, and to draw their attention to various quarters: Being thus situated, a detachment of our troops, together with a sufficient number of marines and sailors began to build betteries, in order to attack the Mora, which were a few days opened, & then assisted by four of our men of war; all of which behaved gallantly, except Capt. John Campbell of the Sterling Castle, who never came so nigh as to share in the engagement, and is now in disgrace. ---- The Cambridge suffer'd most, but they all got off, finding they had no chance for success from their attempts, soon after this the Spaniards used to sally out upon us, but were always beat back with great loss; particularly a few days ago, when about 1000 of them attacked our batteries, with full hopes of victory, having wrote on the front of their hats, neither to take or give quarters; but the Dons soon got such a drubbing as sent 300 of them into the other world, and wounded many; and our loss did not amount to above 100 killed and wounded in this important affair: Our batteries still continued a very hot fire, and had reduced the Mora to a large heap of ruin, and almost dismounted all their guns. We then got full possession of their glacis, and sent some miners into the ditch, who dug a mine under the wall, which was sprung two days ago, and immediately after our people storm'd it sword in hand, and kill'd 400 Of the enemy on the spot, and took 600 prisoners, among which was Don Vellisco, dangerous wounded; he was Commandant of the castle, and made a noble defence: Our loss in this affair was 11 killed and 9 wounded. We are now master of the Great Moor-Castle, which the Spaniards thought impossible, and look'd upon as the strongest place in the world, and the pride of their country. In consequence of this the whole town (large and vastly more elegant than New-York) together with 12 ships of the line, 9 or 10 frigates, and several trading ships in the harbour, must in very little time hence fall in our possession, which makes this a great conquest. The country round looks very delightful, and by every person's opinion who have traveled thro' it, they all agree that it's capable of the best cultivation, but has been greatly neglected by the Spaniards who use it chiefly in raising mules and cattle. All the small stock around this place is already chiefly destroyed during the siege. Our troops lived very well and elegantly for the first three weeks, killing and destroying every thing they could catch: and the Spaniards on the other hand destroying all the small stock that they could not use, in order to prevent our people from being so well supply'd; that betwixt the two, I imagine, by the time we get into town, we shall have very little fresh meat to eat, excepting those who go a great way into the country shooting their wild Cattle."

         I am, your's, &c.

Part of another Letter from Havannah.
—— "The Spanish force at the commencement of the siege, was 12 ships of the line 9 frigates, 2 new ships on the stocks, 4000 regular troops, with marines, sailors, negroes, and militia, all together were supposed to be about 18,000 or 20,000 men.

"The British forces were 23 or 24 ships of the line, 16 frigates & bombs, 12,000 regular troops, which with marines, sailors &c. were supposed to be about 23 or 24,000 brave men. Our troops troops have hitherto suffer'd little, in proportion to those of the enemy, in action; but the fatigue together with the climate has occasion'd a considerable sickness among them, tho' very few but what recovered in a few days, or perhaps a week. The Spaniards, I believe, begin to be very tired of us; and I imagine, because we don't set the town on fire, and attack 'em with greater vigour, they think we soon intend to leave them, but that is not our intention and I'm thoroughly convinc'd, that in a few days, or a week hence, they will find their mistake, and see that we only mean to avoid dangerous attempts with our troops, and make ourselves masters of the town with as small a loss, both to their houses, and to our troops as possible."

The following is further Intelligence we have from Capt. M'Auley who left the Havannah the 7th of August.
—— That our people did not fire a gun on the enemy, from their entering the place, to the time of his sailing; but he was informed from good authority that it was determin'd to make a general attack on the 10th instant, by land and sea; for which purpose batteries were erecting, and 8 sail of the line had orders to enter the harbour, with others to cover them, and that he on the 10th being within hearing of the guns, actually hear the firing begin about 9 in the morning, and continued all day: That the first division of the New-York troops arrived at the Havannah the night before they stormed the castle; but in going thro' the Bahama Straits, the Enterprize man of war, and 5 transports

were lost, but all the troops and ships crews saved: That the second division, from the same place, arrived some days after the storming 5 of the transports being taken, with about 500 soldiers on board by some French men of war, and carried to Cape Francois. That there was the greatest harmony betwixt the land and sea forces, the Admiral having done every thing in his power to forward the service, and the seamen were of the most use in securing the batteries, &c. And tho' the duty was exceedingly hard, yet it was undertaken with the greatest chearfullness by all concerned, and executed in the most speedy manner imaginable: That the fleet had made several prizes, among which were 3 frigates, and a sloop of war: That on the landing of our army the inhabitants of two fine villages left them, tho' the General had forbid any plunder to be made for a number of days, and issued proclamation encouraging them to come back: That our army and navy were in high spirit, hoping soon to be masters of the whole place: And that a 70 gun ship was ordered to be in readiness to carry the glad tiding to England: And, on the other hand, the Spaniards were as obligated and brave as they had been thro' the siege, and resolved to keep the place or lose it inch by inch.

NEW-YORK Aug. 30. Last Week John Harwood, arrived here from Virginia, having come passenger in a Vessel to that Place from the Coast of Africa; and says that he belonged to the Schooner Success, Captain Nathanial Roads, of Rhode-Island; which vessel was cast ashore on the Coast. He came from thence the fifth of May, an informs us, that the following Vessels belonging to Rhode Island, were at Annamaboa, viz.
   Capt. Pinnegar, with 50 Slaves on board.
   Capt. Gardner, with 150 Slaves on board.
   Capt. Flessenan, with 24 Slaves on board.
   Capt. Celeb Gardner, with 10 Slaves on board.
   Capt. Carpenter, with 20 Slaves on board.
   Capt. Peter Allan, in a Brig just arrived.

NEWPORT Rhode-Island Aug. 31. Capt. Wright, Express from Halifax stopt here last-Evening, to put his Pilot on Shore; he left that place last Saturday, and informs, That Lord Colvill was join'd by five Sail of Line from England, and and he had sent an Express to Col. Amherst to hasten his Troops, which were accordingly embarking, in order to Sail Sunday Morning. ——— We hope soon to have the Pleasure of hearing that the French Gentry are going Passengers to England in some of our Ships.

SEPTEMBER 1762

CHARLESTOWN S. Carolina Sept. 4. It's said That Captain Lindsay, of his Majesty's frigate Trent, on the Sterling-Castle, Cambridge, Dragon, and Marlbourough being ordered to batter the Moore-Castle at the Havannah, waited upon Admiral Pocock, and represented to him, that he as he commanded only a frigate, he could be of no service, nor acquire honour; therefore requested, that if any of the four ships lost their Captains, he might be permitted to take command during the cannonade; which the Admiral complied with; and Capt. Lindsay accordingly kept his barge ready, and well manned, and in about 5 minutes the Cambridge threw out the signal for the Captain being killed, when Capt. Lindsay put off instantly, thro' a most terrible fire, got on board the Cambridge, and fought her most gallantly till she, and two ships, were ordered to be towed off.

From Jamaica we have Advice, that Capt. Bendall from Georgia, had carried into Kingston, 16 seamen, which he took up at sea in a longboat, and belonged to a North-American ship that had been taken by a French Privateer.

BOSTON Sept. 6. Extract of a Letter from Halifax, dated August 28, 1762.

"A Number of Transports arriv'd here Yesterday from New-York, which have on board 200 Troops, they are to carry 500 Regulars of our Garrison and 500 Provincials, and the Garrison at Louisbourgh being about 500 more in all about 1700, to retake St. John's; the Expedition to be commanded by Col. Amherst, and will depart from hence in two Days. ——— Lord Colvill is at Newfoundland with four Men of War, of 70, 30, 40 and 20 Guns, and the Massachusetts Province ship Capt. Hallowell, ——— in all probability they will be join'd soon by some Ships from Home."

BOSTON Sept. 6. Thursday last a Gentleman came to Town from Newbury, who arrived there in a Flag of Truce from M. Tournay, Commander of the French Forces by sea and Land at St. John's in Newfoundland: She had 19 Days Passage, and had on board 62 Men, Women & Children, 28 wereof were Heads of Families, all Inhabitants of St. John's and bound to this Port. ——— We are informed that the French Ships had all their Sails bent, and were wooded and watered, but being weakly mann'd they had strengthened themselves by inlisting between 4 and 500 of the Irish, who were constantly exercising the Cannon and Small Arms on board: ——— The Ships it was judged would sail within a Fortnight; A Garrison to be left there of 4 or 500 French Regulars under the command of an Officer who has been with the French in America all the War.

Mr. Tournay says the Inhabitant signed a Paper, wherein they engaged not to take up arms against the French during the War: But this is thought to be a fallacy.

Deserted from Castle-William the 3d instant, William Tricks of his Majesty's 40th Regiment. He is about 5 Feet 3 Inches high, dark complexion, dark brown Hair, black Eyes, well-made, by Trade a Gardiner, born in Old England: Had on when he went away, a brown Jacket, stripped Waistcoat, Scarlet Cloth Breeches, white Stockings. Whoever apprehends said Deserter, and lodge him in any of his Majesty's Goals, or will deliver him to Lieut. Elliott of the 1st or Royal Regiment in Boston, shall receive what is allowed by Act of Parliament for apprehending Deserters, and all reasonable Charges paid.

BOSTON Sept. 6. The following Intelligence from Nassau, in New-Providence July 23, 1762.

On the 21st a most melancholy accident happened here. The privateer schooner Hawke of Philadelphia, commanded by Capt. Archbald, foundered about 1000 yards without our Bar, by means of a violent gust of wind, which took them so suddenly as she stood off and on that she went down in a moment's time, whereby 23 souls are gone to give account of their actions, and others are reserved for other destinies, Very fortunely two seamen were in a boat astern, who, casting out the painter instantly, saved seven people; but the most lucky circumstance was, a Bermudian sloop just coming in at that time, and the pilot boat with her, who saved the rest; but for this, few would have escaped drowning.

NEW-YORK Sept. 6. About 9 o'Clock last Night, Capt. Branscomb, arrived here from St. John's in Newfoundland in a Sloop with 78 Men, Women and Children, belonging to Inhabitants of that Place: He left St. John's the 12th of August, with Provisions scarce enough for one Week, but he put into Farryland, and got a small supply: He confirms the Inhumanity of the French to the English Inhabitants, and that between 4 and 500 of the Fishermen were obliged to enter into the French Service or Stave; that several Parties of the French Soldiers had deserted, and gone to the English at Plecentia, and other Places.

NEW-YORK Sept. 6. The following very Important Intelligence of the Reduction of the Havannah, to His Britannic Majesty's Arms,

We received Friday Afternoon last, by an Express from Philadelphia. It was brought thither the Day before by Capt. Spafford in 14 Days from the Havannah, and confirmed last Night by the arrival here of fifteen Transports under proper Convoy, directly from that Place, which they left the twenty-second day of August, viz.

On Friday, July 30th a chosen Number of Soldiers attacked the Moro, or Moore Castle, and took it by Storm, with the Loss of many Spaniards. From that Day to Tuesday the 10th of August, the Soldiers, and a great Number of Sailors, were employed in raising and compleating of Facine Batteries, for the Cannon and Mortars, on an Eminence that ranges from the Moore Castle along the East Side of the Harbour, abreast with the major part of the City, and their best Fortification. On Tuesday the 10th of August, at 12 o'Clock, my Lord Albemarle sent an Officer with a Drum to the Governor of the Havannah, to demand Possession of the City, and in case of refusal, to acquaint him he would set Fire to it the next Morning. The Governor sent an Answer, that he should not give up the City, that he had six Months Ammunition to defend it. on Wednesday, the 12th of August, at 5 o'Clock in the Morning, all the Batteries began to play on the City, and Forts and kept so warm a Fire on them, that at three o'Clock in the Afternoon our Batteries had dismounted the major Part of their Guns on the City Walls, and in the several strong Forts, and had killed then a great Number of Men, at which Time the Governor sent out 3 Officers, with a Drum, in order to desire them to think of Terms of Capitulation; which was granted. It was said that these Gentlemen Officers desir'd to know, whether the Spanish Admiral, with three other Men of War of the Line, could be permitted to sail to old Spain and to be unsearched or molested; and that our General and Admiral gave for an Answer, that they could not allow them even a Long-Boat; but should have good English Ships to transport them to Spain.

On Saturday the 14th, my Lord Albemarle, with the Grenadiers, marched into the City and took possession of it, and the remainder of the Army encamped without the City Walls.

On Monday of the 16th, Commodore Keppel sailed into the Harbour, and took Possession of the Men of War, which were reported to be nine Ships of the Line, besides 3 or 4 that the Spaniards have sunk across the Harbour's mouth; they had launched one of 110 Guns but a few Days before the arrival of the Fleet. We were informed that the Spanish Admiral told our General, that there was more naval Stores at the Havannah, than would compleatly rig all the Men of War that are there in the Fleet. ——— The Report of the King's Money in the Treasury, was various. Some said 8 and others even 14 Millions of Mill'd Dollars.

On Thursday the 19th, and Friday the 20th several of our largest Men of War went into the Harbour, and also a Number of large Transports, which were designed to carry the Spanish Soldiers to Spain.

The Terms of Capitulation were not known to the publick; but the Spanish Families that had withdrawn from the City to the Country were all returned with their Baggage, and were in possession of their Habitation; and some Soldiers, and English Negroes, were hanged for committing some small thefts on them.

In Addition to the foregoing, we are farther informed by the men of war and transports arrived last Night,---- That there were Five Million Sterling, in specie, found in the Spanish treasury; and it was thought as much more would be got which had been conveyed into the country. That two Galeons likewise were taken in the harbour, and one French 74 gun ship. That four Dutch vessels arrived at the Havannah two days before our fleet appeared off, loaded with Ammunition; and 'tis thought without their assistance the Spaniards could not have held out above a few days. That there were 7 Spanish men of war of the line on float in the harbour, and two of the line and one frigate sunk. That there were two other frigates burnt, one by lightning the other by our shells. --- The Spanish garrison was all embarking for Spain as fast as possible; our troops not to enter the town till they were gone. That Commodore Keppel entered with his division; and that Admiral Pocock with his was under way going in. ---- That we lost a considerable number of officers and private men during the siege; and that the Royal Highland Regiment alone lost at least 17 officers, and Mr. Johnson their chaplain. ---- There were 30 sail of transports left at Havannah for this port; having the 17th regiment, the two battalions of Royal Highlanders, and Montgomery's on board, mostly sick; but only arrived here with their convoy, the Enterprize of 40 guns, and Porcupine man of war, having parted with others two days after they left the Havannah; who 'twas imagin'd join'd the Jamaican fleet of 100 sail, then beating thro' for Europe.

It was the Chesterfield Man that was lost going thro' the old straits of Bahama, and not the Enterprize as lately published.

BOSTON Sept. 8. Wednesday last the Great and General Court of the Assembly of the Province met here, when his Excellency the Governor was pleased to make the following Speech to both Houses, viz.

Gentlemen of the Council and Gentlemen of the Houses of Representatives.

I Have been always desirous to make your attendance in the General Court as unexpensive to yor Constituents and as convenient to yourselves as the Nature and Incidents of the public Business will allow. But as, while the War continues, this Province, however happy in the Operation being removed at a Distance, must expect to bear Share of the Trouble and Expence of it: It will sometimes unavoidably happen that I must be obliged to call you together at an unreasonable Time.

I have now to lay before you a Requisition of His Excellency Sir Jeffery Amherst, who, Observing that the great and important Services which His Majesty's Regular Troops are now employed and the uncertainty of their return, render it absolutely necessary that Provisions shou'd be made in Time for Garrisoning the several Posts on the Continent during the Winter, desires that you would provide for continuing in Pay the same Number of Troops that remained during last Winter: That is, six Captains, thirteen Subalterns and Five Hundred and Seventy two Privates, thus amounting the whole to Five Hundred and Ninety one Men.

I must observe to you that the Necessity of this Request arises from the present vigorous Exertion in the West Indies; which promises effectually to humbel the Pride of the Enemies, and pave Way to Peace. As this glorious Expedition cannot but have your entire Approbation. I doubt not but you will readily embrace the Opportunity to give a public Testimony of it.

The French Invasion of Newfoundland must give you great Concern, upon Account of the National Loss which the Interruption of the Fishery there must have occasioned, although this Province will not, in its own particular, greatly suffer thereby. But I am persuaded that the Reign of the French in those Parts is by this Time near over; and I flatter myself that this Government will have some Share in the Honour of putting an end to it.

Gentlemen of the Council, and Gentlemen of the House of Representatives,

As I have called you together at this Time with Reluctance, so I shall be desirous to dismiss you, as soon as the public Business shall have had due Consideration. This, I apprehend, will take up not many Days: after which I shall be glad to restore you to your several Engagements at your own Homes with as little loss of Time as may be.

Council Chamber September 8 1762. Fra. Bernard.

BOSTON Sept. 13. Wednesday Evening last the News of the Reduction of the Havannah was receiv'd in Town and on Thursday Noon the Guns of His Majesty's Castle William and Batteries of this Town and Charlestown, as also the Field Pieces belonging to the new Artillery Company were discharged in token of Joy of those happy events.

NEW-YORK Sept. 13 Extract of a Letter from on board the Transport of the Second Division which sail'd from New-York for the Havannah.

"On the 21st of July 1762, in Lat. 22. 54. at 4 o'clock in the afternoon, we fell in with a French fleet consisting of two ships of the line with two frigates, one Polacre, and 5 other ships. We saw them take 7 sail of our transports, if there had been half an hour more of day-light we should have shared the same fate; but the night saved us. We put about and stood from them for about 3 hours, and then alter'd our course again. In the morning we found ourselves clear of them, and we saw them no more. The same morning saw two sail which came up with us, notwithstanding our endeavours to avoid them. They proved to be a privateer belonging to New-London, and her consort belonging to New York. We then bore away for Cape Nichola, finding no ships there, we proceede for the Havannah; on the passage we met with the Enterprize man of War and a Transport, going to take troop that had been cast away on the Island of Cuba. On the 20th came in sight of the six ships that was cast away, they were all bilged, but the men all saved. The ships were the Chesterfield man of war of 40 guns, and 5 transports viz. Smiling Nancy, the Industry, the Swallow, the Juno, and the Masquerade."

It is said the Viceroy of Mexico, and Governor of Cartagena, were at the Havannah all the time of the Siege: that the Governor of the Havannah said, that Providence had taken the Place; for that during the Time he had resided there, he never knew a month in which there were not Gales of Wind sufficient to have drove the English Fleet on shore, until the Siege commenced: That the Spanish Officers, it was reported, went to the Governor, in the Time of the general Attack, on the 11th of August, and told him, That the English Fire was so hot, there was no Possibility of standing by their guns with any safety; and that they could not nor would not do it any longer, And that during the ten hours our Batteries play'd on the Town and Fortifications, 600 Spaniards were killed; but the Town was not much damaged, the firing being chiefly against their Forts.

The Connecticut Troops were in the transports that were cast ashore; by an Account received at Connecticut from Colonel Lyman their Commander, dated Havannah the 17th of August, it is said, the Regiment had not suffered much by sickness, since their arrival there, and but few of them died.

NEW-YORK Sept. 13. The Enterprize man of War, John Houlton Esq; commander, who convoyed the transports hither from the Havannah, sail'd from the Hook on Wednesday last for St. John's in Newfoundland, to assist in recovering that Place from the French: On her arrival, there will according to the accounts we have received, be ten English men of war, from 70 to 20 guns besides the Massachusetts frigate: and as this naval force is to be joined by Col. Amherst, with a number of land forces, and a train of artillery, which have long since left this place for Halifax, where there is little doubt made of their success.

BOSTON Sept. 18. Province of Massachusetts-Bay.

Whereas the Town of Boston hath been of late greatly endangered by Bonfires and Fireworks in the Streets of said Town: His Excellency is pleased with the Advice of Council, to direct that the Civil Magistrates and Executive officers in the said Town, do take due Care to prevent all such Disorders on the Evening of the Anniversary of His Majesty's Coronation the 22d Instant.

By order of His Excellency the Governor,
A. Oliver, Secr'y.

Whereas before the Establishment of a Custom House at Falmouth, Casco-Bay, Naval Stores were usually taken on board Vessels loading there, pursuant to Act of Parliament: —— And was much as some Masters of Vessels still presume to continue in said Practice, contrary to the Law of Trade in that Behalf: ——

Notice is hereby given That in future any Master or Owner who shall, before Permit of that Purpose is obtain'd take on board his Vessel either Provisions or Naval Stores previous to his entering into Bonds with the proper Officers for due landing thereof, will subject his Vessel and Cargo to Seizure by the Officers of the Customs in said District or elsewhere. And all Masters are hereby Cautioned against departing said District without Clearance.

By Order of the Surveyor General.

Custom House Falmouth   Fra. Waldo,
September 18, 1762.   Collector.

CHARLESTOWN S. Carolina Sept. 18. We have a confirmation of some parties of Creek Indians being gone to war against the Spaniards. We are likewise informed, that a party of said Indians, who had been sent to Canada, on purpose to see if what we had told them about taking of that country from the French, were true, which the Nation would give credit before, were returned, and reported, that all we said was true, and more; and that this is likely to have a surprizing effect in our favour upon that Nation.

A Month ago we are informed, the garrison of St. Augustine had nothing but flour to subsist on; and since the present war began, our coasts have never been so invested with privateers as for 6 or 8 weeks past; whence we may reasonably conclude, that the distressed situation of the garrison has forced them to send out most of those vessels that have lately annoyed our trade in order to get provisions.

BOSTON Sept. 20. By the Intrepid and Transports arrived at New-York, we have the following particulars and perfect Accounts of the important Conquest of the Havannah, viz.

On Friday July 30th, After 1 o'clock a mine was sprung under the Walls of Mora, at first the Breach was not thought practicable, as not more than three Men could enter a breast; but it was attempted by a chosen Number of Soldiers, who succeeded, put 150 to the Sword in the Fort, and made 300 Prisoners, besides many Spaniards lost in the Water. ——— The gallant amiable Don Velasco, Governor of the Castle was wounded, Don Gonsales, Lieutenant Governor killed; and Don Lewis Velasco, sent to the Havannah.

On the 31st, a Flag arrived, with thanks for the Tenderness shown Don Velasco, and desiring the Body of Don Gonsales, which was not to be found.

August 1. Several Batteries were begun against the Porto and Town.

In the Mora, the Abemarle Battery	4 guns right of the Spanish Redoubts.
5 Guns Saliant.	4 Ten inch Mortars.
10 ditto, Glaces.	4 eight inch ditto.
A Bat. of 13 Inch Mortars.	4 ditto, the free Bat.
5 Guns.	Hawitzers Battery.
8 ditto.	32 ditto on the Barbett
7 ditto.	43 Pieces of Cannon.
Hawitzers.	A Howitzers Battery.

These Batteries were erected on the same Eminence with the Moro Castle, which ranges along the East Side of the Harbour, abreast with the major Part of the City, and its best fortification.

On Tuesday the 10th of August, at XII o'Clock, Lord Albemarle sent an Officer with a Drum to the Governor, to demand Possession of the City, in case of refusal, to acquaint him that he would set Fire to it next Morning. ——— The Governor answered that he had 6 Months Ammunition, and would defend it to the last extremity.

On Wednesday the 11th began at V o'Clock in

the Morning a most tremendous Fire from all the above Batteries till III in the Afternoon, when the Governor sent to desire a Capitulation —— The Execution done by this Fire is scarce credible, most of their Guns on the Walls and strong Forts were dismounted and great Numbers of Spaniards were killed.

The 12th Day was chiefly spent in Messages and Replies. —— The Spanish Admiral was extremely unwilling to give up his Ships; but desired to know whether he with 3 Men-of War of the Line could be permitted to sail to Spain unsearched and unmolested? He was answered, that such permission could not be allowed even to a Long-Boat; but that they should have good English Ships to transport them to Spain: He was at length obliged to comply.

The only Terms Lord Albemarle would grant, were accepted by the Spanish Governor, which almost amount to a Chart Blank.

Previous to the Capitulation the following Letter from the General of the Havannah was sent to Lord Albemarle.

"The Humane Offer I received from your Excellency in your Letter Yesterday, I find myself oblige to listen to, by the cries of the Inhabitants, who have experienced the Misery of War: Therefore the Sentiment I express to your Excellency of holding out the Place to the last extremity are altered. —— I now entreat your Excellency for a Truce of Hostilities for the Space of 24 Hours, during which Time no Works shall be carried on in the Fortifications of the City. That I may regulate and submit to your Excellency the Articles of Capitulation, by which I am ready to surrender the City, May God Preserve your many Years.
    Signed,   Juan Del Prado."

On Monday the 16th, Commodore Keppel sailed into the Harbour, and took Possession of the Fleet, which amounted to Nine Men of War of the Line, two ditto and a Frigate on the Stocks, besides three sank in the Harbour.

The Spanish Seamen were chiefly employed in the sorties and behaved admirably. —— The Blacks sought their Guns.

It is said one of the Men of War had 5 million of Dollars on Board and that 8 Million Sterling in Spicie has been already counted, that Lord Albemarle had declared that the tresure taken at Havannah should be equally divided among the Land and Sea Forces, and that the Share of the two principal Officers would amount to 12,000 Pounds per Annum.

The Capitulation included all the Part of the Island which was under the Jurisdiction of the Governor of the Havannah, but the particulars are not yet known by the Publick.

Our whole Loss was as follows. 400 killed, 600 wounded, 200 of which since dead, 700 dead of sickness.

In the Transports came, the XVIIth, of General Monckton's Regiment, two Battalions of the Royal Highlander, and Montgomery's Regiment, who left the Havannah the 19th of August, merely because they were by sickness rendered incapable of Duty.

The Spirit and Ardour of our Seamen during the Siege was of utmost Consequence. ──── The Service of all our Men were extremely severe, but there was an absolute Necessity for it, or the Design could not have succeeded. ──── The Arrival of Reinforcements from New-York was critical. ──── it is said the Number of our Men fit for Duty was but little more than 3000 but the Spaniards were in a much worse Condition, it is said they had 6000 sick. ──── The Season of this Year, by the Report of the Spaniards has been more favourable for such a design as ours than ever they have known. ──── The Country appears to be exceeding Settled and well cultivated, adorn'd with fine Buildings and Villages; one very large and rich one, within 3 Miles of the Havannah, in which a fine Church and a Monastry, had been abandoned by the Inhabitants before the taking the Havannah, with all the rich Shops of Goods, and Furniture, which were instantly pillaged by our Soldiers.

Lord Albemarle, it is said is to sail for England in October.

BOSTON Sept. 20. By a Vessel arrived at York at the Eastward, from Halifax, which Place she left the 7th instant, we are informed, That the Troops which embarked on board the Transports for the Expedition against St.John's sailed from thence on Monday the 30th of August; they were to stop at Louisbourg, to take the Troops from thence. --- A Vessel was arrived at Halifax from some part of Newfoundland, who on her Passage 5 Leagues from St. John's on the 31st of August, saw Lord Colvill with the Ships which sailed with him, and had not been joined by any from England: It is said the French Ships were not then sailed from St. John's, but were all in readiness; that the number of their Guns were four more than the Ships Lord Colvill had.

BOSTON Sept. 20. On Wednesday last a Person who assumes the Name of James Allen, and has had sundry Passports from several Gentlemen in the neighbouring Governments, with Recommendations for Charity, was convicted before Justice Dana, as a Notorious Deceiver, and Vagrant Beggar, and committed to the House of Correction: ------- He pretended to have been born at Aberdeen, and educated in Herriot's Hospital in Edingburg, and also that he had been a Minister on the Frontiers of Virginia; ------- had suffered the loss of a Wife and 5 Children by the Cherokees, and grievously wounded himself. ------- By these pretences he has imposed on many charitably disposed People in this and neighbouring Governments.

CHARLESTOWN S. Carolina Sept. 25. The Palacre James, John Butler, master from N. Providence for this port, laden with rice, lignumvitae, sugar, &c. was taken off this bar, the 5th inst. as sent to St. Augustine, by a small Spanish Xebeque, mounting only 5 guns, viz. one 6 pounder and a swivel and having about 60 men. She had then been only a few days from St. Augustine, and sent her launch within our bar, to see what vessels were on Rebellion road, where they discovered the Success man of war, &c. --- It was the same Xebeque that chased the brig Betsey, James Walden, master, of and from St. Kitts for Georgia, ashore on the Coffin Land the 3d Inst. and on South Edisto breakers, the Schooner King of Prussia, and Pedee, from this port bound for

Port-Royal. She continued cruizing, till she fell in with his Majesty's sloop Bonnetta, from the Havannah, who fired 60 shot at her, one of which went thro' her quarter, binacle and arm chest, then she avoided coming this way, On the 13th she took the schooner Success, Stuart of and for Rhode-Island from Georgia, with rice and naval stores; on board which Capt. Job Bradford was a passenger. On the 15th she took The Schooner Anne, Williams of and for this port from Georgia, with rice, having 7 negroes on board, and Mr. Henry Toomer of Cape Fear, his wife and child passenger. The same evening, the Spaniards turned all their prisoners, 25 in number into a small leaky boat, in which, with great difficulty, they reached the shore, Among them are, Mr. Toomer, his wife and child, and Captain Stuart, Williams and Bradford.

BOSTON Sept. 27. On the 19th Inst. the Master of a Fishing Schooner arrived at Cape Ann from Louisbourgh, which Place he left about a Fortnight before, and informs, That a Cartel Vessel arrived there in 6 Days from St. John's and inform'd, that Lord Colvill was off St. John's, and had block'd up the French Men of War there. The Transports with the Troops were just sailing from Louisbourgh as he came out.

The Number of Troops consists of 1500 including 500 of this Province that were in his Majesty's Service at Nova-Scotia: there were also Transported a Detachment of the Train of Artillery.

On Friday last arrived here a Vessel from Louisbourgh, by whom we learn, That the Transports with the Troops sail'd from thence upon Expedition to recover St. John's the 7th instant: ——— They had advice at Louisbourgh that upon the first Appearance of Lord Colvill's Fleet off St. John's with French and Spanish Colours flying, they were taken by the French Admiral to be a Reinforcement from Europe: upon which he sent a Schooner with his Lieutenant and 100 Men to assist in conducting them into the Harbour, but the Vessel being detain'd they soon perceiv'd their Mistake, and immediately confin'd all the English that were in the Place, expecting an Attack would soon be made upon them. 'Tis said Lord Colvill had sent several Vessels to Harbour Grace to bring off a considerable Number of People there who were ready to assist him in dispossessing the French of St. John's.

BOSTON Sept. 9. We hear from Montague, in this Province, that on Thursday the 16th Instant, one Mr. Nathan Tuttel, of that district, and his Son Ebenezer Tuttel, observing some fresh Marks of a Bear's being near the Place, they agreed to go out to hunt him, and about sun-set they parted in order to drive a hill, but before they came to the Place where they were to meet again, the young Man saw something move which he took for the Bear, and accordingly fired at it, and immediately ran to secure his Game, when to his great Astonishment he found he had shot his Father, who instantly died; the Ball having gone through his Right Arm and Powder Horn and into his Body: The Jury of Inquest cleared the Young Man, it appearing to be all together Accidental his Father being cloath'd in a black Jacket, and bushy Hair, with a small Hat, and as it was almost Dark, the shade of the Hill hid the lower Part of the Body: He was in the 74th Year of his Age.

Ten Pistoles Reward,

Run away from Baltimore-Town, Maryland, a Convict Servant Man, named Richard Bryant, an Irish Man, but last from London in the Ship Dolphin, Capt. Graymore, a Printer by Trade, a well made Fellow, of about 5 Feet 8 Inches high, and about 28 Years of Age, of a troublesome Address, brown Complexion, short curl'd Hair, had on when he went away, a blue Broad Cloth Coat, with a velvet Cape, black ribb'd worsted Stockings, but had a variety of other Cloaths, some of which he may have taken with him; he also took with him a Violin of which he plays well, and is a good singer, and is supposed to have with him some Cash in Guineas; he was enticed away by one Samuel South, a Convict in the Ship Neptune, Capt. Dawson, to Potomack, (but had Money enough to purchase his Freedom) a Tall lusty Man of a ruddy Complexion, appears somewhat bloated by excessive Drinking, is a Fellow of general

Appearance, and is said to have spent a good deal of Money, and probably has some with him, and has a Pass. Whoever takes up and secures the said Samuel South that he may be brought to Justice and Richard Bryant, that his Master may have him again shall if taken together be intitled to the above Reward, and for Richard Bryant only, Four Pistoles and reasonable Charges Paid by   Barnabas Hughes.

  N. B. The above Samuel South has been heard say that he intended for Halifax, where he has some Friends and Relations.

  BOSTON Sept. 27. We hear from Wilmington in Pennsylvania, dated September 10, 1762.

  On Sunday arrived here Capt. Ralf Walker of this Borough, who, on the 14th of July, was taken in a sloop from hence for Antigua, in lat. 21. 20. long. 61. by a Spanish privateer sloop of 10 guns and 80 men, from Porto-Rico, commanded by Christopher Gonsalo, who stripped him of every thing of value. And, That on the 31st of the same month, having joined a privateer schooner of St. Domingo. of 10 carriage guns and 50 men, they landed on the island of Deseada (lately surrendered by the French with Martinico) and carried off 80 or 90 negroes, robb'd the church, stripped even the women, and treated them otherwise most barbarously, and carried of in money and effects, belonging to the church and inhabitants, to the value of twenty thousand pounds: That the same day they chased Captain Hatton, belonging to Philadelphia, till under the guns of Point-Peter, in Grandterre: That on the 22d they took a brig belonging to Newberry in New-England of 8 guns, and 9 men, Captain Ralse, almost in reach of the guns of Point-Peter: That Capt. Ralse behaved very bravely, keeping the deck, and defending his vessel to the last, even after all his hands fled below: That after the privateer's crew had boarded and taken him, the slash'd and cut him cruelly; and after taking him on board the privateer the Captain would not suffer his wounds to be dressed, until he fainted away with the loss of blood, and then strip'd him almost naked: That on the 23d they landed them at Deseada; from whence they got to Grandterre, where Capt. Walker left Capt. Ralse so bad that his life was despaired of.

BOSTON Sept. Extract of a Letter from New-Providence, Dated August 18, 1762.

"On the 9th Instant an Officer arrived here in a Schooner from Boston, being sent Express from thence to Lord Albemarle and Sir George Pocock, with Accounts that a French Fleet had taken our principal Settlements at Newfoundland: —— This Schooner put in here in order to get a Pilot to the Havannah, which General Shirley immediately provided, and the Vessel sail'd again the same Day. ——

The Transports which sailed from New-York in the 2d division from New-York, and were taken on their Passage to the Havannah, had on board part of his Majesty's 58th Regiment: Those with Major Gorham and Rangers on board, got clear, and arrived safe at the Havannah. ——

We hear that Capt. David Gorham who commanded a Company of Blacks from Jamaica, died at Havannah, with the disorder that is prevalent in the Army and Navy; and which is the effect of a laborious and fatiguing Campaign, more especially in a hot Climate.

NEW-YORK Sept. 30. Capt. Miller informs, that the Garrison sailed from the Havannah for Old Spain, a few days before he sailed: that Admiral Pocock was not sail'd for England: That a Spaniard was apprehended spiking up some Guns on a small Battery: —— And that two others were taken up for murdering a Serjeant belonging to the Royal American Regiment who was to be executed the Day Capt. Miller sailed.

PROVIDENCE Rhode Island Sept. 30. Last week returned here from a cruize, Capt. Smith of this port: About 32 days ago he spoke with the privateer brig Mars, of New-York, from whom he received the following melancholy account. That the day before, the Mars fell in and took a sloop out of a small fleet of merchantmen, and in a few hours after, Capt. M'Gillicuddy fell in with a large French ship and a brig, whom he engaged very warm, but the first or second broadside from the ship, who mounted 24 carriage guns, proved his end, for he was unfortunately torn to pieces by a cannon shot from the enemy: The 2d Lieutenant then took command, the 1st being on board the prize, who was obliged to give over the engagement to repair the damage she had received, and see the last marks of friendship paid to his deceased captain, by having the solemnity performed, of which Capt, Smith was an eye-witness.

OCTOBER 1762

CHARLESTOWN S. Carolina Oct. 2. Extract of a letter from the Havannah, Sept. 23.

"The Royals in general gained great Honour during the siege, but especially the day of the Storm. They first entered the breach (if it may be so called) sword in hand, led by lieutenant Forbes, now a captain in the 42d. the breach did not allow more than one man abreast, and was so situated, that had they missed a step, they must have gone headlong a hundred yards into the sea on one side, or the ditch on the other. Indeed the very men who entered against great and small arms of the enemy, were afraid to return by the same way, lest they should tumble down, even after the place was reduc'd, and the affair all over. It is agreed never was a more desperate attempt, nor more bravely executed. Upon the whole of this expedition, which has been long and severe, both from the enemy and climate, never a man (one excepted) has been known to shew the least backwardness, nor heard to complain of hard duty; tho' many, both officers and men, have been several days in the trenches without being relieved.

"The Don were more obstinate than we expected; but had they known how to dispose and make the most of their strength, they might have increas'd our difficulties. They mustered 6000 men under arms when the place surrendered; and we were not able to bring out more than half that number fit for duty.

"In the King of Spain's warehouses were found a large quantity of tar, and other naval stores in proportion. The prize goods all go to England on account of the captors, except the dry goods belonging to the Royal company, which are to be sold here on the same account. The prize vessels will be left, owing to want of hands, except one ship which carries home sugars to be sold for the benefit of the captors.

"'Tis uncertain when Lord Albemarle and Sir George Pocock will leave us, but imagined, some time in November.

"Things now go on here quiet and easy, the Spanish are brought in pretty good order, and have no reason to complain of any hardships being put upon them by their conquerors. A small detachment of 200 or 400 Men under Major Montgomery, sails in a day or two to reduce Matanzas, an inconsiderable Government, but independant of the Havannah, about 30 leagues distance from hence.

"Commodore Keppel will sail in a few days for Jamaica, with some ships of war, and it is said, will cruise some time off Cape St, Nicholas, as it seems the French men of war and privateers do great damage to the Trade that way."

The privateer brig Charlestown, of this port, Robert Cochranm commander, that sailed from hence on a cruize, 2d June last, was taken off Cape Francois July 1st, by Defenseur of 74 guns, and the Diligent of 32 guns, two French men of war, and carried into Cape-Francois. The French use the prisoners very ill, stripped them of every thing, and put them in goal at the Cape, where they allowed them only bread and water.

CHARLESTOWN S. Carolina Oct. 2. Several vessels arrived here this week from the Havannah, some of which have been out only seven days: Some letters say, that the fatigue the troops underwent in the course of so long a siege in climate are not to be discribed, and their spirit and perseverance not to be equalled: That major general Heppel commanded the storm, and brigadier general Haviland (who arrived here last Wednesday) was second there: That those which arrived from Jamaica after the reduction of the Havannah, were sent back: That a late discovery had been made of 800 chests of money concealed under a terras in the Governor's Castle: That the Morro-Castle, and other works of most importance, were repairing with all possible diligence: That scarce any cannon there, which were all brass, were found serviceable, when the castle was stormed: That the Spanish men of war sunk in the entrance of the Harbour, had not yet been weighed: That since the surrender a Spanish brigantine from Campeachie, went in, nor knowing the place was taken.

The general, in order to prevent impositions on the British soldiers and sailors, has ascertained the price to which provisions should be sold [Which has been generally misunderstood here, that several vessels designed thither from hence now altered their voyage] That Gen Keppel was not made governor, but was thought would be: and that it was imagined brigadier-general Howe will be made Lieut. governor: That the General and Admiral were to sail for England about the 1st of next month: That Mr. William Michie late of this town, was appointed collector there: That there was on the 12th ult. at least 500 sail of vessels in the Havannah, including men of war, Transports, and prizes: That the Mercury man of war said to be ordered to Virginia, may probably come in here in her way: That they had accounts at Havannah of the sailing of the French fleet from the Cape for St. Jago: That Capt. John Campbell and Capt. John French of the 22d regiment, formerly reported dead, were well at Havannah, but that lieut. Barker of Burton's was killed, and lieut. Westal wounded.

BOSTON Oct. 4. Tuesday arrived here Captain Carlsle from Placentia in Newfoundland. He left that Place the 15th of this Instant September, and informs, that the Day before he sailed an Express sloop arrived there from Lord Colvill, for 2 Officers and 70 Marines that had been before landed from the Antelope. ——— The said Express informed that they left Lord Colvill on the 11th instant off St. John's, in which harbour the French Ships still were; that no Ships had then joined him from England: ——— The Express further added, that about two Hours after they left Lord Colvill they met with the Transports having on board Colonel Amherst, with the Troops under his Command from Halifax and of Louisbourg: They had the Wind upon the beam, and no doubt joined the Men of War in less than two

Hours.

BOSTON Oct. 4. Extract from a Letter from Halifax, September 3, 1762.

"On the 27 ult. Colonel Amherst arrived here from New-York, with about 200 Regular Troops, and was joined here by two compleat Companies and a Detachment od Grenadiers of the Royals; two compleat Companies with the Major of the 77th Regiment; one Captain and one Lieutenant of the Royal Train of Artillery, with two Sarjeants, 2 Corporals, 2 Bombadiers, six Gunners, and 25 Matrosses, as also by i Lieut. Colonel, 1 Major, 5 Captains with their Subalterns, and 500 of the Massachusetts Provincials, and are sailed from hence for Newfoundland; but first to stop at Louisbourgh to take on board a Reinforcement from that Garrison,

BOSTON Oct. 7. Deserted His Majesty's Service Dennis Mahoney, an inlisted Soldier, born in Ireland, a Labourer, of light Complexion, light Eyes, brown Hair, down look, 5 Feet 10 Inches hign: Had on a light coloured Cloth Coat, red Jacket, and flop Hat. Whoever shall take up said Soldier, and bring him to Lieutenant Richardson's Quarters at the King's Head, or Serjeant Jordan's at the White Horse at Back-Street, at the North End, or to Castle William, shall have Ten Dollars Reward, and all nacessary Charges paid. ——— If he will return to his Duty within two or three Days he will be received to favour.

All Persons are cautious against concealing or carrying of said Soldier, as they would avoid a severe Prosecution.   Boston Oct. 7, 1762.

NEW-LONDON Oct. 8. Yesterday arrived here the Sloop Gull, Captain Cadwick, in 22 Days from the Havannah, to which Place she had been with Stores for the Connecticut Troops: By this Vessel we have advice, that about ten Days before she sailed, sixteen Transports, under convoy of the Sutherland and Dover Man of War, sailed for Spain, with the Spanish Troops from thence. ——— The Provincials were very sickly there, and it was expected those Troops would shortly return to North America. Captain Stanton of Colonel Lyman's Regiment lately died. It was reported at the Havannah, that the English Forces were to be employed against some other on the Enemy's Settlements in the West-Indies.

BOSTON Oct. 11. A Letter received in Town last Week from an Officer at Crown-Point says, Of the two Thousand Provincial Troops belonging to Massachusetts, but two have died the whole summer.

On Wednesday last a sorrowful Accident happened at Stoughton, as a Number of Persons were raising the Spire of the Meeting-House there, some of the Tackling gave way, whereon Mr. Isaac Penro jun'r fell to the Ground, and was killed in an Instant.

A Vessel arrived at Portsmouth New-Hampshire, the beginning of last Week from Halifax, the Capt. of her says, that he spoke with a 74 Gun ship going into Halifax, which, with two others who were in Company, were dispatched by Admiral Pococke, to join Lord Colvill, in retaking Newfoundland. ——— These Ships vere sent in Consequence of the Advice sent to the Havannah by the Government, on the first certain Intelligence of the French landing at Newfoundland.

No Advice directly from Newfoundland, since our last: ——— It is said the two French Commanders disagree in Opinion: One of them who commands the Land Forces was for destroying the Place, and returning Home in the Vessels they came in, before the English should attempt to dispossess them; but the Commodore of the Fleet, who has the superior Command, was for making a Resistance and retaining the Place; accordingly all the Troops, and those others, whom they have taken in their Service, were very hard at Work to erect new Batteries, and otherways fortifying themselves, being determined not to return the Place in the same Manner it was given them.

Yesterday Afternoon arrived here Capt. Crocker in 14 Days from Louisbourg, who informs, That the Day before he sail'd a Vessel arrived there from a Fisherman that told him all our Troops were safe landed. ——— Capt. Crocker had heard nothing of Lord Colvill's having an Engagement with a number of French and Spanish Men of War, said to be Reinforcement from France, as was rumour'd Saturday last.

NEW-YORK Oct. 11. By his Majesty's ship Cygnet, from the Havannah, we are informed, that 4 companies of the Royals, the 15th and 48th regiment, the 3d battalion of Royal Americans, with all the Provincials, were soon to embark for these parts: That the Spanish soldiers and sailors made Prisoners, at the Havannah, had sailed for Spain: That the Inhabitants had found means to convey off a great part of their Gold, and other valuable effects: That the English had not lost any person of distinction, that the men still continue very sickly and a great many had died.

The Articles of Capitulation are not come to hand, but we understand, that by them, private property is secured, the profession of the Roman Catholic religion permitted and the garrison marched out with all the honors of war.

BOSTON Oct. 12. Deserter from the Snow Bristol Merchant, Robert Kier, Master. The following Seamen, viz. Andrew Smith, Daniel Doraver, John Henery, Stephen Funnall, William Smith, & John Delanesa. If the above Seamen will return to their Duty on board said Snow, now lying at Mr. Griffin's Wharf, they will be kindly received otherwise they will be deem'd Deserters.

LONDON (Whitehall) Oct 12, 1762. This Morning arrived Capt. Campbell of the 22d regiment from St. John's Newdoundland, being dispatched by Lieut. Col. Amherst, with the following letter to the Earl of Egremont.

St. John's Newfoundland, Sept. 20, 1762.
My Lord,

According to the orders I received from Sir Jeffry Amherst at New-York, of which your Lordship will have been informed, I proceeded from New-York to Halifax with the transports, to take up the troops there destined for the expedition. I got into the harbour the 26th of August, and finding Lord Colvill sailed determined to embark the troops there, and at Louisbourgh, as expeditiously as possible and proceed after his Lordship.

The men of war being sailed, who were to have taken part of the troops on board, I was obliged to take up shipping to the amount of 400 tons.

I had everything embarked, ready to sail the 29th but contrary winds kept us in the harbour till the 1st of September, when we got out and arrived at Louisbourgh the 5th. The next day the troops were embarked, and we sailed out of the harbour the 7th in the morning.

I had good fortune to join Lord Colvill's fleet on the 11th, a few leagues to the southward of St. John's; and by intelligence his Lordship had received I was obliged to change my resolution of landing the troops at Kitty Vitty, a narrow entrance near the harbour of St. John's, the enemy having entirely stopped up the passage in, by sinking shallops in the channel.

From the best information I could get, it appeared that Torbay, about 3 leagues to the northward of St. John's was the only place to land troops at within that distance.

Lord Colvill sent the Syren man of war into Torbay with the transports; and it was late at night on the 12th, before they all came to anchor. Capt. Douglas, of his Majesty's ship Syren, went with me to view the bay, and we found a very good beach to land on. It blew hard in the night, and one of the transports with the Provincial light infantry corps on board, was driven out to sea.

I landed the troops early next morning, at the bottom of the bay, from whence a path led to St. John's: A party of the enemy fired some shots at the boats as they rowed in. The light infantry of the regulars landed first, gave the enemy one fire, and drove them towards St. John's. The battalion landed and we marched on. The path for 4 miles was very narrow, through a thich wood, and over very bad ground.

Capt. M'Donell's light infantry corp in front came up with some of the party we drove from the landing place: They had concealed themselves in the wood, fired upon us, and wounded 3 men. A party of Capt. M'Donell's corp rush'd in upon them, took 3 prisoners, and drove the rest off.

The country open'd afterwards, and we marched to the left of Kitty Vitty: It was necessary to take possession of this pass, to open the communication for the landing of the artillery and stores, it being impracticable to get them up the way we came.

As soon as our right was close to Kitty Vitty, the enemy fired upon from a hill on the opposite side. I sent a party up a rock, which commanded the passage over, and under the cover of their fire, the light infantry companies of the Royal and Montgomery's supported by the Grenadiers of the Royal, passed, drove the enemy up the hill, and pursued them on that side towards St. John's; when I perceived a body of enemy coming to their support, and immediately I ordered over Major Sutherland, with the remainder of the first battalion, upon which they thought proper to retreat, and we had just time, before dark to take the post.

Capt. Mackenzie, who commanded Montgomery's light infantry, was badly wounded. We took 10 prisoners. The troops lay this night on their arms.

the next morning, the 14th we opened the channel, where the enemy had sunk the shallops; They had a breast-work which commanded the entrance, and a battery not quite finished.

Lieut. Col. Tullikin, who had meet with an accident with a fall, and was left on board, joined me this day; and Capt. Ferguson commanding the artillery, brought round some light artillery and stores from Torbay in the shallops.

The enemy had possession of two very high and steep hills, one in the front of our advanced posts, and the other nearer St. John's, which two hills appeared to command the whole ground from Kitty Vitty to St. John's. It was necessary that we should proceed on this side, to secure at the same time effectually the landing at Kitty Vitty, from the first hill the enemy fired upon our posts.

The enemy had three companies of grenadiers and two picquets at this post, commanded by Lieut. Col. Belecombe, second in command who was wounded; a Captain of grenadiers wounded and taken prisoner; his lieutenant killed, several men killed and wounded, and 13 taken prisoners.

The enemy had one mortar here, with which they threw some shells at us in the night; also a six-pounder, not mounted, and two wall pieces. This hill, with one adjoining, commanded the Harbour.

The 16th we advanc'd to the hill nearer St. John's, which the enemy had quitted. 29 shallops came in to-day with artillery and stores, provisions, and camp-equipage, from Torbay, which we unloaded. I moved the remainder of the troops forward, leaving a post to guard the pass of Kitty Vitty on the other side. Last night the enemy's fleet got out the harbour. This night we lay on our arms.

The 17th a mortar battery was compleated, and a battery began for 4 24-pounders, and of 2 12-pounders, about 500 yards from the fort; made the road from the landing for the artillery, and at night opened the mortar battery with one 8 inch mortar, 7 cohorns, and 6 royals. The enemy fired pretty briskly from the fort, and threw some shells.

The 18th in the morning, I received a letter from Count de Haussonville of which I do myself the honour to inclose your Lordship a copy, as also of my answers, with copies of other letters that passed, and of the capitulation.

As Lord Colvill, at this time was at some distance off the coast, and the wind not permitting his Lordship to stand in, to honour me with his concurrence in the terms to be given to the garrison, I thought no time should be lost in so advanced a season, and therefore took upon me to determine it, hoping to meet with his Lordship's approbation; and he has given me the greatest pleasure, by entirely approving of every thing I have done.

I must beg leave to say, my Lord, that every assistance we could possibly desire from the fleet, has been given us. Lord Colvill on the short notice of our joining him, having laboured to get together all the shallops he could, and with which we were so apply supplied, was a measure of effectual service; and without which our operation must have been considerably retarded.

The indefatigable labour and preserving ardour of the troops I have the honour to command, so necessary towards compleating the conquest, before the bad season set in, did exceed what I could have expected.

Lieutenant Colonel Tullikin seconded me in every thing I could wish.

Capt. M'Donell of Frazer's regiment, was to have delivered this to your Lordship; but his leg is broken by the wound he received, which keeps him here. May I humbly presume, my Lord, to recommend this gentleman to your Lordship's protection, as a real brave and good officer.

Lord Colvill intends sending his Majesty's ship Syren immediately to England. I send Captain Campbell of the 22d regiment with these dispatches, who will inform your Lordship of any particulars you may desire to know.

I do myself the honour to transmit to your Lordship such returns as I can possibly get in time, to shew the true state of the French troops and garrison here. I am, with the most profound respect,

My Lord, your Lordship's most humble, and most obedient Servant.   Wm. Amherst.

Camp before St. John's, Sept. 16, 1762.

Sir, Humanity directs me to acquaint you of my firm intention. --- I know the miserable state your garrison is left in, and am fully informed of your design of blowing up the fort and quitting it: but have a care, for I have taken measures effectually to cut off your retreat: And so sure as a march is put the the train, every man of the garrison shall be put to the sword.

I must have immediate possession of the fort, in the state it now is, or expect the consequence.

I give you half an hour to think of it.

I have the honour sir to be, sir,
Your most obedient servant,
William Amherst.

To the Officer commanding at St' John's. Translation of a letter from the Count d' Hausonvill, to Lieut. Col. Amherst, St. John's, Sept. 16, 1762.

With regard to the conduct that I shall hold, you may, Sir be misinformed. I wait for your troops and your cannon: and nothing shall determine me to surrender the fort, unless you shall have totally destroyed it, and I shall have no more powder to fire.

 I have the honor to be Sir,
Your most humble, & most obedient Servant,
    The Count D'Haussonville.
Count D'Haussonville to Lieut. Col. Amherst.
Sir,

Under the uncertainty of the succours which I may receive from France or its allies, and the fort being entire, and in good condition for a long defence, I am resolved to defend myself to the last extremity. The capitulation which you may think proper to grant me, will determine me to surrender this place to you, in order to prevent the effusion of blood of the men who defend it. ——— Whatever resolution you come to, there is one left to me, which wou'd hurt the interest of the Sovereign you serve.

Fort St. John,   I am, Sir, &c.
Sept. 18, 1762   Le, Count d'Haussonville.
Camp before St. John's Sept. 18, 1762.
Sir,

I have just had the honor of your letter. ———
His Britannick Majesty's fleet and army cooperating here, will not give any other terms to the garrison of St. John's, than their surrendering prisoners of war.

I don't thirst after blood of the garrison; but you must determine quickly, or expect the consequence,
 I am, Sir, &c.   Wm. Amherst.
To Count d'Haussonville.
Copy of the letter from the Count d'Haussonville to Col. Amherst, dated St. John's Sept. 18th.

I have received, Sir, your letter, which you did the honor to write me. ——— I am as averse as you to the effusion of blood. I consent to surrender the fort in a good condition, as I have already acquainted you, if the demands which I have enclose herein are granted to my troops.
 I am, Sir, &c.   Le Count d'Haussonville.
   Articles of Capitulation
Demands of the garrison of St. John's, and, in general the troops that are in it.
The French troops shall surrender prisoners of war.

―――― Answer. Agreed to.

The officers and subaltern officers shall keep their arms, to preserve good order among the troops.

―――― Answer. Agreed to.

Good ships shall be granted to carry the Officers, grenadiers and private men either wounded or not, in the space of one month on the coast of Britany.

―――― Answer. Agreed to. Lord Colvill will embark them as soon as possible.

The goods and effects of both officers and soldiers, shall be preserved.

―――― Answer. His Majesty's troops never pillage.

The gate will be taken possession of this afternoon, and the garrison will lay down their arms.

This is to be signed by
Lord Colvill, but it will
remain at present as after
in full force.

(signed)
William Amherst.
Le Counte d'Houssonville.

Total of the French prisoners. 1 Colonel, 1 Lieut. Colonel, 13 Captains, 4 Ensigns, 27 Serjeants, 45 Corperals, 40 Sub-Corperals, 12 Drummers and 533 Fusiliers.

Total of the killed wounded and missing of our troops from the 13th of September inclusive.

―――― Lieut. Schyler, and 11 rank and file killed.

―――― Captain M'Donnell, Bailie and M'kenzie with 2 Serjeants, 1 drummer, & 32 rank and file wounded.

BOSTON Oct. 18. Last Friday the Province Ship King George, Capt. Hallowell, arrived here from Newfoundland, with the agreed News of the retaking of St. John's in Newfoundland, by Col. Amherst, on the 18th of September last.

An Account of the Expedition against St. John's in Newfoundland, commanded by Lieutenat Colonel William Amherst.

Aug. 16. Col. Amherst sail'd from New-York with two Companies of light infantry, form'd from recover'd Men of the different Corps that had been sent to New-York from the Army in the West-Indies, having Transports with him for the Troops he was to take from Halifax and Louisbourgh, with plenty of Stores and a fine Train of Artillery.

Aug. 25. Arrived at Halifax, and having embarked the Light Infantry and Grenadier Company of Royals, with three Companies of Montgomery's Highlanders, and 500 Provicials, he immediately proceeded to Louisbourgh.

Sept. 5th. Arrived at Louisbourgh.

Sept. 6th. In the Morning 5 compleat Companies of the 45th Regiment embarked.

Sept. 7. The whole Fleet sail'd out of Louisbourgh Harbour.

Sept. 8. Lord Colvill with his Squadron being Cruizing before St. John's, he received an Account from Col. Amherst of his being at Halifax with a Body of Troops and was to proceed to Louisbourgh and there to take on board the detachment of the 45th Regiment, and proceed to invest St. John's; on which Intelligence Lord Colvill immediately station'd himself about 4 Leagues to the Westward of the Harbour and procured all the Shallops that was possible to be had, and put them under the care of the several Ships in his Squadron, in order to land the Troops on their arrival.

Sept. 9. A Cartel came out of St. John's for Halifax, who informed that the Ships and Garrison were determined to remain and oppose any Attempt that should be made for the reduction of that Place.

Sept. 10. Lord Colvill received Intelligence That Mons. Tournay and his Squadron was determin'd to come out next Day, having on board the greater Part of the Garrison: upon which his Lordship with his Squadron proceeded before the Harbour.

Sept. 11. About 7 o'Clock discovered 11 Sail the S. W. which his Lordship steer'd for, and about 12 came up with the Ships, in which was Col. Amherst and the Troops; the Night being almost calm made little way towards Torbay.

Sept. 12. Came in Anchor in Torbay.

Sept. 13. In the Morning the Army, consisting in whole of 900 Regulars, and 500 Massachusetts Provincials, made their Landing good, having but little opposition, and only 3 Men wounded; the Landing was covered by Capt. Douglass, who commanded his Majesty's Ship Syren: No sooner was the Army landed, that Col. Amherst began his march to Kitty Vitty, about 9 Miles from Torbay, a Post absolutely necessary for the Army to take possession of for landing the Provisions, Artillery, Stores, &c. The Army was a good deal harrassed in their March by different Parties of the Enemy, and the badness of the Road made the March very fatiguing. On the Army's arriving near Kitty Vitty, they found the Enemy, amounting to about 300 Men, in Possession of this Post, and all the commanding Grounds naturally very strong, being surrounded with high Craggy Mountains, covered with Rocks, which made it extremely difficult to approach yet it was resolv'd immediately to dislodge them; and the Light Troops having receiv'd their Orders for that Purpose, and being under Cover of the Men of War, began to Attack with their usual Bravery, and in less than half an Hour drove the Enemy from all the Posts; and part of the Army too Possession and secured the Entrance by Water to Kitty Vitty: Here Captain McKenzie was dangerously wounded. The Army halted there all Night.

Sept. 14. About 20 Shallops with Artillery, Stores, Provisions, &c. sailed from Torbay, and arrived safe to the Army at Kitty Vitty about 3 in the Afternoon. The Army having received two Days Provisions, and such Artillery and Ammunition as were immediately wanted being landed, it was resolved to attack the Enemy as soon as possible, who still continued in Possession of the Ridge of Mountains that runs from Kitty vitty to the Mouth of the Harbour of St. John's and hangs over and commands the Fort. The Ships off St. John's, and covering the landing of the Shallops.

Sept. 15. Half an Hour before Day break, the Troops attack'd the Enemy and drove them from the Ridge of Mountains, killed several of them and took some Prisoners, among them was a Captain of Grenadiers, who was very much wounded; ——— Capt. M'Donald, who commanded a Company of Light Infantry, and Capt. Ballie of the Royals were both wounded, and Lieut. Schuyler killed:

―――― Most of this Night and Day it rain'd very hard, the Wind from the E. N. E. the Ships beating off the Sea: At 6 o'Clock in the evening the Wind shifted to the Westward, but still continu'd foggy, under which Cover the French Ships made their Escape, cutting their Cables and leaving Count Hosson De Ville, and all the Royal Marines, consisting of 5 Companies of Grenadiers: Notwithstanding there was a Party of 300 Men posted at the Entrance of the Harbour, the Ships got out undiscovered.

Sept. 16. The Army marched from Kitty Vitty in the Afternoon to within a Mile of the Garrison.

Sept. 17. Early this Morning a Detachment with a Working Party was sent to a convenient Hill near the Fort, to throw up an Entrenchment and made a Bomb Battery; about Evening it was finnish'd and at half an Hour after 7 o'Clock the Eight Inch Mortar and about Eleven Cohorns began to play on the Town, and continued till Seven o'Clock in the Morning of

Sept. 18. When an Officer with two Drums came out of the Fort having the Chamade, and about Noon the Garrison surrendered themselves Prisoners of War: ―――― Le Compte De Hosson Ville, and other Officers and Men, amounted to upward of 700, among which were 5 Companies of Grenadiers.

Sept. 19. Lord Colvill. with Part of the Squadron, went into St. John's.

Sept. 20. The Rest of the Ships with all the Transports got in, with three Ships of the Line and one Frigate, who arrived the Night before from England, after a Passage of 6 Weeks and 3 Days, but see nothing of the French Ships.

Sept. 21. Ships Wooding and Watering, and Transports getting ready to receive the French Garrison, and about 60 more which were taken Prisoners during the Siege.

Sept. 22. Duty going on as before.

Sept. 23. His Majesty's Ship Syren sailed expressed for England, after being detained two Days by contrary Winds. This Day all the French Prisoners embark'd and would have sail'd, but being little Wind could not get out.

Sept. 24. The Transports sailed.

Sept. 25. His Majesty's Ship Gosport sailed for New-York having all the Sick and Wounded and 113 of the Troops from that Place, with a Transport, having the remainder. In the Evening his Majesty's Ship Enterprize arrived from the Havannah.

Sept. 26. The King George sail'd with a Transport, both of which having the Detachment of the 45th Regiment for Louisbourgh, and the 28th all the Troops of the several Corps were to embark for the different Stations, except 300 Regulars left to garrison St. John's. This Day Captain M'Kenzie died of his wounds.

Oct. 3. The King George arrived at Louisbourgh, landed the Troops, and took on board 100 Provincials and landed them at Halifax the 10th.

The Killed, Wounded and Missing of the Enemy was upward of 100. That on our Side was about 20 killed and 15 wounded.

The following Men of War arrived at St. John's from England on the 20th of September, two Days after the Place surrendered, having been out six Weeks and three Days, viz.

Men of War	Guns	Commander
Shrewsbury	74	Capt. Pallester
Bedford	74	Capt. Martin
Superb	74	Capt. Rowley
Minerva	32	Capt. Peters

The Enterprized arrived from Havannah the 25th of September.

We hear that the Articles of Capitulation were but three, and those very short; that the Garrison surrender Prisoners of War, to be sent to France, and were to be transported by the 18th instant, tho' 'tis tho't they are near home by this Time.

We hear that our Provincial Troops who were in the above Expedition behaved with the greatest Spirit and Resolution; particularly Captain Barrons of Lincoln, in this Province; who with his company assisted the Light Infintry in dislodging the Enemy from their strong Posts at Kitty Vitty, and who with his Men climb'd up Rocks and Precipices, before tho't inaccessible and from which the enemy did not expect an

Assault could be made, and put them into such surprize and confusion that they were soon drove from a 6 Gun Battery the had advantageously erected there, and defended by 300 Grenadiers of France, who were entirely put to flight with considerable loss in kill'd and wounded. Our whole Number in this Attack amounted to but 170 Regulars and Provicials, of which we lost only 4 or 5: The gallant behaviour of Capt, Barrons and his Party, 'tis said merited the particular Notice of Col. Amherst, and has done great Honor to themselves and Country.

BOSTON Oct. 18 We hear from Biddeford in the county of York that their inferior court lately held there a remarkable cause was tried between Thomas Hammet of Berwick, in said county, Yeoman, Plaintiff and Peter Staple of Kittery, in said county, Gentleman, defendant; for the defendant's debauching, ravishing and carnally knowing the plaintiff's wife &c. and that after a full hearing of six hours, the jury brought in their verdict for the plaintiff is to recover against the defendant one thousand pounds L. M. damages and cost.

CHARLESTOWN S. Carolina Oct. 20. Our Accounts from the Creek nation contain the following intelligence, viz. That in June last some Lower-Creeks, from the place called the Point, went to Pensacola, and brought 56 Kegs of rum into the nation; that only 6 of them were presents, and the rest bought with shrouds, callico, &c. That some time after near 500 men of the Lower Towns resolved to go to war against the Spaniards at St. Augustine, and actually set out; but the Coweta's, and particularly the Young Lieutenant, sent different Indians after them and dissuaded them from their purpose; however none of them would had succeeded had not an old fellow from the Point (who had great influence) gone on the same errand. That the Young Lieutenant lately delivered a talk to be sent to one or both the governors of Carolina and Georgia; in which he said, "That the governor of St, Augustine had sent him, and one or two other headmen out of every town an invitation to come and partake of some English guns, shrouds, &c.

of which he had them plenty; at the same time informed him of the great number of English men that died or were killed at Havanna;" and he desired, "That his brothers the two governors, would not encourage, or pay for, the bringing of Spanish scalps to them; otherwise perhaps some mad people might kill Englishmen in their room," And that soon after this, the Young Lieutenant, and a few other headmen, set out to go to St. Augustine.

BOSTON Oct. 21. We hear that at a Salem Court last Week one Benjamin Ellingwood was tried for murdering one Jacob Poland at Beverly on the 16th of August last, by stabing him: The Jury convicted him of Manslaughter only: for which he was burnt in the Hand. The Court it is said were in Opinion that the Crime was aggrivated, and if not Murder, that it bordered on the Line of Murder; they therefore inflicted the highest Penalty the Law enabl'd them to do. viz. to suffer Twelve Months Imprisonment, and pay cost.

PHILADELPHIA Oct. 21. Terms of Capitulation proposed by the French Garrison and Troops at St. John's in Newfoundland.

I. The French Troops shall surrender Prisoners of War.   (Agreed to)

II. The Officers superior and inferior, shall retain their Arms for to keep their Troops in Order.   (agreed to)

III. Proper Vessels shall be provided, in the Space of a Month, to carry the Officers, Grenadiers, and Soldiers, both wounded and not wounded to the Coast of Bretagne. in France.
(Agreed to: Lord Colvill will of course embark them as soon as he possibly can)

IV. The Effects of the Officers and Soldiers shall be preserved to them. (His Majesty's Troops never pillage.)

The Gate will be taken Possession of this Afternoon, and the Garrison will lay down their Arms.

   Signed.   WM. Amherst.
         Le Comte d'Haussonville.

This is also to be signed by Lord Colvill, and shall remain in Force.

Camp before St. John's, September 18, 1762.

PORTSMOUTH New-Hampshire Oct. 22. Last Saturday Evening came to Town the Capts. Coffin and Farnall, having been taken, capt. Coffin in a Ship, and capt. Fernall in a Sloop, and carried into Porto-Rico, where, they with between 30 and 40 other capts of Vessels were closely confined in Goal for 3 Months, not having any thing allowed them the whole Time for Food but cattle Gutts, &c. the Spaniards telling them that Beef was to good for Englishmen. The 3d of September the above capts. with 8 others were released out of Goal, with paying a Ransom of 20 some odd Dollars for each man; and when they came out left 200 Englishmen in Goal there, with Nothing but the above Food to feed upon, which, (together with their being informed that the Governor of Antigua had denied to settle a cartel, was their Occasion of their lying there.) cause many of them to enter on board Spanish Privateers to cruize against their own countrymen.

BOSTON Oct. 25. Province of Massachusetts-Bay.

Whereas an English Girl, whose name is Malone, was captivated with her Father some Years ago, either at Contocook or Penicook, and is now at St. Louis Falls in Canada, which Girl is now about 16 Years of Age: If the Father (who was released about 4 Years ago) or any other of the Girl's Friends will apply to the Secretary's Office in Boston they may be informed how she may be recovered from the Indians.

NEW-YORK Oct. 25. By Captains Colgan, Durham and Tanner from the Havannah in 14 Days, we have the account that the provincials were to embark for the continent in 5 days after they sailed, under convoy of his Majesty's Ship Intripid, of 64 guns, and that a private soldier share of the cash found at the Havannah, would amount to about 30 dollars.

PHILADELPHIA Oct. 28. From St. Criox in the West-Indies we are informed that the Sloop Charming Betsey, Captain John Knox, bound from Georgia to Antigua, having put in at the West end of St. Croix, for Provisions and Water, while the Captain was on Shore, the 3d of October, William Foster and John Bettle, with two other Men ran away with the Sloop and Cargo after putting the Mate ashore. If the said Sloop should put into any Part of the Continent, it is hoped she will be secured for the Owner.

    WILLIAMSBURG Virginia Oct. 29. The Ship Lockhart, Capt. Coats, from Glasgow has arrived in James River: About 80 leagues off the capes she was taken by a French frigate from the Missisippi, bound home; who, after taking out most of her provisions (of which they were much in want) and such goods as they stood in need of, to the value of 500 Pounds besides rummaging the mens chests for their cloaths, &c., ransomed her for 4500 pounds sterling.

NOVEMBER 1762

BOSTON Nov. 1. Extract of a letter from South Carolina, September 29, 1762.

"The two French Frigates lately carried into New-Providence by the General Shirly Privateer of that Port, had each 12 guns mounted: they sailed from Cape Francois the 7th instant, bound for Old France, with 5 ships of the line and two frigates, having a Spanish battalion of 600 men on board, bound for St. Jago de Cuba. Lieutenant Anstruther and Mackensey, and two other officers and 30 men of the 2d division that sailed from New-York for Cuba, and were taken by the French were on board the prize.

Major Rogers is arrived at New-York from South Carolina, and was to set out for Albany last Monday.

CHARLESTOWN S. Carolina Nov. 3. The garrison of St. Augustine, according to some late accounts, is in greater distress than ever, for want of provisions, having had no supply from these provinces since April last, except what rice their xebeque-privateers took in Captain Butler's vessel, the 5th of last month, upon the coast: The two schooners of Capt. Stuart and Capt. Williams, which were taken by the same xebeque on the 12th and 15th, were with her, totally lost going in, and no part of their cargo saved; since which, the rice taken in Butler being almost expended, the Spaniards are obliged to subsist chiefly on fish. At the same time the garrison dare not stir-out for a stick of wood, for fear of the Creek Indians; and they are extremely uneasy with daily apprehensions of a visit: However they were equipping two privateers, to look out for more provisions this way, which were to put to sea the beginning of next month, one of them a sloop of 14 guns (carriage and swivels) one of 10, and a third (if any) of less force; of which we hope his Majesty's sloop Bonnetta, commanded by capt. Carie (now ready to sail on a cruise) will soon give a good account.

On Thursday last arrived here from England, his Majesty's ship Epreave commanded by Peter Blake, Esq; sent hither with Outassite or Judd's Friend and the other Cherokee Indians, that went from Virginia in said vessel, Great attention was paid to these Indians in England by his Majesty's ministers, of which they are very sensible, as well as the care Capt. Blake has taken of them. Yesterday Outassite had an audience of his Excellency the Governor in council, when he expressed his attachment to the British nation. His Excellency has sent off a message to the Cherokee country with accounts of their arrival here; and has ordered carriages to be provided for carrying up the presents they received in England from the King. The ministry was not a little embarassed, in regard to those Indians, by their interpreter's dying soon after they left Virginia; and no person capable of speaking the Cherokee language could be found in or about London, that all possible means were used for that purpose.

NEW-YORK Nov. 8. On the 25th October Captain Mackey from Londonderry fell in with Captain Macgachan, from Africa, having on board 300 Negroes, bound for Virginia. They had lost their masts and had 7 feet water in the hold, the Slaves had also rose, on which near 50 of them were killed, and having met with Capt. Mackey, the white people left the ship and went on board him, and was arrived at Philadelphia.

On Monday last Capt. Friend arrived at Philadelphia from England, in whom came Passenger Benjamin Franklin, Esq; late Agent for the Province in London.

CHARLESTOWN S. Carolina Nov. 10. Sir George Pococke sailed the 2d instant from the Havannah for England. The Mercury man of war, with several other vessels bound here, came out with him. On board the Mercury is the bishop of St. Jago and some other principal ecclesiasticks of the island of Cuba, who were taken for some dangerous practices, and are to be put ashore at St. Augustine.

On Monday put in here being leaky the ship Mary, Capt. Days, and the ship Blackate, Capt. Franklin, with about three hundred Spanish officers, soldiers, sailors and marines from the Havannah for Cadiz or the first port to Spain.

The same day put in here, being in the like condition, the ship Amity's-good-intent, with about sixty New-York provincials, sent home from the Havannah.

It is said the provincials will be immediately embark on board the transport ship Betsy, Capt. Hutton ready to sail for New-York; and that the Spaniards will be obliged to remain here till the vessels they came in are refitted.

PHILADELPHIA Nov. 11. The following is an Account of the melancholy disaster that befell the Phænix, of London, Captain M'Gachery, in Lat. 37. and Long. 72. bound to Maryland from Guinea, with 332 Slaves on board.

"On Wednesday the 20th of October 1762, at six o'clock in the evening, came on a most violent gale of wind at the south, with thunder and lightning, the sea running very high, when the ship sprung a leak, and we were obliged to lie under bare poles. The water gained on us, with both pumps continuously working. At ten P. M. endeavoured to put the ship to the wind, to no purpose. At 12 the sand ballast having choaked our pumps, and there being 7 feet water in the hold, all the casks afloat, and the ballast washed to the leeward, cut away the rigging of the main and mizen-mast, both which went instantly close by the deck, and immediately the foremast was carried away about 20 feet above. Hove overboard our guns, upon which the ship righted a little. We were then under a necessity of letting all our slaves out of irons, to assist in pumping and bailing. Thursday morning being moderate, having gained about 3 feet on the ship, found every cask in the hold stoved, so that we only saved a barrel of flour, about 10 lb. of bread 25 gallons of wine, beer and shrub, and 25 gallons of spirits. The seamen and slaves were employed all this day in pumping and bailing, the pumps were frequently choaked, and brought up great quantities of sand. We were obliged to hoist one of the pumps up, and put it down in the quarter-deck hatchway. A Ship this day bore down upon us, and tho' very near, and we making every signal of distress, she would not speak to us. On Friday the men slaves being very sullem and unruly, having had no sustenance of any kind for 48 hours, excepting a dram, we put half of the strongest in irons. On Saturday and Sunday all hands, night and day, could scarce keep the ship clear, and we were constantly under arms. On Monday morning many of the slaves had got out of irons and were attempting to break up the grating, and the seamen not daring to go down the hold and clear our pumps, we were obliged for the preservation of our own lives, to kill 50 of the ring-leaders and stoutest of them. ——— It is impossible the misery the poor slaves underwent, having had no fresh water or food 5 days. Their dismal cries and shrieks, and most frightful looks, added a great deal to our misfortune; four of them were found dead, and one drowned herself in the hold. This Evening the ship gained on us, and 3 seamen dropt down at the pump with fatigue and thirst, which could not be quenched, tho' wine, rum and shrub, were given them alternately. On Tuesday morning the ship had gained, during the night, above a foot of water, and the seamen quite worn out, and many of them in dispair. About 10 in the forenoon we saw a sail; about 2 she discovered and bore down upon us; at 5 spoke with us, being the King George, of Londondarry, James Mackey, master; he immediately promised to take us on board, and hoisted out his yawl, it then blowing very fresh; the gale increasing, prevented him from saving any thing but the white peoples lives (which were 36 in number) not even any of our cloaths, or one slave, the boat being scarce able to live in the sea the last trip she made. Capt. Mackey, and some Gentlemen passengers he had on board treated us with great kindness and humanity."

BOSTON Nov. 15. At a meeting of the Freeholders,

and other Inhabitants of the Town of Boston, duly qualified and Lawfully warned, in Public Town Meeting assembled, on Tuesday the 11th Day of May 1762.

Whereas the Inhabitants of the Town of Boston are greatly imposed upon, with respect to the Admeasurement of Wood and Bark, brought to Market in Carts and Sleds, and thereby great Fraud and Deceit is often practiced: For preventing the same,

It is therefore voted and ordered, that from and after the Tenth of September next ensuing, all Wood and Bark as they come into Town, shall be measured, and a Certificate of the Measure thereof shall be given to the Owner or Driver of the Cart or Sled.

It is further Ordered, That a suitable Person or Persons be from Time to Time think fit, to measure all such Wood and Bark brought in Carts or Sleds; and the said Person or Persons shall be under Oath to do Justice between Buyer and Seller; and shall attend from Sun-rising to Sun-setting, and shall make an entry of all Wood and Bark they measure.

And it is furthered Ordered, That there be allowed to the said Person for every load of Wood or Bark so measured Two Pence, to be paid by the Person who buys the same, or in case of his Absence at the Time of measurement, then be paid by the Owner or Driver of the Cart or Sled, who shall be reinbursed by the Buyer.

It is further Ordered, That after the tenth Day of September next, if any Person or Inhabitant of the Town of Boston aforesaid, shall buy any Wood or Bark thus brought to Market without the same being first measured as above, He, She, or they, shall forfeit and pay three Shillings for every Load brought.

Voted. That the aforegoing By-Law and Order of the Town be presented to the Court of General Sessions of the Peace to be holden at Boston within and for the County of Suffolk, for their Allowance and Approbation.

   A true Copy as appears of Record.
 Attest,   William Cooper Town-Clerk.

Last Wednesday Afternoon one Nathaniel Pain,

of Malden, an elderly Man, was detected and committed to Goal for stealing Goods, off three several Shop-Windows near the Town-Dock; he pretended to be very serious and conscientious, and for Excuse said that he was often disordered in his Mind, at which Time the cunning Adversary was apt to take the Advantage of him.

BOSTON Nov. 15. Yesterday Morning arrived here Capt. Marshall from Halifax, having on board a Number of the Massachusetts Provincials, which have been doing Duty at Nova-Scotia the Summer past; several other Vessels with the remainder of the Troops were ready to sail for this Place when Capt. Marshall came away.

We hear that Mr. William Chapman, a young Gentleman belonging to this Town, having been trading at Detroit was murdered by two of his Negro Servants as he was crossing Lake Erie in a Canoe on his return Home; the Negroes were soon after apprehended by the Indians, and delivered up to the commanding Officer of the Fort at Pittsburgh, where no doubt they will receive the just punishment of so horrid a Deed.

ANNAPOLIS Nov. 18. Last Monday arrived here from Bristol, the ship Betsey, Capt. Nicholas Andrew, with 79 Passengers of note, who are destined to tarry in his Majesty's American Plantations for the term of 7 Years.

BOSTON Nov. 22. Last Evening a Boy about 8 Years old, Son of Mr. Joseph Spear, fell from the Wharf near the South Battery, and was accidentally discovered under the Water, 'tis tho't about a Quarter of an Hour after he fell in; was taken up motionless and to all Appearances dead, but being carried to a House he was stripp'd and covered over with fine Salt, and in 12 or 15 minutes there appeared in him some faint Signs of Life, and in two Hours after he was so far recovered as to be able to speak, and is now in a fair Way of doing well. ———— 'Tis remarkable several Persons have been recovered by this Method after having lain in the Water a considerable Time, and given over for dead.

NEWPORT Rhode Island Nov. 22. Yesterday se'nnight two transports arrived here from Albany, and brought part of the regiment in the pay of this colony, which served this year at Fort Stanwix: The remainder of those who served in that quarter (except those who were retained for the winter service) are returning by land, and some of them have already reached this place. We hear they have been remarkably healthy.

It is said that the people in England were much dissatisfied with the proposals of peace with France and Spain; and that after the Duke of Bedford's return from Paris, he was insulted by the populace.

PHILADELPHIA Nov. 25. On Sunday last a Portuguese sailor stabb'd a young man, a butcher, in so dangerous a manner that he is since dead. He likewise cut another man very badly, but he is like to recover. —— The Sailor is in custody.

PORTSMOUTH New-Hampshire Nov. 26. Last Saturday a melancholy accident happened on board a ship at the north end of this town, as some men were fixing a pair of spars in order to hoist in masts; and one of the men being out on the bowsprit, by some accident the spars fell, and struck the bowsprit with such force that it hove the man 10 or 12 feet into the air, and as he fell struck his head against the bowsprit, and from thence overboard, he was immediately taken up, tho' bruised in such a manner that he died on Tuesday last.

NEW-HAVEN Nov. 27. The first of October last died at the Havannah, in the 23d Year of his age, Doct. Nathaniel Hubbard, [youngest Son of Col. Hubbard of this Town] Chief Physician to the Connecticut Regiment, that assisted in the Reduction of the Havannah. —— He was a young Gentleman possessed of many excellent and agreeable Accomplishments, that rendered him a useful Menber of Society; and his Death is justly lamented by all his Friends and Acquaintances.

BOSTON Nov. 29. By a Vessel arrived at Martha's Vineyard in a short Passage from the Havannah we learn, that the Spanish Bishop there, together with the Viceroy of Mexico, had concerted a scheme for the recovery of that Place, the former having collected upwards of 3000 Stands of Arms, and near 5000 Spadoes in one of the Churches; and the latter got together quite a considerable Body of Men some distance from the City, in order as soon as the Admiral and General were sail'd for England, to make a general Massacre of the English in the Place; But that Lord Albemarle being aprized of this plot, sent for the Bishop, and after having examined him, immediately put him on board one of the Men of War and sent him to England.

BOSTON Nov. 29. We hear from the Parish at Ware River at the Westward, that on Friday Evening the 19th Inst. a young Man about 19 Years of Age, Son to the Widow Thomas of that Place, went from Home with two Pails to get Water some considerable Distance from the House, and having a Colt to lead at the same Time, 'tis supposed he imprudently put the Rope over his Shoulder, and by some Means the Colt having took Fright, the Rope catch'd round his Neck and was thereby hung, and drawn about, as he was found next Morning tied to the Colt with his Head and Body bruised in such a Manner. His Death was much lamented by his Neighbours as he was a promising Youth, and more so by his sorrowful Mother and the rest of the Family, he being greatly their Dependance.

We hear from Stonington, that last Week as a Boy about 14 Year of Age, named Gallop, was driving an empty Cart on the side of a Hill in that Town, it overset and fell upon him, by which Accident he was instantly killed.

BOSTON Nov. 29. Captain Waterman, who arrived here last Monday from Philadelphia, inform us, That 15 Days before off Ready-Island, he met with a small Sloop, from which one Capt. Jones came on board him, and informed that on his Passage from North Carolina to Rhode Island he was taken but two Days after he came out by a small Spanish Privateer Schooner from St. Augustine; that they gave him and his People the Boat with which they went ashore at Virginia, from thence he took Passage for Philadelphia, but meeting with Capt. Waterman he came with him and landed at Tarpaulin-Cove. ——— It is not a Month since Captain Jones was taken. ——— The Captain of the Privateer had dismissed the Pilot which he took in the Summer up Chesapeak-Bay; as he had the Charts and was now well acquainted with the Southern Coast: He gave out that he intended to continue Cruizing that way for some Time. ——— It is tho't that, it would be no difficult Matter, especially now the Havannah is ours, to starve the Garrison of St. Augustine, or oblige them to surrender, by two Frigates from South Carolina, alternately blocking up the Port.

BOSTON Nov. 29. Last Thursday se'nnight a Transport arrived at New-York from the Havannah, having on board Major Gorham, with the surviving Officers of his corps of Rangers, as also those who were promoted in the Room of such as died at the Havanaah.

Names of the Officers returned to New-York.
Joseph Gorham, Major Commandant.
Andrew Watson, Captain of the 2d Company of Rangers, purchased of Capt. Danks, Sept. 23, 1762
John Walker, Captain Lieutenant.
1st Lieutenants Thomas Dixon, Marquis de Compte.

Promoted to 1st Lieutenant, Edward Crosby, from 2d Lieut. James Johnston from Serj. Major. James Tute, from America. Joseph Hayland from the Manur. Joseph Hiller, 2d Lieut. from the Intrepid. Constintine Doberty, Surgeon, from Gen Hospital.

Name of the Officers of Major Gorham's two Company of Rangers who died at the Havannah.

First Lieutenant William Shipton, William How, Elisha Waterman, Christopher Gorham. Second Lieutenant, Samuel Shipton. Surgeon, Abraham Dupee.

Charles Proctor and John Waterman Volunteers, both died after being promoted to 2d Lieutenants.

All the Privates remaining of this Corps of Rangers, amounting to 128 Men, are draughted into the Regiment left at the Havannah, tho' it was tho't by the Surgeons not above one Third of them would recover of the Disorder with which they were Afflicted.

The above Transport sailed from the Havannah in Company with about 40 sail, under Convoy of the Intrepid and 'tis said about 50 Officers are on board them who are coming on the recruiting Service.

The six Woman who went from America witn Major

Gorham's Corps are also dead.

NEW-YORK Nov. 29. On Monday arrived here from the Havannah in about 5 Weeks, the Ship James, Capt. Kosster, and three or four other Transports, with sundry Officers and Men Belonging to different Regiments of the Regulars and Provincials some of whom come to raise recruits, and others to recover their Healths. We hear some of the sick were immediately order'd to Rhode Island. These Ships are part of the Fleet that left the Havannah under Convoy of the Intrepid, from whom they were separated in a hard Gale of Wind on the Coast, about a fortnight ago. We don't hear the Intrepid is yet arrived.

DECEMBER 1762

PHILADELPHIA Dec. 2. Last week interred in one Grave, three Children of one Family in this City, who lost their Lives by a most unfortunate Accident. It had been proposed, it seems, to prepare their Bodies for the Small-Pox by giving them some Cream of Tartar, which was accordingly sent for to an Apothecary's Shop; by Mistake Tartar Emetic was delivered and administered instead of it, which by the Excee Quantity and voilent Operation, soon brought on Death. The Grief of the Parents, who have no other Children, is inexpressible.

"How careful ought the Venders of Medicine to be, that none but discreet and intelligent Persons are suffered to attend and serve in these shops."

PROVIDENCE Rhode-Island Dec. 4. Last Saturday the Brig Britannia, Capt. Dudley Saltonstall, arrived at New-London in 40 Days from Coracoa; in whom came Passenger Mr. John Snow of this Town, late Mate of the Brigantine Industry, Captain Philamon Williams, who had been gone near twelve Months without ever being heard of. —— Mr. Snow gives us the following Account of the Loss of said Vessel on the Voyage from Barbados to Saltertuda and the many difficulties and Hardships they afterwards undervent, viz. On the 3d of April last, they sailed from Barbados in a Fleet for Saltertuda and were to touch at Martinico, but their Vessel leaking and an Extreme heavy Sailor, they soon lost sight of the Fleet; and after many fruitless Efforts to get into Martinico, they bore away for Saltertuda: but were by strong Currents and adverse Winds, were driven so far to Leeward, that on the 17th of April, about 4 o'Clock in the Morning, they unfortunately run ashore on the Spanish Main, at a place called Cora: where they were soon after boarded by 150 Savages from the Shore, who plundered them of every Thing that could be of any Service to them and turn'd them ashore (seven in Number) without any Kind of Provisions to subsist on, with Directions to go to Maricry, a Spanish Settlement about 300 Miles from thence. They accordingly set out on their journey, through a Country they were unacquainted with, and after travelling three Days in the greatest Distress for want of Subsistence, and continually exposed to wild Beast of Prey, and more Savage Natures, they were luckily over taken by seven Spaniards, who supplied them with Refreshments, and conducted them to the Spanish Town. As soon as they arrived they were immediately imprisoned, without Distinction in a Loathsome Goal, where they all continued for five Months, except one, who embraced the Roman-Catholic Religion, after a Month's Comfinement, and was set at Liberty; and treated with great Kindness. At length the Spanish Governor ordered the six that kept fast to their Faith, on board a Dutch Sloop that was trading there, in which they got to Caracoa. Captain Williams died on the 19th Ult, on his passage Home after a few Days Illness.

BOSTON Dec. 6, The Snow with Provincial Troops arrived here last Saturday Se'nnight, is called the Friendship, William Sherry, Master, in who camed Captain Lemuel Dunbar and 180 Troops belonging to this Province: The Account of the disasters that befel them are as follows, viz. That on the 6th of November they left Halifax in the Morning, and about 7 o'Clock in the evening as they were going about 7 knots, their Rudder broke just above the Water, and all the lower Part went off; a violent Storm then came on whereby they could not carry the least Sail, but were obliged to lay at the Mercy of the Sea to the 10th of the Month, on the Morning of which they discovered Land on both Sides of the Vessel, and being unable to put their Ship about were drove before the Wind till they were within a Mile of the Land, where they dropt Anchor, which held them till the next Day; just at Light they described a Schooner, and making signals she came to them, and informed them that they were at the Entrance of the East Passage of Cape-Sables, call'd Barrington's-Bay; by the help of the Schooner the Snow was carried in, and had a Rudder fixed by the 17th; in the evening of that Day 6 of the Soldiers being ashore hired two of the Inhabitants to carry them on board in a Canoe; the Wind blowing very fresh the Canoe filled and over-set, five of them got on the Bottom and continued there for the space of an Hour, the owner of the Canoe continued on her Bottom an Hour longer, when he was heard from the Shore, upon which they got a Boat and took him up, and being carried on board the Snow informed them of the Loss of the six Soldiers, whose names were as follow: ——— Clement Crane, of Brantree; Benjamin Johnson, jun'r, Nathaniel Ramsdell, and John Pratt, of Bridgewater; Ignatious Cushing of Duxbury; David Mosse, of Plymouth; and one of the Inhabitants that was hired to bring them off.

BOSTON Dec. 6. Silent Wilde, the Western News-Carrier. Hereby signifies his Desire to those that have employed him, that as the first half Year of his last Engagement expir'd the Beginning of the present Month, that they would be so kind as to leave their Money for him at the several Places where they respectively have received their Papers, as soon as may be. ———

N. B. supposed it is needless to remind my Employers that as I engag'd for one whole Year (which I am determined to fulfill) at Two Dollars each, so that the half, Year already expired is one Dollar each: ——— tho' some don't remember the Time payment.   Silent Wilde.

NEW-YORK Dec. 6. The 10th of November, the Ship Duke, Samuel Sparrow, Master, foundered in Lat. 32 and a half, but all the Crew was taken out by the Intrepid, Capt. Hale; and 4 Days after Captain Hale was obliged to put 40 Hands on board the Cæsar, John Morton, Master, to preserve her from sharing the same Fate; tho' she was left with 3 Feet Water in her Hold.

In the above Ships, several Officers as well as Regulars and Provincials, are arrived here. Those of Connections are, General Lyman, Colonel

Putnam, Major Dirkee; Lieutenant Parks, Chalker, Wells and Nolson; and Ensign Denny and Anderson. Of the same Corps the following Officers died at the Havannah, viz. Capts. Spalden, Patterson and Stanton; Lieuts. Brown, Pirkin, and I. & W. Thompson; also Ensign Dounar.

 Tuesday last his Majesty's ship Intrepid, John Hale Esq; Commander, arrived at Sandy Hook from the Havannah after a very tedious Passage of 40 Days: She was Convoy to about 30 Transports that sailed from thence for this Port, with Provincials that was sent from this Continent to assist at the reduction of that very important Place; of which Fleet the following Vessels are arrived. viz. Vulture, Diamong, Francis, Oliver, James, Elizabeth, Venus, Resolution, Nancy, Margery, Young Samuel, Jane and Elizabeth, Hopewell. The Patience, Lydia, York and Halifax, bore away for Providence, being leaky; the Marlborough for S. Carolina; and the Duke of York, Ceasar, Temple, and five or 6 others unknown are not yet arrived.

 NEWPORT Rhode Island Dec. 9. Last Night, broke out of His Majesty's Goal in Newport, one John Shearman a Prisoner under the Sentence of Death for Burglary. He is near 5 Feet 10 Inches high, about 48 Years of Age of a dark Complexion, hath a very flat Nose, and walks a little stooping: He wears a dark coloured Coat, whoever apprehends him, and delivers him to the Subscriber, or secure him in any of His Majesty's Goals, shall receive Eight Dollars Reward.

        Joseph G. Wanton Sheriff.

 CHARLESTOWN S. Carolina Dec 11. We hear that the prince of Chotih has sent down a talk to the governor, from Ninety-Six, wherein he acquaints his excellency, that he was there on his way coming down, but meeting with Judd's-Friend, and hearing with pleasure the talk bro't from the great king George, he should return to the Cherokee nation: That he and all the Warriors, however, desire to meet and see his excellency, at Ninety-Six, in the spring, and to have a trade established at Gourdy's as formerly; and he concludes with assurances, that he and all the warriors are of one mind, as brothers and friends to the English, and children and subjects to the same king.

On the 12th ult. eight unknown Indians came into the Catawba nation, killed and scalped Capt. Day. one of their warriors, and made off, without leaving any marks whereby it could be discovered of what nation they were; but the Catawba's suspected them to be Cherokees and have sent down for advice how to act: They at the same time repeat their complaints of the North Carolinians continuing to incroach upon their lands.

CHARLESTOWN S. Carolina Dec. 11. Last saturday night arrived in town from Seewee-bay where they were put ashore the night before, part of the crew of the brigt. Friendship of this port, taken by a French privateer sloop commanded by one Martin (but manned entirely with Spaniards) the thursday night preceeding, off Edisto. The privateer is the same from whom Mr. Isaac Waldon (one of our pilots) so happily escaped friday last week. She anchored, with our prize, the same evening off Bull's island inlet, stripp'd the brigt. of some sails and rigging and set her on fire; then put all her prisoners ashore, except two very valuable negro men (belonging to capt. Thomas Tucker and Alexander Rase, Esq;) and proceeded to sea. From the Spaniards burning the prize and setting their prisoners on shore, it was imagined that she had finished her cruize; but on saturday she chased a shooner belonging to Henry Laurens, Esq; coming from Winyah, laden with indigo and naval stores, back to the port she came from, Sunday afternoon she was discovered at anchor just without the point of the North-Island within Winyah bar, but not suspected of being the enemy: That night, at about 12 o'clock, a party of the privateer's crew guided by capt. Tucker's fellow (who was bound) surprized Mr. Bromley the pilot's House, siezed therein Mrs. Bromley, a child about two years old, Mr. Joseph Dubourdieu, and several negroes, and stripped the house of every thing of least value; (the rev. Mr. Pearce, rector of that parish, who had been in the house some days, having come there from George Town for his health, was happy enough to escape their search; and the negroes, while the enemy were plundering, all made their escape) they likewise seized a sailing boat of Mr. Dubourdieu's, having stoved the sloop's only one in landing, into which they put all their prisoners and plunder, and went down to the point of the island, but the wind being contrary, and a heavy sea, they could not then reach the sloop: After being about 15 hours in this boat (Spaniards, prisoners and plunder) without a mouthful of provisions, and scarce any water, she lost her rudder; whereupon the Spaniards determined to, and did return to Bromley's house, which they pillaged a second time, then seized a large new ship's long-boat that lay there ready rigged, gave Mr. Dubourdieu his own, and went off, but did not get out till dark. The next morning (Monday) the boat was seen by Mr. Dubourdieu, from the beach, endeavouring to get to the sloop, which had weighed at 9 o'clock, and was in chace of a ship and a snow that appeared plainly in of offing; as the sloop sailed well, and the wind blew fresh at N. E. Mr. Dubourdieu supposed both ship and snow to be taken, and he doubts if the privateer's prize-boat got on board; he rather believes she is in some one of the inlets on this side off Winyah Wednesday afternoon several guns were heard off Winyah bar, whence it was concluded, that the privateer had returned to look for her boat and the party she had landed to surprize Bromley, but he with his boat fortunately happened to be up the river. ——— By the questions asked of Mr. Dubourdieu, it seemed to be the intention of the Spaniards, if they had Bromley, to have surprized George Town, and pillaged all the plantations along the river; amongst other things, they made earnest inquiries about provision vessels.

BOSTON Dec. 13. We hear from Williamsburg in Virginia of the following barbarous Affair transacted at Porthsmouth in that Province, on Sunday the 24th ult. A transport Ship from the Havannah, having a considerable amount of Spanish Soldiers and Sailors on board, among whom was Don Pedro the second in command in the

Sea-Service, with his Family, having sprung a leak, put into Hampton Road to refit: the Spaniards had liberty to tarry on shore at Portsmouth, where they behaved exceedingly well; but several Sailors belonging to his Majesty's Ship Arundel, being likewise on shore, they proposed to rob them, imagining they had a great quantity of Money with them: The Sailors began with quarelling, than proceeded to Blows, and drove the Spaniards into a House, then fired upon them, killed one, wounded several, which died of his wounds, they set Fire to the House in which the Spaniards had lock'd themselves and some of them actually went for powder to blow them up; they also burnt into the Commander's House, beat and wounded him, one of the Captains, and all the Domesticks, except two who had hid themselves.
—— A stop was put to any further Attempts by Capt. Manwaring's going ashore and dispersing his people.; The Norfolk Militia was raised to apprehend all concerned in this affair, some of whom are already committed to Goal. —— The Spaniards have a grateful Sense of the kindness of the Inhabitants, in their Assistance to rescue them from the Hands of such Ruffians.

Out of a detachment of 212 Men from the Colony of Rhode Island, that were at the siege of the Havannah, only 100 have return'd alive; the remainder, except 2 kill'd by the enemy, died of Sickness.

BOSTON Dec. 13. For Jamaica, the Ship Oxford, Burthen 640 Tons, mounts 24 Guns, 20 Swivels, and small Arms in Proportion; John Ross, Commander. —— Has Letters of Marque against the French and Spaniards, and will sail from Falmouth about the last of December.

All able bodied Seamen, and able-bodied Landmen, that has a Mind to go on said Ship, may come to Falmouth in Casco-Bay, where they shall be kindly received on board, and shall enter into Monthly pay from the Day they set out from Boston, or any other Place, and be allowed all reasonable Expences by Land or Water, provided they come on board in thirty Days from the Date hereof. Wages for able Seamen Three Pounds Sterling per Month, Land-Men Forty-five Shillings per Month, and may be discharged in Jamaica, or proceed the Voyage from thence to London. All Prizes taken by said Ship, to be shared or divided amongst the Captors as customary. There is Thirty-five Men on board, and intend to carry Seventy. In Case it be Peace with France and Spain before sailing from Falmouth, its expected Wages will be in Proportion.

    Falmouth 22d November 1762.   John Ross.
N. B. Captain Alexander Ross, of Falmouth, will give Security for the Performance of agreement.

BOSTON Dec. 13. Ran Away on Sunday Night the 5th of December, Instant, from Widow Martha Jerauld, of Medfield, a Mulatto Servant, mamed Cesar about 4 Feet 9 Inches high born in Medfield, aged 30 Years, speaks fast and thick: Had on when he ran away, a thick all wool Coat, a blue Broad-Cloth Jacket, and an old Flat Hat, wears a Cap. Whoever shall take up said Fellow, and convey him to the Subscriber, shall have Two Dollars Reward and necessary Charges paid by
  Medfield Dec. 11, 1762.   Martha Jeraulds.

NEWPORT, Rhode Island Dec. 13. Last Wednesday Evening John Shearman, who received sentence of death at the last superior court, for burglary, and had been reprieved by the Hon. Assembly for the term of 14 months to obtain his Majesty's pardon, broke out of our goal and made his escape.

CHARLESTOWN S. Carolina Dec. 15. Saturday last, we received the following further information of the Spanish privateer that has the hardiness to infest our coast, while two of his Majesty's ships are upon a cruize in quest of her, viz.

That on Thursday the 9th instant, the longboat taken in the night of the 5th at North-Island near George Town, having missed the privateer, had come down the coast as far as Racoon Keys: That the Spaniards went ashore upon one of them (called Mr. Lynch's island) the same day, where they killed some of the cattle and hogs, and took two negroes belonging to Mr. Mazyck, who had been dispatched to alarm some plantations on Santee and stop a rice-loaded schooner from coming out of that river; but one of the negroes made his escape. And that every day last week, till Friday the 10th, the privateer either was seen, or her signal guns for the boat heard, sometimes off Winyah, sometimes off the Cape, and lately off Racoon Keys.

Upon this intelligence given to Capt. Goodall, of his Majesty's ship Mercury, he immediately ordered a barge out, well manned, to proceed as far as the said Keys, in quest of the above long-boat; but this morning she returned without seeing her, and account that she got on board the privateer Friday evening off Bull's Island.

Yesterday morning we had the following further account of the said privateer, viz.

That on the 7th instant, she was off shubrick's island, and gave chace to a large snow which however got away: That the same day he took the ship Black Prince, Andrew Dodd master, from New York bound for this port, about 9 leagues E. N. E. from this bar: That on the 8th, in the same cruizing ground, he took the brigt. Catharine, Andrew Elton Wells, master (of St. Kitt's) from St. Croix bound for Georgia, and ordered her to St. Augustine: That after capt. Dodd had struck his colours, while he was hoisting out his long boat, (his yawl being stove along-side) the commander of the privateer discharged a blunderbuss at him, which shot his hat thro', cut off some of his hair, slightly wounded him in one ear and leg: That the privateer continued cruizing in the same station till Friday the 10th when capt. Dodd was permitted to ransom his ship for 600 dollars; but she was pillaged, and capt. Wells with all his crew, (except two men) put on board: And that on Saturday she went in chace of the Brigantine that came from the northward, which is thought to have escaped. —— This intelligence we have of capt. Wells, who landed here yesterday morning from on board the Black Prince, which got in over the bar the evening before. He informs us further, that capt. Dodd spoke with capt. Blake, in his majesty's ship Epreuve, on Sunday, and gave him such information that he immediately went in the course the privateer took. Capt. Wells discribes the privateer thus; "She is a new sloop New-England built, burthen about 65 tons, with a quarter-deck, crane irons along it 6 feet long, and a white bottom much weather beaten; belongs to St. Augustine, and is commanded by Don Maria del Manza; her sides have been sawed for 10 ports, which are arched over with iron, but she had only 8 carriage guns mounted; her mast is very taunt, stands well, and had a square-sail, yard and boom across; she had against top-sail bent to her top-mast, but occasionally carries a square-top-sail; her sails are old and much weather beaten, and her main-sail has 3 remarkable large patches of new cloth in it, each about 12 or 13 yards."

Wednesday morning sailed on a cruize, in Quest of the above privateer, his majesty's ship Mercury, Capt. Goodall.

BOSTON Dec. 20. Extract of a letter from the Havannah.

"So many whizzing messengers of distruction have terrified my ears in some of out attacks that the greatest usurer you have, had he known the danger I stood in, would have been unwilling to have given six hours purchase for my life in an annuity. When (at last) the Spaniards were so terribly troubled within fallen sickness, sickness, that not one man in five was able to keep on his legs, four minutes at out advancing, death, like an ill-natured fellow, having made the ground so slippery; and providence afforded us nothing but the scent of sweat, blood & gun powder to refresh our nostrils with, in so dangerous a situation. It was very surprising to observe the courage of our brave fellows in this hot work; for in every attenpt though never so difficult, their resolution and bravery still procured them success. I was very much surprized at the hardiness of one fellow, in the 72d regiment, who was very near Col. K———, and had his left arm taken off by a cannon ball from the Moro Castle, upon which he muttered out these words: "What an unfortunate son of a whore was I to put my tobacco-box in my left pocket, that now I cannot easily come at it with my right hand, to refresh myself with a chew."

NEW-YORK Dec. 20. Tuesday last the Ship Oliver, Capt. Sterling, bound to Boston in going through Hell-Gate run on the Hogs-Back, and received so much damage, that the hull 'tis thought will be entirely lost.

PHILADELPHIA Dec. 23. Extract of a Letter from an Officer at Detroit, to his friend at Williamsburg, dated October 26, 1762.

"The settlement is about 15 miles long, the land extremely good, and the people might live very happy were they industrious; but instead of cultivating their lands, they pay a most exorbitant price for almost all necessaries of life, and only carry on a little dirty trade with the Indians.

The 19th of this month was the most extraordinary dark day, perhaps ever seen in this world. At nine in the morning it was scarce lighter than at day-break and so continued till about 12 o'clock, the air being very full of smoke accompanied with a strong smell, as of wood, straw and other combustibles when burning. At half after one it was so dark, that we were obliged to light a candle to dine by: At this time it rained a little, with which fell such quantities of black particles, like ashes, as turned every thing black it fell upon, even the river, which was covered with a froth, which, when scummed off the surface, resembled the lather of soap, with this difference, that it was black and greasy. At 7 in the evening, the air was more clear, & the disagreeable smell considerably abated. ——— We have been since informed, by people who were 20 miles from hence that day, that the darkness, rain, and smell was the same with them."

NEW-LONDON Dec. 24. Last Wednesday Evening two Indians being on board a Canoe in the Cove at the lower end of this Town, they were heard to have some high Words together and soon after one of them was heard to fall overboard; and altho' help was immediately obtain'd he was drowned. The Body was found the next Morning, when the Coroner's Inquest convened and brought in their Verdict, that the Wounds and bruises found on the Body was not mortal. Their names were John & Solomon Peters, belonging to Sonington, and were brothers; the latter was drowned, and former was taken into custody. They were both in Liquor.

We are credibly informed that a certain ensign in Colonel Lyman's Regiment, which went to the Havannah, inlisted 26 Men into the Regiment; and that all but one of them died of sickness.

When the City of Havannah surrendered, there was computed to be about 50,000 Souls in it; who were reduced to the greatest Distress by sickness and the destruction of the siege.

BOSTON Dec. 27. We hear from the Town of Hebron in Connecticut, that of 18 Soldiers which went from that Place, in the Expedition to the Havannah, 15 are dead, two are sick at New-York, and one only is returned.

JANUARY 1763

NEW-YORK Jan. 3. A Letter from the Havannah, dated Nov. 27, says They had Advice that Commodore Hepple had taken off Cape Francois 11 sail of Ships from Bourdeaux, with 2000 Troops on board; and that he had taken 9 Sail from the Cape bound home. under convoy of a 60 Gun Ship. No doubt the Publick will be highly pleased when they hear this piece of News confirmed.

BOSTON Jan. 4. Province of Massachusetts-Bay. The Officers who were employed in the service of this Providence the last Year, that are concerned in making up the Pay Rolls, are directed to attend at Boston, as soon as may be upon a Committee appointed by the General Court to examine the said Rolls: And the Suttlers who were employed in the said Service are, also, directed to attend the said Committee with their accounts. By Order of His Excellency.
Tho. Goldthwait Secr'y of War.

PORTHSMOUTH New-Hampshire Jan. 7. By a Vessel a few Days ago from Newfoundland, the Master of which informs, that sometime about the middle of November was drove on shore a considerable Quantity of Furrs and Skins in St. Mary's Bay, and that a Part of some Vessel's stern was also drove on Shore upon which was wrote, The Bonetta.

CHARLESTOWN S. Carolina Jan. 8. The back parts of this province will soon be better settled then ever, abundance of people coming daily from the Northward to view the lands, who being much charmed with its fertility, and finding the weather exceedingly more moderate than in the northern climates, intend to apply for grants for the same.

BOSTON Jan. 10. Last Saturday four Oyster-Men being employed in the Hold of their Vessel lying at the Town Dock, opening of Oysters over a

Pot of Charcoal, one of them soon after found himself so much disordered by the Steam of the Coal, that he got out upon Deck as quick as possible, but before he could get Assistance to help the other three out, they were so far suffocated as to be deprived of all Senses of Motions, and were near an Hour before they could be perfectly recovered.

Notice is hereby Given, That by a Decree of the Governor and Council, my Marriage with Hannah Story, who calls herself Hannah Davidson, was declared null and void, upon Proof being made of her prior Marriage to Thomas Story, who is still living. All persons are therefore hereby cautioned against trusting her on my Account.

Boston 8th January 1763.   William Davidson
(a Gardner.)

NEW-YORK Jan. 10. Yesterday arrived here, from Philadelphia, Captain William Montgomery, late of the Schooner ----- belonging at this Port, who sailed from Spanish Town for this Place, on the 20th of October last, and on the 24th, in Lat. 20, 20. Long. 64, 20. after 30 Hours Chace, was taken by Captain Don Diego, in a Sloop of 10 Guns, belonging to Spanish St. Domingo. The People were strip'd of every Thing, save Shirt and Trowsers, and the Schooner dispatch'd for that Place. The People remain'd on board the Privateer 16 Days, when they fell in with a Sloop bound to Statia on board which they were ill put, and on the 14th of November they arrived at that Island. From thence they went to St. Kitts, and from thence sail'd Dec. 2d, and arrived the 29th at Philadelphia. The Captain reports they are great numbers of Spanish Privateers in the West Indies.

On Friday last, a Son of Mr. Isaac Martin, on Canon's Dock, about 3 Years old fell from a Window of the second Story, into the Stoop below, where Mr. Martin was sitting. The Head of the Child first striking the Floor, his Scull was fractured and he remained some time deprived of Sense; but skilful Surgeons being immediately called in, he was trepanned and properly dressed. He is now in a fair way of recovery almost out of Danger. ——— This may be a Caution to others, not to trust Children without a careful Attendant, in upper Rooms, where the Windows are not secure by Bars.

BOSTON Jan 17. Tuesday last arrived here Capt. Davis in 7 Weeks from Bristol & Swanzey, by whom we have the following most interesting Article, viz.

From the London Gazette.
Whitehall, Nov. 9 1762

Early Yesterday Morning, Mr. Monet, one of the King's Messengers, arrived at the Earl of Egremont's Office, his Majesty's principal Secretary of state, with the Instrument of Preliminary Articles of Peace, signed at Fontainbleau the 3d Instant, by his Grace the Duke of Bedford, his Majesty's Plenipotentiary with those of the most Christian and Catholic Kings.

LONDON Nov. 9.

Yesterday Morning the following Letter was received by the Right. Hon. the Lord Mayor.

To the Right. Hon. the Lord Mayor
"My Lord,
I am directed by my Lord Egremont to acquaint your Lordship, that one of his Majesty's Messengers has this Moment brought an account of the Duke of Bedford's having signed the Preliminary Articles of Peace with France and Spain, at Fontainbleau, on the 3d Inst. The Secretary of State's intention for making this immediate Communication to your Lordship, of the first Account relating to the Signature of the Preliminaries, which has been transmitted to his Office by the King's Minister at Paris, is in order to have it publickly known in the City without loss of time. Your Lordship will, no doubt, take such Steps as are most proper to answer the Purpose.   I am,
   With the greatest Respect,
      My, Lord,
         Your Lordship's most obedient
            humble Servant,
                           Rob. Wood."
LONDON Nov. 9.
POLITICAL.

The principal Articles of the preliminary Treaty signed on the 3d Instant at Fontainbleau between England, France and Spain, are said to be as follows:

I. Portugal to be immediately evacuated by by Spanish and French Troops.

II. Newport and Ostend to be evacuated, and Dunkirk to be demolished.

III. France and England to withdraw their Armies out of Germany, and Regulations agreed upon for sucouring their respective Allies in case the Houses of Austria and Brandenbourgh go to with their War.

IV. Minorez to be restored in England.

V. Belleisle to be restored in France.

In AFRICA.

VI. Senegal remains with England.

VII. Goree restored to France.

In ASIA.

VIII. The French Army may, if they please, rebuild Pondecherry, and have Settlements on the Caramandel Coast; but to be excluded fron having any Establishments in the Kingdom of Bengal, except those Comptoirs or Factories, with more than 16 Men to garrison each.

In The WEST-INDIES.

IX. Martinico, Guadaloupe, and Marigalante, to be restored to France.

X. Grenado and the Grenadillas to remain with England.

XI. St. Lucia to belong to France.

XII The other three Neutral Islands, Tobago, Dominica, and St. Vincents, to belong to England.

XIII. Spain to have back the Havannah, and to cede to England St. Augustine, and the whole Country called Florida; the Right of the English to cut Log-Wood allowed; The Spanish Claims to Newfoundland Fishery given up.

NORTH AMARICA.

XIV. The French are excluded from the Fishing in the Gulf of St. Lawrence on the Bays of Cape Breton, St. John's, Antiecosta, and Gaspee; but may erect Stages between Cape Riche and Bonivista, to cure the Fish they shall catch on the Shores between the above Capes. They are to be allowed to have Harbours at Miquelon and St. Peter's in which Islands they may have a Fort with only fifty Men as Garrison, and subject to the Inspection of an English Commissary. None but French Ships to be allowed to touch at Miquelon and St. Peter's.

XV. The whole of Canada to be ceded to England; and the most valuable Part of what the French used to call Louisiana; the River Missisippi being declared the boundry between the Colonies of the two Nations on the Continent of North-America; The English to have Navigation of the Missisippi down to the Sea.

(As many people suppose that a peace is concluded when preliminaries are signed, it is fit to inform them that preliminaries articles are certain propersitions agreed to previous to the Treaty of Peace, which are to be subject of discussion, during the negotiation, till the Treaty is absolutely finished, so that altho' preliminaries of each are settled, yet no peace may ever ensue in pursuance of such articles, which, in effect, do only open the treaty, or point out the subjects of the negotiation.)

BOSTON Jan. 17. The Speech of His Majesty Francis Bernard, Esq; Captain General and Governor in Chief, in and over His Majesty's Province of the Massachusetts-Bay, in New-England, and Vice-Admiral of the same.

To the Great and General Court of Assembly of said Province.

Gentlemen of the Council, and Gentlemen of the House of Representatives,

It is with great Pleasure to me, that I am able, at the opening of this Session, to inform you, That the Preliminaries of Peace have been agreed by the Ministers of England, France and Spain.

I cannot but consider it as a happy Circumstance, that this Event, the just object of War, and desirable, where it most successful, is like to be brought about at a Time when the Glory of Great Britain is at so great a height, and her Power is so well established, as to enable her to require not only a Security for the future, but also an indemnification for what is passed.

Whatever may be the Terms upon which a general Peace shall be concluded, you may assure yourselves they will be advantageous to this Country. The Eyes of Great-Britain are fixed upon it: She sees the importance of her North-American Dominions. The Defence of them was the first occasion of the War; The Safety will be a principal object of the Peace.

   Gentlemen of the House of Representatives,

   I have nothing now to ask of you for the King's immediate Service: There will be wanted a supply to make good your former Grants; for which purpose the Treasurer will have order to lay before you the present State of the Treasury. I shall be glad when all extraordinary Expences shall cease, and the People shall be left to enjoy the fruits of their Labours without any apprehension of Danger.

   Gentlemen of the Council, and, Gentlemen of the House of Representatives,

   The Business of the Session will probably be confined to the domestic Policy of the People; in regard to which I shall communicate to you what occurs to me as occasions shall require. I hope that the Time is nor far off when your Council will be wholly directed to the internal Welfare and Prosperity of the Province; in which you may be assured of my Concurrence by all legal means of my Power.

   Council Chamber Jan. 12, 1763.   Fra. Bernard.

(The Definitive Treaty of Peace and Friendship, between His Britannick Majesty, the Most Christian King and the King of Spain, concluded at Paris, the 10th Day of February, 1763.)

FULLNAME INDEX

All names appear as they were originally published

1ST REGIMENT, 38 280
4TH REGIMENT, 90
15TH REGIMENT, 101 150 302
17TH REGIMENT, 146 150 152-154 283 (XVIIth) 38
22ND REGIMENT, 57 77 84 90 152 190 299 302 306 Of Foot (XXII) 64 Of Foot (XXIInd) 44
23RD REGIMENT, (XXIII) 38
27TH REGIMENT, 101 150 153
28TH REGIMENT, 101 150 312
35TH REGIMENT, 63 101
38TH REGIMENT, 150
40TH REGIMENT, 101 150 238 280
42ND REGIMENT, 101 150 190 297
43RD REGIMENT, 101 150
45TH REGIMENT, 309 312
46TH REGIMENT, 233
48TH REGIMENT, 101 150 302
58TH REGIMENT, 244 295
72ND REGIMENT, 336
77TH REGIMENT, 300
ABBOT, Capt 212
ACTEON, (ship) 225
AITKENS, John 135
ALBEMARLE, Earl 246 Earl Of 248 Lord 209 268 281-282 288-290 295 298 324
ALCIDE, (ship) 137 248
ALCOCK, John 72
ALDFIELD, Capt 104
ALICE, (ship) 248

ALLAN, Peter 277
ALLEN, Ebenezer 237 James 291 Joseph 62 Martin 73 Mrs 171 237
AMHERST, Col 278-279 286 299-300 308-310 313 Gen 4 13-14 19-20 44 50 63 71 91 100 104 146 154 199 205-206 253 Jeffery 150 255 Lt Col 302 306-307 Lt Col William 308 Sir Jeffrey 170 208 212 284 Sir Jeffry 187 302 William 306 308 Wm 306-307 314
AMITY'S GOOD INTENT, (ship) 319
AMITY'S ASSISTANCE, (ship) 152
ANDERSON, 183 Ens 330 John 182
ANDREW, Nicholas 322
ANGLESOY, (ship) 47 49
ANNE, (ship) 292
ANSON, (ship) 106
ANSTRUTHER, Lt 317
ANTELOPE, (ship) 158 257 261 264 268-269 299
APPOWIN, Capt 110
ARBUTNOT, Capt 209-210
ARCHBALD, Capt 280
ARCHIBALD, David 14
ARMIGER, Col 150
ARMSTRONG, Wm 35
ARSON, (ship) 106
ARTILLERY, Royal Regiment Of 151
ARUNDEL, (ship) 90 333
ARWOOD, Samuel 159
ASHLEY, 182
ASSISTANCE, (ship) 78 83 110
ATKIN, Edmond-Death Of 140

ATKINS, Capt 252 John 156 Silas 251
ATKINSON, Theodore Esq 177 Theodore Jr 177
AUDRE, (ship) 66
AULDBOY, Capt 107
AUSTIN, Mr 143
AVERY, John 96 227
BAFFETT, Capt 107
BAGLEY, Col 26
BAGMIER, Capt 106
BAILIE, Capt 308
BAIRD, Capt 263 John 266
BALL, Capt 107 Charles 75
BALLIE, Capt 310
BANKS, Capt 235
BARBEIT, Ross 157
BARBER, Lt 84
BARCELONA, (ship) 240
BARCLAY, Lt 193
BARKER, John 235 Lt 299
BARNES, Samuel 118
BARNSWELL, George 115
BARRONS, Capt 312-313
BASS, Capt 160
BASSET, Capt 157
BATTALION CORPS, 87
BAXTER, John 223
BAYARD, (ship) 71-72 William 186
BAYNTON, William 172
BAYONNE, 66 72
BAYONNE CASTLE, (prison) 61
BEALE, Benjamin 174
BEDFORD, (ship) 312 Duke Of 323 341
BELCHER, 144 J 2 Jonathan 1 203 Mr President 49
BELECOMBE, Lt Col 304
BELL, Mr 37
BENDALL, Capt 279
BENEY, John 159
BENSON, Capt 189
BERNARD, Fra 42 50 80 106 163 171 188 209 212 230 260 285 Francis 11 13 40 49 79 104 163 187 210 343-344 Gov 232

BERRY, John 173 188
BETSEY, (ship) 205 291 322
BETSY, (ship) 319
BETTLE, John 315
BIGREY, Thomas 75
BILLANDER TARTAN, (ship) 239
BIRD, Mary 40
BLACK PRINCE, (ship) 238 335
BLACKATE, (ship) 319
BLACKENEY, Lord 150
BLACKS, Company Of 295
BLAGDEN, Samoel 106
BLAIR, John 114 182
BLAKE, Capt 33-34 48 72 335 Edward 101 Peter 318
BLENAC, M 228
BOLT, Charles 75
BONETTA, (ship) 339
BONNETTA, (ship) 292 318
BOON, (ship) 244
BOONE, Gov 154 Thomas 152
BOOTH, Mr 47 Mrs 47
BOSHER, Thomas 139
BOUNTY, To Be Paid To Enlisted Soldiers 50
BOURAN, De 217
BOWIES, Capt 110
BOX, Mr 143
BOYNTON, William 172
BRADDOCK, Capt 253
BRADFORD, Capt 232 Job 292
BRANSCOMB, 281
BRAY, George 233-234
BREME, Capt 20
BREMFIELD, Thomas 7
BRERETON, Capt 242
BRETON, William 73
BREWER, Jonathan 5 19
BRIGS, John 159
BRISTOL, (ship) 110
BRISTOL MERCHANT, (ship) 302
BRITANIA, (ship) 256
BRITANNIA, (ship) 242 274 326
BRITANNICUS, 197
BRITON, (ship) 274
BROMLEY, 332 Mr 331 Mrs 331
BROOKS, James 258
BROTHERLY LOVE, (ship) 35 152

BROUGHTON, Capt 253
BROWN, 10 Lt 330 Mr 80-81
BROWNE, Francis 205
BRUCE, Capt 204 James 75
BRYANT, Richard 293-294
BUCK, Capt 107
BUCKLER, Daniel 204
BUCKLEY, R 2
BULKELEY, Rich 203
BULL, Gov 144 Wiliam 126 William 121 128
BULLFINCH, 182
BURFORD, (ship) 106
BURIALS AND BAPTISMS, Boston 167
BURNET, Capt 169
BURNHAM, Capt 225
BURTON, Col 77 84 104 146 233 Lt 77
BUSHINGTON, John 237
BUTLER, Capt 317 John 291 Thomas 101
BYRD, Col 15 78 99 102-104 112 114 121-122
BYRN, Capt 57
BYRNE, John 57
BYVANEK, Capt 33
CADETS, Company Of 206
CADWICK, Capt 300
CAESAR, (ship) 329
CALL, Celeb 137
CALLOE, Mr 245
CAMBEL, Ens 84
CAMBRIDGE, (ship) 274 279
CAMERON, Ens 145
CAMPBEL, 3
CAMPBELL, 199 Capt 77 114 302 306 James 152 John 146 152 274 299
CANADA, Ceded To England 343
CANADIANS, Conditions In Quebec 67 Deplorable Conditions In Montreal 39 Love For Extravagant Dress 39
CANER, Rev 2
CANOYS, Indians 93
CAPTAINS KING AND BULLFINCH, (ship) 159

CAPTIVES, 236 From Massachusetts To Be Listed 66
CAREFUL, (ship) 159
CAREY, (ship) 34
CARIE, Capt 318
CARLSLE, Capt 299
CARLSON, R 13
CARPENTER, Capt 277
CATAWABA INDIANS, 95
CATAWBA INDIANS, 32 74 82 96 116 127 331
CATHARINE, (ship) 335
CAWATA INDIANS, 80
CAYTON, Andrew 40
CAYUGAS, Indians 93
CEASAR, (ship) 330
CENTURION, (ship) 263
CHABERLAND, Ens 265
CHACTAW INDIANS, 80-81
CHALKER, Lt 330
CHAMBERS, Capt 73 212
CHANDLER, Jonathan 46
CHAPMAN, Benja 165 William 322
CHARLESTOWN, (ship) 206 298
CHARMING BETSEY, (ship) 225 315
CHATAHS INDIANS, 78
CHEESMAN, Joseph 71-72
CHEROKEE PEACE TERMS, 120 125-131 135
CHEROKEES, 3-4 8 16 22-23 29-32 37-38 43-44 57 64 71 74-75 77-78 80-88 90 92 96 98-100 102 110 113 115-117 120 122-123 126-130 139 144 146 151 153-154 159 227-228 233 236-239 291 318 330
CHESTERFIELD, (ship) 233 238 283 285
CHICASAH INDIANS, 82
CHICASAW INDIANS, 95 116
CHICESAW INDIANS, 127
CHICKASAW INDIANS, 81
CHICKESAW INDIANS, 32 81 130
CHIKESAW INDIANS, 37 74 80 238
CHOCTAW INDIANS, 29

CHOCTAWS, 19
CHURCH, Capt 257
CIVAN, 182
CLANARD, 267
CLARK, 165
CLASTON, Capt 34
CLEAR, Peter 159
CLEMENS, 33
CLOUGH, Benjamin 73
COATS, Capt 315
COBB, Capt 96 Sivanus 49
COBHAM, Rober 157
COCHRANM, Robert 298
COCKBURN, Capt 190
COCKLE, James 81 240
COCKRAN, 199 Capt 258 William 250
COFFIN, Capt 315
COL, Grant 131
COLBERT, Capt 95 James 37
COLDEN, Cadwallader 102 Lt Gov 236
COLDTHWAIT, Ezekiel 25-26
COLEFOX, Capt 107
COLGAN, Capt 315
COLLINS, 182 Capt 35 204
COLLODEN, (ship) 17
COLQUHAUN, Lt 57
COLVIL, Lord 44 314
COLVILL, Lord 250 269 277 279 291-293 299 301-303 305-306 308-309 311
COLVILLE, Lord 9
COMPANIES, Maj Hamilton's 14
COMPANY, Blake's 33-34 48 Byrn's 57 Corce's 33 Davis's 33 Demere's Independent 44 Hay's 98 Motte's 33 Newhall's 33 Parker's 27 33 Peabody's 33-34 48 Phodey's 89 Rogers' Independent 44 Walter's 57 Whipple's 26 33
CONBERFORD, William 225
CONGAREES, 146
COOKE, Mr 176

COOPER, Rev Mr 2 William 36 40 98 118 133 235 269 321
COPELAND, Eph Jr 234
COPPER INDIANS, 130
CORCE, Capt 33
CORNAL, Mr 80
CORNE, 10
CORNETTE, 215
CORONACRE, 147
CORPS OF ENGINEERS, 77 85
COTTLE, Joseph 172
COWETA INDIANS, 22 80 313
COWETAW INDIANS, 30-31
COYTMORE, Mr 10
COZENS, Abraham 223 Phebe 223
CRADOCK, George 109
CRAIG, 182
CRAMONT, (ship) 261
CRANE, Clement 329
CRAWFORD, Capt 107
CREEK INDIANS, 4 8 14-15 19 21-23 29-32 37 65 75 77 80 86-87 90 100 112 114 130 199 239-240 253 287 313 317
CROCKER, Capt 301
CROSBY, 210 Edward 325 Richard 233
CROWN POINT, 24 26 101 160 171 178 192 231 301
CULVER, 3 Lt 2
CURRY, Maj 238
CURTIS, Capt 146
CUSHING, Capt 212 Ignatious 329
CYGNET, (ship) 302
D'ARC, M 259
D'AUTUN, Bishop 247
D'HOUSSONVILLE, Le Counte 308
DAGBRIEN, Magarete Berbury 169
DANIELS, Capt 74
DANKS, Capt 325
DARBY, Lt Col 150
DAVIDSON, 274 Capt 114 Hannah 340 William 340
DAVIES, Magaret 238 Rev Mr Samuel 17

DAVIS, Capt 33 46 152 341 Solomon 144
DAWSON, Capt 293
DAY, Jane 234 Mrs 225 Thomas 225
DAYS, Capt 319
DEAGAN, Capt 139
DEBOURAN, Mons 213
DEFENSEUR, (ship) 298
DEFIANCE, (ship) 157
DEJANO, Capt 64
DEL MANZA, Don Maria 336
DEL PRADO, Juan 289
DELANCY, James 102
DELANESA, John 302
DELAP, Capt 113
DELAWARES, Indians 93
DELIGHT, (ship) 57
DEMERE, Capt 90 104 Paul 44
DENKE, Capt 110
DENNIS, Capt 16
DENNY, Ens 330
DEPTFORD, (ship) 242
DESERTERS, 260 302
DETROIT, 44 76 337 Rogers Takes 19
DEW, Richard 233
DEXTER, Jeremiah 73
DIAMOND, (ship) 227
DIAMONG, (ship) 330
DIANA, (ship) 253
DICKENSON, Capt 148
DIEGO, Don 340
DILIGENT, (ship) 298
DIRKEE, Maj 330
DISPATCH, (ship) 158
DIXEY, Capt 177
DIXON, Thomas 325
DOBERTY, Constintine 325
DOBLIN, (ship) 113
DOBSON, Capt 242
DODD, Andrew 335 Capt 335
DOGGET, Samuel 246
DOLPHIN, (ship) 69-70 78 159 242 251 293
DONELE, Daniel 71
DORAVER, Daniel 302
DOUBLEDAY, Capt 77 89
DOUGLAS, Capt 303

DOUGLAS (cont.) Com 158 Commodore 93
DOUGLASS, 265 Capt 250 309 Com 193 Commodore 46 225 242 James 113 Mr 104 Sir James 238 242
DOUNAR, Ens 330
DOVER, (ship) 3 146 174 300
DOW, James 188
DRAGON, (ship) 279
DREW, Thomas 72
DROUGHT, In New Hampshire 264
DUANE, Mr 179
DUBLANC, Capt 89
DUBLIN, (ship) 113
DUBOURDIEU, Joseph 331 Mr 332
DUFF, Capt 101
DUKE, (ship) 329
DUKE OF YORK, (ship) 330
DUNBAR, Lemuel 328
DUNBIBIN, Donald 138
DUPEE, Abraham 325
DURHAM, Capt 315
EARTHQUAKE, Boston 145 New Jersey 186
EDDY, Capt 107
EDES, Mr 154
EDGAR, (ship) 209
EDMUNDS, Hanna 97 Nehemiah 97
EDWARD, (ship) 152
EDWARDS, Henry 63
EGREMONT, Earl Of 302 341
ELIZABETH, (ship) 47 330
ELIZABETH AND ANNE, (ship) 78
ELIZABETH AND MARY, (ship) 238
ELLINGWOOD, 269 Benjamin 314
ELLIOT, James 25 Maj 8-9 18
ELLIOTT, Capt 107 Lt 280
ELLIS, Gov 14
ELLOITT, Lt 237
ENTERPRIZE, 312 (ship) 206 224 244 276 283 285-286 312
EPREAVE, (ship) 318
EPREUVE, (ship) 335

ESKIMAUX, 271
EVERIT, Capt 9
EYES, John 237
EYRE, Col 106
FAHRINGTON, Capt 85
FALKLAND, (ship) 44 90
FANEUIL HALL MARKET, Burned 6-7
FANNY, (ship) 158 238
FANUEIL, Peter 7
FARLEY, Samuel 245
FARNALL, Capt 315
FARREL, Capt 158
FEAVIER, John 98
FERGUSON, 182
FERGUSON, Capt 304
FISH, Mr 243
FISHBOURNE, (ship) 85
FISHER, William 14
FISKE, Banjamine 137
FITCH, Tho's 166 Thomas 166
FLEETS, Misters 243
FLEMING, 110
FLESSENAN, Capt 277
FOBES, Abner 44 Phebe 43
FORBES, Lt (Capt) 297
FORCES, French 280 His Majesty's 91 Provincial 224 Regular 223 233
FORT BEAUSEJOUR, 72
FORT CHISSEL, 71
FORT COMBERLAND, 72
FORT CUMBERLAND, 177
FORT DETROIT, 3 106 253
FORT DOBBS, 104
FORT EDWARD, 24
FORT GEORGE, 24 147 236
FORT HALIFAX, 139
FORT JOHNSON, 95 142
FORT LOUDOUN, 4 15 20 116 121 123 126
FORT PITT, 3
FORT PRINCE GEORGE, 3 10 14-15 21 36-37 57 73 77 82-83 88-89 95 99 102 110 115 135 138 140-141 145-146 151 153 160 233

FORT PRINCE WILLIAM, 100
FORT ROYAL, 181-182 189-191 195-196 Surrender Of 197
FORT SANDUSKY, 109
FORT ST JOSEPH, 76
FORT ST PIERRE, 181
FORT STANWIX, 322
FORT WILLIAM, 266
FOSTER, Capt 107 204 Col 34 William 315
FOWEY, (ship) 225
FOWLER, Capt 156
FOX, (ship) 10
FRANCIS, (ship) 330
FRANKLIN, B 243 Benjamin 318
FRAYNE, Richard 159
FRAZER, William 81
FREEMAN, Capt 250 Edmond 250
FRENCH, Christopher 146 Christopher 152
FRENCH, John 299
FRENCH GRENADIERS, 193
FRENCH NEUTRALS, 271
FRENCH PRISONERS, 77 89
FRENCH PRIVATEER, 83 96
FRENCH SAILORS, Kindness Of 61-62
FRIEND, Capt 318
FRIENDSHIP, (ship) 179 328 331
FROST, Capt 46 48 62 158-159 John 47 60
FUNNALL, Stephen 302
FURLONG, Capt 8-9
GAGE, Gen 65 89 Gov 28 Thomas 163 165
GALLOP, 324
GAMBELL, Andrew 14
GARDNER, Capt 198 277 Celeb 277
GARLAND, (ship) 221
GASCOIGN, Capt 113
GEMMEL, Andrew 18
GENERAL SHIRLEY, (ship) 317
GEORGE, Capt 46
GEORGE II, King Of England 15 24 161 Death Of 2
GEORGE III, King Of England 13 24 185 233 330

GERMAN FLATS, False Reports Of Indian Attack 265
GILL, Mr 154
GLADWIN, Maj 106 109
GLASSEL, Mr 265-266
GLOVER, 166
GOLDTHWAIT, Ezerkiel 8 Joseph 199 Tho 51 79 95 104 188 194 210 222 225 339 Thomas 72 260
GOLDTHWAITE, Ezekiel 17
GOLDTHWAIT, Ezekiel 199
GONSALES, Don 288
GONSALO, Christopher 294
GOOD, Dorothy 103
GOODALL, Capt 335-336
GOODRICH, Capt 265
GOODWIN, Capt 242
GORHAM, Christopher 325 David 295 Joseph 185 325 Maj 64 244 295 325
GOSPORT, (ship) 269 312
GOSS, Ephran 240
GOULD, Widow 234
GOURDY, 330
GRAMONT, (ship) 251 255 264
GRANBY, (ship) 110
GRANSTON, Caleb 205
GRANT, Alexander 35 Brig 201 Col 22 30 38 44 57 73-74 77-78 80-89 95 98-100 102-104 110-117 120-126 129-130 135 139-141 146 160 174 Gen 153 James 3 Lt Col 150
GRAY, James 173
GRAYHAM, Andrew 73
GRAYMORE, Capt 293
GREEN, 193
GREENWOOD, Capt 114
GREGSON, John 72
GRENADIERS, 202 220 262 282 300 304 309-311 British 200-201 French 313
GREYHOUND, (ship) 36 57 89

GRIFFIN, (ship) 158 Mr 302
GROVES, Capt 3
GUINARD, Mr 219
GULES, Capt 107
GULL, (ship) 300
HALE, Capt 329 John 330 Robert 101
HALEQUIN, (ship) 206
HALIFAX, 171 (ship) 98 330
HALL, Charles 256 Dr 3 George 256
HALLOWELL, Benj 57 Capt 143 228 269 279 308
HALRON, (ship) 166
HAMILTON, 83 John 73 Maj 14
HAMMET, Thomas 313
HANCOCK, Mr 49 205 Thomas 203
HANDGRAVE, Charles 72
HANDY, Capt 172
HAPPY RETURN, (ship) 72
HARDY, Gov 137
HARGILL, Christopher 46
HARLEQUIN, (ship) 242 246
HARLEY, 182
HARLOW, Capt 247
HARMAN, John 73
HARWOOD, John 277
HASSET, Capt 33
HATHORN, Capt 107
HATTON, Capt 294
HAUSONVILL, Count D' 306
HAUSSONVILLE, Count D' 307 Count De 305 Le Comte D' 314
HAVANA, Attack On 274-276 Reduction Of 281-283 285 288
HAVANNAH, To Be Attacked 209
HAVILAND, Brig 202 Brig Gen 298 Col 150 182
HAWKE, (ship) 280
HAWKE, Sir Edward 147
HAY, David 98 Ens 72
HAYLAND, Joseph 325
HAYT, Capt 98
HAZZEN, Lt 19
HEARN, Capt 267 Mrs 85
HEARSEY, Israel 97 Tabitha 97

HENERY, John 302
HEPPEL, Maj Gen 298
HEPPLE, Commodore 339
HERO, (ship) 19 239
HERRIOT'S HOSPITAL, 291
HIBERNIA, (ship) 26 33
HIGGINS, 183 John 182
HIGHLANDERS, 35 43-44 57
  Montgomery's 77 90 151
  283 309 Murray's 150
  Royal 101 290 Royal
  1st Battalion 201
  Royal Scotch 151
HILL, Jack 75
HILLER, Joseph 325
HOAR, Col 103 222 227
HOLBROOK, Samuel 234
HOLEYOKE, Edw 134
HOLLAND, Stephen 185
HOLLOWELL, Benjamin 166
HOLMAN, Stephen 149
HOLMES, Adm 63 Capt 24
  John 23 Mr 85 89
HOLTON, John 206
HONNONVILLE, Marquis De
  267
HOPE, (ship) 238 250
HOPEWELL, (ship) 138 330
HOPSON, (ship) 159
HOSSON DE VILLE, Count
  311
HOSSON VILLE, Le Compte
  De 311
HOULSTON, Capt 224
HOULTON, John 286
HOW, Abygail 26 John 185
  188 Joshua 137 173 178
  William 325
HOWARD, Capt 4 139
HOWE, Brig Gen 299 Col
  273
HUART, Le Baron De 217
HUBBARD, Col 323
  Nathaniel 323 Thomas 6
HUBER, Martin 186
HUDSON, Seth 137 185 188
HUGHES, Barnabas 294
  William 73
HULL, Joseph 256
HUNTER, Capt 139

HUSSEY, Daniel 159
HUTCHINS, Robert 179
HUTTON, Capt 319
HYLANDERS, 38
INDEPENDENT TROOPS, Sick 45
INDEPENDENT COMPANIES 38 238
  From England 3
INDEPENDENT COMPANY,
  Demere's 104 Rogers' 104
INDIAN, Allakallakulla 74
  Arrakullakulla 128
  Attakillakulla 128
  Attakullakulla 120 125-126
  128 140 144 151 153 160
  Caesar 80 Cappy 153 Capt
  Day 331 Duvull's Landlord
  29 Fool-harry 22 Half
  Breed Will 115 Harry 115
  Hougougsaniyonde (Thomas)
  160 Judd's Friend 153 233
  318 330 King Hagler 21
  Little Carpenter 15 37 74
  87 102 111-112 115 117
  120-121 124 128-131 140
  144 146 151 154 160
  Mistifico 19 Nottowegas 29
  Occunastotah 140
  Occunnastota (The Great
  Warrior) 153 Old Ceasar
  102 Old Ceasar Of Hywassih
  115 Old Hop 153 Old Hopp
  115 Oucannosstota 15
  Oucanostata 102
  Ouccanostato 110-111
  Outassite 318 Prince Of
  Chote 151 Prince Of Chotih
  330 Salloue 102 Serowih 15
  Silver Heels 154 193
  Silverheels 30-31 88
  Standing Turkey 111 140
  153 233 Tale Of Eftatowih
  78 The Great Warrior 135
  139-141 The Mankiller 15
  95 99 115 The Mortar 22 80
  87 The Raven Of Hywassih
  115 The Raven Of Naucasih
  115 The Slave-catcher 111-
  112 The Wolf 4 31 The
  Young Lieutenant 22 313-
  314

INDIAN (cont.)
  The Young Warrior 112
  140-141 236 The Young
  Warrior Of Estatoe 146
  The Young Warrior Of
  Estatoey 87 Tiftoe 111
  Tiscoey 151 Tistoe 236
  Waybukcumigut 269
  White Owl 95 99
  Wilanawah 115
  Willanawaw 102 Wolf
  King 20 21 28-29 32
  Yellow Bird 96 Young-
  twin 22
INDIAN CORPS, 86 88
INDUSTRY, (ship) 286 327
INFANTRY, Scott's 193
INGERSOL, Col 221-222 227
INGOLLS, Benjamin 33
INTREPID, (ship) 169 288
  325-326 329-330
INTRIPID, (ship) 233 235
  238 315
IRISH SETTLERS, of Nova
  Scotia 138
IVEA, Enoch 222
JACKSON, Joseph 230
  William 230
JAMES, (ship) 238 326 330
  Joseph 159
JANE AND ELIZABETH,
  (ship) 330
JARVIS, Capt 269 Col 206
  Leonard 13
JEDIAC, Tribe 76
JERAULD, Martha 334
JERAULDS, Martha 334
JERMIN, Lt 190
JOHNSON, Benjamin Jr 329
  Capt 204 John 266 Mr
  283 Sir William 4 91
  106 109 152 Thomas 99
  William 246
JOHNSTON, Dr 77 James 325
JOLISS, Capt 209
JONES, 182 Capt 107 324
  John 159
JORDAN, Sgt 300
JUNKINS, Capt 107
JUNO, (ship) 286

JUTT, Hugh 15
K----, Col 336
KATTER, Capt 114
KENNEDY, Capt 86-88 92 154
  Gen 150 John 72 256
  Quintin 146 152 Quintyne 8
  74
KEPPEL, Commodore 282-283
  289 298 Gen 299
KERR, Walter 253
KERSTEAD, Capt 242
KESLEY, Capt 266
KIDNEY, Mr 80
KIER, Robert 302
KING, Capt 107 Thomas 75
KING GEORGE, (ship) 56 143
  228 269 308 312 320
KING OF PRUSSIA, (ship) 291
KINGMAN, Lemuel 237
KINGSMAN, Lemuel 237
KNIGHT, Ens 84
KNOX, John 315
KOSSTER, Capt 326
KUNCHE, 157
LA FORTUNE, (ship) 89
LA MARIAN, (ship) 265
LAFAOUR, Capt 107
LAKE CHAMPLAIN, 24
LAKE GEORGE, 101
LANDER, Capt 222-223
LANE, Charles 173 188
LARK, Joseph 174
LAROUCHE, Mr 202
LATOUCH, Mons 191
LATOUCHE, 217 Gen 214 La
  Vassor 219-220 Le Vessor
  De 215 M 90 Mons 195-196
  Mons Lavassor 213 Mr De
  209
LAUCESTON, (ship) 252
LAURENS, Henry 331
LAVECOMPT, 182
LAWRENCE, Capt 66 254
LAWRENS, Lt 21
LAWTON, William 192
LEACH, John 221
LEE, James 193
LEFYEAR, Mr 198
LERETTO, 68
LETCHERS, 182

LEVANT, (ship) 46
LEWIS, Capt 107 172 223
    John 266 Maj 71
LICKENS, John 221
LIGHT INFANTRY, 84 193
    200 202 303-304 309-
    310 312 Gage's 89 106
LIGHTNING STRIKES, 243
LIKENS, John 186 Mary 186
LILLIE, Capt 254
LINDSAY, Capt 279
LION, (ship) 237
LISH, George 63
LITTLE, Capt 157
LIZARD, (ship) 44 64 90
    235-236 244
LLOYD, John 135-136
LOCKHART, (ship) 315
LOMPRE, M 90
LOO, (ship) 18
LORING, Benjamin 234
    James 237
LOUISIANA, Ceded To
    England 343
LOVE AND ANN, (ship) 157
LOVETT, Capt 107
LUKE, M 194
LYDIA, (ship) 330
LYELL, Capt 91
LYFORD, Wm 206
LYHIN, Mary 169
LYMAN, Capt 300 Col 46
    286 338 Gen 329
LYNCH, 166 Mr 334
M'AULEY, Capt 276
M'CUNNINGHAM, 117
M'DONALD, Capt 310
M'DONELL, Capt 306
M'DONNEL, Capt 303
M'DONNELL, Capt 308
M'GACHERY, Capt 319
M'GILLICUDDY, Capt 242
    295
M'INTOSH, Capt 21 44
M'KENZIE, Capt 308 312
M'PHERSON, Capt 242
MACDONALD, John 35
MACGACHAN, Capt 318
MACINTOSH, Capt 57
MACKENSEY, Lt 317

MACKENZIE, Alexander 35 57
    Capt 38 304
MACKEY, Capt 318 320 James
    320
MACKIE, Mr 265-266
MACKINTOSH, Capt 77 145 236
    Lauchlane 10 Launchlane 21
    Mr 16
MACNAB, 35
MAHONEY, Dennis 300
MAJOR ROGERS, (ship) 205
MALCOM, Capt 24 John 18 23
MALONE, 315
MANCKTON, Gen 232
MANSFIELD, Lord 106
MANUR, (ship) 325
MANWARING, Capt 333
MARBLE, Benjamin 240
MARGERY, (ship) 330
MARINES, French Royal 311
MARLBOROUGH, (ship) 330
MARLBOUROUGH, (ship) 279
MARLOWE, Capt 78
MARS, (ship) 242 295
MARSH, Edward 72
MARSHAL, Capt 18-19
MARSHALL, Capt 213 322
MARTIN, Capt 205 312 Isaac
    340
MARTINECO, Accounts Of
    Proceedings 192-193 199-
    202 Articles Of
    Capitulation 213-220
    Artillery At 196 Attacked
    181 Description Of Battle
    Of 190-191 Success At 195-
    198
MARY, (ship) 319
MARY FLOWER, (ship) 159
MARY THE SECOND, (ship) 238
MASQUERADE, (ship) 286
MATHEWS, Capt 182
MATROSS, Edmond Smith 25
MAZYCK, Mr 334
MCAULEY, Capt 273
MCCLOWING, Joseph 75
MCDONALD, Capt 21 Ens 37
MCINTOSH, Capt 151 Lt 37
MCKENZIE, Capt 310
MCLELAND, 274

MCNUTT, Alexander 14 18 138 Col 138
MCPHERSON, Capt 16 158
MCTAGGART, Capt 72 Peter 73
MCTAGGET, 182
MEGEDERNE, Aguste De 146
MELVILL, Gov 90
MELVIR, James 95
MERCHANT, 182
MERCURY, (ship) 35 75 299 318 335-336
MESSASAGA INDIANS, 269-270
MICHIE, William 299
MICHILIMAKINAK, 253
MICHILLMACHINAC, 20
MICKMACK, Tribe 76
MIDDLETON, Col 21 84 87 141 145
MIFLIN, Mr 21
MILITIA, Accident In New Haven 222 Norfolk 333
MILLER, Capt 295 Christopher 142
MILLIGAN, Dr 186
MILN, Mr 10 15 37
MINERVA, (ship) 312
MIRIMICHI, Tribe 76
MISHILIMACINAC, 152
MITCHEL, James 205
MITCHELL, Capt 238
MOCKTON, Gen 14
MOCKTON, (ship) 242
MOHAWKS, 3-4 8 21 29-32 88 95
MOHICONS, Indians 93
MONCHTON, Robert 235
MONCKTON, Gen 73 138 150-151 182 200 202 209 213 290 Gov 236 Maj Gen 150 Robert 145 147 241
MONET, Mr 341
MONEYPENNY, Alex 154
MONRO, 157 John 84
MONTGOMERY, 103 Col 34-35 44 Maj 150 298 Wm 340
MONTGOMERY'S HIGHLANDERS, 309
MONTGOMERY'S REGIMENT, 290
MONYPENNY, Alexander 152
MOODY, George 145 Mrs 145
MORRISON, Mr 5
MORSE, Lt 100 Mrs 75
MORTALITY REGISTER, 178
MORTON, Capt 204 John 329 Joseph 18
MOSSE, David 329
MOTTE, Capt 33
MULATTO, Cesar 334
MULATTOES, 215
MUNDS, Capt 244
MUNRO, Mr 35
MURPHY, 243
MURRAY, Col 222 Gen 65 Ld 150
MURRELL, Robert 73
NADAU, 215
NANCY, (ship) 330
NAPIER, Capt 146
NATICOKES, Indians 93
NEGRO, Cumber 119 Cyrus 135 Daniel 172 Fortune 192
NEGRO SOLDIERS, 238
NEGROES, 4 38 47 78 91 96 215-216 220 227 242 246 263 265 283 292 294 318 322 331-332 335
NEPTUNE, (ship) 159 293
NEW HARLEQUIN, (ship) 242
NEWHALL, Capt 33 46
NIAGARA, 106 270
NICCOLL, Capt 107
NICHOLL, Capt 91
NICHOSON, Capt 198
NIGHTINGALE, (ship) 3 151-153 Ebenezer 237
NINETY-SIX, 21 104 135 141 146-147 151-153 160 236 330
NIXON, Capt 231
NOBLE, Arthur 234
NOLSON, Lt 330
NORTON, Capt 78 110 William 83
NORWICH, (ship) 89
OBRIEN, Mary 169
OFFICERS, Massachusetts 339 Provincial 329 Regular 329

OGDEN, Capt 98
OLD MONK, (ship) 47 60
OLIVE, (ship) 212
OLIVE BRANCH, (ship) 156
OLIVER, (ship) 330 337 A 13 66 80 106 163 212 287
ONEIDA NATION, 160
ONONDAGO INDIANS, 93 265
ORDIORNY, Capt 38
ORDOGRIEZ, Don Pedro 263 265
OTIS, Mr 176
OTWAY, Lt Gen 150
OUTWAY, Gen 104
OXFORD, (ship) 209 333
PAIN, Nathaniel 321
PALACRE JAMES, (ship) 291
PALLESTER, Capt 312
PALMER, 254 Capt 253
PARKER, Capt 33 Lt 145 Peter 26
PARKMAN, Sam 173
PARKS, Lt 330
PARRON, Matthew 14
PARTIZANS, 16
PATIENCE, (ship) 330
PATTERSON, Capt 330
PAXTON, Cha 10 Charles 47 49 109 149
PEABODY, Capt 33-34 48
PEARCE, Capt 148 Edward 75 Mr 230 Rev Mr 331
PEARNE, Capt 223 Wm 224
PEARSAL, Capt 3
PECK, William Augustus 239
PEDEE, (ship) 291
PEDRO, Don 332
PEGGY, (ship) 158
PEIBODY, Oliver 14
PELLAMY, Richard 179
PENRO, Isaac 301
PENROSE, James 239 Tho 239
PERCIVAL, Capt 146
PERKINSON, Stephen 4
PERRIGREEN, James 237
PETERS, Capt 312 John 338 Solomon 338

PHAENIX, (ship) 319
PHILADELPHIA, Numbers Of Houses Counted 44
PHILIPS, John 72-73
PHILLIPS, 182 Capt 251 Col 206
PHILLIPSON, Ballard 204
PHIPPS, Capt 143
PHIPS, Capt 167
PHODEY, Capt 89
PHOENIX, Capt 181
PINNEGAR, Capt 277
PIRKIN, Lt 330
PITT, Secretary 40 46
PITTSBURGH, 106
PLAYFORD, Samuel 186
POCOCK, Adm 209 232 238 252 268 279 283 Sir George 242 273 295 298
POCOCKE, Adm 301 Sir George 228 318
POE, George Jacob 260
POGINOUCH, Tribe 76
POLACRE, (ship) 285
POLAND, Jacob 314 Mr 269
POLLY, (ship) 33 274
POLLY AND SALLY, (ship) 242
POPKINS, John 234
POPULATION, 168
PORCUPINE, (ship) 233 238 244 283
PORT ANTONIO, (ship) 250
PORT ROYAL, 193
PORTER, 8 Capt 9
POTTORIE, De La 215
POWER, Thomas 18
POWEY, (ship) 40
PRATT, John 329
PRETTY SALLY, (ship) 274
PRICE, Mr 47 William 198
PRINCE GEORGE, (ship) 72
PRISONERS, French 252 308
PRIVATEERS, 19 114 205-206 212 221 238 242 246 249 253-254 256 261 263 266 280 287 294 317 332 French 46 48 72 107 259 265 279 298 331 New York 89 Spanish 228 315 324 334-336 340

PROCTOR, Charles 325
PROVINCIAL REGIMENTS, 101
　Completing Of 79
PROVINCIALS, 15 77 84-85 87 89 101 238 244 302 309 330 Connecticut 101 Davis's 46 George's 46 Massachusetts 101 301 322 New Hampshire 101 New York 319 Newhall's 46 Rutlidge's 48 To Be Raised From Connecticut 64
PUTNAM, Col 330
QUINCY, Edmond 72 Edmund Jr 138
RACHEL, (ship) 238
RAISONABLE, (ship) 137 192-193
RALSE, Capt 294-295
RAMLEY, Capt 204
RAMSDELL, Nathaniel 329
RAMSEY, 182
RANDELL, Capt 60
RANDLE, Mr 47-48
RANGER, (ship) 159
RANGERS, 4 19 21 82 87 90 154 193 242 248 2nd Company 325 Bosher's 139 Deagan's 139 Demere's 90 Gorham's 64 185 244 295 325-326 Hayt's 98 Ogden's 98 Provincial 139 Rogers' 90 Russell's 139 Scott's 193 Thompson's 14 36-37 139
RANSOM, Thomas 72
RASE, Alexander 331
RATCLIFF, William 188
RECRUITMENT, In Boston 194 210In Connecticut 194 In New Hampshire 194
RECRUITS, Provincial 208
REGAN, Miles 73
REGIMENT/REGIMENTS, 137 210 Amherst's 91 150 Armiger's 150

REGIMENT/REGIMENTS(cont.)
　At Quebec 65 Bagley's 26 Blackeney's 150 Burton's 84 104 146 Campbell's 146 Frazer's 306 French 262 French's 146 Hoar's 103 222 227 In Quebec 67 Ingersol's 221-222 227 Kennedy's 146 150 Lyman's 300 338 Massachusetts 224 Middleton's 21 141 145 Militia 206 Mockton's 14 Monckton's 150 290 Montgomery's 34 290 304 New Jersey 73 New Jersey Provincial 220 North Carolina 99 Otway's 150 Outway's 104 Payment Of 171 Provincial 222 326 Provincial Ranger 139 Reduced From 1000 To 700 Men In Each 44 Regular 227 245 326 Regular Deserters 237 Rhode Island 322 Royal 146 280 297 302 304 Royal American 248 295 Royal Artillery 98 Royal Highland 283 Saltinstall's 221-222 Saltonstall's 103 227 Seton's 146 The General's 57 Thuing's 72 Thwing's 95 Thwing's Provincial 179 To Be Raised 41 50 Townshend's 150 Virginia 245Waddle's 104 Webb's 150 Whitmore's 14
REGIMENT OF FOOT, Provincial 139
REGULAR FORCES, Recruiting 221
REGULARS, French 209 280
REPULSE, (ship) 44 90
RESOLUTION, (ship) 330
REVENGE, (ship) 159 205
RICHARDSON, Capt 225 Lt 300
RIDGEWAY, Elizabeth 186
RIPPON, Capt 78
RISING SUN, (ship) 204
RITCHIE, Andrew 135

RIVERS, Capt 246
RIVIERE, De La 218-219
ROACH, Capt 107
ROADS, Nathanial 277
ROBERT, (ship) 209
ROBERTS, Capt 87
ROBERTSON, Archibald 35
ROBINSON, 144 John 179 Mr 180
ROBUSLE, (ship) 257
ROCHEMORE, De 214
ROCHESTER, (ship) 169 170
RODNEY, Adm 182 209 213 222 G B 220
ROGERS, Capt 65 104 112 205 Maj 5 16 19-20 25 36 44 199 233 253 317 Robert 90 203 Takes Fort Detroit 3
ROLLES, Capt 245 248
ROLLO, Lord 44 90 94 98
ROSE, Samuel 46
ROSS, Alexander 334 Capt 264 Ezibilon 38-39 Jaremiah 38 John 333-334
ROUILLE, Gov 214
ROWLEY, Capt 312
ROYAL AMERICAN REGIMENT, 248 295
ROYAL AMERICANS, 48 91 198 3rd Battalion 101 150 302
ROYAL ANN, (ship) 147
ROYAL HIGHLANDERS, 150 283 290 1st Battalion Of 101 2nd Battalion Of 101
ROYAL REGIMENT, 280 302
ROYAL REGIMENT OF ARTILLERY, 151
ROYAL SCOTS, 34 48-49
ROYALL, Brig 206 Isaac 71
ROYALS, 77 84 300 Grenadier Company Of 309
RUBY, (ship) 18
RUSSELL, 193 Charles 139
RUTILEGE, Capt 34
RUTLIDGE, Capt 48

RUTLIGE, Capt 33
SAILORS, Wages For 333
SAINT ANDREW, (ship) 198
SAINT LUKEBYCORN, 198
SALLY, (ship) 23 35 159
SALLY AND POLLY, (ship) 16
SALTINSTALL, Col 221-222
SALTONSTALL, Capt 107 Col 103 227 Dudley 256 327
SAMPSON, 33 Thomas 158-159
SAMUEL, (ship) 81
SANDERS, (ship) 9
SARAH, (ship) 114
SAUNDERS, Adm 63
SAVAGE, Lt 21
SCAILE, Capt 233
SCARBOROUGH, (ship) 35 70
SCHUYLER, Lt 310
SCHUYLER'S COPPER MINES, 192
SCHYLER, Lt 308
SCOT, 182
SCOTT, Capt 70 Col 193
SEAFLOWER, (ship) 16
SEARLE, Capt 252
SEMINS, Capt 107
SENECA INDIANS, 109
SENNET, Capt 242
SERENE, (ship) 250
SETON, Sir Harry 152 Sir Henry 146
SHARPE, Gov 233
SHAWANESE, Indians 93
SHEARMAN, John 192 330 334
SHEPHERD, Capt 266
SHERRY, William 328
SHIPTON, Samuel 325 W W 185 William 325
SHIRLEY, Gen 35 295
SHIVERICK, Capt 113
SHORE, Jane 115
SHREWSBURY, (ship) 312
SHUBRICK, 335
SHUTE, Mrs 198 Sergeant 198
SIMPSON, Capt 118
SIX NATIONS, 43
SKEEN, Maj 193
SLATTEN, Widow 234
SLAUGHTER, John 26
SLAVES, 73 215-216 218 242 277 320

SMALL, Mr 139
SMALL POX, 2 17 25-26 36 326
SMILING NANCY, (ship) 286
SMITH, 274 Andrew 302 Benjamin 124 Capt 91 148 295-296 Edward 99 William 75 302
SNOW, John 327
SOLDIER, Provincial 225
SOLDIERS, Connecticut 73 French 20 French- desertion Of 281
SOTHERLAND, (ship) 44
SOUTERLAND, (ship) 64
SOUTH, Samuel 293-294
SPAFFORD, Capt 281
SPALDEN, Capt 330
SPARROW, Samuel 329
SPEAR, John 237 Joseph 322
SPRAGUE, Obadiah 119
SPRANGUE, Obadiah 120
SPRY, (ship) 98
SQUARREL, (ship) 233
SQUIRREL, (ship) 21
STANFORD, (ship) 245
STANTON, Capt 300 330
STAPLE, Peter 313
STERLING, Capt 337 John 95 Lord 137
STERLING CASTLE, (ship) 274 279
STEVENS, Jacob 137 John 136
STEVENSON, Capt 9
STEWART, Capt 33
STIRLING CASTLE, (ship) 9
STORK, (ship) 62
STORY, Hannah 340 Thomas 340 William 21 47 49 81 241
STOTE, Capt 35
STUART, Capt 46 48 292 317 John 4 20 120
SUCCESS, (ship) 292
SUPERB, (ship) 312
SURENE, (ship) 264
SUSANNA, (ship) 245
SUTHERLAND, (ship) 90 300

SUTHERLAND, Maj 304
SUTTLERS, Massachusetts 339
SUTTON, 267 Capt 245-246 John 75
SWABRIDGE, Capt 24
SWAIN, James 174
SWALLOW, (ship) 246 286
SWANTON, Com 193 Commodore 44
SWATRIDGE, Capt 62
SWETT, Thomas 101
SYLVESTER, Quarter Master 104
SYMMES, Capt 221
SYREN, (ship) 303 306 310- 311
SYRENE, (ship 247 (ship) 268-269
TABER, John 159
TAMBROW, John 64
TANNER, Capt 315
TARDY, John 158
TARTAR, (ship) 209
TAYER, Jacob 234
TAYLOR, Capt 158 209
TEMPLE, (ship) 330 John 163 166 Mr 137 Rob 10 Robert 47 49 109
TERRELL, John 188
THOMAS, Mr 255 Widow 324 Wiliam 266
THOMPSON, 81 Andrew 66 I 330 John 156 Maj 3 14 21 36-37 139 Mr 80 W 330 William 90
THREE FRIENDS, (ship) 159
THUING, Col 72
THURSTON, Capt 242
THWING, Col 95 179
TICONDEROGA, 24
TIEL, Nadau Du 215
TONYA, Capt 40
TOOLE, John 73
TOOMER, Henry 292
TOSH, Capt 248
TOURNAY, Commodore De 267 M 280 Mons 309
TOWNSEND, William 15
TOWNSHEND, Gen 150
TRACY, Keturah 256

TREATY, Between England France And Spain 342-343
TREATY OF PARIS, 344
TRENT, (ship) 279
TRICKS, William 280
TROOPERS, 249
TROOPS, 18 35 44 138 170 209 314 British 23 British At Martineco 189 Connecticut 286 French 262 264 307 His Majesty's 3 77 In Havana 273 Massachusetts Provincial 231 309 New York 276 Pay And Enlistment Of 187 Provincial 8 33-34 57 160 227 233 279 292 300-301 312-313 328 Provincial-raising Of 229 Raised By Connecticut 45-46 Raised By New York 45 Raised By Rhode Island 46 Regular 16 57 279 284 300 309 313 Rhode Island 333 Royal 147 The King's 153 To Be Raised In New Haven 187
TROOPS OF GUARDS, 206
TROY, John 26
TRUE BLUE, (ship) 252
TRUE BRITON, (ship) 238
TUCKER, 182 Edward 96 Thomas 331
TULL, 182 Capt 204
TULLIKIN, Lt Col 304 306
TURNBULL, John 99
TURNER, Lewis 21
TURNWE, Capt 107
TUTE, James 325
TUTELOES, Indians 93
TUTTEL, Ebenezer 293 Nathan 293
TWO BROTHERS, (ship) 238
UDANG, Rev Mr 65
VANS, Mr 247

VARNETT, 182
VAUDREUIL, Gov 39 Marquis De 247
VELASCO, Don Lewis 288
VELLISCO, Don 275
VENUS, (ship) 330
VERNON, Widow 245
VILLE, Compte De Hosson 255 Dount De Hosson 252
VIRGINIA FORCES, 104
VIRGINIANS, 99
VOLUNTEER CORPS, 74
VOUGHAM, Col 64
VULTURE, (ship) 330
WADDLE, Col 104
WAIT, Capt 5 19
WALDEN, James 291
WALDO, David 99 Fra 287 Joseph 99
WALDON, Isaac 331
WALKER, Capt 295 John 325 Martin 159 Ralf 294
WALLACE, Capt 58
WALLIS, 33
WALTER, Capt 57
WALTH, Brig 202
WANTON, Joseph G 330
WAR, Declared On Spain 206
WARREN, Capt 107 Job 158
WATERMAN, Capt 324 Elisha 325 John 325
WATNER, 182
WATSON, Andrew 325
WATTS, Capt 111-112 115 141
WEBB, Capt 173 242
WELCH, John 173 188 Lt Col 150
WELD, Edward 143
WELL, Maj Gen 150
WELLS, Andrew Elton 335 Capt 335 Lt 330 Mr 91 93
WENTWORT, Gov 113
WENTWORTH, Gov 177
WESTAL, Lt 299
WETHERED, Mrs 185
WHALING, Patrick 75
WHIPPEL, Stephen 27
WHIPPING, Public 40
WHIPPLE, Capt 33 Gidion 159 Stephen 26

WHITE, 182 Capt 181 Col
    240 Elizabeth 174
    Isaac 174 Mary 221
    Moll 169 William 72
WHITING, Col 46 John 46
WHITMORE, Gen 14
WHITTY, Capt 18
WICKHAM, Capt 227
WILDE, Silent 329
WILKINSON, Mr 37
WILLE, Le Compte De
    Hosson 252
WILLIAMS, Capt 227-228
    292 317 328 Mrs 143
    Philamon 327

WILLINGTON, John 240 Mary
    240 244
WILLOUGHBY, William 185
WILMOT, (ship) 23
WIMBLE, Capt 245
WINTER, Capt 16
WIRT, Mr 233 Uriah 210
WOOD, Rob 341
WOODRECK, Thomas 75
WOODSIDES, John 244
WRIGHT, Capt 242 277 Gov 96
    199 Lt Gov 14 William 233
YORK, (ship) 330
YOUNG, Capt 228
YOUNG SAMUEL, (ship) 330

Other Heritage Books by the author:

1767 Chronicle

Boston, the Red Coats, and the Homespun Patriots, 1766-1775

Central Colonies Chronicle: The Freeman, the Servants, and the Government, 1722-1732

French and Indian War Notices Abstracted from Colonial Newspapers
Volume 2: 1756-1757
Volume 3: January 1, 1758 to September 17, 1759
Volume 4: September 17, 1759 to December 30, 1760
Volume 5: January 1, 1761 to January 17, 1793

Jolly Old England

Journal of Occurrences: Patriot Propaganda on the British Occupation of Boston, 1768-1769

Newspaper Datelines of the American Revolution
Volume 1: April 18, 1775 to November 1, 1775
Volume 2: November 1, 1775 to April 30, 1776
Volume 3: May 1, 1776 to November 1, 1776
Volume 4: November 1, 1776 to January 30, 1777

Pontiac's Conspiracy and Other Indian Affairs: Notices Abstracted from Colonial Newspapers, 1763-1765

www.ingramcontent.com/pod-product-compliance
Lightning Source LLC
Chambersburg PA
CBHW072132220426
43664CB00013B/2221